TIGERS IN TROUBLE

Financial Governance, Liberalisation and Crises in East Asia

CONTRIBUTORS

Muhammad Ali Abdusalamov, Tashkent State University of Economics; Visiting Fellow, Institute of Southeast Asian Studies (ISEAS), Singapore (until March 1998).

Yilmaz Akyüz, (PhD, East Anglia), Chief, Macroeconomic and Development Policies, UNCTAD, Geneva.

Walden Bello (PhD, Princeton), Professor, University of the Philippines, Diliman, Quezon City and Co-Director, Focus on the Global South, Bangkok, Thailand.

Nicola Bullard, Senior Associate, Focus on the Global South, Bangkok, Thailand.

C.P. Chandrasekhar (PhD, JNU), Associate Professor, Centre for Economic Studies and Planning, Jawaharlal Nehru University, New Delhi, India.

Chang Ha-Joon (PhD, Cambridge), Assistant Director of Development Studies, Faculty of Economics and Politics. University of Cambridge, Cambridge, England.

Jayati Ghosh (PhD, Cambridge), Associate Professor, Centre for Economic Studies and Planning, Jawaharlal Nehru University, New Delhi, India.

G.K. Helleiner (PhD, Yale), Professor, Economics Department, University of Toronto, Canada; Coordinator, G-22.

Jomo K.S. (PhD, Harvard), Professor, Faculty of Economics and Administration, University of Malaya, Kuala Lumpur, Malaysia.

J.A. Kregel (PhD, Cambridge), Professor, Economics Department, University of Bologna and Professor, Johns Hopkins University, Bologna, Italy.

Laurids S. Lauridsen (PhD, Roskilde), Associate Professor, Roskilde University Centre, Roskilde, Denmark.

Joseph Y. Lim (PhD, Pennsylvania), Associate Professor, School of Economics, University of the Philippines, Diliman, Quezon City, Philippines.

Kamal Malhotra, Co-Director, Focus on the Global South, Bangkok, Thailand.

Manuel F. Montes (PhD, Stanford), Senior Fellow, Institute of Southeast Asian Studies (ISEAS), Singapore and Senior Fellow (on leave), East-West Center, Honolulu, USA.

TIGERS IN TROUBLE

Financial Governance, Liberalisation and Crises in East Asia

edited by

Jomo K.S.

 HONG KONG UNIVERSITY PRESS
Hong Kong

 IPSR BOOKS
Cape Town

 UNIVERSITY PRESS LTD
Dhaka

 WHITE LOTUS
Bangkok

 ZED BOOKS LTD
London and New York

TIGERS IN TROUBLE
was first published in 1998 by
Zed Books Ltd
7 Cynthia Street, London N1 9JF, UK

Copyright © Zed Books Ltd 1998

Distributed in the USA exclusively by
St Martin's Press
Room 400, 175 Fifth Avenue, New York, NY 10010, USA

Printed and bound in Malaysia

A catalogue record for this book is available from the British Library

Library of Congress Cataloging-in-Publication Data
Tigers in trouble : financial governance and the crises in East Asia /
[edited by] Jomo K.S.
 p. cm.
A collection of 11 essays by the editor and other authors.
Includes bibliographical references and index.
ISBN 1-85649-661-9 (hc.). — ISBN 1-85649-662-7 (pbk.)
 1. Capital market—East Asia. 2. Financial crises—East Asia.
3. Monetary policy—East Asia. 4. International Monetary Fund.
5. International finance.   I. Jomo K. S. (Jomo Kwame Sundaram)
HG5770.5.A3T54   1998
332.1'095'09049—dc21   98-27307
                                                         CIP

ISBN 1 85649 661 9 Hb
ISBN 1 85649 662 7 Pb

Published in Hong Kong by Hong Kong University Press
/F Hing Wai Centre, 7 Tin Wan Praya Road, Aberdeen, Hong Kong
ISBN 962-209-475-9

Published in South Africa by IPSR Books
Community House, 41 Salt River Road, Salt River 7925, Cape Town, South Africa
ISBN 0-9584224-4-3 Hb
ISBN 0-9584224-3-5 Pb

Published in Bangladesh by The University Press Ltd
Red Crescent Building, 114 Motijheel C/A, PO Box 2611, Dhaka 1000
ISBN 984-05-1445-8

Published in Burma, Cambodia, Laos and Thailand by White Lotus Company Ltd
GPO Box 1141, Bangkok, 100501, Thailand
ISBN 874-8434-59-1

Support from the Institute On Governance is gratefully acknowledged.
Institute On Institut sur   122, rue Clarence St., Ottawa, Canada KIN 5P6
Governance   la gouvernance   Tel: (613) 562-0090   Fax: (613) 562-0097
                               Website: http://www.igvn.ca

CONTENTS

Contributors   ii
Tables and Charts   viii
Glossary   ix
Foreword   xi
Acknowledgements   xii
In Lieu of a Preface   xiii

1 Introduction: Financial Governance, Liberalisation and
  Crises in East Asia   1
  Jomo K.S.

    Macroeconomic Concerns   3
    Collapse: The Bubble Bursts   5
    Lessons   6
    Policy Challenges   8
    Changed International Financial System   9
    Implications of Financial Liberalisation   11
    Analytical Catch-up   13
    Understanding the Southeast Asian Currency Crisis   16
    IMF Intervention   18
    This Volume in Brief   21
    Roots of the Crisis: Challenges of Governance   23

2 The East Asian Financial Crisis: Back to the Future   33
  Yilmaz Akyüz

    The Crisis: Surprising or Predictable?   34
    The Policy Response   37
    Global Implications   38
    Conclusions   42

3 East Asia is not Mexico: The Difference between
  Balance of Payments Crises and Debt Deflation   44
  J.A. Kregel

    An Interpretation of the Asian Crisis   45
    A Financial Crisis of International Capital Market Failure   51
    Stage Two: The Cure is Worse than the Disease   57

4 Hubris, Hysteria, Hope: The Political Economy of
   Crisis and Response in Southeast Asia   63
   C.P. Chandrasekhar and Jayati Ghosh

   Background to the Current Crisis   63
   The Financial Crisis   68
   The IMF Response   74
   Foreign Finance, Governments and People   78
   The Prognosis   80

5 Taming the Tigers: The IMF and the Asian Crisis   85
   Nicola Bullard with Walden Bello and Kamal Malhotra

   The IMF and Thailand: A Cosy Relationship   85
   The IMF and Indonesia: Under the Volcano   92
   The IMF and South Korea: Teaching the Tiger a Lesson   100
   Social Impact of the Crisis   109
   The Role of the IMF   120
   Conclusions and Recommendations   132

6 Thailand: Causes, Conduct, Consequences   137
   Laurids S. Lauridsen

   Excessive Short-term Borrowings and Casino Capitalism   138
   Financial Institutions and the Financial Crisis in the 1980s 140
   Financial Liberalisation in the 1990s   142
   Economic Slowdown, Loss of Competitiveness and
      Currency Crisis   143
   The Politics of the Financial Crises   145
   Financial Crisis and Breakdown of Investor Confidence   147
   The IMF Medicine   149
   The Chuan Government: Financial Clean Up and
      Sticking by the Terms   151
   From Financial Crisis to Socioeconomic Crises   153
   Concluding Remarks   157

7 Indonesia: Reaping the Market   162
   Manuel F. Montes and Muhammad Ali Abdusalamov

   Setting the Stage   163
   Asian Crisis Erupts   171
   Conclusions: Understanding the Political Economy   179

8 Malaysia: From Miracle to Debacle   181
   Jomo K.S.

   Policy Responses: Solution or Problem?   184
   Denial and Distraction   185
   Bail-outs for 'Cronies'   186
   The Changing Budget as a Reflection of Changing Stance   189
   Finally, the Tide Turns   190
   Confidence Restoration   192
   Political Fallout   194

9 The Philippines and the East Asian Economic Turmoil   199
   Joseph Y. Lim

   Economic Phases in the Last Two Decades   199
   Analysis of the Causes of the Crisis   213
   Prospects for the Future   219

10 South Korea: The Misunderstood Crisis   222
   Chang Ha-Joon

   Understanding the Crisis   222
   Immediate Causes   223
   Deeper Causes   226
   What Future for Korea?   229

Afterword: The East Asian and Other Financial Crises –
Causes, Responses and Prevention   232
G.K. Helleiner

   Causes   232
   Issues in Crisis Management   233
   Crisis Prevention and Damage Control   236

Bibliography   239
Index   248

TABLES

P1   Distribution of Loans by Country of Origin   xv
P2   Lending by BIS Reporting Banks by Country and by Sector   xv
P3   Maturity Distribution of Lending of BIS Reporting Banks   xvi
1.1   Selected Indicators for Four Countries in Southeast Asia   31
1.2   International Bank Lending by Banks, as of end-June 1997   32
1.3   Total Exposure of BIS Area Reporting Banks to
Non-BIS Borrowers, end-June 1997   32
1.4   Savings Rates in Selected Southeast Asian Countries, 1981-96   32
3.1   External Financing of Korea, Indonesia, Malaysia,
Philippines and Thailand   55
3.2   Asian Countries: Investment as Percentage of GDP, 1986-95   55
3.3   Asian Countries: Current Account Balances as a
Percentage of GDP, 1989-97   56
3.4   Asian Countries: Fiscal Balances as a Percentage of GDP, 1988-97   56
4.1   East Asia: Export Growth Trends   64
4.2   East Asia: Export Growth Rates in Selected Categories, 1995-96   64
4.3   East Asia: Aggregate Net Resource Flows   84
5.1   Approximate Contributions to IMF Loans   104
5.2   Thailand National Budget, January-December 1998   113
7.1   Indonesia: Inflation and Monetary Aggregates   164
7.2   Indonesia: Ratios of M2 and TAFI* to
GDP and to Each Other, 1970-91   168
7.3   Indonesia: Status of Bank Credit, 1993-1995   170
7.4   Indonesia: Monetary and Banking Data, 1990-96   172
7.5   Indonesia: Macroeconomic Fundamentals, 1990-96   173
8.1   Malaysia: Key Macroeconomic Variables, 1989-96   198
9.1   Some Macro Indicators for the Philippines, 1981-97   201
9.2   Philippines: Balance of Payments, 1990-97   206

CHARTS

P1   Southeast Asian Vulnerability   xiii
P2   IMF Prescription/East Asian Dilemma   xiv
7.1   Indonesia: Growth and Type of Banks, 1979-96   167
7.2   Rupiah/US Dollar Movements, 1 July–27 November 1997   176
7.3   Rupiah/US Dollar Movements, 1 December 1997–6 February 1998   177

GLOSSARY

AFTA	ASEAN Free Trade Area
AMC	Asset Management Corporation (Thai)
AMF	Asian Monetary Fund
APEC	Asia-Pacific Economic Cooperation
ASEAN	Association of South East Asian Nations
AWSJ	*Asian Wall Street Journal*
BAFIA	Bank and Financial Institutions Act, 1989 (Malaysia)
BBC	Bangkok Bank of Commerce
BIBF	Bangkok International Banking Facility
BIS	Bank of International Settlements
BMB	Bangkok Metropolitan Bank
BNM	Bank Negara Malaysia (Malaysian central bank)
BoT	Bank of Thailand
BSP	Banko Sentral Pilipinas (Philippine central bank)
CP	Chart Pattana (Thai political party)
CPI	consumer price index
EIU	Economist Intelligence Unit
EMS	European Monetary System
EPF	Employees Provident Fund (Malaysia)
ESCAP	United Nations Economic & Social Commission for Asia
EU	European Union
FDI	foreign direct investment
FEER	*Far Eastern Economic Review*
FIDF	Financial Institutions Development Fund
Fincos	finance companies
FRA	Financial Restructuring Agency (Thai)
G-7	Group of 7… (countries)
GATT	General Agreement on Tariffs and Trade
GDP	gross domestic product
GM	General Motors
GNP	gross national product
HIPC	heavily indebted poor countries
ICMI	Ikatan Cendekiawan Muslimin Indonesia (Indonesian Muslim Intellectuals Association)
IDL	Industrial Development Law (South Korea)
IFC	International Finance Corporation
IIF	Institute of International Finance

IMF	International Monetary Fund
IOFC	International Off-shore Financial Centre
ISA	Internal Security Act (Malaysia)
KCTU	Korean Confederation of Trade Unions
KLCI	Kuala Lumpur Composite Index
KLSE	Kuala Lumpur Stock Exchange
KUB	Koperasi Usaha Bersatu (Malaysia)
M1	currency and demand deposits
M2	M1 plus savings deposits
MAI	Multilateral Agreement on Investment
MISC	Malaysian International Shipping Corporation
MMC	Malaysian Mining Corporation
MOF	Ministry of Finance
NAP	New Aspiration Party (Thai)
NBFIs	non-bank financial institutions
NEAC	National Economic Action Council (Malaysia)
NFPE	non-financial public enterprise
OBI	Office of the Board of Investment (Thai)
OECD	Organisation for Economic Cooperation and Development
PLMO	Property Loan Management Organisation (Thai)
PNB	Permodalan Nasional Berhad (National Equity Limited)
PT	Perusahaan Tersendiri (Limited Company)
R&D	research and development
RAB	Radhanasin Bank (Thai)
SBI	Sertifikat Bank Indonesia (Bank of Indonesia Certificate)
SBPU	Surat Berharga Pasar Uang (banker's acceptance instrument saleable to)
SC	Securities Commission (Malaysia)
SEC	Securities and Exchange Commission
SES	Stock Exchange of Singapore
SMEs	small and medium-sized enterprises
SMIs	small and medium industries
TAFI	total assets of financial institutions
TDRI	Thailand Development Research Institute
TPI	Thai Petrochemical Industry Co. Ltd
UEM	United Engineers Malaysia
UK	United Kingdom
UMNO	United Malays National Organisation (Malaysia)
UN	United Nations
UNCTAD	United Nations Conference on Trade and Development
US	United States
WTO	World Trade Organisation

FOREWORD

Around the world, the way in which power is shared, decisions are made, and various interest groups are accorded a voice in the shaping of public policy, is in a state of profound change. This is particularly true in East Asia, where rapid social and economic development in the past few decades has been the subject of countless publications, seminars and dialogues around the world. Much of the discussion on East Asia has underlined the link between governance and social and economic development. If governance factors contributed to the rapid growth in East Asia, what role does governance continue to play through the financial and economic crisis? What can we learn from this experience which will be useful, not only in Asia, but in other developing and developed countries around the world?

If governance is to be made more effective, we must first ask questions like these and then ensure that analytically sound, balanced views, are brought to the debate. With that in mind we, at the Institute On Governance, are pleased to be able to contribute to the publication of *Tigers in Trouble: Financial Governance, Liberalisation and Crises in East Asia.*

This book provides a holistic and balanced analysis of the crisis. It outlines the role of deregulation, financial liberalisation and globalisation. It analyses the policy responses of the IMF and examines the quality of macroeconomic and financial governance in the region. The authors agree that macroeconomic management in the region has not been seriously awry. They argue that the undermining of national financial governance by the forces of financial liberalisation has played a role in the crisis, and must be considered in the debate over recovery. Finally, the book discusses factors such as cronyism and rent seeking, which have played more complicated roles in the crisis than popularly assumed in recent discourse.

It is our pleasure to congratulate the authors of *Tigers in Trouble* for their balanced approach, sound analysis and commitment to the process of discussion and debate on important governance and development issues at both international and national levels.

Robert Giroux
Chairman
Institute On Governance
Ottawa, Canada

Kathleen Lauder
Director
Institute On Governance
Kuala Lumpur, Malaysia

ACKNOWLEDGEMENTS

Robert Molteno of Zed Books first approached me to undertake this volume last year. Not knowing enough about the other economies in the region as well as the international financial system, I initially declined. However, in late January 1998, at a meeting in Oslo organised by some Norwegian colleagues, I discovered that several other colleagues were developing very similar analyses of the currency and related liquidity crises in Southeast Asia and South Korea. With encouragement from various friends, I began preparation of this volume.

This volume would never have materialised without the co-operative support of all the contributors to the volume, who promptly responded to my every request. I am also appreciative of the willingness of the publishers to put this book on a 'fast track' in view of the urgency of influencing public discourse on an ongoing crisis which has generated tremendous debate internationally. I am also grateful to Elsevier for allowing us to include a slightly revised version of the South Korean chapter by Chang Ha-Joon which appeared in the August 1998 issue of *World Development*. The same issue also contains earlier versions of the contributions by Laurids Lauridsen and myself.

I am also grateful for the financial and human support generously provided by the Southeast Asian office of the Institute On Governance based in Ottawa. I especially want to thank Kathleen Lauder, Brenda Melles, Mary John and Tony Tsou for their prompt and careful help with proof-reading and indexing, going well beyond the call of duty. As always, Foo Ah Hiang has given me sterling support in preparing this volume for publication, while Robert Molteno, Anne Rodford and Farouk Sohawon have been consistently supportive from the Zed offices in London. Meanwhile, Chong Ton Sin and Lai Kwong Onn have been helpful with attending to production matters and the cover design respectively.

As usual, my loving children, Nadia and Emil, and my mother have taken the brunt of my involvement in yet another project of this nature. All I can say is 'sorry and thank you'.

Jomo K.S.
June 1998

IN LIEU OF A PREFACE

Chart P1
Southeast Asian Vulnerability

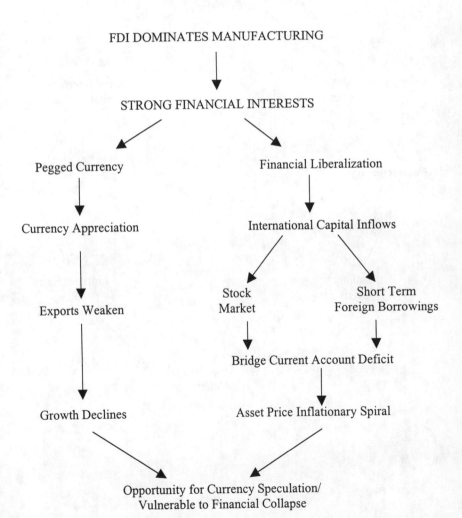

FDI DOMINATES MANUFACTURING

STRONG FINANCIAL INTERESTS

Pegged Currency

Financial Liberalization

Currency Appreciation

International Capital Inflows

Exports Weaken

Stock
Market

Short Term
Foreign Borrowings

Bridge Current Account Deficit

Growth Declines

Asset Price Inflationary Spiral

Opportunity for Currency Speculation/
Vulnerable to Financial Collapse

Chart P2
IMF Prescription/East Asian Dilemma

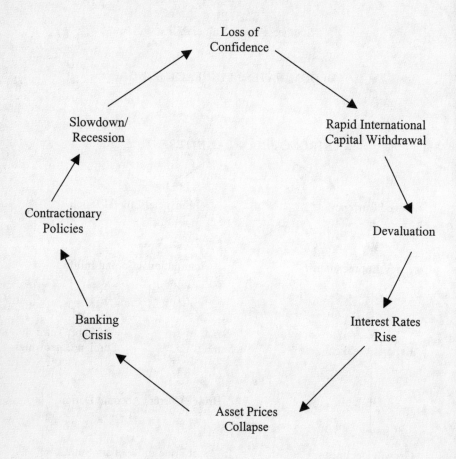

Loan Distribution

Table P1
Distribution of Loans by Country of Origin — End June 1997
(US$ million)

Claims on	*Grand Total*	*France*	*Germany*	*Japan*	*UK*	*US*
Indonesia	58,726	4,787	5,610	23,153	4,332	4,591
South Korea	103,432	10,070	10,794	23,732	6,064	9,964
Malaysia	28,820	2,934	5,716	10,489	2,011	2,400
Philippines	14,115	1,678	1,991	2,109	1,076	2,816
Thailand	69,382	5,089	7,557	37,749	2,818	4,008

Source: Bank of International Settlements (BIS).

BIS Bank Lending

Table P2
Lending by BIS Reporting Banks by Country and by Sector — End June 1997
(US$ million)

	Total	*Banks*	*Public Sector*	*Non-bank Private Sector*
Indonesia	58,726	12,393	6,506	39,742
South Korea	103,432	67,290	4,390	31,680
Malaysia	28,820	10,486	1,851	16,460
Philippines	14,115	5,485	1,855	6,772
Thailand	69,382	26,069	1,968	41,262

Note: Consolidated cross-border claims in all currencies and local claims in non-local currencies.

Source: Bank of International Settlements (BIS).

Loan Maturity

Table P3

Maturity Distribution of Lending of BIS Reporting Banks — Up to June 1997

(US$ million)

	Total			Under 1 Year			1-2 Years			Over 2 Years		
	June 96	Dec. 96	June 97	June 96	Dec. 96	June 97	June 96	Dec. 96	June 97	June 96	Dec. 96	June 97
Indonesia	49,306	55,523	58,726	29,587	34,248	34,661	3,473	3,589	3,541	14,177	15,331	17,008
South Korea	88,027	99,953	103,432	62,332	67,506	70,182	3,438	4,107	4,139	13,434	15,884	16,366
Malaysia	20,100	22,234	28,820	9,991	11,178	16,268	834	721	615	7,425	7,326	8,248
Philippines	10,795	13,289	14,115	5,948	7,737	8,293	531	565	326	3,710	4,111	4,001
Thailand	69,409	70,147	69,382	47,834	45,702	45,567	4,083	4,829	4,592	14,931	16,344	16,491

Note: Consolidated cross-border claims in all currencies and local claims in non-local currencies.
Source: Bank of International Settlements (BIS).

1
INTRODUCTION: FINANCIAL GOVERNANCE, LIBERALISATION AND CRISES IN EAST ASIA

Jomo K.S.*

Since July 1997, the currencies of all three second-tier Southeast Asian newly industrialised countries (NICs) have fallen precipitously, with the stock markets responding in tandem. The Philippines has also been similarly affected although not as badly. At the end of 1997, despite its rather different economic structure, South Korea too went into free fall, arguably with more disastrous consequences. Most other economies in East Asia have also been under considerable pressure, either directly (e.g. with the attack on the Hong Kong dollar) or indirectly (e.g. due to the desire to maintain comparative cost advantage against the now greatly devalued currencies of Southeast Asian exporters).

Contrary to the impression conveyed by many economic journalists and commentators as well as by the International Monetary Fund (IMF), there is little agreement on how to understand and characterise this crisis. One manifestation of this has been the debate between the IMF and its critics over the appropriateness of its negotiated programmes in Thailand, Indonesia and South Korea. Some critics also point out that the Philippines has not been spared despite being under an IMF programme since the mid-1980s. The Suharto government's plans to establish a currency board in Indonesia have also generated much debate along different lines.

While the policy debates have understandably captured the most attention, especially with the public at large, the East Asian crisis has also challenged economists, especially international economists. Some still see the crisis as essentially a currency crisis, although perhaps of a new type, different from those previously identified with either fiscal profligacy or macroeconomic indiscipline.

* I am grateful to Jan Kregel, Al Alim Ibrahim, Din Merican and Warren Bailey for their useful critical feedback, but implicate none of them.
There continues to be considerable debate over the principal causes and consequences of the recent currency and financial crises in Southeast Asia. This essay is deliberately polemical as there is clearly no shared understanding of the various contentious issues involved. As far as possible, the language is not technical, in order to be accessible to as wide a readership as is feasible. Since events are still unfolding, such reflections should be open to revision with the passage of time, events and trends, and the benefit of hindsight. Hence, criticisms and suggestions are especially appreciated.

Approaching it slightly differently, other economists see it as a balance of payments crisis, emphasising the current account deficits sustained by most of the economies affected. A growing number maintain that the crisis started off as a financial crisis, though most agree that it has already had and is likely to have tremendous consequences for the real economy, either because of its consequences for the financial sector or because of the consequences of official policy and other responses.

There is also considerable debate about the implications of this crisis for economic development, particularly for the debate over whether the East Asian experience of the last three decades offered different lessons and prescriptions for development from those advocated by the 'counter-revolution' against development economics. As is now well known, this neo-liberal reaction has maintained that development economics and its prescriptions were bad economics, based on distortions of neo-classical welfare economics, which exaggerated the extent and implications of 'market failure' and underestimated the likelihood of 'state failure' and its consequences.

Influential economists at the World Bank and elsewhere are already citing the East Asian financial crisis to criticise the Bank's (1993) *East Asian Miracle* volume as flawed. In particular, the critics denounce part of the study's acknowledgement of the success of 'directed credit' and what has come to be known as 'financial restraint' — said to have been authored by the Bank's current senior vice-president and chief economist, Joseph Stiglitz, who has also dissented on the appropriateness of IMF prescriptions for the current financial crisis.

With the mid-1997 crisis starting not long after Paul Krugman's (1994) claims that East Asian growth is not sustainable because it is based primarily on factor accumulation — eventually subject to diminishing returns rather than productivity growth ('perspiration rather than inspiration') — many critics from across the political spectrum have seen the East Asian financial crisis as evidence of Krugman's argument, or of some variation thereof. Often, there is more than a touch of neo-liberal triumphalism in hasty pronouncements of the end of the Asian miracle or in word plays of 'miracle or debacle', 'tigers or fat cats' and the like.

Meanwhile, in recent years, there has been growing recognition of major structural and systemic differences among the eight high performing Asian economies (HPAEs) studied by the World Bank (1993), namely Japan, South Korea, Taiwan, Hong Kong, Singapore, Malaysia, Thailand and Indonesia. The last three have been increasingly grouped as second-tier or second-generation Southeast Asian NICs, with characteristics quite different from the others, and of course, even among themselves. It has been argued that industrial policy or selective state intervention has been of much poorer quality and less effective in these economies for various reasons; instead, there has been much other state intervention motivated by less developmentalist considerations, especially in

Malaysia and Indonesia (Jomo *et al.* 1997). It appears that such interventions bear some of the responsibility for the vulnerability of the second-tier Southeast Asian NICs to the factors which have precipitated the mid-1997 financial crisis in the region.

Macroeconomic Concerns

Rapid economic growth and structural change, mainly associated with industrialisation in the region, are generally traced back to the mid-1980s. Devaluations in all three countries as well as selective deregulation of onerous rules helped create attractive conditions for the relocation of production facilities in these countries and elsewhere in Southeast Asia and China, especially from Japan and the first-tier or first-generation newly industrialising economies (NIEs) of South Korea, Taiwan, Hong Kong and Singapore. This dynamic growth sustained export-oriented industrialisation well into the nineties, but was soon accompanied by the growth of other manufacturing, services as well as construction.

This is not to suggest that the fundamentals were all alright in Southeast Asia. Although high growth was sustained for almost a decade, during most of which fiscal balances were in order, monetary expansion was not excessive and inflation was generally under control, some other indices have been awry. The export-led growth of Southeast Asian economies since the late 1980s has been followed by a construction and property boom, fuelled by financial sectors favouring such 'short-termist' investments — involving loans with collateral which bankers like — over more productive, but often more risky investments in manufacturing and agriculture. The exaggerated expansion of investment in such 'non-tradables' has exacerbated current account trade deficits. Although widespread in East Asia, for various reasons, the property–finance nexus was particularly strong in Thailand, which made it much more vulnerable to the inevitable bursting of the bubble.

Financial liberalisation from the 1980s also saw major ramifications in the region, as foreign savings supplemented the already high domestic savings rates in the region to further accelerate the rate of capital accumulation, albeit in increasingly unproductive activities owing to the foreign domination of most internationally competitive industries in the region. Consequently, several related macroeconomic concerns had emerged from the rapid growth of the last decade by the mid-1990s:

First, the *savings-investment gap*, which was 5 per cent of GNP in 1997, *lay behind the current account deficit*,[1] which has exceeded RM12 (almost US$5) billion since 1994. The gap had been bridged historically by heavy reliance on foreign direct investment (FDI). But high FDI and foreign debt have, in turn, caused growing investment income outflows abroad.[2] In recent years, the current account gap has been temporarily bridged by short-term capital inflows, as in 1993 and since 1995, with disastrous consequences later with the subsequent reversal of such flows. Many recent confidence restoration measures seek to induce such short-term inflows once again, but they cannot be relied upon to address the underlying problem in the medium to long term.[3]

Although always in the minority, foreign investment institutions 'made' the stock markets in the region, shifting their assets among securities markets as well as among different types of financial investment options all over the world. In the face of limited transparency, the regional nature of their presence, the nature of fund managers' incentives and remuneration and the short-termism of their investment horizons, foreign financial institutions were much more prone to herd behaviour and contributed most to the regional spread of contagion.

Second, there was a *recent explosion of private sector debt, especially from abroad*, not least due to the efforts of 'debt-pushers' associated with greater competition in bank lending.[4] The ratio of loans to Gross National Product (GNP) has risen rapidly in recent years. Meanwhile, commercial banks' foreign liabilities more than tripled between 1995 and 1997. This is partly why the standard insistence on raising domestic interest rates is quite misleading as much of the recent increase in corporate borrowings has come from abroad. This has exacerbated the impact of the current crisis, with triple pain caused by currency depreciation, stock market collapse and rising interest rates.

Meanwhile, the *over-investment* of investible funds, especially from abroad, in *'non-tradables'* only made things worse, especially for the current account. Only a small proportion of commercial bank and other lending has gone to manufacturing, agriculture, mining and other productive activities; the percentage is likely to be even smaller with foreign borrowings, most of which have been collateralised with assets such as real property and stock.[5] In other words, much of the inflow of foreign savings actually contributed to an *asset price inflation*, mainly involving real estate and share prices. Insofar as such investments did not contribute to increased production of 'tradables', they actually exacerbated the *current account deficit*,[6] rather than alleviated it — as they were thought to be doing. This, in turn, worsened the problem of 'currency mismatch', with borrowings in US dollars invested in activities not generating foreign exchange. Insofar as a high proportion of these foreign borrowings were short term in nature and were deployed to finance medium to long-term projects, an additional 'term mismatch' problem also arose.

More generally, the foreign exchange risk of investments generally increased, raising the vulnerability of these economies to the maintenance of the *quasi-pegs* of their currencies to the US dollar,[7] which had, in turn, encouraged a great deal of *unhedged borrowing* involving an influential constituency with a strong stake in defending the peg regardless of its adverse consequences for the economy. Owing to foreign domination of export-oriented industries in Southeast Asia, unlike Northeast Asia, there was no strong domestic export-oriented industrial community to lobby for floating or depreciation of the Southeast Asian currencies despite the obvious adverse consequences of the peg for international cost competitiveness. Instead, after virtually pegging their currencies to the US dollar since the advent of flexible exchange rates, from the early 1990s and especially from the mid-1990s, most Southeast Asian central banks resisted downward adjustments in their exchange rates, which would have reduced, if not averted some of the more disruptive consequences of the recent currency collapses.[8]

According to the Bank of International Settlements (BIS) (*Asian Wall Street Journal*, 6 January 1998), well over half of foreign borrowings from commercial banks were short term in nature, i.e. coming due soon: Malaysia 56 per cent, Thailand 66 per cent, Indonesia 59 per cent and South Korea 68 per cent. There is growing evidence of continued lending by continental European and Japanese banks to East Asian customers despite warnings by the BIS and others well before the crisis broke in July 1997 (Raghavan 1998).

Collapse: The Bubble Bursts

Contrary to the claim that 'the market' will exact swift and painful punishment on governments and economies which do not have their macroeconomic house in order, the timing, nature and consequences of the mid-1997 financial crisis in Southeast Asia underline the imperfect nature of financial markets. This has been reflected in the long delay in 'rectification'. For example, current account deficits were more serious in 1995 compared to 1997, but there was no rectification then, let alone punishment of the culprits, i.e. current account deficits in Malaysia and some other neighbouring economies had reached all time highs, without any commensurate adverse effect.[9]

In the wake of the Mexican crisis in early 1995, even the IMF had stepped back momentarily from its advocacy of virtually unfettered financial liberalisation. Unfortunately, the short-termism of financial markets extends to human and institutional memories as well as to related policy-making and advocacy. The recent crisis has also seen a market where the magnitude of 'overshooting' exceeds that of the 'correction' many times over. Further evidence of market-induced anarchy can be found in the 'herd behaviour' underlying the 'contagion' or 'domino' effects. While some governments and economies have been badly affected by the crisis since mid-1997, there is little evidence that the private sector culprits have suffered most as a consequence, i.e. not only is the market neither efficient nor swift, it is also unjust.

Perceiving the Southeast Asian region as much more integrated than it actually is (e.g. in terms of trade links excluding Singapore, the regional entrepôt), the panicky investment decisions of fund managers based outside the region — e.g. in Wall Street or the City of London — have often been 'herd-like',[10] causing a 'contagion' or 'domino' effect throughout the region. The very logic and magnitude of hedge fund operations[11] have tended to exacerbate these phenomena, with disastrous snowballing consequences for the region. Other international, regional and, increasingly, local currency speculators and hedgers have also been responsible, but mainly reacting in their own self-interest to perceived market trends, rather than as part of some grand conspiracy.

Lessons

Obviously, one cannot wish away the present situation by simply claiming that East Asian economic fundamentals are fine, even if that were true. Unfortunately, as East Asia has painfully learnt, the market is driven by sentiments as much as by fundamentals. Hence, although much more serious current account deficits in 1995 did not result in crisis, the authorities have to be careful to minimise vulnerability due to the economy's openness.

One cannot, for example, liberalise the capital account, and then complain when short-term portfolio investors suddenly withdraw due to their whims and fancies. That is why, even Chile, the darling of the Chicago monetarists, makes it very difficult — and costly — to rapidly withdraw capital from its economy, and treats foreign direct investment (FDI) very differently from portfolio investment. Some other authorities may try to go further to distinguish those who are simply short-termist from, say, pension funds with a more medium-term orientation. After all, one cannot expect more birds to fly into rather than out of an open birdcage indefinitely since the basic premise of financial liberalisation is 'easy come, easy go'.[12]

In recent years, many Southeast Asian economies became excessively reliant on such short-term capital inflows to bridge their current account deficits. This was exacerbated by excessive imports to make more non-exportables such as buildings. Ostensibly prudent financial institutions often preferred to lend for real property and stock purchases, and thus secure assets with rising values as collateral, rather than to provide credit for more productive ends.

While foreign banks were happy to lend US dollars at higher interest rates than available elsewhere, Southeast Asian businesses were keen to borrow at lower interest rates than available domestically. The costs of hedging — a hundred basis points or so for ringgit-dollar, a few hundred for baht-dollar or rupiah-dollar — now look cheap in hindsight. The existence of a well-developed swap market allows Southeast Asian companies to tap into foreign capital markets, at a not unreasonable cost, by swapping away the currency risk. The problem was ultimately one of greed: the combination of much lower foreign interest rates and seemingly fixed exchange rates caused borrowers to gamble and not prudently pay the cost for some insurance by hedging.

Hence, most such loans remained unhedged as Southeast Asian currencies seemed pegged to the US dollar in recent years despite the official fictions of exchange rates moving with the basket of currencies of major foreign trading partners. The boom in bank lending in the region in recent years led to intense competition reminiscent of lending to Third World governments in the late seventies (which built up to the debt crisis of the early eighties). However, the new fiction in international policy-making circles was that such accumulation of private sector debt did not matter as long as public sector debt was reined in.

Meanwhile, portfolio investors moved into the newly emerging stock markets of Southeast Asia with encouragement from the International Finance Corporation, an arm of the World Bank. In Malaysia, for example, they came in a big way in 1993, only to withdraw even more suddenly in early 1994, leaving most retail stockholders in the lurch. But unfortunately, policymakers seem to have short memories and did not learn the lessons from that experience as the new unsustainable build-up from 1995 sent stock prices soaring once again despite declining price–earnings ratios. The rest is history, but as a wise man once said, when history repeats itself, the first time it's tragedy, the second time farce.

Thus, the Southeast Asian currency and financial crises since mid-1997 have been partly due to financial liberalisation and its consequent undermining of monetary and financial governance. The 'quasi-pegs' of the region's currencies to the US dollar and the encouragement of foreign capital inflows — into the recently opened-up stock markets as well as in the form of borrowings, often on a short-term basis[13] — to close the current account deficit, also ensured that foreign savings supplemented the already high domestic savings rate to raise investment rates in the region, contributing to a spiralling inflationary bubble of share and real property prices. The quasi-peg not only encouraged unhedged borrowing from abroad, but also became a target for currency speculators as regional currencies appreciated with the US dollar despite declining export competitiveness and growth. Meanwhile, financial liberalisation allowed lucrative opportunities for taking advantage of falling currencies, thus accelerating and exacerbating the collapse of regional currency and share markets. All this, together with unjudicious official responses, transformed the inevitable 'correction' of overvalued currencies in the region into a collapse of the currencies and the stock markets of the region as panic set in, exacerbated by herd behaviour and contagion.

Although the financial systems in the region are quite varied and hardly clones of the Japanese 'main bank' system, as often wrongly alleged, they have nevertheless become prone — owing to particular policy conjunctures — to the same financial-property 'bubble' phenomena, albeit for somewhat different reasons. Arguably, the more bank-based systems of Thailand, Korea and Indonesia had a stronger nexus of this sort compared to, say, Malaysia's much more stock market-oriented financial system. Rapid growth, on the basis of export-oriented industrial-isation from the late 1980s, gave rise to unregulated financial expansion, which contributed to a property boom and asset price bubbles, both in the more market-oriented or 'Anglo-Saxon' Malaysia as well as the more bank-oriented Thailand.

With the currency collapses, the assets acquired by short-term portfolio and other investors in the region depreciated correspondingly in value, precipitating an even greater sell-out and panic, causing herd behaviour and probably causing contagion to spread across national borders to the rest of the region. In Malaysia and perhaps elsewhere, further property market and stock market collapses seem imminent in view of anarchic over-building and the property–finance nexus. Thus, many will be hit by this 'triple whammy' from the currency, stock and property markets.

The higher interest rates being demanded by the financial community will add salt to the wound, and has shown little success so far in increasing short-term capital inflows. But even when higher interest rates succeed in doing so, such flows can only be temporarily sustained and retained, at great and permanent cost to productive investments in the real economy. And if such outflows are eventually reversed in the precipitous manner experienced by Southeast Asia in the second half of 1997, much collateral damage will be experienced again.

Policy Challenges

As a consequence of recent developments, Southeast Asia now faces domestic policy reform challenges relating to four factors, namely *greater exchange rate flexibility*, the *urgency of financial sector reform*, as well as *handling asset price bubbles* and *current account deficits*. Before addressing the challenges on the domestic and international fronts, it is useful to summarise these four dimensions of the current crisis.

Without the advanced economies stabilising exchange rates with regard to one another's currencies, the *virtual* or *quasi-pegging* of an economy's foreign exchange rate has become very *dangerous*, as the recent crisis has demonstrated. Short-term capital inflows may temporarily supplement domestic savings, but the reversal of such flows can create severe disturbances. While such flows may be influenced by economic fundamentals in the long term, they are determined by speculative sentiments in the short term. Short-term exchange rate adjustments — with disruptive consequences for domestic prices and wages — are then deemed necessary to stem sudden outflows, but these, in turn, offer an opportunity for currency speculators.

Financial sector reform has to be thought of not only in terms of the liberalisation insisted upon by international financial interests, but also the *new regulation needed* to anticipate and respond to new challenges. While the problems caused by excessive as well as inappropriate regulation are often emphasised by advocates of liberalisation, liberal banking policies can result in a weak domestic banking sector[14] unable to withstand competition from abroad, and even the collapse or costly bail-out of weak banks. For most developing economies, policies of '*financial restraint*' are also *still needed* to 'direct' credit[15] to finance productive investments instead of asset purchases or consumption. Greater capital account convertibility, related financial innovation and the proliferation of non-bank finance companies as well as 'private banking' (discreet services for rich clients) also pose new challenges for financial regulation.

Easy credit, partly due to capital inflows, resulted in meteoric rises in real property as well as share prices desired by most of those involved. Banking regulation to minimise such asset price inflation deserves the highest priority, and is always difficult to achieve in 'good times' without precipitating an asset price meltdown. It will be easier to achieve now that the asset price bubble has burst.

Current account deficits have been considered 'natural' in Southeast Asia, as in many other fast growth situations, supposedly reflecting the excess of domestic investment over domestic savings; hence, they were not seen as a source of policy concern in certain policy-making circles. Since the debt crisis of the early and mid-eighties, the cutting of fiscal deficits gained top priority at the behest of the Bretton Woods institutions and others. Developments since the Mexican tequila meltdown of early 1995 suggest that the current account deficit was the Achilles' heel of the Southeast Asian economies, precipitating financial meltdowns beginning with the collapse of their currencies 'quasi-pegged' to the US dollar, inadvertently encouraging massive unhedged private borrowing from abroad.

Changed International Financial System

Malaysian Prime Minister Mahathir Mohamad's criticisms[16] of the role of international currency speculation in precipitating the recent East Asian crisis as well as the IMF policy responses have largely been dismissed outside of Malaysia except for those who recognise his remarks as reflecting confused frustration in the face of a new phenomenon not satisfactorily explained by conventional economic analysis. Hence, dismissing Mahathir would be tantamount to throwing the baby out with the bath water as Mahathir was trying to address a real problem, albeit incorrectly. After all, as many have already pointed out, the international financial system and its further liberalisation have favoured those already dominant and privileged in the world economy, at the expense of the real economy and of development in the South.

Ironically, Mahathir's arch-nemesis, the international financier George Soros has recently argued, quite correctly, that the unregulated expansion of capitalism, especially finance capital, threatens to undermine its own future, i.e. that capitalism has to be saved from itself. While admitting that he himself has profited greatly from financial liberalisation, Soros argued — in Keynesian mode — that excessive liberalisation has been resulting in virtual anarchy, dangerous for the stability so necessary for the orderly capitalist growth and democratic development desired by his liberal vision of a Popperian 'open society'.

The prevailing system of flexible exchange rates was introduced a quarter of a century ago, inaugurating a new international monetary regime with very mixed consequences. Hence, the current regime is relatively new, only beginning after US President Nixon's 1971 unilateral withdrawal from the Bretton Woods' regime of fixed exchange rates — which had pegged the dollar to gold at US$35 per ounce and other currencies to the US dollar. Under the new regime, the volume of foreign exchange spot transactions had grown to more than 67 times the total value of the international trade in goods by 1995, or more than 40 times the value of all international trade (including 'invisibles' or services).[17] Viewed from a historical perspective then, such currency trading is hardly natural, inevitable or even desirable. For most of human history, including that of capitalism, it has not been 'integral to global trade in goods and services', as claimed by US Treasury Secretary Robert Rubin. In fact, as is well known, various critics have offered various alternatives to the present system such as returning to fixed exchange rates, the gold standard and so on.

In a world economy where foreign exchange spot transactions are now worth more than 70 times the total value of international commodity trade transactions, the financial sector has become increasingly divorced from the real economy. With the recent proliferation of new financial instruments and markets, especially in Malaysia, the financial sector has an even greater potential to inflict damage on the real economy. Ever since Lord Keynes advocated 'throwing sand' into the financial system to check the potentially disastrous consequences of unfettered liberalisation, Keynesians — and others — have been wary of the financial liberalisation advocated by ideological neo-liberals and their often naive allies.

In a telling episode at the beginning of September, IMF deputy head, Stanley Fischer pointed out that although the current account deficits in Southeast Asia had emerged quite some years ago, markets had failed to adjust — contrary to the predictions of conventional economic theory. (In response, instead of recognising the failure of market mechanisms, US Federal Reserve Chair Alan Greenspan gently chided Fischer, expecting the IMF to 'inform' Wall Street.)

Nobel laureate in economics James Tobin has called for a tax on foreign exchange spot transactions to enable more independent national monetary policy, discourage speculative capital movements and increase the relative weight of long-term economic fundamentals against more short-termist and speculative considerations. As a bonus, the tax collected would also more than adequately fund the United Nations system and programmes, not leaving it hostage to the whims of US leadership, as has recently been the case. Another Nobel laureate, Lawrence Klein has mentioned two other options to be considered besides the Tobin tax, namely regional monetary arrangements as well as the introduction of mechanisms analogous to what are popularly known as 'circuit-breakers' into the system — a suggestion also made by the World Bank's senior vice-president and chief economist, Joseph Stiglitz.

But the lobby for financial liberalisation remains much stronger and far more influential, dominating most of the business media and the key financial institutions internationally, especially in the US. Acknowledging that money is not just another commodity, the *Wall Street Journal*, for example, continues to promote currency boards (instead of central banks) and the pegging of other currencies against the US dollar, while attacking most other international monetary alternatives, rarely acknowledging the advantages that dollar pegs have given to the US, such as having the rest of the world finance its huge deficits.

Implications of Financial Liberalisation

An explosion of international financial flows followed the substitution of the Bretton Woods system of fixed exchange rates with a new system of flexible exchange rates. Strong speculative motives are generally ascribable to international capital flows. However, the loosening of fixed exchange rates was also associated with a loosening of capital controls, permitting many investors to diversify to their advantage. In any case, the trend picked up momentum from the 1980s, leading to a US$1,250 billion daily foreign exchange market by 1997, and the proliferation of new financial instruments. Yet, many of the alleged benefits of financial liberalisation have not been realised, as the following summary of recent findings by Lord Eatwell (1997a) shows.

* First, financial liberalisation was expected to move resources from capital-rich to capital-poor countries,[18] when in fact, *net flows* of finance — and of real resources — have been very *modest*, and mainly towards the capital-rich.[19] Of course, most net flows to the 'capital-poor' were mainly to 'emerging markets' such as those in East Asia, which arguably contributed to asset price bubbles and, eventually, to financial panic and currency and stock market collapse.
* Second, while liberalisation was expected to enhance opportunities for savers and lower costs to borrowers, savers have benefited most from *higher real interest rates*.[20]
* Third, the *new financial derivatives* — expected to improve risk management — have actually *generated new systemic risks*, especially vulnerable to sudden changes in sentiment.[21]
* Fourth, improved macroeconomic performance — with greater investment and growth expected from better allocative efficiency — has not been realised; in fact, *overall macroeconomic performance* has been *worse* than before liberalisation.[22]
* Fifth, financial liberalisation has introduced a *persistent deflationary bias* on economic policy as governments try to gain credibility to avert destabilising capital flows, instead of the 'healthy discipline' on governments expected to improve macroeconomic stability.

Financial markets seem to function in such a way as to impose their own 'expectations' on the real economy, thus defining their own 'fundamentals' and logic, which in turn become self-fulfilling prophecies. In other words, they do not just process information in order to efficiently allocate resources. Since financial markets operate like beauty contests and the real economy has no automatic tendency to converge to full-employment growth, the presumed analytical assumptions of other market participants become imposed on the economy.

The threat of instability in the now massive capital market forces both government and private investors to pursue risk-averse strategies, resulting in low growth and employment creation. A deflationary bias in government policy and the private sector emerges in response to the costly risks of violating the rules of the game. This is exacerbated by the high costs of debt due to high real interest rates owing to efforts to maintain financial stability in a potentially volatile world. Thus, 'long-term price stability' supersedes a 'high and stable level of employment' as the policy priority. Such a monetarily stable system, involving relatively slow growth and high unemployment, can last indefinitely.

A sophisticated liberalised financial system, prioritising flexibility or the possibility of easy exit, is necessarily fragile, as reflected in:

- liquidity crises, *reducing real output*;
- private sector risk aversion, encouraging *short-termism*;[23]
- public sector risk aversion, resulting in a *deflationary policy bias*;
- persistent pressure for ever *greater flexibility*, increasing the ease of exit.

The benefits that the reduction of financial controls have brought to 'emerging markets' must be weighed against the increased instability due to *enhanced ease of exit*. While increased flows of (real) FDI generally require agreement to unrestricted profit repatriation, this is quite different from the 'instant exit' conditions demanded by financial markets.[24]

There is considerable evidence that in the longer term, economic development has been associated with developmentalist states. The post-war Golden Age — which saw high levels of output and employment as well as short-run efficiency — was premised on active macroeconomic management under the Bretton Woods system. Post-war European reconstruction was achieved with tight capital controls. On the other hand, the recent rush to convertibility and capital control deregulation in Eastern Europe has resulted in Russia becoming a significant net capital exporter![25]

Some dangers associated with financial liberalisation have now become quite evident, but most are not being sufficiently recognised, let alone debated and addressed. Most initiatives in this regard cannot be undertaken unilaterally without great cost, as market reactions to Malaysian Prime Minister Mahathir's critical remarks have made clear. The very few options available for unilateral initiatives need to be carefully considered, and only implemented, if deemed desirable.

Selectively invoking instances of bad or incompetent policy-making or implementation does not justify leaving things to liberalised markets that render systematic policy-making impossible. Instead, it emphasises the importance of creating an environment and developing the capability for good and competent policy to be effective.

Many need to be actively pursued through multilateral initiatives, for which the governments need the support of neighbours and others. Given the power of the dominant ideology which infuses the prevailing international system, it is virtually impossible to assert control over the financial system without a fundamental change in priorities and thinking by the major governments involved. However, the currencies of a small number of major governments — the US, Japan, Germany and the UK — were involved in over three-quarters of currency transactions in 1995. Hence, acting together, they have the capability to control capital flows, but of course, only if they abandon faith in the alleged superiority of neo-liberalism.

Analytical Catch-up

It seems fair to say that no one fully anticipated the current crisis in East Asia. There were, of course, sceptics who regarded the claims of an East Asian economic miracle as somewhat exaggerated, albeit for different reasons, e.g. because they had not achieved much productivity growth and would eventually run up against diminishin`g returns (Krugman 1994); others argued that the performances of the Southeast Asian newly industrialising countries (NICs) were significantly inferior compared to Japan and the first-tier NIEs (Jomo *et al.* 1997).

Some had warned, in the aftermath of the Mexican meltdown of early 1995, that current account deficits in Southeast Asia were worryingly high, and that the region was not immune to financial difficulties. But even such pessimists never expected the financial crisis in the region as it has unfolded since mid-1997. They only expected some kind of conventional currency crisis, followed by a temporary slowdown before recovery on a more sustainable basis. Even people like Krugman expected the longer-term slowdown to set in more gradually, with the lead geese affected first.

What happened in East Asia has been far more dramatic than Mexico in early 1995 as well as much more complicated, with asset prices collapsing, banks and other financial institutions failing, many companies going bankrupt, and probably a far more severe and protracted downturn than even the most pessimistic expected. It is now clear that the East Asian crisis differs from conventional currency crisis scenarios in at least several important ways (Krugman 1998):[26]

- the absence of the usual sources of currency stress, whether fiscal deficits or macroeconomic indiscipline;[27]

- the governments did not have any incentive to abandon their pegged exchange rates, e.g. to reduce unemployment;
- the pronounced boom-bust cycles in asset prices (real property and stock markets) *preceded* the currency crisis, especially in Thailand, where the crisis began;
- financial intermediaries have been key players in all the economies involved;
- the severity of the crisis in the absence of strong adverse shocks;
- the rapid spread of the initial crisis in Thailand, even to economies with few links or similarities to the first victims.

Very importantly then, the traditional indices of vulnerability did not signal a crisis as the source of the problem was not to be found in the governments *per se* or in national income accounts. The (mainly private) financial intermediaries were 'not part of the governments' visible liabilities until after the fact'. For Krugman (1998) then, one cannot adequately make sense of the crisis in terms of conventional currency crisis models; for him, *the crisis has mainly been about bad banking and its consequences, and only incidentally about currencies.*[28]

Rejecting the conventional views that blamed either fiscal deficits or macro-economic indiscipline, for Krugman (1998), the East Asian crisis has been brought about by 'financial excess and then financial collapse', involving asset price bubbles and then collapses, 'with the currency crisis more a symptom than a cause of this underlying real malady'. East Asian financial intermediaries 'were perceived as having an *implicit government guarantee*, but were essentially *unregulated* and therefore subject to *moral hazard* problems.[29] The excessive and risky lending of these institutions created *inflation* — not of goods, but of *asset prices*. The overpricing of assets was sustained, in part, by a sort of circular process, in which the *proliferation of risky lending drove up the prices of risky assets*, making the financial condition of the intermediaries seem sounder than it was.'

The crisis was thus precipitated by the bursting of the bubble: '*The mechanism of crisis... involved that same circular process in reverse: falling asset prices made the insolvency of intermediaries visible, forcing them to cease operations, leading to further asset deflation.* The circularity, in turn, can explain both the remarkable severity of the crisis and the apparent vulnerability of the Asian economies to self-fulfilling crisis — which in turn helps us understand the phenomenon of contagion between economies with few visible links' (my emphases).

The East Asian vulnerability to crisis contagion was also unanticipated.[30] In light of the limited trade and investment relations among Southeast Asian economies (barring Singapore) and the fact that other economies elsewhere producing the same exports have not been similarly affected, popular explanations — invoking regional proximity, linkages and competition — do not stand up to much careful scrutiny. The plight of South Korea, further away and economically quite different, has also undermined such easy explanations, encouraging instead new hypotheses about East Asia more generally, implying that those affected are mutant flying geese with Japanese-type economies and problems. As the chapters in this volume show, Krugman's suggested sequencing seems more relevant for understanding Thailand, whereas the sequencing in the rest of the region appears to have been different.

Other issues also need to be taken into account for an adequate analysis of the East Asian crisis:

* financial *crises* have very severe effects on growth because they *disrupt* the *productive contribution of financial intermediation*;
* the East Asian crises have not only involved excessive investments, but also *unwise investments*;
* the huge real currency *depreciations* are likely to *cause large declines in output*;
* other kinds of market failure, e.g. herd behaviour, need to be taken into account.

While the analysis offered in this volume is not inconsistent with Krugman's emphasis on asset price bubbles, excessive investments and other problems caused by moral hazard due to implicit government guarantees for weakly regulated financial intermediaries, a more adequate analysis must also account for various other phenomena including:

* the implications of the growth in currency trading and speculation in the post-Bretton Woods international monetary system;
* the reasons for the Southeast Asian monetary authorities to defend their quasi-pegs against the strengthening US dollar despite its obvious adverse consequences for export competitiveness and hence for growth;
* the consequences of financial liberalisation, including the creation of conditions which have contributed to the magnitude of the crisis;
* the role of herd behaviour in exacerbating the crisis;
* other factors accounting for the contagion effects.

A number of policy issues also deserve careful consideration, including the nature and implications of IMF 'rescue' programmes and the conditionalities imposed by the Fund, as well as of policies favoured by the international as distinct from the domestic financial communities, and others affected. The adverse consequences of financial disintermediation and grossly undervalued currencies for economic development also deserve special attention, especially as the crisis threatens the future of growth and structural change in the region, not only directly, but also as a consequence of policy responses. The contractionary policies favoured by the IMF, the international financial community as well as others, recently including Malaysia's financial authorities, may well throw out the baby of economic development with the bath water of financial crisis.

Understanding the Southeast Asian Currency Crisis

In late 1997, Manuel Montes (1998) published the most serious attempt to understand the crisis in Southeast Asia. He begins by considering the most oft-cited popular explanations, suggesting that the crisis stemmed from the banking sector due to imprudent expansion and diversification of domestic financial markets, fuelled by short-term private borrowings. Montes (1998: 3) suggests that this was especially true of Thailand, but less so for Indonesia, Malaysia and the Philippines (in order of decreasing relevance), underlining the significance of the contagion effect; 'the differences raise questions about how sensitive the currency knockdown (and the associated divestment from these economies) are to economic fundamentals'.

Despite large current account deficits for the affected countries, more for Malaysia and Thailand compared to Indonesia and the Philippines, he notes that macroeconomic conditions were otherwise sound. He shows high growth and savings rates, and low inflation in the 1990s for the four most affected Southeast Asian economies, with the Philippines a bit of a laggard. By the mid-1990s, all had fiscal surpluses. Instead, Southeast Asian vulnerability was 'as in a classic credit crunch, from an over-extended mismatch in the maturity and currency unit between sources and uses of credit' (Montes 1998: 2).

Montes (1998: 7) sees the Thai crisis as 'the latest in a series of such crises in which a currency attack follows on (or is justified by) an unhealthy domestic banking system, following an episode, of say three to five years, of vigorous external capital inflows'. The currency collapse weakens the domestic banking system by increasing the range of non-viable investments based on the previous exchange rate, thus magnifying the crisis. Such crises have resulted in lower growth, higher unemployment and the deployment of taxpayer funds to salvage the financial system and related asset holdings.

Montes cites Kaminsky and Reinhart's (1996) study of 71 balance of payments crises and 25 banking crises during the period 1970-95. There were only three banking crises associated with the 25 balance of payments crises during 1970-79, but 22 banking crises which coincided with 46 payments crises over 1980-95, which they attribute to financial liberalisation from the 1980s, with a private lending boom culminating in a banking crisis and then a currency crisis. Thus, *Montes attributes the Southeast Asian currency crisis to the 'twin liberalisations' of domestic financial systems and opening of the capital account.*

Montes argues that financial liberalisation induced some new behaviour in the financial system, notably:

- domestic financial institutions had greater flexibility in offering interest rates to secure funds domestically and in bidding for foreign funds;
- they became less reliant on lending to the government;
- regulations, such as credit allocation rules and ceilings, were reduced;

• greater domestic competition has meant that ascendance depends on expanding lending portfolios, often at the expense of prudence.

Meanwhile, liberalising the capital account has essentially guaranteed non-residents ease of exit as well as fewer limitations on nationals holding foreign assets, thus inadvertently facilitating capital flight.

Historically, developing countries in Southeast Asia have successfully induced capital inflows, often by subsidising them through a variety of investment incentive programmes. Montes (1998: 11) argues that 'removing controls on capital inflows effectively subsidises net outflows, a self-defeating stance for a capital-needy economy to take'. Opening the capital account has also provided foreign fund managers with access to domestic bond and stock markets, and given the domestic financial system access to lower cost funds from abroad. Thus, offshore banking operations financed intermediation growth as well as competition among domestic financial groups.

The lending boom increasingly involved asset purchases fuelled by rising property and stock prices. Montes argues that the Thai authorities hesitated to prick the asset price bubble for two reasons. The dominant liberal economic ideology deemed it inappropriate for government authorities to bother about private sector-driven current account deficits. Similarly, it was felt that greater regulation would undermine healthy financial sector development.

To defuse upward pressure on the exchange rate, the Thai authorities engaged in costly sterilisation operations.[31] Montes emphasises that sterilisation measures put upward pressure on domestic interest rates, increasing the differential with foreign interest rates, thus inducing even more inflows. With the exchange rate peg and sterilisation measures, the interest rate differential widened, especially as international interest rates declined. Montes argues that the Thai authorities failed to protect the long-term viability of their banking system through prudential regulation, which would have required curbs on the massive increase of financial intermediation for asset purchases.

Montes argues that 'three guarantees' exacerbated the problem of moral hazard, contributing to the banking/currency crisis. First is government support for the domestic financial system.[32] The commitment to an open capital account and the adoption of a virtually fixed exchange rate or quasi-peg effectively subsidised short-term foreign borrowings, supporting foreign equity investments as well as offshore banking facilities. With these three guarantees, and arguably the expectation of IMF protection of their interests in the event of a crisis, international lenders are encouraged to lend more while not having much incentive to effectively monitor the deployment of their loans. The quasi-pegging of Southeast Asian currencies to a strengthening US dollar since the mid-1990s gave non-US dollar lenders to the region unrealised exchange rate gains as well.

In a useful chapter (Chapter 4) on fundamentals and sentiments, Montes points out that international financial analysts and macroeconomists mean different things when they speak of fundamentals. Private asset managers seem to refer to 'factors that support the one-year to year-and-a-half stability of key asset prices, especially exchange rates' whereas economists and public officials usually think of the medium term in terms of three years and consider fundamentals 'in terms of the impact of asset prices on real economic variables, such as output growth, exports, and employment' (Montes 1998: 29).

Montes goes on to identify the following as key fundamentals of the affected Southeast Asian economies:

- viability of domestic financial systems;[33]
- domestic output and export responsiveness to nominal devaluations;[34]
- sustainability of current account deficits;[35]
- high savings rates and robust public finances.

Despite the sound fiscal situation before the crisis, the Southeast Asian economies are now expected to have even larger fiscal surpluses despite the need for greater public financing of physical infrastructure and social services. To restore confidence in their currencies, they are being asked to cut their current account deficits besides government spending, with ominous implications for economic recovery and sustainability.

Recognising a limited but still significant scope for monetary independence in the Southeast Asian economies, Montes maintains that economic liberalisation should not be allowed to frustrate the sound development of the financial system and improvements in the productivity of investment. He warns that sound macro-economic fundamentals do not guarantee immunity from contagion and crisis. The scope for monetary independence partly depends on the soundness of macro-economic management as well as political will. Favouring flexible exchange rates, he warns that capital controls and other efforts to prop up a currency under attack are ineffective and actually subsidise further speculative actions. International co-operation and co-ordination have often been the best response during such episodes, but are also important for effective prudential and regulatory initiatives as well as to reduce 'policy arbitrage'. He also advocates measures to insulate the domestic banking system from short-term volatility through regulatory measures and capital controls as well as stricter prudential regulation for the region.

IMF Intervention

The challenge at the international level is formidable, especially with the vested interests underlying American as well as European positions on systemic reform. Yet, there have been many misgivings elsewhere too about the nature and vola-tility of the international financial system, with renewed attention to particular aspects with each new crisis. Southeast Asians need to work with others who are like-minded and to draw upon the rich critiques which have developed over the years in developing reform proposals which are likely to gain broad international support.

That is why it is distressing that at the September 1997 Hong Kong annual meetings of the IMF and World Bank, the IMF's policy-making Interim Committee — which represents all 181 IMF member countries via 24 ministers — gave the IMF a mandate to alter its Articles of Association so that it would have additional 'jurisdiction' over the capital account as well as over the current account of members' balance of payments, which it has had for many decades.[36]

In December 1997, the World Trade Organisation also concluded its financial services agreement which basically commits member countries to scheduled accelerated liberalisation of the trade in financial services. The *Wall Street Journal* noted that the agreement would primarily benefit the US and Europe since it is most unlikely that the South is in a position to export financial services to the North. It is therefore likely that countries of the South will face even greater problems with their balance of payments as their services, and hence current account deficits worsen. Many of the nascent financial services which have emerged under protection in these countries are unlikely to survive international competition from transnational giants enjoying economies of scale and other advantages.

As recent press discussion of the IMF's record and capability suggests, there is growing international scepticism about the IMF's role in and prescriptions for the ongoing East Asian crisis. Perhaps partly out of force of habit in dealing with situations in Latin America, Africa, Eastern Europe and elsewhere, where fiscal deficits have been part of the problem, the same prescription ('one size fits all') seems to underlie the recent IMF interventions in East Asia.

Many of its programmes are effectively contractionary in consequence, with little regard for the social and other adverse consequences of swallowing its medicine. Thus, what starts off as a currency or financial crisis leads, partly due to IMF-recommended policy responses, to economic slowdown, if not recession. For example, although all the affected East Asian economies have been running fiscal surpluses in recent years (except Indonesia which had a small deficit in 1996), the IMF has forced all the governments to slash public expenditure and increase their budgetary surpluses.

There has been considerable doubt as to whether the IMF actually recognised the novel elements of the crisis and their implications ('old medicines for a new disease'), especially at the outset. The apparent failures of the IMF — to anticipate the current crisis in its generally glowing recent reports on the region, and also to stem, let alone reverse the situation despite interventions in Thailand, Indonesia and Korea — have certainly not inspired much confidence. Nor has the fact that though the Philippines had long been under an IMF programme, it was not spared the contagion.[37]

The Fund does not seem to be sufficiently cognisant of the subjective elements contributing to the crisis, and seems to approach the crisis as if it were solely due to macroeconomic or other weaknesses. For instance, by closing down banks in Indonesia, the IMF undermined the remaining shreds of confidence there, inducing wholesale panic in the process. Also, while the IMF insists on greater transparency by the affected host government and those under its jurisdiction, it continues to operate under a shroud of secrecy itself.

The IMF's double standards, as reflected by its apparent priority for protecting the interests of foreign banks and governments, has also compromised its ostensible role as an impartial party working in the interests of the host economy. The burden of IMF programmes invariably falls on the domestic financial sector and, eventually, on the public at large — through the social costs of the public policy response, usually involving bail-outs of much of the financial sector if not the corporate sector more generally — who thus bear most of the costs of adjustment and reform, while commitments to foreign banks are invariably met, even though both foreign and domestic banks may have been equally irresponsible or imprudent in their lending practices.

As the BIS noted in its latest *Report on the Maturity and Nationality of International Bank Lending* (Raghavan 1998, Vadarajan 1998), 'In spite of growing strains in Southeast Asia, overall bank lending to Asian developing countries showed no evidence of abating in the first half of 1997.' In the year from mid-1996 to mid-1997, South Korea received US$15 billion in new loans, while Indonesia received US$9 billion. Short-term lending continued to dominate, with 70 per cent of lending due within a year, while the share of lending to private non-bank borrowers rose to 45 per cent at the end of June 1997. The banks were also actively acquiring 'non-traditional assets' in the region, e.g. in higher yielding local money markets and other debt securities. Most of this lending was by Japanese and continental European banks.

Thus, Western banks will emerge from the crisis not only relatively unscathed, but also relatively stronger. Some merchant banks and other financial institutions will also be able to make lucrative commissions from marketing sovereign debt as the short-term private borrowings — which precipitated the crisis — are converted into longer-term government-guaranteed bonds under the terms of the IMF programmes. Thus, the bail-out programmes are primarily for the foreign banks rather than the East Asian economies or people.

The limited willingness of the US to contribute to the IMF bail-out packages to Thailand, Indonesia and South Korea — now exceeding a hundred billion US dollars — has also reflected new US priorities in the post-Cold War context. Despite its own unwillingness to commit more, the US administration also blocked Japanese and other regional initiatives to develop a regional facility for fear that it might enhance the Japanese role and leadership in the region and diminish the US's standing. However, since the end-October 1997 global stock market panic, the US administration seems to have taken a leading role despite the limited exposure of US banks to the region. US concerns about a possible global financial meltdown, the US dollar's role as the leading reserve currency and the opportunities for US banks and other investors to take advantage of the situation seem to have influenced this change of stance.

Almost in tandem with financial liberalisation, IMF intervention is generally recognised to undermine and limit national economic sovereignty.[38] Particularly damning is the clear abuse of imposed IMF conditionalities in the Korean aid package to resolve outstanding bilateral issues in favour of the US and Japanese interests (Chossudovsky 1998). Legislation and other new regulations enabling greater foreign ownership of as well as increased market access to the Korean economy — which have little to do with the crisis or its immediate causes — have been forced upon the Korean government. Even more damaging has been the further dismantling of many key institutional features which have made possible the Korean economic miracle since the 1960s. Meanwhile, Japanese banks have insisted that the Korean government guarantee repayment as a condition for rolling over Korean short- term debt.

More generally, throughout the region, there is a 'fire-sale' going on at bargain basement prices, with foreign investments taking up the best assets available for a song. If one accepts that the currency as well as more general financial crisis means that these assets are grossly under-priced by international standards, one cannot claim any welfare improvement (Krugman 1998), given the likelihood that the new foreign owners need not be more efficient to be able to buy up these assets.

The recent currency and financial crises in Southeast Asia suggest that the Southeast Asian economic miracle has been built on some shaky and unsustainable foundations. Recent growth in both Malaysia and Thailand has been increasingly heavily reliant on foreign resources, both capital and labour. Limited investments and inappropriate biases in human resource development have held back the development of greater industrial and technological capabilities throughout the region.[39] Southeast Asia's resource wealth and relatively cheap labour sustained production enclaves for export of agricultural, forest, mineral and, more recently, manufactured products, but much of the retained wealth generated was captured by business cronies of those in power, who contributed to growth by also re-investing captured resource and other rents in the 'protected' domestic economy in import-substituting industries, commerce, services, and privatised utilities and infrastructure.

This Volume in Brief

This volume essentially makes three closely related arguments involving liberalisation and governance. First, financial liberalisation has undermined previously existing governance institutions and mechanisms without creating adequate alternatives in their place. Second, domestic governance arrangements, including those involving the financial system, have been shaped or abused by those with influence for their own advantage. Third, in some instances, especially in Thailand, Malaysia and Indonesia, in the absence of adequate crisis response arrangements, official responses have been unduly influenced and compromised by vested interests as well as other considerations.

After critically examining the nature of the East Asian financial crisis as well as the policy responses, Yilmaz Akyüz considers various likely implications of both. He highlights the gross inadequacy of existing arrangements for global financial governance in order to avoid the recurrence of similar crises. Although capital is more mobile than other factors of production and financial markets are far more integrated than product markets, global governance of international financial transactions is woefully inadequate and tends to discipline borrowers rather than to regulate lenders. Existing arrangements seek to manage rather than to avoid crises, often at considerable cost to human welfare and economic development, and do not provide for either dispute settlement or adequate checks against 'beggar thy neighbour' policies. He also highlights the absence of effective, orderly and adequate arrangements for liquidity provision by an international lender of last resort as well as for orderly workouts of international debtor–creditor relations.

As Jan Kregel's chapter shows, many aspects of the East Asian financial crisis were neither completely unprecedented nor unanticipated. But referring to historical precedent can not only be misleading, but even dangerous, as has been the tendency to see the East Asian crisis as analogous to the 1994-95 Mexican 'tequila' crisis. To emphasise the differences, Kregel reviews recent developments in East Asia in a global context and from a historical perspective, highlighting its novel features, relevant antecedents as well as systemic elements contributing to it.

C.P. Chandrasekhar and Jayati Ghosh consider the political economy of recent growth in Southeast Asia. They locate Southeast Asia's vulnerability prior to the crisis in the decline of export growth, exacerbated by the appreciation of currencies in the region, particularly against the Chinese renminbi devalued in 1994. They also address the questions of why international banks were so heavily exposed in Southeast Asia, and why the affected Southeast Asian economies — with among the highest domestic savings rates in the world — needed the huge capital inflows in the first place. The latter part of their chapter is devoted to the nature and likely implications of IMF intervention in response to the crises in East Asia.

Nicola Bullard, with Walden Bello and Kamal Malhotra, critically assess the IMF's role and performance in the East Asian financial crisis. They show that the Fund has prescribed wrong and socially disastrous medicine for the region's ills, grossly exceeded its mandate in its Articles of Agreement, conducted itself arrogantly and reflected the interests of the US. The result of the Fund's failures has been to exacerbate the human and macroeconomic impact of the crisis. Drawing upon the variety of criticisms of the Fund which have emerged in the last half-year from across the political spectrum, they argue that the IMF should serve as the lender of last resort during balance of payments crises, while opposing any changes to the Fund's Articles of Agreement, such as extending its jurisdiction to include capital account liberalisation, as well as the variety of conditionalities recently associated with IMF funding. They also call for new mechanisms for the effective and just resolution of private sector debt crises and the regulation of international capital flows, especially of short-term speculative capital, to reduce their capacity for economic destabilisation.

The remaining chapters in this volume are country studies which identify the origins and circumstances of the financial collapses as well as their economic and other implications in the four Southeast Asian economies of Thailand (Laurids Lauridsen), Indonesia (Manuel Montes) Malaysia (Jomo K.S.) and Philippines (Joseph Lim), as well as South Korea (Chang Ha-Joon). There is some inevitable unevenness as well as redundancy in coverage, but also a striking unanimity about the international and systemic origins and sources of the recent currency and financial crises in the region.

Roots of the Crisis: Challenges of Governance

The roots of the crisis can usefully be summed up in terms of various challenges of governance, at both international and national levels. At the international level, governance issues have been raised by the transformations of financial, especially capital markets. Flexible exchange rates and other related developments have increased the scope for and activity in currency speculation. Increased international flows of investment funds have also contributed to currency volatility. Most of these funds are of a portfolio nature, and hence more liable to enhance volatility, while the share of direct investments continues to decline.

Financial liberalisation has also reduced monitoring and supervision of financial, including banking operations and transactions, including those of a prudential nature. There has also been a significant increase in 'private banking' as well as increased banking transactions across borders with the proliferation of 'international offshore financial centres' and other international banking facilities. The growing dollarisation of the world economy, including international finance, has also skewed the nature of these developments in important ways.

Liberalisation of financial services as well as of investment regulations, including liberalisation of the capital account, have otherwise also reduced national oversight and management of financial flows, which created the conditions conducive to the recent Southeast Asian and South Korean crises. The scope for national macroeconomic — including monetary — management has been considerably reduced by various dimensions of financial liberalisation. Options for developmentalist as well as rentier initiatives have been significantly reduced as a consequence.

The variety of regimes in East Asia do not allow easy generalisations for the entire region. It has been tempting for observers to contrast the economies and regimes which have experienced major crises since the second half of 1997, i.e. Thailand, the Philippines, Indonesia, Malaysia and South Korea, with the other high performing East Asian economies which have not, namely Japan, Taiwan, Hong Kong and Singapore, as well as China. There is no systematic evidence that the difference lies primarily in the extent of corruption, rent-seeking, government intervention, industrial policy, export-orientation, productivity growth, FDI or democracy. Although all the economies affected have liberalised their capital accounts, this may only be a necessary, but certainly not a sufficient condition for the crisis. The big difference seems to have been that the former have not had much foreign exchange in reserve unlike the latter, which have the highest reserves in the world, and hence were not vulnerable to currency attack.

The extent to which macroeconomic fundamentals were awry among the affected economies varied considerably and, by themselves, cannot explain the financial collapses, although they suggest their greater vulnerability to currency attack and the greater likelihood of panic. This crisis has underlined the significance of sentiments, and there is no convincing explanation for what happened, especially herd behaviour, which does not take account of market psychology. Hence, confidence restoration must necessarily be at the top of the agenda for any recovery programme, but this, in turn, raises the dilemma posed by the temptation of reviving confidence in a potentially volatile set of arrangements, which can easily turn against the national economies concerned and their regimes' ambitions — as the recent crises have shown.

Previously hegemonic neo-liberal explanations of the East Asian miracle were effectively challenged from the late 1980s (White 1988, Amsden 1989, Wade 1990) and developed in sophistication (e.g. see Chang 1994) and nuance (Jomo *et al.* 1997) in the mid-1990s. The World Bank's (1993) influential response suggested that the political, bureaucratic, cultural and institutional circumstances of the rise of Japan and the first-generation or first-tier East Asian NIEs of South Korea, Taiwan, Hong Kong and Singapore were so exceptional as to be beyond emulation. Instead, it was suggested that other developing countries should seek to emulate the second-tier Southeast Asian NICs of Malaysia, Thailand and Indonesia, which had, according to the World Bank, achieved rapid growth and industrialisation after liberalising in the mid-1980s.

In response, Jomo *et al.* (1997) argued that the Southeast Asian NICs achievement has been much more modest than that of the first-tier East Asian NIEs in several important respects, and that the sustainability of their growth, industrialisation and structural change was much more suspect as a consequence. Their volume also suggested that the former's rapid export-oriented industrialisation from the mid-1980s was partly due to a favourable conjuncture — involving Southeast Asian currency depreciation coinciding with Japanese and first-tier East Asian NIE currency appreciation and rising production, especially labour costs — as well as liberalisation of some existing regulations inimical to attracting such investments and their replacement with a new investment regime much more conducive to promoting export-oriented industrialisation.

Many other features of the old regime have been retained, while 'rentrepreneurs' creatively utilised features of the new regulatory environment to advance and pursue their own interests. These features have all contributed to industrial organisation and structure in these economies. Thus, while some regulations have undoubtedly enhanced growth and structural change, often by offering rents and incentives to encourage desired investments, others have also strengthened rentier abuse. While much of this may be analytically distinguishable, with the latter relatively easily isolated and checked through policy intervention, others may be much more difficult to unravel from developmentalist rents.

Simplistic perspectives and gross generalisations do not recognise and distinguish between developmentalist rents and rentier abuse. Policy reforms which fail to do so will encourage throwing out the developmentalist baby with the bathwater of abuse, with disastrous consequences for developmentalist ambitions and projects. Of course, the willingness to check rentier abuses is ultimately determined by the regime's independence of such rentier interests, its consequent 'political will' and its capacity to bring about the necessary reforms.

Finally, as economic and business historians remind us, there have been important precursors to the recent crises in East Asia, even within the region. Unfortunately, the market — which is increasingly being left to its own devices — has neither an institutional memory nor a capacity to develop natural immunity. It is therefore left to policymakers to build the necessary institutions and to design and redesign the needed institutional features of governance to ensure that tragedy does not become farce.

Notes

1. Meanwhile, the 'financial analysts' have become so fixated with the current account deficit that this indicator, almost alone, has become the fetish of financial analysts, especially since the Mexican meltdown of early 1995. In earlier, different times, some economies sustained similar deficits for much longer, without comparable consequences. As noted in the immediate aftermath of the Mexican crisis of 1995, several Southeast Asian economies already had comparable current account deficits then despite, or rather because of rapid economic growth. Yet, as IMF deputy head, Stanley Fischer observed, the currency markets failed to adjust earlier in Southeast Asia.

2. Of course, the availability of cheap foreign funds — e.g. due to a low real interest rate — can help to temporarily close both domestic savings-investment as well as foreign exchange gaps, especially if well invested or deployed.

3. In this connection, it is interesting to note that the Chicago school-influenced Chilean government has maintained strict controls on the capital account. Portfolio investments in Chilean stock are permitted in the New York Stock Exchange, rather than in the Santiago stock market, while unlike FDI, portfolio capital inflows into Chile are subjected to conditions which inhibit easy exit.

4. In some countries, government-owned non-financial public enterprises (NFPEs) have been very much part of this private sector debt growth phenomenon.

5. There is also no evidence that the stock market boom in recent years has more effectively raised funds for productive investment; in fact, the converse seems more likely as financial intermediation has switched from commercial banks to the stock market in the last decade.

6. While the Southeast Asian economies have been running current account deficits, so has the US, especially with the region, except that it has different consequences given the actual and 'quasi' dollar pegs prevailing in much of the world today.

7. While the US economy has been strengthening, the Southeast Asian economies were growing even faster.

8. In the mid-1990s, as the US dollar strengthened with the US economy, both the Japanese and the Germans allowed their currencies to depreciate against the US dollar, with relatively little disruption, in an effort to regain international competitiveness.

9. For example, the Malaysian current account deficit as a share of GDP was lower in 1996 and 1997 than in 1995.

10. In the face of limited information and a novel, rapidly changing situation, such behaviour is often considered rational by market players, even if unfortunate.

11. Hedge funds may, however, go in different directions, for instance, when one fund's currency sell-off provokes another fund to snap up bargain equities, e.g. foreigners were often persistent net buyers of Japanese stocks throughout the bursting of the bubble there in the 1990s.

12. Financial liberalisation means investors have a choice as to when they 'come and go', and, of course, the very existence of that choice may encourage them to stick around in certain circumstances.

13. Short-termism — encouraged by financial liberalisation — has also accentuated the bias against longer-term productive investments.

14. As in Chile in the early 1980s.

15. These can involve savers being encouraged with tax policies that do not punish them for putting money away. While banks should still make lending decisions based on economic criteria alone, systemic biases towards short-termism need to be mitigated. The government can prioritise and favour certain types of investments by subsidising them through taxes or loan guarantees for those sectors or activities it deems important.

16. It has been very difficult for Malaysia to credibly take the high moral ground on currency and other types of speculation because of the well-known behaviour of Bank Negara in the 1980s. The Malaysian central bank was known to take very aggressive, short-term speculative positions in the major currencies with a view to making a profit. This went on for several years until the Bank lost several tens of billions of ringgit in 1992 while betting on sterling and then withdrew to tamer activities. There is a similar sense about the tin cartel in the early 1980s (Jomo 1990). Mahathir's comments are hence seen as insincere abroad in that he is seen to have directed the government to undertake speculative activities in the

past and was able to do so because the international currency and commodity markets are so open. It has been difficult to gain sympathy about non-Malaysian speculators after having approved of such activities before.

17. Since trade-related currency trading is greatly exceeded by investment-related currency trading, it is not surprising that the volume of currency trading is so large. One key question is how much of those investment-related trades are 'healthy', 'appropriate' or 'desirable'. International investors want to hedge their personal income and wealth by spreading their investments across many countries and adjusting them quite frequently as conditions change, thus contributing to market volatility.

18. Recent results show that national savings tend to equate national investment, suggesting that flows of capital to 'the best possible use' are far from universal and much smaller than simple theories predict. Lack of information or other risks and uncertainties tend to reduce cross-border capital flows.

19. Eatwell suggests a negative correlation between dependence on 'foreign savings' and economic performance. This is true if we do not break down the nature of foreign savings. The numbers are strongly biased by the inclusion of short-term money market flows, which may include efforts by governments to prop up their currencies with high interest rates which temporarily suck in money from overseas. Mexico, Brazil and especially Venezuela typified this a few years ago. If only long-term direct investment or equity investment was considered, a lot of poorly performing Latin American economies would be screened out. Southeast Asian countries, especially Singapore and Malaysia, would then rank high on both foreign savings (measured 'appropriately') and economic performance.

20. Currently, high interest rates represent a very unhappy situation for the region. They are intended, in part, to prop the currency up to maintain confidence but, perhaps more importantly, to allow local companies to pay off their foreign debts. The cost of this is slower growth. With lower interest rates and lower exchange rates, which help the economy grow and help consumers, mismanaged local companies would have to reorganise themselves, or otherwise lose their equity (which they deserve, in many cases, to forfeit). Foreign creditors who were stupid enough to lend dollars to mismanaged companies should see their bank loans and bonds defaulted on. Bankrupt local companies could be bailed out and re-capitalised, with 100 per cent equity ownership then going into mutual funds or pension funds distributed equally to the masses of ordinary citizens.

Liberalisation is generally associated with higher interest rates. However, lower interest rates could have been due to a combination of pegged exchange rates, capital controls and the deployment of funds inside such economies. Pegged exchange rates are enforced by capital controls which 'trap' a pool of savings inside an economy. The trapped savings are typically exploited by governments or banking cartels which may keep interest rates too low, even below inflation rates. The capital controls may thus force savers to accept low interest rates and stop them from getting a fairer return elsewhere. The cheap savings may get loaned to undeserving corporations or for other purposes, possibly at the direction of the government.

21. One could argue that some of this is the result of greed, stupidity, and lack of education or regulation. If used carefully, derivatives are ultimately insurance contracts.

22. There is, however, evidence of a strong positive correlation between financial openness, foreign investment, GDP growth and per capita income for the East Asian countries, though the region seems to be exceptional.

23. Due to the separation of ownership and management of portfolio investments, though it may be in the interest of investors to 'buy and hold', it is difficult to write contracts to motivate pension managers, mutual funds and other intermediaries to stay put.

24. Of course, liquidity is one of the features which induces otherwise risk averse investors to buy into a situation. Furthermore, in any transaction, there is a buyer for every seller.
25. Of course, capital flight is not an inevitable consequence of financial liberalisation, but may reflect the fears and consequent hedging behaviour of locals.
26. Paul Krugman's (1998) attempt at theoretical catch-up is particularly worthy of consideration in light of his own previous attempts at understanding related international economic phenomena as well as East Asian economic growth. As the crisis is still unfolding, such an attempt can hardly be definitive, especially since we do not even have the advantage of complete hindsight. Yet, as policy is very much being made on the hoof, his attempt to highlight certain relationships may well be illuminating. Hence, Krugman argues that:

> it is necessary to adopt an approach quite different from that of traditional currency crisis theory. Of course Asian economies did experience currency crises, and the usual channels of speculation were operative here as always. However, the currency crises were only part of a broader financial crisis, which had very little to do with currencies or even monetary issues *per se*. Nor did the crisis have much to do with traditional fiscal issues. Instead, to make sense of what went wrong we need to focus on two issues normally neglected in currency crisis analysis: the role of financial intermediaries (and of the moral hazard associated with such intermediaries when they are poorly regulated), and the prices of real assets such as capital and land.

27. None of the fundamentals usually emphasised seem to have been important in the affected economies: all the governments had fiscal surpluses and none were involved in excessive monetary expansion, while inflation rates were generally low.
28. Krugman (1998) argues:

> The boom-bust cycle created by financial excess preceded the currency crises because the financial crisis was the real driver of the whole process, with the currency fluctuations more a symptom than a cause. And the ability of the crisis to spread without big exogenous shocks or strong economic linkages can be explained by the fact that the afflicted Asian economies were... highly vulnerable to self-fulfilling pessimism, which could and did generate a downward spiral of asset deflation and disintermediation.

29. According to Krugman, East Asian financial intermediaries 'were able to raise money at safe interest rates but lend at premium rates to finance speculative investments.' He shows that they had 'an incentive not merely to undertake excessively risky investments, but (even) to pursue investments with low expected returns'. Krugman argues that the moral hazard problem involving over-guaranteed, but under-regulated financial intermediaries not only distorted investments, but also led to overinvestment at the aggregate level as well as over-pricing of assets. He also suggests why East Asian businesses became extremely leveraged by Western standards as well as their tendency to be over-optimistic about their investments. Access to world capital markets allowed moral hazard in the financial sector to translate into excessive real capital accumulation.

He then concludes that such a moral hazard regime with overpriced assets was vulnerable to financial crisis as disintermediation set in. For Krugman, 'the days of cheerful implicit guarantees and easy lending for risky investment are clearly over for some time to come' as 'financial intermediaries have been curtailed *precisely because they were seen to have lost a lot of money*' (Krugman's italics). The problem is exacerbated by a magnification effect caused 'by the circular logic of disintermediation: the prospective end to intermediation, driven by the losses of the existing institutions, reduces asset prices and therefore magnifies those losses.' His analysis offers 'a story of self-fulfilling financial crises, in which plunging asset prices undermine banks, and the collapse of the banks in turn ratifies the drop in asset prices.'

However, Krugman's model assumes that the financial intermediaries do not invest capital of their own, thus leading to the prediction that they will almost always need financial bailouts; in fact, if they invest their own capital, financial intermediaries will have something to lose as well, which would presumably check their conduct.

30. Krugman's model focuses on domestic financial intermediaries, whereas foreign institutions have played a major role in the East Asian crises.

31. In contrast to portfolio investment to buy domestic financial assets, FDI flows for new plant, equipment and intermediate inputs have different macroeconomic implications, with a limited impact on reserves, money supply and domestic interest rates (Montes 1998: 22). FDI is also less easily withdrawn.

32. Montes (1998: 27) points out that incentives in international markets tend to intensify, rather than moderate, over-optimism or over-pessimism due to herd behaviour and other factors.

33. Montes emphasises that sentiments can either favourably or unfavourably influence fundamentals and the health of financial systems; in particular, the collapse of the Southeast Asian currencies due to sentiments would adversely affect the viability of investments made in different exchange rate conditions, which could in turn further exacerbate the domestic banking crisis.

34. Montes argues that the rural-based economies of Southeast Asia have been better able to carry out real devaluations from nominal changes in currency value, while their export sectors have not been too tied down by supply side inflexibilities to respond to real devaluations. After asserting that stock markets have served to share risks among asset owners rather than raise financing, he argues that except for financial system weaknesses, Southeast Asian real sectors have been relatively immune from the recent asset market frenzy.

35. Montes points out that equity and portfolio investments have overtaken direct investment, loans and trade credit in providing external financing in the 1990s. He cites Reisen's warning (Montes 1998: 34) that offers of foreign financing should be resisted if they would 'cause unsustainable currency appreciation, excessive risk-taking in the banking system, and a sharp drop in private savings.' Hence, in a market-sentiment driven world, currencies become too strong with offers of strong external financing and too weak when capital withdraws.

36. I am grateful to Anthony Rowley for confirming these details with Kunio Saito, director of the IMF's new Tokyo regional representative office on 17 December 1997.

The executive board of the Fund is currently holding a series of meetings to discuss the detailed implementation of this mandate and will report again to the Interim Committee on the *modus operandi* at the spring meeting. Thereafter, individual member governments have to ratify the change, but a simple majority will be sufficient. In other words, a unanimous vote is not needed to approve the change in the Fund's Articles.

However, other colleagues — including Professor Gerald Helleiner of the University of Toronto and Dr. Yilmaz Akyüz of UNCTAD — suggest that the situation is not as dire as the above account suggests because the approval process is much more complicated.

37. Arguably, the Philippines currency has not taken quite as hard a hit, in part because their (colonial-inherited) banking and accounting standards are considered relatively better, but also because short-term capital inflows have been relatively less, given the recentness of its economic recovery.

38. However, invoking 'national economic sovereignty' may become very dubious when it is clearly hijacked by special interests.

39. While the low productivity growth critique popularised by Krugman (1994) may be theoretically and methodologically faulted, there is little doubt that East Asian growth has generally been boosted by high savings and investment rates. While this might give the impression of 'all perspiration, no inspiration', as suggested by TFP critics, the dominance of FDI in the internationally competitive export-oriented industries suggests the transfer or import of 'inspiration' embodied in new plant and equipment as well as the necessary technological learning to get the jobs done.

Table 1.1
Selected Indicators for Four Countries in Southeast Asia

	GDP Growth %	Export Growth %	Import Growth %	FDI Growth %	Import/ GDP %	Current Account US$ bil.	Current Account % GDP
Indonesia							
1991	7.0	13.5	18.5	35.5	35.5	-4.3	-3.7
1992	6.5	16.6	5.5	19.9	35.9	-2.8	-2.2
1993	6.5	8.4	3.8	12.8	29.5	-2.1	-1.3
1994	7.5	8.8	12.9	5.2	31.1	-2.8	-1.6
1995	8.2	13.4	27.0	106.2	31.9	-7.0	-3.6
1996	7.9	9.7	5.7	–	32.1	-8.7	-3.9
Thailand							
1991	8.4	23.8	15.8	-17.6	41.4	-7.6	-7.6
1992	7.8	13.7	6.0	4.9	39.4	-6.3	-5.7
1993	8.3	13.4	12.2	-14.6	40.2	-6.4	-5.1
1994	8.9	22.2	18.5	-24.3	40.9	-8.1	-5.6
1995	8.7	24.7	31.6	51.4	42.9	-13.6	-8.1
1996	6.7	-1.9	0.8	13.0	–	-14.7	-8.2
Malaysia							
1991	8.4	18.6	27.4	71.4	35.5	-4.2	-8.8
1992	7.8	9.7	0.6	29.6	35.9	-2.2	-3.9
1993	8.3	17.0	15.8	-3.4	29.5	-3.0	-5.0
1994	9.2	26.8	32.7	-13.3	31.1	-4.5	-6.2
1995	9.6	20.3	24.8	-4.8	31.9	-7.4	-8.8
1996	8.2	6.5	1.4	–	32.1	-5.2	-5.3
Philippines							
1991	-0.5	14.5	11.1	2.6	20.0	-1.0	-2.2
1992	0.3	2.8	11.5	-58.1	20.9	-1.0	-1.9
1993	2.1	22.0	29.9	443.0	23.8	-3.0	-5.7
1994	4.4	15.5	16.7	28.5	23.6	-3.0	-4.3
1995	4.8	28.7	22.4	-7.1	22.2	-2.0	-2.7
1996	5.7	18.7	24.0	–	23.2	-7.7	-4.3

Note: Exports are f.o.b., imports are c.i.f. except for Thailand.
Source: IMF, *International Financial Statistics*, various volumes.

Table 1.2
International Bank Lending by Banks, as of end-June 1997 (US$ billion)

	South Korea	Thailand	Indonesia	Malaysia	Developing Countries
Total Borrowings	103.4	69.4	58.7	28.8	744.6
Banks	67.3	26.1	12.4	10.5	275.3
(%)	(65.1)	(37.6)	(21.1)	(36.5)	(37.0)
Private Non-bank	31.7	41.3	39.7	16.5	352.9
(%)	(30.6)	(59.5)	(67.6)	(57.3)	(47.4)
Government	4.4	12.0	6.5	1.9	115.6
(%)	(4.3)	(17.3)	(11.1)	(6.6)	(15.5)
Short-term					
December 1996	67.5	45.7	34.2	11.2	
January 1997	70.2	45.6	34.6	16.3	
(%)	(67.9)	(65.7)	(58.9)	(56.6)	

Source: Raghavan, C., "BIS Banks Kept Shovelling Funds to Asia, Despite Warnings", *Third World Economics*, 177: 12-13.

Table 1.3
Total Exposure of BIS Area Reporting Banks to Non-BIS Borrowers, end-June 1997
(US$ billion)

Total	1,054.9
Germany	178.2
Japan	172.7
USA	131.0
France	100.2
UK	77.8
% of Private Non-bank Borrowers	45%

Table 1.4
Savings Rates in Selected Southeast Asian Countries, 1981-96 (as % of GNP)

	1981	1985	1990	1996
Indonesia	33.3	29.8	36.7	33.7
Malaysia	28.8	32.7	33.4	38.8
Thailand	22.0	24.2	34.7	35.3
Philippines	26.8	18.8	18.7	20.5

Note: The main problem of most studies on savings in less developed countries is the unreliable nature of the savings data. The basic issues is that savings tends to be calculated as a residual. As a result, it inherits all the statistical problems of other components of national income, in particular of investment.

Source: Nasution, Anwar (1998: Table 1).

2
THE EAST ASIAN FINANCIAL CRISIS: BACK TO THE FUTURE*

Yilmaz Akyüz

The world economy is perhaps experiencing the most serious financial crisis since the breakdown of the Bretton Woods system in the early 1970s, in terms of both its scope and its effects. Its impact is much more global than the other financial crises we have seen in the past two or three decades, including those in Latin America. Today, global financial integration is much more pervasive, and the East Asian countries have a much higher share of world trade and production. For the first time, a financial crisis in the South has had a profound impact on capital markets in the North. It is also expected to cause a significant drop in global growth.

Regarding the causes and consequences of the crisis, there is a tendency among the commentators to lump together the East Asian countries which are directly or indirectly affected by the current financial crisis. This is particularly notable among those who consider the crisis as the end of the 'Asian model of development'. However, those who are more familiar with the region know that there are considerable variations among these countries in the policies pursued, the institutions established and the level of development reached. There is at least a distinction between the first-tier newly industrialising economies (NIEs), that is the so-called four tigers (Hong Kong, South Korea, Singapore and Taiwan), and the second-tier newly industrialising countries (NICs) (Indonesia, Malaysia and Thailand). Again, among the first-tier NIEs, Hong Kong is distinguished by its *laissez-faire* policies, while the others are known to have followed a more interventionist, dirigiste approach. Of these, two dirigiste economies, Singapore and Taiwan, are so far virtually untouched by the crisis. In Southeast Asia too, the problems faced by Indonesia and Thailand are quite different from those in Malaysia, which has again pursued somewhat more interventionist policies than the former two.

---

* An earlier version of this chapter was presented at a seminar on 'Impacts of the Asian Currency Crisis on Europe's Growth Prospects', European Institute for Asian Studies, Brussels, 20 January 1998. The opinions expressed do not necessarily reflect the views of the UNCTAD secretariat, and the designations and terminology used are those of the author. This chapter owes a great deal to discussions with Jan Kregel, Andrew Cornford and Richard Kozul-Wright.

The Crisis: Surprising or Predictable?

The crisis in Southeast Asia did not come to us as a complete surprise. In its analysis of East Asia, the United Nations Conference on Trade and Development's (UNCTAD's) 1996 *Trade and Development Report* made a clear distinction between the first- and second-tier NIEs in terms of their policies, performances and prospects. While praising the successful policies of the second-tier NICs which have helped establish competitive resource- and labour-intensive industries, the *Report* pointed out that the easy stage of export promotion was coming to an end, and that these countries could suffer from loss of competitiveness. The *Report* sounded a clear warning, noting that growth in the region relied excessively on foreign resources, both labour and capital:

> Thus, the second-tier NIEs may be unable to sustain large current-account deficits over the longer term; they need to reduce their trade deficits so as to minimise the risk of serious balance of payments problems and a sharp slowdown in growth. Much will depend on their success in enhancing their export potential through upgrading…. The fact that in Malaysia and Thailand wage pressures can only be mitigated by large-scale immigration suggests that these economies may be having difficulty in achieving the necessary upgrading…. Without upgrading… FDI will remain footloose and the economy would be highly vulnerable to interruptions of capital inflows. Concerns over such a possibility have been growing in Thailand and even more in Malaysia in view of their large current account deficits (UNCTAD 1996: 104, 123).

However, the Korean crisis is more surprising. With hindsight, we seem to have overlooked the significance of three important trends that were under way, which were eventually responsible for the crisis: first, the sustained appreciation of the currency; second, massive short-term borrowing abroad by the private sector; and finally excessive investment in a number of industries. A stable real exchange rate was always a main policy objective in post-war South Korea and the recent appreciation constitutes a major departure from that policy. Again, South Korea tapped external finance in its post-war industrialisation primarily through borrowing from international banks, but this was almost always subject to government approval and guarantee. Finally, while private investment was the driving force of Korean industrialisation, policy always played a major role in co-ordinating investment decisions in order to avoid excessive competition and capacity creation as well as to benefit from scale economies.

Departure from such practices during the past few years partly reflects the pressures of globalisation. For instance, as the Korean firms became multinationals, their activities became less transparent and more difficult to monitor, a factor which appears to have played a major role in overborrowing and overinvestment as well as risky financial operations by some firms. But of much greater significance, a more liberal stance towards finance over the past few years has meant abandoning many checks and balances which had underpinned the Korean success.

It is notable that these departures from post-war practices coincided with Korea's bid for the membership of the Organisation for Economic Cooperation and Development (OECD). Far from being considered as policy errors by the orthodoxy, they were recommended as necessary if Korea was to adapt to a globalising world. Even now, complete removal of barriers against access of the private sector to international financial markets is advocated as a solution to the crisis. In this view, the problem is not liberalisation as such, but the absence of effective prudential regulation and supervision of the banking system.

There can be little doubt that prudential limits on bank lending, capital adequacy requirements and currency matching conditions for assets and liabilities that are properly enforced can help prevent excessive risk-taking by banks, thus containing the adverse effects of widespread defaults. However, it is not clear how domestic credit expansion could be prevented when capital inflows lead to a rapid liquidity expansion. Unless the central bank is willing and able to sterilise the impact of foreign capital inflows on domestic liquidity, there will be an increase in domestic lending which will eventually spill over from the financing of safe and productive investments to risky and speculative assets. The lending spree in turn raises the collateral values of assets financed by such lending, thereby encouraging belief in the appropriateness of these values. Such a process of Minskyan endogenous fragility (Minsky 1982, 1986) was experienced not only in East Asia, but also in the banking system in Mexico in the early 1990s and in the US in the 1980s.

This process contains a major contradiction. As the investment bubble continues, growth remains strong, eventually leading to a deterioration in the external balance. An unstable dynamic is created in which increasing domestic interest rates to slow the economy and improve external payments serve to attract additional capital inflows and expand bank liquidity and lending further. But eventually, loans become non-performing and banks are weakened. Thus, deterioration of the external balance and weakening of the financial sector are two sides of the same process of excessive capital inflows. The basic problem is not in the control and supervision of the banking system, but in the absence of instruments to restrict capital inflows and contain their impact on macroeconomic and monetary conditions. But these instruments are usually discarded with the adoption of liberalisation designed to remove 'financial repression'!

Furthermore, domestic banking regulations cannot prevent excessive non-bank private sector borrowing abroad. This is not always appreciated, even though in East Asia an important part of private borrowing from international banks is by non-bank firms: one-third in South Korea, around 60 per cent in Malaysia and Thailand, and even more in Indonesia (Bank for International Settlements 1998a: Table 1). Control over such borrowing would call for various restrictions, including (Chilean-type) non-interest-bearing deposit requirements — something that qualifies as 'financial repression' rather than prudential regulation (Helleiner 1997, Le Fort and Budnevich 1997). On the other hand, it is not clear whether the Anglo-American type of corporate governance based stock-market discipline could prevent excessive borrowing and risk-taking by non-bank private business — witness the experience of the US in the 1980s, where firms accumulated large stocks of debt to acquire highly risky assets. Nor do international financial markets impose the right kind of discipline over private debtors in emerging markets. All too often, they manifest herd-like, pro-cyclical behaviour in both giving and cutting back loans. Indeed, until the turmoil in the currency markets, East Asian banks and firms enjoyed very high marks from Western rating agencies and banks.

What we have in East Asia is a typical private sector external debt crisis, very much like the so-called Southern Cone crisis in Argentina, Chile and Uruguay in the late 1970s and early 1980s. As will be recalled, these countries too had allowed the private sector unrestricted access to external finance in the belief that, for private firms, the difference between domestic and external debt was net significant, since they were expected to assess carefully the costs and benefits on which their survival depended. The experiment ended with private sector over-borrowing, subsidised debt servicing *via* preferential exchange rates and eventually the nationalisation of private external debt and a *de facto* socialisation of the banking system (Diaz-Alejandro 1985).

It also appears that the so-called non-debt-creating financial inflows, that is acquisition of property and securities by non-residents, have also played some role in sustaining speculative bubbles in equity and property markets in Southeast Asia. Indeed increased access by non-residents to securities markets (as well as greater access by residents to dollar assets) tends to establish a close link between the two inherently unstable markets, namely currency and equity markets. This generates destabilising feedbacks: a currency crisis could easily lead to a stock market collapse, while a bearish mood in the equity market could easily translate into a currency crisis. Again, one may need more direct measures to control such destabilising linkages, including restrictions over foreign acquisition of domestic securities (Akyüz 1995).

Recent experience shows that almost every domestic financial crisis (asset price deflation or banking crisis) in developing countries tends to translate into a currency turmoil, payments difficulties and even an external debt crisis. Similarly, in such countries reversal of external capital flows or attacks on the currency almost invariably threaten the domestic financial system. By contrast, currency turmoils in industrial countries do not usually spill over into domestic financial markets (e.g. the 1992-93 European Monetary System (EMS) crisis); nor do domestic financial disruptions necessarily lead to currency and payments crises (e.g. the S&L crisis and the 1987 stock market collapse in the US). External indebtedness, together with dollarisation of the economies in the South, accounts for much of this difference. The East Asian crisis can be described either as excessive borrowing abroad by the private sector, or as excessive lending by international financial markets. In any case, there is a failure of free capital markets to produce an optimal global allocation of capital. As pointed out by Alan

Greenspan, it is clear that more investment monies flowed into these economies than could be profitably employed at modest risk. In this sense, it is a global crisis with a regional trigger. Perhaps one can also fault East Asian governments for failing to prevent market failure — an approach that underpinned successful policy intervention in post-war East Asia.

The Policy Response

For the first time, a major disagreement has emerged among mainstream economists over the appropriate policy response to a financial crisis in developing countries. The policy package to be adopted can be expected to address two problems: first, it should help restore confidence, thereby halting the turmoil in the currency and asset markets; second, it should correct the underlying fundamentals.

There is a growing concern that IMF policies are not helping to restore market confidence. A factor contributing to the continued market volatility and yo-yo movements in exchange rates and equity prices is no doubt lack of consensus among mainstream economists about the appropriateness of the orthodox policy package. But neither do markets appear to have been impressed by the policies promoted so far. For example, although Indonesia and Thailand have kept their interest rates higher than Malaysia, they have experienced greater difficulties in their currency and stock markets. By the same token, strict adherence to the orthodox programme has not protected the Philippines against contagion.

Regarding fundamentals, there was certainly a need for correction in exchange rates and external balances. However, so far, declines in the currencies in the region have more than corrected the earlier appreciation; baht, won and rupiah have certainly overshot the levels that can reasonably be considered as compatible with sustainable current account positions. There is not a strong case for a drastic reduction in domestic absorption and growth to bring about the adjustment needed in external payments. Indeed, many prominent mainstream economists have criticised the IMF programmes of fiscal austerity and tight money, arguing that, while these could be appropriate under conditions of monetary and fiscal dis-equilibrium, this is not the case in East Asia. It is rightly argued that targeting very low inflation when currencies have lost half of their value could simply drive these economies into deep recession. Furthermore, voices are increasingly heard from the region that conditionality is abused, promoting the bilateral interests of the major industrial countries in areas which have very little to do with the management of the crisis, and drastically restricting national autonomy and raising the danger of political backlash.

A useful lesson on what needs to be done under conditions of debt deflation can be drawn from recent US history. As will be recalled, recovery in the US during the 1980s was driven by spending financed by increased indebtedness relative to income. Business firms, consumers and the government all raised their indebtedness to unprecedented levels, while financial institutions increased their lending against risky assets including real estate, and financed mergers and acquisitions. These meant that both corporate and household incomes and spending became increasingly sensitive to interest rates. The Fed started tightening after the 1987 crash in order to check asset price inflation, and this policy was complemented by tax increases and less expansionary fiscal policy. The result was one of the deepest post-war recessions. However, in reaction to the weakness in the financial system and the economy, the Fed started to reduce short-term interest rates in the early 1990s, almost to negative levels in real terms, thus providing relief not only for banks, but also for firms and households, which were able to ride the yield curve and refinance debt at substantially lower interest servicing costs. This eventually produced a boom in the securities market, thereby lowering long-term interest rates, and helping to restore balance-sheet positions, producing a strong recovery at the end of 1993. Clearly, the US economy is unlikely to have enjoyed one of the longest post-war recoveries if the kind of policies advocated in East Asia had been pursued in the early 1990s in response to debt deflation.

It is true that monetary relaxation did not make much of a dent in the Japanese case, but largely because Japan was too hesitant in pursuing a similar policy for fear of creating another bubble. It was also unable to put together a financial restructuring package or address its structural problems through appropriate measures to deregulate the economy (Akyüz 1998).

It is often suggested that easy money is not a policy option in East Asia since asset price deflation is associated with currency turmoil. However, high interest rates are not securing stability in the currency markets. Indeed, they are actually undermining a positive response to the recent shift in exchange rates owing to their effects on the banking sector and companies' capacity to meet their financial obligations. The credit crunch seems to be so deep that, despite favourable exchange rates, firms are unable to export as their access to trade credit is curtailed. Thus, an important part of the improvement in the current-account balances of South Korea and Thailand so far seems to have been due to import cuts rather than export expansion. Provision of adequate external liquidity to support the exchange rate would have avoided such an outcome by allowing these countries to pursue a more accommodating monetary policy to deal with debt deflation.

Global Implications

The developing countries in Asia have become major actors in the global economy, playing a crucial role in generating global demand. A sharp decline in their growth rates and a reduction in their contribution to global demand will make it especially difficult for industrial economies, in particular Europe and Japan, to expand at rates needed to reverse the upward trend in their unemployment rates.

There can be little doubt that the crisis will have serious consequences for regional growth dynamics and integration in East Asia. These are built on the so-called *flying geese* process, whereby countries at different levels of industrial-isation and development move together on the basis of a progressive upgrading of their industries. Intra-regional trade and investment both play a major role in this process by helping to locate production according to comparative advantages determined by relative levels of productivity and wages. A stable pattern of exchange rates throughout the region is absolutely essential for this process to be driven by the real economic forces of thrift and productivity.

These foundations of the flying geese process have been shaken by recent shifts in the exchange rates among the currencies of the region through what look like competitive devaluations. Currency instability causes unexpected shifts in the relative positions of individual countries, and creates considerable uncertainty regarding the competitiveness of various industries across the region, thereby undermining investment in tradables, including intra-regional investment. If restrictive policies are pursued to restore stability, the overall speed of regional growth will be reduced.

Regarding the global impact of the crisis, there has been a certain degree of ambivalence. While on the one hand it is increasingly argued that we are now all living in a global village as a result of significantly increased integration of markets and interdependence of economies, it is at the same time maintained that the impact of the East Asian crisis on the global economy can be expected to be negligible since their share in global trade and production is small. However, greater realism appears to have started to influence the views of major inter-national organisations, which have come to recognise that the global impact of the crisis will be serious, leading to a significant loss of growth, as much as over one percentage point from the baseline.

But what is less appreciated is that this is coming on top of existing imbalances in the world economy. Indeed, on the eve of the crisis, there was already a major inconsistency: virtually all major industrial countries except the US were expecting faster growth on the basis of increased exports, while the contribution of the US to global demand was expected to slow down. The surplus countries (Europe and Japan) were employing restrictive fiscal policies and attempting to increase their export surpluses to preserve growth. By contrast, with the notable exceptions of China and Taiwan, the fast-growing economies of East Asia were major contributors to global demand, running large deficits financed by private capital inflows. However, as US and European interest rates had started to edge up, capital flows were expected to be diverted from developing countries, forcing them to cut their external deficits and hence their contribution to global demand.

Perhaps the single positive contribution of the East Asian crisis is that it has halted the moves towards monetary restriction and higher interest rates in the US and Europe. This emerged when the crisis led to a global stock market break in late October 1997, and has been motivated primarily by concerns over the possible impact of higher interest rates on financial markets in industrial countries. Moreover, the slump in East Asia appears to have eased the preoccupation of central bankers with the risk of inflation, and has even raised some concerns about deflationary pressures.

However, the crisis has done nothing to reduce global imbalances; indeed, it has tended to worsen them. Although exchange rates have now turned more favourable, firms in East Asia also face a greater need to earn foreign exchange in view of cutbacks in lending and the prohibitive cost of foreign borrowing. Furthermore, the rise in domestic interest rates has increased their domestic debt servicing while, together with fiscal retrenchment, depressing domestic demand. Consequently, East Asian firms can be expected to pursue an aggressive export strategy in markets where they have already gained competitiveness — namely, in the US, Europe and Japan. Although the expected export boom is not yet in sight because of their credit crunch, it should not come as a surprise if these countries eventually succeed not only in eliminating their external deficits, but also in creating large trade surpluses, not as in Latin America in the 1980s through drastic import cuts, but by rapid increases in exports. The tighter the domestic policy stance, the greater the tendency to seek markets abroad in industrial countries.

This means that a positive adjustment should have two components. First, loans should be rolled over and rescheduled to allow the countries concerned to service them from future export earnings and not through increased external borrowing at penalising rates. Second, it is necessary to raise global growth to provide markets in which the East Asian countries can earn the foreign exchange needed to pay off their foreign currency debt. Thus, the solution to the problem is not to be found simply in the restructuring of the financial sector of the Southeast Asian economies, necessary as it may be, or in their macroeconomic policies. Rather, a crucial component must be removing the deflationary bias in the macroeconomic policies in Japan and Europe. Until these two areas initiate domestic demand-led growth and reduce their external surpluses, the global economy will continue to be vulnerable to the risk of financial instability and recession, and the crisis in Southeast Asia will continue to contribute to the decline in global growth and trade frictions.

The crisis will tend to aggravate the difficulties faced by Japan. While the yen has been falling against the dollar, it has appreciated against the East Asian currencies. This means that Japan may not get an additional overall stimulus from shifts in exchange rates, but its trade surplus with the US may grow, triggering reaction particularly if the US economy is slowing and its trade deficit rising. Further declines of the yen to gain competitiveness against East Asian NIEs will also mean declines against the dollar, which can again cause trade frictions. Japanese firms may not be able to respond to loss of competitiveness by out-sourcing through foreign direct investment (FDI) to East Asia as they did previously: the Japanese banks already have large exposure in the area and there is excess capacity. This means that Japanese profits will be squeezed, putting pressure on wages and unemployment.

It is often held that the EU will be relatively untouched by the crisis since its exports to the region are a small proportion of GDP. However, for some countries in the EU, exports to East Asia have been the most dynamic component of aggregate demand in recent years. Moreover, it is important to recognise that European banks have larger exposures than Japanese and US banks not only in Asia, but also in Eastern Europe and Latin America, where vulnerability to contagion remains high. Moreover, the crisis can be expected to influence policies in developing countries and transition economies with large external deficits. They may be inclined to restrict domestic demand and cut their imports and external deficits in order to reduce their vulnerability to an interruption of capital flows. This would be deflationary, not only for the countries concerned, but also for their trading partners including Europe. Declines in net exports to developing countries, together with restrictive fiscal policies designed to meet the conditions for the European Monetary Union (EMU), may make it more difficult for the EU to halt the rise in unemployment. Growth may further be depressed if the European currencies appreciate *vis-à-vis* the yen; although the latter may be greeted as a success for the EMU, it would only aggravate the unemployment problem.

The crisis may also pose an additional challenge for the EMU. It is generally recognised that desynchronisation of cycles among the participating countries, together with restrictions on individual countries' budgetary policies and the absence of a strong fiscal centre *a la* US, can cause frictions regarding interest rate and exchange rate policies, particularly since initial conditions with respect to external payments and labour markets differ widely. Such frictions would also emerge if the EMU received asymmetric external shocks that required a different monetary policy response for the different participants (Feldstein 1997). In that respect, the coincidence of the Asian crisis with the launching of the EMU could be a cause for concern.

Another unknown element in the evolution of the crisis is China. While the country itself is not exposed to speculative attacks in the same way as the others in the region, Hong Kong is its Achilles' heel. Should Chinese exports slow sharply as a result of increased competition from the region and its growth rate fall considerably below the 8 per cent set by the government, markets may try to test the resolve of the government to maintain a fixed exchange rate — very much as they did in France in 1993. Since China cannot politically afford to abandon the peg in Hong Kong, it may choose to devalue its own currency, using the interest rates in Hong Kong to defend the peg. However, if it does not succeed in keeping the peg, the crisis could intensify significantly.

To sum up, the East Asian crisis has unleashed forces that tend to aggravate the existing imbalances in the global economy, raising once more the spectre of deflation and protectionism. Certainly, increased trade imbalances and reduced growth will provide humus to protectionist sentiments and such pressures may intensify, as much in Europe as in the US. Moreover, these pressures could succeed in attaining their goals if surplus countries do not pursue expansionary macroeconomic policies as developing countries start cutting their trade deficits.

Another potential threat is competitive devaluations. This was a major concern for the architects of the Bretton Woods system, and that concern increased after the collapse of the system in the early 1970s. However, it receded when inflation became a major problem. Because of the implications for price stability, countries were unwilling to use their exchange rates to export unemployment. The threat of competitive devaluations is much more serious now than at any time since then, because the danger now is deflation, not inflation. There were some signs of it during the currency crisis in Europe a few years ago when some countries pulled out of the EMS and devalued to import some demand. If the crisis deepens global deflation, there may be more action of this kind. This is why it is important to have expansionary policies in the countries with external surpluses.

Perhaps the worst scenario is the emergence of redundant capacity on the other side of the Pacific too. In Japan the post-Plaza recovery was based on a very strong investment boom, but only to result in excess capacity subsequently. Again, the current difficulties in East Asia are traced back to excessive investment in the region since the beginning of the decade. Increased trade frictions may become unavoidable should the US investment-led expansion come to an end in the same way.

Conclusions

The East Asian crisis shows once more that there are serious systemic problems in the global monetary and financial arrangements. Indeed, it has long been maintained by many observers that it is not possible to speak of a 'system' of international money and finance. The East Asian financial crisis has increased awareness of the need for global governance of finance so as to prevent the recurrence of similar crises. Hopefully, the international community will be forced to reconsider whether or not existing arrangements regarding international payments and finance are compatible with stability and growth.

The main problem is that, even though financial markets are much more integrated than product markets and capital is much more mobile than other factors of production, there is no global governance of international financial transactions analogous to that found in the area of trade. Moreover, the present international arrangements are not only inadequate, but also asymmetrical; they are designed to discipline borrowers rather than regulate lenders. This stands in sharp contrast with the way national financial systems are designed. Moreover, international arrangements are designed to manage rather than to prevent crises. Further, the measures to stave off international banking crises tend to be at the expense of living standards, stability and development in debtor developing countries.

Second, with greater financial integration, the global impact of interest- and exchange-rate policies has become much more important. This is true not only for the major industrial countries but also for many developing countries, where policies are seen to have had serious regional or global repercussions. There is no effective surveillance in these areas and there is no way of preventing 'beggar thy neighbour' policies affecting key monetary and financial variables. Moreover, there is no mechanism for dispute settlement regarding macroeconomic and financial policies, such as exists for trade policies. If a country puts up its tariffs on imports of cars from its neighbour, the latter can go to the World Trade Organisation (WTO) and complain, but no forum exists where a country can make analogous representations about a rise in a major country's interest rates and a consequent increase in its debt burden, or about a devaluation which has the same effect on its exports as higher tariffs.

Third, there are no effective, rule-based and adequately funded arrangements for the provision of liquidity by an international lender of last resort.

Finally, there is a need for a system of orderly workouts based on rules and bankruptcy procedures governing international debtor–creditor relations.

Several proposals to fill these gaps are worth considering. The international community needs to turn its attention to these issues as part of efforts to improve the governance of international finance.

3

EAST ASIA IS NOT MEXICO: THE DIFFERENCE BETWEEN BALANCE OF PAYMENTS CRISES AND DEBT DEFLATION

J.A. Kregel

What was different about the collapse of the Asian emerging markets in 1997? The free fall of the Mexican peso and the collapse of the Mexican Bolsa produced a 'Tequila effect' that spread through most of South America, but did not create a sell-off in the global financial markets similar to that which occurred on 27 October 1997. Normally, sharp declines in prices in emerging equity markets produce a 'flight to quality', in which international investors shift their funds back into developed country markets and local investors seek to protect their wealth by diversifying into developed country assets. Yet, the collapse in the Asian emerging markets, that started in Thailand, spread to the other second-tier newly industrialising economies (NIEs), and eventually extended to the first-tier NIEs produced the largest absolute declines ever experienced in the major developed country equity markets. If equity markets can suffer from what Alan Greenspan has called 'irrational exuberance', the Asian crisis suggests that they may also suffer from 'irrational pessimism'. Yet, there is much to indicate that in this case the financial markets in Japan, Europe and the US were quite rational in assessing the global implications of the financial crisis in Asia.

The developing countries in Asia have come to play a crucial role in global growth. In the 1990s, they accounted for roughly half of global expansion. The immediate implication of the Asian crises is that the collapse of growth in the region would produce a global deflation. This would make it more difficult for developed economies, particularly Europe and Japan, to expand at rates necessary to generate sufficient investment to produce reductions in unemployment. Recovery in the developed world outside the US and the UK is thus at risk as a result of declining Asian growth. Indeed, if the US cannot continue its current expansion, there is a clear risk of a global depression similar to that of the 1930s.

The stage for the decline in growth in the Asian region has been set by what may be called a series of competitive devaluations amongst the currencies in the region. The combination of globalisation of production and economic development in these countries has advanced to the point that a substantial proportion of their trade is now within the Asian region (including Japan), rather than with the developed economies.[1] It has been based on a progressive upgrading of the value added to production, as represented in the idea of the 'flying geese'. But, the logic of the 'flying geese' model is that progress to more advanced stages of development is determined by relative rates of increase in productivity, income per capita and real wages. Since much of the trade is linked to a division of labour within the region, with Japan and the more advanced NIEs exporting capital equipment and semi-finished goods to be assembled in Southeast Asia and then shipped on to others before final export to developed country markets, stable relative costs and prices have played an important part in regional integration and development. Currency instability is very disruptive to this process, causing random shifts in the relative position of individual countries and in their development plans. Thus, the entire logic of the Southeast Asian development process would be disrupted by volatile cross rates of exchange of the currencies of the countries in the area creating changes in relative competitiveness independent of changes in productivity and per capita income levels. If restrictive policies are necessary to restore the currency stability required to allow the 'flying geese' system of relative positions on the value-added ladder to function, then growth will fall and the demand for exports from the developed countries will decline.

While it is true that neither the US nor Europe depend on Asia for a substantial proportion of their exports (the US exports less than 20 per cent and Europe little over 5 per cent), it is an integral part of the process of globalisation; while the US may not export much to Asia, US companies do import to and export from their production facilities in Asia, so that the overall impact on US income will be much higher.[2] And these companies are primarily in the high technology area, that has been at the basis of the restructuring of the US economy and the performance of US equity markets. But how was it possible for one of the most successful development areas to suffer a virtually complete reversal of fortunes in less than a year?

An Interpretation of the Asian Crisis

The Asian crisis was not a typical balance of payments crisis, such as those experienced with such frequency under the Bretton Woods system, or the Mexican peso crisis of 1994/5. In Mexico, rapid liberalisation of domestic markets caused imports to grow much more rapidly than exports. Tight monetary policy to reduce inflation produced high interest rates, which attracted foreign capital inflows to deregulated and liberalised domestic financial markets which financed the trade gap, while it also caused real appreciation of the peso which further worsened the trade balance by turning relative prices against exports. The capital inflows also encouraged import growth as foreign borrowing allowed domestic banks to compete for domestic market share by lending to households to finance consumption and to arrange foreign exchange loans to domestic business at international interest rates. The result was a continually increasing Mexican payments deficit, along with record increases in banks' non-performing loans, a fall in private savings and low domestic investment, with slow growth and rising unemployment accompanying a fall in the rate of inflation and a government budget surplus.

Irrespective of the reversal of US interest rate policy, which was initiated in February 1994, the real appreciation of the peso would eventually have collided with the increasing external deficit, and Mexico would have experienced an exchange rate crisis that would have been aggravated by a domestic financial crisis due to bad bank loans to households and foreign currency exposure of business clients.[3]

The Asian crisis of 1997 has been very different. Most countries have been near surplus on their trade balance, if not on their current account balances, and have a long-term record of fiscal rectitude. Imports were not dominated by luxury consumption goods, savings ratios were extremely high and banks were not financing unsustainable consumption booms. Foreign exchange reserves were high and exchange rates had been stable throughout the 1990s. Yet, there was a discernible tendency towards deterioration in the foreign account caused by a fall-off in the rapid growth of exports in most countries. But, this was caused not by changes in what had until that time been successful internal stabilisation policy, but rather by changes in the external environment, over which they had little control and there were few policy responses available. This is a characteristic of the world of increased economic interdependence and free global capital flows.

External Balance

Current account balances had already started to show weakness throughout the region in 1994. This was, in part, due to the sharp fall-off in import growth in the developed countries. For the developed countries as a whole, the rate of increase in imports fell from 11.0 per cent in 1994 to 7.6 per cent in 1995 to 5.2 per cent per annum in 1996. In Japan, the rate of growth of imports fell from 13.6 per cent in 1994 to 3.5 per cent in 1996; in the US, the decline from 1994 to 1996 was from 12.0 per cent to 6.4 per cent; and in Europe, from 9.1 per cent to 5.3 per cent for the same period. As external positions deteriorated, most countries responded with restrictive policies and external imbalances had started to improve in 1997 (cf. UNCTAD 1997: Chapter 1).

By historical comparison, the trade deficits were not large. Ostrey (1997: 20-3) points out that they cannot be traced to 'excessive private consumption'. He further argues that there is 'relatively strong' evidence in favour of the long-term 'sustainability' of the deficits given the 'strength of savings and investment' — which 'implies that the resources needed to enlarge future productive capacity are in place and, therefore, that rapid economic growth... is likely to persist. In addition, the allocation of investment appears to be efficient, judging from the strong performance of total factor productivity and exports, as well as the absence of significant relative prices distortions in these economies.... In addition, both the absence of significant exchange rate misalignment together with relatively open trade and investment regimes have tended to foster diversification of the export base in the ASEAN countries, making the trade balance less sensitive to terms of trade shocks, and reducing the risks associated with terms of trade shocks.'[4] On this reasoning, the external account should not then have been a cause of crisis.

Capital Flows

The other side of the slowdown of developed country imports is an increase in capital flows from the developed economies into the Asian economies starting in 1993-4. This was further stimulated by the tightening in monetary policy to reduce the deterioration in the foreign balance and by the reaction of international investors to the Tequila crisis in Latin America. There was a sharp increase in the proportion of bank lending into the region, representing a radical change from past experience. In 1993, the banks in the Bank of International Settlements (BIS) reporting area listed US$14.8 billion of assets representing bank lending to Asia. In 1994, the figure jumped to US$47.8 billion and in 1995 nearly doubled to US$86.3 billion. The figure for 1996 was down slightly at US$72.3 billion.

Capital flows require both a borrower and a lender, but they are usually arranged by an intermediary. Thus, in addition to the fall in returns in developed countries that led to a search for higher returns in emerging markets, global investment banks were seeking alternative sources of revenue to help them emerge from their difficulties in the US in the 1980s. One of the ways that they could do this was by earning fee and commission income by arranging structured derivative packages which allowed emerging market borrowers access to funds at low interest rates prevailing in developed country markets, while offering assets earning high emerging market interest rates to developed country investors. A popular means of arranging lending was by means of equity swaps in which high-yielding debt issued by emerging market firms or banks was repackaged into investment trust vehicles which could be sold to institutional investors in developing countries as if they were investment-grade assets. Although the technical aspects of these packages are complicated, they almost all depend on the stability of exchange rates, since the exchange rate risk is borne not by the underwriting bank, but by the buyer or the seller.[5]

Financial liberalisation also made it possible for financial institutions in emerging economies to increase their role as intermediaries. The issue of bonds by Asian entities increased from US$25.3 billion in 1995 to US$43.1 billion in 1996. Korean entities alone accounted for US$16 billion, and Hong Kong, Indonesia and Thailand raised about US$4 billion each (IMF 1997c: 77). Many of these bonds served as the basis for derivatives contracts (discussed above) and were intermediated by offshore investment funds.[6] The result was a sharp increase in foreign exchange reserves, which further strengthened expectations of exchange rate stability.

The increase in capital inflows produced a sharp increase in foreign exchange reserves, which further strengthened expectations of exchange rate stability. However, as central banks attempted to keep their currencies from appreciating relative to the dollar, the rise in foreign exchange reserves was translated into increased liquidity for the domestic banking sector and in expanded domestic lending.

Exchange Rate Misalignments

However, this attempt to keep exchange rates stable to prevent loss of competitiveness was only partially successful since the dollar was itself on a strengthening path from the end of 1995, but this only started to become visible in real exchange rate appreciations in a number of countries from 1996. For example, the IMF's *Expanded Competitiveness Indicators System* (Turner and Golub 1997) reports that Indonesia's real effective exchange rate (the exchange rate of the rupiah corrected for changes in costs and prices in Indonesia relative to its trading partners, weighted by the amount of Indonesian trade with each trading partner), marginally depreciated in 1990-94, and only regained its 1990 level by 1995. In Thailand, the real effective exchange rate in 1994 was the same as in 1990, and rose only marginally in 1995. In Korea, the real effective exchange rate depreciated substantially in 1990-93, and remained at a roughly constant level until 1995. Malaysia and Singapore show marginal rises from 1990-92, and then stability thereafter. Only Hong Kong and the Philippines show substantial and sustained declines in competitiveness due to real exchange rate appreciation over the period 1990-95. This study supports the conclusion of the absence of substantial exchange rate readjustment cited above.[7]

Domestic Banks and Domestic Credit Expansion

Throughout this period, Asian countries were under pressure from both the IMF and the World Trade Organisation (WTO) to modernise, liberalise and deregulate their banking and financial systems. In 1993, Thailand created the Offshore International Banking Facility. The BIS notes that its existence 'was an important reason for the upsurge in cross-border inter-bank credit to Thailand' (BIS 1995: 19)[8] in 1994.[9] Ostrey (1997: 20-21) notes that 'in Thailand, risk-weighted capital-asset ratios were increased for both commercial banks and finance companies in order to comply with BIS standards, and now approach 10 per cent for local banks. In addition, required provisions for doubtful assets were increased, and limits on banks' net open foreign exchange positions were tightened. While banks have been successful in broadly matching the maturity structure of their assets and liabilities, rapid growth in foreign exchange lending has nevertheless created concerns of increased foreign exchange risk. In Malaysia, the position of the banking system has strengthened in recent years.' At the beginning of 1994, Korea initiated the conversion of short-term finance companies into investment banks, as part of an attempt to introduce features of developed countries' financial systems such as commercial paper markets and investment banking, such as the creation of offshore investment funds that were the major vehicles for the sale of derivative products of Korean banks and corporations. These effectively created a commercial paper market and provided new sources of foreign borrowing.

An IMF Working Paper (Montgomery 1997: 25, 19) notes the completion of the modernisation of the Indonesian banking system. It cautions that the basic problem is no longer the absence of appropriate regulation, but the supervision of the banks to ensure that regulations are respected, especially with regard to the rapid expansion of real estate lending, and to the reliability of the figures on bank capital adequacy. The paper also reports that the ratio of net foreign exchange liabilities to bank equity reached a high of 161 per cent in 1992/3, but had fallen back to little over 100 per cent in 1994/5.

These and other types of liberalisation throughout the region provided a fertile ground for the inflows of foreign investors' funds, which multilateral agencies such as the Organisation for Economic Cooperation and Development (OECD) and the IMF were actively encouraging. However, given the high savings rates in most Asian countries, and the preponderance of foreign direct investment (FDI, foreign companies' direct investments in productive capacity) flows in others, and the relative absence of demands for consumption finance, bank lending was directed primarily into two areas.[10] One was in providing loans to domestic firms, using the supply of cheaper foreign funds to offer interest rates below domestic rates. The other was to finance non-manufacturing initiatives, such as financial services, real-estate investments, and other types of infrastructure investment that previously had been rationed by government policies directing credit towards export-oriented manufacturing industries. With rates of growth averaging 8-10 per cent, and given the increasing importance of the globalisation of production in Asia, it was relatively easy for bankers to justify financing the rapidly expanding needs for new office space, leisure centres, golf courses and recreational residences. The exceptional returns that they expected on such investment could, of course, only be justified on the basis of continued global expansion. Unfortunately, it was coming to an end.

Asia is not Mexico

Thus, unlike Mexico, it is impossible to argue that excessive domestic bank lending and excessive real exchange rate appreciation led to a consumption and import boom which eventually created an expanding foreign deficit that specu-lators recognised as unsustainable since both the real exchange rate appreciations and the increased domestic bank lending occurred well after the beginning of the decline in trade balances and the increase in foreign bank lending. Rather, the process appears to have been the opposite. It was the rise in short-term bank inflows and the decline in developed country demand in the presence of liberalisation of domestic financial markets that led to the deterioration in the trade balance, which was then further aggravated by dollar appreciation and rapid domestic credit expansion. It is for this reason that the crisis was not a foreign exchange crisis caused by a payments imbalance, since there was no clear evidence that exchange rates were inappropriate. Reserves were extremely large,[11] external balances were moving in the right direction and official international agency assessments of country fundamentals suggested that the external positions were sustainable at existing exchange rates.

The Beginning of the Crisis

The crisis broke at the weakest link in the Asian economies, i.e. the recently liberalised and deregulated private domestic banking systems. Weakness in the financial sector in Indonesia was evidenced by its first private bank failure in 20 years in 1992, and the rescue of a major state bank in 1995 (Montgomery 1997: 13). In Thailand, where the expansion of the banking sector had been the most rapid,[12] the central bank had since 1996 been practising a policy of 'forbearance' (frequently used by developed country central banks, in particular the Federal Reserve), that is, central banks lending to support banks in difficulty in the hope that they can be rescued without public notice and without creating market panic. Given the degree to which Thai banks and finance companies had been financed through foreign currency lending to their new offshore banking centre, this meant using foreign exchange reserves for their internal function of lender of last resort. A similar process appears to have been at work in Korea from the spring of 1996. However, in Korea, the first signs of difficulty were in a run of bankruptcies starting with Hanbo steel in January 1997. But, despite increasing information of difficulties in Asian banks,[13] a Thai land development company failing to meet a foreign debt payment, and numerous bankruptcies in Korean corporations, foreign capital inflows into Asia continued unabated during the first half of 1997.

But the failure by the Bank of Thailand to arrange the rescue of the country's largest finance company, Finance One, in the Spring of 1997 concentrated the attention of international lenders and the feared reversal of short-term lending started. The failure took on special importance because it occurred against the background of increased uncertainty in international capital markets concerning the evolution of international interest rate differentials. At the beginning of May 1997, the view that the Japanese economy was engaged in a full-fledged recovery gained increasing support (although there was virtually no hard evidence to support this belief) and there was a sharp appreciation of the yen and a sudden rise in Japanese short-term interest rates on expectations that the Bank of Japan would move quickly to raise its discount rate.[14] As a result, funds that had been borrowed at low interest rates in Japan and Hong Kong, and invested at substantially higher rates in Asia, were quickly withdrawn and returned to Japan, supporting the appreciation of the yen and putting increasing pressure on Asian reserves and exchange rates.

The Thai financial crisis could not have avoided becoming an exchange rate crisis, given the degree to which foreign reserves had already been used to shore up banks through the 'lender of last resort' function and the fact that the reserves were not nearly sufficient to meet the liquidation of the entire amount of foreign lending while the foreign balance was continuing to deteriorate. A domestic banking crisis, which could have been handled by the central bank through creation of domestic currency in a relatively closed capital market, became a foreign exchange crisis because of the open capital market and the size of foreign capital inflows into the Thai banking system through the Bangkok International Banking Facility (BIBF). Since the Bank of Thailand could not print dollars, it could not act as lender of last resort for its own domestic banks' exposure in US dollars, while its use of its foreign exchange reserves to do so made it helpless to support the exchange rate.[15]

Thus, even though Thailand had a savings ratio of around 40 per cent, foreign exchange reserves that were three times the size of the 1996 current account deficit, slowing import growth as well as domestic consumption, and predominantly long-term capital inflows, the baht was floated on 2 July and the IMF called in at the end of the month to formulate a bail-out.

A Financial Crisis of International Capital Market Failure

The crisis could thus be explained as a case of 'market failure' of two different types. First, a failure of free, competitive international capital markets to produce the optimal allocation of capital. Funds continued to flow to Asian financial institutions after it was clear that financial instability was widespread. In the words of Alan Greenspan: 'In retrospect, it is clear that more investment monies flowed into these economies than could be profitably employed at modest risk' (Greenspan 1997: 1-2). Second, is a failure of privatised free-market 'banking systems, [that] were not up to the task of effectively absorbing and channelling to productive use large foreign capital inflows as well as the large amount of domestic savings of these economies.... Such weakness led to the misallocation of resources' (Hormats 1997: 1). On the other hand, Stanley Fischer notes that 'the maintenance of pegged exchange rate regimes for too long... encouraged external borrowing and led to excessive exposure to foreign exchange risk' (Fischer 1998: 2) — which suggests that international bankers and businessmen are incapable of identifying exchange rate misalignments.[16]

The rapid deterioration in conditions in Thailand — especially the change in exchange rate policy which led to substantial losses for foreign investors who had presumed that the probability of exchange depreciation was negligible — led to a reassessment of investors' expectations for exchange rate adjusted returns on their investments in the rest of the region. Speculators, having succeeded in Thailand, started to look for other possible candidates for depreciation.

The balance of payments deficit in the Philippines had been increasing for some years and attention quickly shifted to the exchange rate of the peso. The central bank responded with an increase in the overnight interest rate from 15 per cent to 24 per cent and the discount rate to 32 per cent, but under pressure, the peso was allowed to float within a fluctuation band on 11 July. Once the peso had fallen, it was clear that every country in the region was a potential target. Malaysia had the next worst balance of payments position, and its foreign borrowing from banks had been increasing rapidly. Although steps had already been taken in March 1997 to reduce exposure of financial institutions to real estate and financial investments, Malaysia quickly followed the Philippines and allowed the ringgit to float on 14 July. Singapore followed on 17 July, allowing a depreciation of the Singapore dollar, and although Indonesia had also tightened monetary policy in an attempt to support its currency, once Malaysia and Singapore had given up the dollar peg, Indonesia introduced enlarged fluctuation bands on 21 July. Thus, in the space of less than three weeks, Thailand, Philippines, Malaysia, Singapore and Indonesia gave up exchange rates that had been stable against the dollar for extended periods.

Had it been a typical Bretton Woods balance of payments crisis, it should have been over at this point; tight monetary and fiscal policy would have reduced imports and increased the demand for domestic assets, while the currency depreciations should have increased exports. The balance of falling imports, rising exports and increased demand for domestic assets — due to high interest rates and expectation of subsequent appreciation — should have brought equilibrium to the foreign currency markets and, following the Mexican example, growth and currency stability should have resumed after a period of high inflation. With an average of around 15 per cent of GDP in bad loans, it would have ranked on the high side of recent financial crises, but not out of the range of Mexico and Venezuela, and much lower than Chile. This was clearly the expectation of the IMF and most international observers. However, the move to floating exchange rates did not bring stability, but instead brought increased pressure. The reason, as noted above, was that this was not a typical balance of payments crisis, but a financial crisis.

Contagion and Capital Flows

As exchange rates continued to fall, it became clear that what had been a relatively stable process of adjusting trading patterns without sectoral adjustment crises would be permanently disrupted. As a result, Taiwan — even though it had a massive trade surplus, massive foreign exchange reserves, a budget surplus and no visible speculative pressure on its exchange rate — decided to recover its relative competitive position in the region and devalued its currency by 10 per cent on 17 October. This quickly extended the crisis from Southeast Asia to Northeast Asia and the first-tier newly industrialised countries (NICs). It suggested difficulty in even the strongest of the Asian economies. Given the pivotal role of Hong Kong between Taiwan and China and its recent change to special administrative region status under Chinese control, the result of the devaluation in Taiwan was to raise the possibility of a devaluation of the Hong Kong dollar, or even the Chinese renminbi.[17]

Given that the Hong Kong dollar was one of the few currencies in the region showing clear evidence of overvaluation and a deteriorating external balance, there was an instant flight of investors. The fact that the Special Province operated a currency board, in which domestic currency is 100 per cent backed by foreign exchange reserves, may have contributed to the panic. Investors in Hong Kong now ran the risk of a depreciation of the exchange rate or of a collapse of the prices of their financial assets, or both. The depreciation of virtually every other currency in the region suggested that there would be pressure on competitiveness and thus on the exchange rate. But, the operation of the currency board meant that even if the defence of the exchange rate was successful, this in itself would have negative impact on equity prices. Even if the board did not run out of US dollars, by selling dollars against Hong Kong dollars, it would sharply reduce the domestic money supply, producing a sharp increase in interest rates, and internal deflation, which would certainly create difficulty for domestic banks and property companies that were primarily involved in real estate lending and other financial ventures. Thus, even if the exchange rate held, in doing so, it would certainly bring about a collapse in the stock market. The obvious, safe course of action for a foreign investor facing this choice was to sell both Hong Kong stock and the Hong Kong dollar. The market was already under pressure in August and September, but fell 6 per cent on 22 October and another 10 per cent on 23 October, after the Taiwanese depreciation. As a result of sales of Hong Kong dollars, overnight interest rates rose from 7 per cent to 300 per cent and suggested that the domestic costs of exchange rate stability would be very large. Since a devaluation in Hong Kong would certainly have meant a devaluation of the Chinese currency, this would have ushered in a series of beggar-my-neighbour devaluations reminiscent of the currency instability of the 1920s and 1930s which led to the Great Depression. Faced with this prospect, the New York financial markets led the rest of the world's developed equity markets in a record absolute collapse on 27 October 1997.

Despite the bankruptcies of large manufacturing conglomerates (*chaebols*) and increasing concern for the Korean banks that had lent to these firms, given that many of the *chaebols* carried leverage ratios in excess of 500 per cent (i.e.

borrowed funds were five times owner's equity capital), markets continued to treat these as purely internal difficulties. Korean bank credit ratings were reduced in August, but it was only after the global equity market collapses at the end of October that markets focused on the viability of the Korean producers in conditions of global depression. Given the exchange rate changes in the region, the Korean currency was now clearly overvalued, its production was heavily concentrated in semiconductors (whose price had fallen from around US$50 per chip to US$5 in less than two years), and it was attempting to further expand in the international automobile market where excess capacity dominated. Finally, its current account had been deteriorating rapidly.

This would have been enough to raise the concerns of international investors, but at the same time, a series of Japanese bank bankruptcies occurred. Since the largest proportion of lending to Korea was from Japan, it was feared that they would recall their loans to Korean conglomerates, forcing more bankruptcies in Korea. Korea thus experienced the same withdrawal of foreign lending which had been occurring in the rest of the Asian region since the summer.

In November, it became clear that the Bank of Korea had for some time been using its foreign exchange reserves for lender of last resort lending to domestic banks unable to roll over their foreign borrowing. It also emerged that the level of short-term foreign lending was much higher than had been presumed. Thus, with around US$6 billion in foreign reserves and around US$100 billion of lending to be repaid to foreign lenders, the Bank of Korea allowed the won to float, and it went into free fall, much as the other currencies in the region, and the IMF was called in to provide support.

Given that Japanese banks were the largest lenders in the region, and had substantial exposure to increasingly shaky Korean companies, the collapse of the won created panic in Japan and the Bank of Japan had to inject some US$23 billion into the banking system on 29 November to keep the inter-bank money market from collapsing as Japanese banks withdrew credit, even from other Japanese banks. The rise in the yen which had started in the spring was thus reversed and it started to weaken against the dollar during November 1997.

This closed the first phase of the crisis, with Thailand, Indonesia and Korea accepting IMF conditional lending, and a number of other countries such as Malaysia, Hong Kong and Taiwan introducing similar policies independently of any international commitment of funds. Table 3.1 gives evidence of why these measures have been unable to reintroduce currency stability in the region. The withdrawal of commercial bank lending, plus current account financing and the sale of portfolio equity total US$58.9 billion, over two-thirds of the accumulation of reserves over the period 1990-96 of US$76.2 billion. In one year (in fact, since the outflows only started in earnest in July, the relevant period is closer to six months), the region was called upon to reimburse lending and make current payments equal to the accumulated reserves of the previous seven years. This is

Table 3.1
External Financing of Korea, Indonesia, Malaysia, Philippines and Thailand

Five Asian Economies: (US$ bn.)	*1994*	*1995*	*1996*	*1997ᵃ*	*1998ᵇ*
Current Account Balance	-24.6	-41.3	-54.9	-26.0	17.6
Net External Financing	47.4	80.9	92.8	15.2	15.2
– Direct Equity Flows	4.7	4.9	7.0	7.2	9.8
– Portfolio Flows	7.6	10.6	12.1	-11.6	-1.9
– Commercial Bank Lending	24.0	49.5	55.5	-21.3	-14.1
– Non-Bank Private Lending	4.2	12.4	18.4	13.7	-3.3
Net Official Flows	7.0	3.6	-0.2	27.2	24.6
Reserves (- = increase)	-5.4	-13.7	-18.3	22.7	-27.1

Notes: ᵃ estimate, ᵇ forecast.
Source: Institute of International Finance, 29 January 1998: 2.

Table 3.2
Asian Countries: Investment as Percentage of GDP, 1986-95

	1991-95	*1986-90*
Singapore	34.1	32.4
Malaysia	39.1	23.4
Indonesia	27.2	26.3
Thailand	41.1	33.0
Philippines	22.2	19.0
Korea	37.4	31.9
China	35.3	27.8

Source: Own calculations based on data from Asian Development Bank, *Key Indicators of Developing Asian and Pacific Countries*.

Table 3.3
Asian Countries: Current Account Balances as a Percentage of GDP, 1989-97

	1989	*1990*	*1991*	*1992*	*1993*	*1994*	*1995*	*1996*	*1997*
Hong Kong	11.5	8.5	6.6	5.3	7.0	2.1	-3.4	-1.0	-1.0
Singapore	9.6	8.3	11.2	11.4	7.3	15.9	17.7	15.0	13.7
South Korea	2.4	-0.9	-3.0	-1.5	0.1	-1.2	-2.0	-4.8	-3.9
Taiwan	7.6	6.9	6.7	3.8	3.0	2.6	1.9	3.8	3.1
China	-1.3	3.9	4.3	1.4	-2.7	1.3	0.2	0.9	1.2
India	-2.3	-2.2	-1.5	-1.5	-1.5	-0.9	-1.7	-1.2	-1.1
Indonesia	-1.2	-2.8	-3.7	-2.2	-1.3	-1.6	-3.4	-3.4	-3.6
Malaysia	0.8	-2.0	-8.9	-3.7	-4.4	-5.9	-8.5	-5.3	-5.9
Philippines	-3.4	-6.1	-2.3	-1.9	-5.5	-4.4	-4.4	-5.9	-4.5
Thailand	-3.5	-8.5	-7.7	-5.7	-5.6	-5.9	-8.0	-8.0	-4.6

Source: Asian Development Bank.

Table 3.4
Asian Countries: Fiscal Balances as a Percentage of GDP, 1988-97

	1988-93	*1994*	*1995*	*1996*	*1997*
Hong Kong	2.3	0.8	-0.3	0.1	1.4
Singapore	6.8	4.0	7.6	6.7	5.1
South Korea	0.5	0.6	0.5	-0.3	-0.5
Taiwan	-1.6	-6.3	-7.4	-8.0	-5.0
China	-2.6	-2.4	-1.3	-1.2	-1.3
India	-7.4	-6.5	-5.8	-5.1	-4.9
Indonesia	-0.6	-0.4	0.8	0.7	0.5
Malaysia	-3.7	-0.2	1.2	-0.7	1.6
Philippines	-3.3	0.7	0.5	0.3	0.4
Thailand	3.3	1.5	3.0	2.2	-0.7

Source: Asian Development Bank.

equivalent to a massive 'bank run' on the region, without any lender of last resort. Just as no bank can ever repay all its deposits at sight, no country which is open to international capital flows can repay virtually all of its short-term borrowing instantaneously without a collapse in the exchange rate and substantial disruption of the real economy. It is for this reason that the basic problem in the region was not mistaken domestic policy, or fundamental disequilibrium, or even lack of transparency in the banking sector, although there is no question that weakness in the banking sectors of many of the countries aggravated the crisis, but was primarily caused by the reversal of the excessively rapid rise in capital inflows and the fall in global demand.

Indeed, these are simply two sides of the same coin, excess saving on the part of the developing world outside the US, visible in the form of capital flows into the region, meant that domestic investment was increasingly substituted for export sales. This may be called an excess savings crisis. Alternatively, it may be termed an over-investment crisis, which, in a way similar to Japan, has caused massive over-investment and over-capacity which will produce downward pressure on the prices of traded goods and thus deterioration in the terms of trade of these countries. Indeed, it is ironic to recall that at the beginning of the 1990s, most official institutions were announcing that it would be a decade of savings shortage as the demand for capital by developing countries outstripped the supply of savings, and that high real interest rates would be the natural result. Less than half-way through the decade, there is instead massive excess capacity, a risk of a global glut of production. Yet, high real interest rates seem still to be considered the answer to the crisis.

Stage Two: The Cure is Worse than the Disease

The second stage of the crisis came in the policy response, largely based on the conditional lending by the IMF. The IMF also mistook the crisis for a traditional balance of payments crisis and applied the same measures that they had used with modest success in the Tequila crisis. These involved increasing interest rates to restore confidence in the currency, tightening government budgets to slow demand for imports, control of monetary aggregates to keep the rate of inflation from eroding the benefits to export competitiveness of devaluation and reform of the banking system. The idea was basically to put household and bank balance sheets back in equilibrium and to allow firms to create an export surplus. However, as noted above, the collapse of exchange rates had not been due to banks financing excess demand for imported consumption goods, but rather, financing imports of capital goods by firms. It was the firms' balance sheets that were generally at risk. And the IMF conditions only made their positions worse. First, the flight of foreign capital meant that they had to replace their short-term financing, but at sharply higher rates from domestic banks. Second, with falling global demand, firms became increasingly dependent on domestic demand, but fiscal policy was ensuring that demand would be falling. Thus, firms had rising short-term financing costs and falling income flows to meet them. Third, firms that had borrowed abroad had to repay foreign lenders. Given the long period of relatively stable exchange rates, much of this borrowing had not been hedged, and thus had to be repaid in foreign currency. But, export receipts were falling and the value in domestic currency was rising daily. All three of these factors meant that firms went from being in a position of illiquidity, i.e. of not being able to convert their assets into foreign currency quickly enough, to positions of insolvency, i.e. of having the value of their assets fall below their liabilities. That is, they were technically bankrupt. At the same time, domestic banks that had acted as intermediaries, borrowing foreign currency to lend to domestic firms, found themselves in the same position. But, their position was aggravated by the fact that if they charged higher interest rates, this simply made it more likely that their clients would go bankrupt and be unable to repay anything. The dispute with the IMF was thus over the impact of interest rate policy. The IMF wanted rates set at levels that were high enough to generate demand for domestic currency, while the firms and banks and most affected Asian governments wanted interest rates set low enough to allow firms and banks to make their payment commitments.

Given the fact that the only way that firms and banks could escape bankruptcy was by repaying their foreign currency loans as fast as possible, this set in train what Hyman Minsky, following Irving Fisher, has called a debt deflation process. In order to meet their current commitments, a firm is forced to sell assets, inventory, current output, anything that will prevent it from having to close its books as bankrupt. But this is a self-defeating process, for as they increase supply, they drive down the price of the assets they are trying to sell, reducing their ability to liquidate their assets for a value that will cover their commitments. For Asian firms, the proceeds of the sales reduced domestic asset prices, while their demand for foreign currency drove up its price, thus driving the terms of trade against them. In such conditions, there is no interest rate high enough to stop the sale of domestic investments and the sale of the domestic currency. Indeed, high interest rates only make the process worse. As firms and banks scrambled to save themselves from bankruptcy, they also drove down the value of the currency.

Indeed, the IMF seems incapable of accepting the idea that higher interest rates might increase the demand for foreign currency by more than it increases supply in a period of crisis and thus aggravate conditions. For example, Camdessus (1998: 2) notes that 'the key lesson of the "tequila crisis" [was] a timely and forceful tightening of interest rates... to make it more attractive to hold domestic currency'. Fischer (1998: 4) uses virtually identical language. But, they both refer to examples of the successful use of high interest rates to *defend* a fixed exchange rate, not to the success of the policy in conditions *after* the devaluation had already taken place.[18] In this regard, it is interesting to note that BIS (1997: 108) refers to 'the increases in (or continued high) real interest rates... in Indonesia and

Thailand... and in Malaysia' that had been put in place already during 1996 and early 1997.

After a substantial devaluation, for a company with foreign exposure, a higher interest rate only makes bankruptcy more probable. For a foreign lender seeking to recover funds, there is no increase in interest rates that can offset the bankruptcy of a creditor. Again, it is interesting to note that BIS (1997: 111) refers to the successful experience of both the US and Sweden of using low interest rate policies to resolve collapsing asset and real estate prices.

At the same time, the breakdown of the financial system made it impossible for firms to increase production or exports, so that while trade balances improved sharply, this was primarily the result of massive falls in imports, rather than increased exports. Thailand and Korea both showed surpluses by the end of 1997, but this had little positive impact on exchange rates. For the month of January 1998, imports in Korea fell at a 40 per cent annual rate, and in Thailand at a 30 per cent annual rate.

Since banks were also part of this process, the equivalent for a bank of the distress sale of assets is to call in loans, or to refuse to make loans. The result was that short-term inter-bank and commercial paper markets disappeared in many countries, and firms were unable to get financing for imports required for production, or even to obtain credit to finance exports. Further, the decision to reform the banking system by requiring rapid bank closures created widespread distrust in the remaining banks, and in many economies, including Hong Kong, there were large scale withdrawals of deposits from the banks, pushing even solid banks to difficulty and reducing even further their ability to lend to support production. Thus, the policies introduced created conditions of full-scale debt deflation in which banks and firms were forced to sell assets to make payments, driving down prices in both stock markets and foreign exchange markets. Thus, the second stage of the crisis involved the sustained meltdown of asset markets throughout December 1997 and January 1998. By the time the IMF had been convinced to introduce additional freedom (the conditions on all three lending agreements were reviewed and rewritten with more lenient conditions on fiscal positions and interest rates in the beginning of 1998), conditions had deteriorated to the point that it is unlikely that there will be positive growth in the region in 1998 and there is some question about 1999.

This phase of collapsing production and income in Asia is reflected in the sharp falls that have occurred in primary commodity prices and oil prices. Thus, the greatest negative impact from the crisis outside Asia has been in other developing countries and in the petroleum producing countries. It would not be surprising if a number of the former should have to apply to the IMF for balance of payments support as a result of the Asian crisis.

Clearly, a more reasoned response to the crisis would have been to attempt to slow the withdrawal of foreign lending and to ease the conditions of payment.

Low, rather than high interest rates would have been indicated, along with policies to stimulate growth. But, most important would have been rapid policies to reschedule foreign loans to stop the mad rush to sell assets and buy foreign currency. This has now started to occur in the case of Korea, which has reached agreement with international bank lenders to roll over the short-term debt owed by Korean banks.

The first step in the third phase of the crisis will then be to restore stability to asset markets, which means having both buyers and sellers, borrowers and lenders. This will allow producers to increase exports and the process of adjustment to begin. However, much of the productive capacity will in fact be closed by bankruptcy. And the fall in prices will be less than the change in exchange rates due to the fact that most Asian exports are import-intensive, so that import costs will be rising in dollar terms. Domestic costs will also be rising as the impact of depreciation on the domestic price level works through to domestic costs. It is also likely that capital flows will return, through foreign purchases of domestic productive capacity (to operate or to close, as occurred in East Germany). It is for this reason that it is difficult to determine appropriate exchange rates. At current exchange rates, this process should be extremely rapid, and will certainly bring calls from developed countries, swamped with imports, for protection measures. It would be ironic if the liberalisation of capital flows, which the IMF has now declared as its major objective, should lead to a deterioration in the free trade in goods and services, which was to be its original objective. The crisis suggests that the two are interdependent, and perhaps cannot be achieved simultaneously. Given that this is precisely the scenario which was the prelude to the global crisis of the 1930s, the collapse of global capital markets in response to the crisis was simply playing according to the script. It remains to be seen if policy can be crafted so as to avoid a repeat of the 1930s.

Notes

1. In 1994, the exports of the ASEAN-4 (Malaysia, Thailand, Indonesia, Philippines) plus the first-tier NIEs (Korea, Taiwan, Hong Kong, Singapore) to developing East Asia plus Japan was US$172 billion and to the other developed márket economies US$168 billion, with another US$44 billion to the rest of the world (UNCTAD 1996: Table 24, p. 88).

2. For example, in 1997 the percentage of total imports into the US from affiliates of US companies was over 19 per cent from Thailand, over 18 per cent from Malaysia, and nearly 14 per cent from Indonesia. The share for Hong Kong was over 50 per cent and Singapore over 80 per cent. Korea was less than 3 per cent, while the Philippines was just over 5 per cent.

3. The Mexican crisis did differ from prior experience because of the large build up of foreign holdings of domestic financial assets, including government securities, such as Tesobonos that paid returns linked to the US dollar. The IMF bail-out package thus served primarily to provide an exit for foreign holders of peso-denominated Tesobonos while preserving currency convertibility. The IMF funding, rather than supporting current account convertibility, was thus used for the first time in history to ensure capital account

convertibility. The Mexican crisis might thus be said to be the mid-point between a standard Bretton Woods style exchange rate crisis caused by a current account deficit under restricted capital flows, and an exchange rate crisis caused by capital account outflows and a collapse of financial asset prices under free global movement of capital.

4. While Ostrey (1997) notes that any external deficit represents a potential risk in the case of external shocks, it points out that deficits in the 1980s had been much higher without generating difficulty.

5. It is for this reason that when the Thai baht devalued, it represented a major event, since all contracts which had been purchased on the high probability of exchange rate stability automatically changed in value, and frequently passed from positive to negative values, leading investors to sell them, which was the equivalent of withdrawing capital from the Asian economies.

6. For example, according to the Korean Securities Supervisory Board, 28 Korean securities houses operated over 100 funds with assets of nearly US$3 billion located in Malaysia, Ireland and France. Investment banks were also active in operating offshore funds. Roughly two-thirds of the assets of these funds were in Korean companies. The losses of these funds are estimated at over US$1 billion (cf. *Korean Times*, 19 February 1998).

7. Since the Mexican crisis the IMF has produced a number of studies attempting to identify indicators of future exchange rate and banking crises. The indicator which appears as significant in all of them is real appreciation of the exchange rate, which the IMF studies cited above suggest was not a major factor in Asia.

8. The commentary refers to flows in 1994. The report also notes that 'tight monetary conditions help to explain the large banking inflows into South Korea'. An IMF Working Paper (Johnson, Darbar and Echeverria 1997: 38) notes that 'net private capital inflows were larger as a percentage of GDP in Thailand than in the other countries and a large part of these inflows through the international banking facility were short term in nature, which may have increased Thailand's vulnerability to a reversal of such flows.'

9. The *1996/97 Annual Report* (BIS 1997: 112-3) noted that 'the difficulties of Thailand's banking system can be traced in part to the creation... of the Bangkok International Banking Facilities (BIBF), which, as well as promoting Bangkok as an international financial centre, allowed local banks to borrow in dollars.... The Bank of Thailand has taken a number of measures to limit the growth of the BIBF on lending to the domestic market. From September 1995 local banks' net foreign exchange liabilities were made subject to ceilings (e.g. 20 per cent of assets). In addition, foreign deposits were excluded from the calculation of the statutory loan-to-deposit ratios that banks have to maintain.'

10. Composition of Bank Loans, 1993 (percentages)

East Asia	Home Mortgages	Consumer Credit	Enterprises	Government
Indonesia	4.1	6.9	70.7	2.2
Korea	12.7	11.7	74.5	1.1
Malaysia	13.9	11.2	30.1	0.5
Thailand	8.3	4.1	58.8	0.7

Source: BIS 1998b: 40.

11. According to the IMF (1997b: 64), emerging economies accumulated US$575 billion in reserves between 1990 and 1996, representing 49 per cent of the total flows; US$202.2 billion were to the Asian region, but only US$76.4 billion were to Asia excluding India and China (cf. IMF 1997b: 197-8). However, they are concentrated in China, Taiwan, Singapore and Hong Kong. Thailand's reserves increased by US$27 billion, and Singapore's by US$56 billion over the period.

12. Bank assets as a percentage of GDP for three Southeast Asian countries, 1989-94 (percentages)

Bank Assets/GDP	1989	1990	1991	1992	1993	1994
Indonesia	49.3	60.5	64.2	63.0	58.8	57.3
Malaysia	92.4	96.0	101.9	95.0	92.9	99.9
Thailand	72.7	79.2	82.2	85.0	94.6	109.5

Source: Montgomery 1997: Table 1, p. 7.

13. For example, both Korea First and Seoul Bank were known to be in difficulty as a result of corporate bankruptcies in early 1997. Figures for the end of 1996 showed 12.6 per cent of the loans of the eight nation-wide Korean commercial banks were impaired. International rating agencies had issued warnings on Thai banks and at least one international organisation had noted that the Southeast Asian economies were 'vulnerable to interruptions of capital inflows' (UNCTAD 1996: 102).

14. The move was all the more important because it 'was of a magnitude that market participants considered quite unlikely, even as late as 5 May. As the yen appreciated rapidly between 5 May and 9 May (the market) began to reflect a significant probability of large further appreciations' (IMF 1997c: 19).

15. However, it did operate actively in the forward market for baht, employing the technique of the bear squeeze (first employed in Berlin in the 19th century and by Poincaré in the famous stabilisation of the French franc, see Einzig 1937) to try to support the exchange rate. The Bank bought baht from speculators for exchange at a future date at an exchange rate determined by the relative interest costs of lending baht for the period. At the future expiry date of the contract the speculator had to sell baht to the Bank at the previously agreed price. If the baht had devalued by the future date, then the speculator could purchase in the market the baht he had to sell to the Bank at a lower dollar price than that he would receive, the difference representing speculative profit. In a bear squeeze the Bank makes it as difficult as possible for speculators to buy the baht that they have to deliver by restricting the Bank's sale of baht to speculators in the offshore markets. The speculators thus have to borrow the baht at extremely high rates (rates went as high as 1,300 per cent) to honour their contracts and take a loss. It is estimated (IMF 1997c: 35) that speculators lost as much as US$1.5 billion in the bear squeeze applied by the Bank of Thailand through the beginning of July. The problem with such a policy is that the central bank has to have enough foreign exchange to meet the forward sales of baht coming due until speculation is stemmed.

16. As, presumably, is part of the IMF Research Department, cf. Ostrey 1997, quoted above. See also IMF (1997c: 69): 'Among currencies not affected by the contagion was the Korean won, even though there were many parallels in economic circumstance with Thailand... observers have noted that this was perhaps because Korea's debt levels were lower, because the substantial depreciation of the won during the last year and a half had left it at a more appropriate level, or because the recent appreciations of the yen would have greater benefits for Korea than its neighbours. While these factors may have played a role, it should be noted that unlike... the Asian economies that were attacked, Korea restricts won credit to foreign residents, and the foreign exchange markets... are underdeveloped. Simply put, this makes it difficult for foreign investors to speculate against the won.'

17. Fred Bergsten (1997) has suggested that the Taiwanese move, which came on the eve of Jiang Zemin's visit to the US, was made in order to embarrass China.

18. Although the IMF has also criticised the Asian countries for the stability of their exchange rates, cf. Fischer (1998).

4
HUBRIS, HYSTERIA, HOPE:
THE POLITICAL ECONOMY OF CRISIS
AND RESPONSE IN SOUTHEAST ASIA

C.P. Chandrasekhar and Jayati Ghosh

The 'East Asian miracle' could be described as the second major attempt in the post-war period — after the oil price hikes of the 1970s — to significantly alter the distribution of income across the regions of the world. The current economic crisis in the region suggests that this effort, like its predecessor, has failed in terms of its ultimate goal — that of achieving a sustainable and substantial transfer of income from the core capitalist nations to a section of the periphery. While this issue is by no means definitively resolved, it is certainly true that both the recent crisis and the era of high growth that preceded it in Southeast Asia, have qualitative importance for the international economy that extends far beyond the immediate quantitative implications. Indeed, it can be argued that this crisis heralds a new conjuncture in post-war development.

The convergence of recent economic disaster across the East and Southeast Asian economies should not blind us to the fact that their development trajectories and levels of performance have differed substantially. South Korea is known to have pursued a state-directed and highly regulated export-led growth strategy, which delivered very high growth for more than two decades, and which only recently has given way to a more liberalised regime. Malaysia and Thailand, by contrast, have a much more recent history of rapid economic growth, characterised by more open economic regimes, within which foreign direct investment (FDI) played a crucial role in delivering both output and export growth. Oil revenues and a strong state have played an important role in Indonesia's development path. The Philippines was never really much of a 'tiger' except in the matter of export growth, and that has not translated yet into any major transformation of domestic productive structures.

Background to the Current Crisis

Even at the start of the crisis in mid-1997, economic performance in the region differed substantially, although all these countries had recorded a significant deceleration in export growth in 1996 (Table 4.1). Thailand, for example, had recorded a one percentage point decline in its exports in the previous year and was saddled with a huge current account deficit on its balance of payments. It

Table 4.1
East Asia: Export Growth Trends
(annual percentage change in US$ values)

Country	1990-96	1994	1995	1996
China	16	32	23	2
Korea	12	17	30	4
Taiwan	10	10	20	4
Malaysia	18	25	26	6
Thailand	16	23	25	-1
Indonesia	12	9	13	10
Developing East Asia	6	10	12	-5

Source: World Trade Organisation (1997), vol. 2, p. 63.

Table 4.2
East Asia: Export Growth Rates in Selected Categories, 1995-96 (percentages)

	% of Total Exports	1995	1996
China			
Total exports		23.00	2.00
Iron and steel	2.4	212.03	-29.59
Machinery & transport equipment	23.4	43.27	12.57
Office machinery & telecom. equipment	11.4	44.73	18.56
Automotive products	0.4	45.77	-4.67
Textiles	8.0	17.77	-12.99
Clothing	16.6	1.34	4.10
Korea			
Total exports		30.00	4.00
Iron and steel	4.0	15.62	-3.36
Machinery & transport equipment	52.1	39.51	2.95
Office machinery & telecom. equipment	24.5	40.22	-4.07
Automotive products	8.9	56.63	26.06
Textiles	9.8	15.15	3.29
Clothing	3.3	-12.31	-14.85

Table 4.2 (continued)
East Asia: Export Growth Rates in Selected Categories, 1995-96 (percentages)

	% of Total Exports	1995	1996
Taiwan			
Total exports		20.00	4.00
Iron and steel	2.2	50.14	15.90
Machinery & transport equipment	51.3	27.97	8.22
Office machinery & telecom. equipment	30.6	36.13	9.01
Automotive products	1.6	18.22	12.78
Textiles	10.4	15.81	1.40
Clothing	2.8	-5.63	-1.35
Malaysia			
Total exports		26.00	6.00
Iron and steel	0.7	20.40	21.34
Machinery & transport equipment	55.1	29.45	6.20
Office machinery & telecom. equipment	44.5	33.06	6.63
Automotive products	0.4	27.40	7.53
Textiles	1.7	35.86	15.15
Clothing	3.0	9.42	4.59
Thailand			
Total exports		25.00	-1.00
Iron and steel	0.8	76.95	
Machinery & transport equipment	37.8	26.05	10.96
Office machinery & telecom. equipment	24.0	28.26	14.75
Automotive products	1.2	-43.62	35.80
Textiles	3.4	17.61	-1.39
Clothing	7.2	11.09	-19.53
Indonesia			
Total exports		13.00	10.00
Iron and steel	0.7	22.01	-11.14
Machinery & transport equipment	10.0	25.57	30.57
Office machinery & telecom. equipment	6.2	21.33	35.42
Automotive products	0.3	64.56	16.15
Textiles	5.7	8.61	4.50
Clothing	7.2	5.30	6.37

Source: WTO (1997).

had experienced a slowing of FDI inflows in recent years, which, given its pattern of growth, spelt a weakening economy and growing dependence on short-term financial flows to finance an increasingly import-dependent production and consumption pattern. Malaysia, similarly, had a large current account deficit, financed, to a lesser degree, by 'hot' money flows made possible by the open capital account, and also some of the typical effects of 'overvaluation', including excess resources directed towards real estate. Indonesia, on the other hand, had much less of a current account problem, and did not even suffer so much of a deceleration in export growth. South Korea, whose current account deficit and public debt amounted to just three per cent of GDP, appeared economically stronger than many Organisation for Economic Cooperation and Development (OECD) countries when it recently won membership of the rich nations' club. Hence, the deceleration in exports appeared to be a mere cyclical downturn that could be dealt with, as still appears to be true in the case of China. This was supported by the fact that unlike other countries in the region, while the growth of export value in South Korea fell from 30 per cent in 1995 to 4 per cent in 1996, the growth in the volume of exports only fell from 24 per cent to 19 per cent.

These differences suggest that the same or similar economic fundamentals could not have led to the 'crisis' in these economies. Nevertheless, in all of these countries, the *crisis has taken the same form of a collapse of currencies and stock markets*, and there has been a *high degree of synchronisation of such capital market collapse*. To fathom this common denouement to widely varying plots, we need to turn to the realm of finance, and this is explored in the section below. But it is also necessary to identify the proximate 'real causes' of the dramatic decline in economic performance in virtually all these countries.

Insofar as it is possible to isolate the original sin in this particular Asian drama, it must lie in the deceleration of export growth experienced by the entire region from about the middle of 1995. In the decade preceding this year, as is well known, the Asian region, and particularly East and Southeast Asia, was the most economically dynamic part of the world. Both in terms of the GDP growth rate and the rate of export growth, the developing economies of Asia, in the aggregate, outperformed any other grouping. In addition, the dominant share of capital flows to the developing world was absorbed by Asia, and by a small set of countries (such as China) within Asia, but the jury is still out on whether this was the cause or the effect of high growth.

Most Asian countries have experienced deceleration or decline in their manufactured exports since the middle of 1995, and the causes for this sudden drop have still not been adequately explored. Two factors have been most commonly cited: the saturation of developed country markets, particularly for machinery and transport equipment, semiconductors and office automation equipment, which accounted for a significant share and constituted the most dynamic segment of the total exports of many of these countries; and the increased protectionism (despite the General Agreement on Tariffs and Trade, GATT, and the World Trade Organisation, WTO) by industrial countries in the area of textiles and clothing imports, which remain the mainstay of newly industrialised country (NIC) exports (Table 4.2). Such export patterns were not accompanied by equivalent reductions in imports, thus leading to widening trade and current account deficits throughout most of Southeast Asia. The decline in export growth not only hit the profitability of domestic exporters and employment in export-oriented industries, but also adversely affected investor expectations, which had become dependent upon very high growth rates; this proved to be a catalytic factor in the subsequent financial debacle.

According to one school of thought, these current account imbalances led to precipitous declines in foreign investor confidence and consequently to the current crisis. Implicit in that judgement is the presumption that relatively mobile capital constituted a major chunk of foreign investment in the region, which, it is now clear, was indeed the case. According to the Institute of International Finance (IIF), a think-tank funded by global financial institutions, net private capital flows to the five East Asian economies afflicted by the crisis (Indonesia, Malaysia, Philippines, South Korea and Thailand) fell sharply in 1997. While in 1996, these economies attracted net capital flows to the tune of US$93 billion, they suffered an outflow of US$12 billion in 1997, or a loss of US$105 billion in terms of net inflows.[1] This amount equals two-thirds of the capital funnelled into all of Asia the previous year. According to this report, South Korea alone received US$50 billion less than it did the year before (Andrews 1998). Much of this outflow occurred, it appears, because of the refusal of international banks to rollover the large sums of short-term credit they had provided these countries with in the recent past.

It must be noted that this decline in funding to Asia was not the result of a decline in capital flows to all developing countries. The IIF's report estimates that private capital flows to large emerging economies, excluding the five Asian economies mentioned above, increased from US$202 billion in 1996 to US$212 billion in 1997. There were, in fact, two significant trends with regard to international capital flows: first, a sharp shift in favour of Latin America, which received 45.2 per cent of all flows; and second, a sharp increase in flows in the form of net equity investment (US$133 billion), either in the form of FDI or portfolio flows. This clearly indicates that banks which had, in herd-like fashion, rushed into East Asia in the recent past had suddenly chosen to pull out of the region, at a time when other foreign investors were putting new money into other regions of the world. As the Chief Economist of Dresdner Bank described in an interview to the *New York Times*: 'You can't imagine how much these countries were in the driver's seat. We were all standing in line to help these countries borrow money.'

The Financial Crisis

There are two obvious questions that arise in this context. First, why did banks increase their exposure to a degree where they would have to pull out, on a massive scale, in the course of a few months? Second, why did economies which boasted of such high domestic savings rates require these huge capital inflows at all? The answers must be sought in the functioning of capital markets and changes in the control regimes of Asian emerging markets over the past decade.

Many observers have noted that central to the 'globalisation' of the past decade has been the globalisation of finance. In recent years, as a result of a range of developments, particularly in the developed countries, banks, pension funds and international institutional investors have been awash with liquidity. With such agents in search of avenues for investment that yield quick returns, financial capital has proved unusually mobile, seeking out new areas of investment in 'emerging markets' and pulling out, in bandwagon style, at the slightest hint of risk. Despite the risks that such mobility involved for recipients, this certainly gave developing countries an unprecedented degree of access to international finance. Most developing countries liberalised their financial markets in the early 1990s to benefit from this situation.

This resulted in one commonality in all East Asian countries, namely their growing exposure to international finance in the wake of financial liberalisation. In the form of investments in stock markets and foreign debt incurred by banks and corporate groups, the presence of internationally mobile capital was unusually high in all of them. Such reliance on mobile foreign finance meant that any factor that spelt an economic setback, however small or transient, triggered an outflow of capital as well. As mentioned earlier, the 1995-97 period witnessed a number of developments which spelt such a setback.

As discussed in greater detail elsewhere in this book (see chapter six on Thailand by Lauridsen) the response to these developments, in the form of a loss of investor confidence and capital flight, began in Southeast Asia's weakest link: Thailand. The flow of portfolio capital slowed down substantially and creditors refused to roll over short-term debt. That turn of events encouraged currency speculators, both domestic and foreign, to enter the picture, leading to a collapse in currency values. Once this process began, however, the 'contagion' spread to other countries with far stronger economies and larger foreign reserves. Given developments in the world economy and the region, there was always some adverse 'fundamental' that could provide the basis for a loss of investor confidence. In South Korea, for example, it was the fact that banks had been under pressure to lend to overextended business groups, that were taking a beating in international markets and consequently could not cross-subsidise their loss-making operations with profitable ones as effectively as they had done in the past. Banks had therefore to take on huge short-term loans to keep these *chaebols* afloat, resulting in the fact that such loans were estimated at more than US$100 billion at the time of the crisis. When creditors refused to roll over those loans, a collapse of reserves and of the won ensued. This meant that even weak and transient signals of adverse economic performance were enough to set off the train of events that ended with a speculative attack on the currency. Thus, currency volatility, being the immediate consequence of the volatility of investor confidence and international financial flows, became a common symptom of widely varying economic difficulties.

The developing country debt crisis of the 1980s, and the rescheduling exercises that followed, had important effects on the expectations of international banks. While such banks have remained essentially wary of developing country lending, they have also become convinced that the losses they incur in developing country markets are limited by the implicit sovereign guarantee of loans to private borrowers, by governments in both the developed and developing countries. This is a problem which was not adequately recognised in most mainstream analyses until recently. Krugman (1998) has argued that the serious problem of moral hazard involving financial intermediaries, whose liabilities were *de facto* guaranteed by the government, operated in the Asian case, so that these financial institutions were able to raise money at safe interest rates, but lend that money at a premium to finance speculative investments. As a consequence, none of the standard prudential norms were closely followed by either bank creditors or other investors. The fact that the domestic banking and finance sectors in these countries were subject to prudential regulation was not an adequate safeguard against this moral hazard problem, because of the high recent dependence on external commercial borrowing, which turned out to have extremely dire implications for the borrowing countries.

This points to the futility of believing that capital account convertibility, accompanied by domestic prudential regulation, will ensure against such boom-bust volatility in capital markets. Even Georges Blum, the Chairman of the Swiss Bank Corporation and of the IIF, had to grudgingly declare, when releasing the IIF report quoted earlier: 'One has to say on the side of the banks that there has been some lack of prudence. There have been policy mistakes.' The fact that the IMF-negotiated bail-out in South Korea involved banks converting US$24 billion of short-term debt into medium-term debt guaranteed by the government, at interest rates ranging from 2.25 to 2.75 percentage points above the London Inter-Bank Offer Rate (LIBOR), illustrates once again why such policy mistakes occur. International banks have to pay little penalty, if any at all, for their lack of diligence. As Akyüz (chapter 2) has noted, 'The basic problem is not in the control and supervision of the banking system, but in the absence of instruments to restrict capital inflows and contain their impact on macroeconomic and monetary conditions. But these instruments are usually discarded with the adoption of liberalisation designed to remove "financial repression"!'

The real question therefore is why the East Asian economies chose to approach the international financial markets for such funds despite their high domestic savings rates. The explanation lies in the 'autonomous' tendencies generated by financial liberalisation in these economies over the past decade. By allowing domestic financial agents to approach foreign financial institutions directly, liberalisation has had two consequences. First, it provides them a source of 'easy finance' when they find themselves over-stretched domestically, because corporations or institutions to whom they have overexposed themselves are finding it difficult to service past credit without access to new loans. Second, they have a source of finance which can be used to fund risky activities (like those accompanying a property or stock market boom), since the 'original' investors ask few questions. Such tendencies can be damaging because of a more fundamental consequence of both trade and financial liberalisation: the dissociation of any increase in foreign exchange commitments of individual agents from their ability to contribute to the earnings of foreign exchange needed to service those debts.

It is true that Indonesia and Malaysia have had open capital accounts for a very long time, but these could be effectively regulated because such a large proportion of the transactions before the 1990s were effectively state controlled. In the 1990s, the external capital transactions of private agents within these economies became much more pronounced, and the freedom regarding commercial borrowing from abroad allowed private companies to completely de-link the taking on of foreign exchange obligations from the ability to service them in foreign exchange. The case of Thailand is instructive because it shows how misplaced is the general obsession with government deficits as creating the only unsustainable external imbalances. Initially, Thai current account deficits — which reflected the excess of private sector investment over private savings, since the government account was typically in surplus — were financed with FDI inflows, which also supported the country's export effort and raised the rate of growth. However, the situation changed from 1990. While FDI inflows were slowing, exports were not growing fast enough to finance burgeoning imports. The 'structural deficit' in Thailand's current account, stemming from the openness of its economic regime, was no longer accompanied by adequate inflows of private direct foreign investment. To finance its external deficits, therefore, Thailand had to resort to borrowing from international credit markets, implying a rapid increase in external debt. Much of this was necessarily short-term debt, which is very susceptible to the level of investor confidence. Financial markets had been concentrating on the rate of export growth, rather than external imbalance, as the single most important indicator of creditworthiness, and after export deceleration increased the current account deficit, pressure on the baht began. The pressures and the likely prospect of decline forced domestic operators with foreign exchange service commitments in the near future to rush into the market to acquire dollars and reduce their losses in terms of the domestic currency, triggering a run on the currency fuelled by financial speculators.

The relatively prolonged period of exchange rate stability in these countries, with most currencies pegged to the US dollar, also created complacency about possible changes, and high export growth also lulled policy makers into believing that continued access to foreign exchange would never be a problem. As a result, the capital account transactions in virtually all these countries began to reflect substantial market failures in ways that went largely undetected. The most obvious failure, in terms of foreign exchange balancing, has already been mentioned.

Of course, all this begs the question of why financial liberalisation occurred to such a wide-ranging extent in many of the countries of this region in the 1990s. While Indonesia and Malaysia have had open capital accounts for more than a quarter century, this has reflected their ability to access foreign funds because of political considerations, as well as the close nexus established over this period between domestic capitalists, foreign investors and the state in these countries. The forces making for financial liberalisation in countries like Thailand and the Philippines, related to dependence on foreign capital inflows, has already been mentioned. But the recent financial liberalisation in countries like South Korea is the outcome of a different process, which deserves a closer look.

It is widely accepted that finance was one of the prime instruments with which the state in South Korea guided industry along directions which made it an international industrial powerhouse. State-owned or backed financial entities were allowed to mobilise resources, both domestically and through borrowing abroad, to fund industrial investment. Using these financial institutions as instruments of control, the government forced industry to comply with its industrial growth strategy, and induced investments in less profitable areas with differential interest rates that implied negative real (or inflation-adjusted) interest rates in some sectors. The financial sector was powerful, not merely because it was the conduit for cheap investment funds, but because it functioned as an arm of the state's economic apparatus in encouraging and monitoring industrial investments.

Such a system certainly did have several advantages over stock market based systems such as that of the UK or US economies, and indeed, it was precisely this system that was associated with the high output growth rates and dramatic transformations of productive structures of the previous two decades. However, it is also true that there can be at least two problems with such a financial system. First, they fail to deal with the question of who is to monitor the monitor. South Korea's banks, backed by politicians and bureaucrats, lent heavily to a few private business conglomerates (*chaebols*), who diversified into a wide range of areas based on cheap credit and an initially cheap and docile labour force. It should be remembered, as observed by Veneroso and Wade (1998), that the high corporate debt-equity ratios also reflected the high domestic savings rates, and the resulting high rates of loan intermediation to GDP. This is why there is a 'strong financial rationale for co-operative, long-term reciprocal relations between firms, banks and government' in such a system, as well as a need for restrictions on firms' and banks' freedom to borrow abroad and other similar regulations. It was this combination which helped to deliver South Korea's successful emergence as an internationally competitive producer. But it also meant that these business groups were over-geared, with the ratio of debt to equity used to finance their investments often ranging between 300 and 500 per cent. Further, banks not only accepted property as collateral for their excessive lending, but themselves resorted to speculative investments in the property market which, as in much of Southeast Asia, registered a boom along with industrial growth. Thus, both the structure and the extent of loans pointed to the financial fragility of the system in terms of vulnerability to sudden shocks.

The shock itself, as Chang (1998a) has emphasised, emerged from liberalisation and deregulation, rather than from excessive regulation. Two significant aspects of the deregulation of the 1990s are worth mentioning. First, the government abandoned its traditional role of co-ordinating and regulating private investment activity, which allowed excess capacity to build up in important industries like steel, shipbuilding, automobiles and petrochemicals. Second, the financial liberalisation policies allowed for a rapid build-up of short-maturity commercial borrowing by private borrowers, including from external sources. The slowdown of industrial and export growth from mid-1995 onwards meant that many of South Korea's conglomerates were unable to service their huge loans. This, together with the end of the property boom, meant that South Korea's banks were saddled with huge volumes of non-performing assets. This, in turn, required the closure of some financial institutions and the restructuring of others. This has constituted the core of South Korea's crisis. Since the state was closely tied to these financial intermediaries, it had no choice but to take responsibility for depositors' funds and for restructuring the financial system. This is why the South Korean government now requires resources estimated at US$60 billion simply to ensure the survival of the domestic banking and productive system.

The second problem characterising the South Korean strategy stems from the immense power it gave to a newly emerging financial class. Being functionaries of the system, rather than owners of the capital which the state helped them accumulate, the members of this class would have had very different attitudes to the state than South Korea's state-sponsored industrial class. Since they effectively became the principal link with foreign capital in a country which resorted to large scale commercial borrowing even while it discouraged foreign investment in industry, the attitude of these financiers to integration with the international economy tended to be more positive than other elements in the country. This, in turn influenced the conduct of economic policy in the more democratic political regime demanded by the militancy of South Korea's student community and its working class. Democracy has meant that the close links between the state and industrial capital, involving mutual favours and pay-offs, is increasingly under challenge. Politicians and industrialists have had to pay a price for the corrupt nexus that democracy helped reveal. But democracy has also brought with it the pressure for a greater degree of openness *vis-à-vis* the international system. There is reason to believe that this pressure towards openness in the economic sphere comes more from the financial sector, rather than from industry, which gained its foothold in international markets on the basis of state support and a protected economic regime.

This helps to explain the response to the current crisis as well as the controversy surrounding it. To start with, although the incipient crisis in the banking system was public knowledge for quite some time, the government, under some influence, chose to ignore the problem, rather than to opt for the harsh measures that may have been necessary. Second, when the crisis finally had to be faced, the fundamental premise of the response was that the financial system needed to be bailed out, even if subsequent restructuring becomes unavoidable. This has made the cost to the state of dealing with the crisis quite substantial. If all non-performing loans of the banks are to be 'funded', the sums involved would equal almost 13 per cent of GDP. Finally, the government has chosen to finance the bail-out with foreign funds under IMF auspices. It may be true that some foreign exchange is needed to tide over the immediate balance of payments problem and its impact on foreign reserves. But this would be far less than needed to 'bail-out' the financial system in the name of restructuring. The remaining resources for a financial-restructuring exercise that places new controls on finance, which tries to monitor the monitor, could come from where it normally comes from, namely the 'lender of last resort', the central bank.

Choosing the domestic central bank, rather than the IMF, as the 'lender of last resort' would have had important implications. It would have meant that controls over the financial sector, rather than greater financial liberalisation, would be at the core of the restructuring exercise. It would also have meant that, at the risk of some inflation, the system would avoid a real economic 'crunch' because of the liquidity that would be pumped into the system. That is, such a restructuring exercise would favour the real economy over the financial system. On the other hand, the conditionality accompanying an IMF-sponsored loan package would require greater liberalisation of the financial system, greater freedom for foreign financial institutions and a deflationary fiscal strategy, which reduces real growth and places the burden of adjustment on society as a whole, rather than the financial system. The problem in South Korea is that it is not just subject to pressures from international finance, but also from the powerful financial class its own successful strategy has created. This may help to explain why the South Korean state appears to have chosen the path that is likely to be much more painful for most of its citizens.

The IMF Response

The unusual speed and severity of the financial downfall, which converted the aggressive 'tiger' economies of the beginning of 1997 into wounded and limping objects of international succour in just a few months, has been much commented upon. But the other surprising aspect of the recent East Asian crisis has been the fact that even after these economies had been duly subdued and harsh doses of IMF medicine had been forced upon them, the downturn continued apace. This makes the recent East Asian experience quite different from that of Latin America — especially Mexico — in 1995. There, the pure financial crisis lasted only two months at most, with the currency plummeting and foreign exchange reserves dwindling. The US-led bail-out, which also involved some money from the IMF, seemed like a lot of money at the time, involving a credit line of US$40 billion. But this amount pales into insignificance when compared with the amounts — in excess of US$100 billion — which have already been promised to the troubled Asian economies. Yet, the promise of money in Mexico, along with that country's acceptance of the IMF guidelines, was enough to stop the immediate crisis, even though it led to a deep economic depression with falling living standards, from which Mexico has not yet fully recovered.

The contrasting experience in these two regions may be explained in terms of the role of the US government, which was determined to prevent the financial crisis in Mexico from spiralling into a major collapse of international proportions. The US government not only provided its own credit guarantee, but also arm-twisted US-based multinational banks with heavy exposure in Mexico to renew the inflow of resources. This turned out to be critical in halting the decline of the peso and the collapse of domestic financial assets. The crisis-ridden countries of East Asia simply do not have the same strategic importance to the US as its immediate neighbour did, and this is especially true after the defeat of communism internationally. Indeed, there was even a sense of glee in Washington and New York at the humiliation of the former 'tigers' and the undoing of their claims to an alternative 'Asian model' of capitalist development, as long as analysts there were confident that the contagion would not spread to their own stock markets. So, while the US has formally supported the IMF-led financing packages and insisted on compliance with the Fund's conditionalities, the US government's own offers of financial support have been extremely stingy, and it has done relatively little to pressurise private investors to stay in these countries. The Japanese, who could have played this role, have been beset by their own economic difficulties. And so, combined with the need of domestic companies in these countries to buy dollars to service their foreign debt, the outward pressure emanating from private international investors continued to cause purchases of dollars in these currency markets.

Part of the reason for the inadequacy of official response in stemming the slump may also lie in the sheer magnitude of the collapse of foreign capital inflows into the region. Even the period of greatest severity of Latin America's debt crisis — 1982 to 1984 — did not involve such a dramatic reversal of capital flows, and such a sudden turnaround of this extent may also be unprecedented in modern capital markets internationally. The magnitude of the reversal also suggests that a large part of the recent crisis was created by the crisis itself, in its earlier cumulative effect on capital flows from the middle of 1997. Thus, what began as a tentative trickle in terms of the reduction of FDI and then portfolio capital, became a deluge because of the combination of the herd instinct of international investors, and the tendency of some domestic companies to take on further external commercial debt in an effort to borrow themselves out of what appeared to be temporary trouble.

As mentioned earlier, one of several novel features of the recent East Asian debacle has been the relative inability of the IMF to reverse the process of capital outflow from the region, and the associated slump in currency and capital markets in these countries, despite more than six months of explicit intervention and promises of huge funds for the region. Beginning with the agreement with the Thai government in July, and followed by the first deal with Indonesia, the later agreement with South Korea and the second negotiated agreement with Indonesia, the IMF has already provided substantial funds to some of the most beleaguered countries, and promised in excess of US$100 billion in the near future. Nevertheless, this appears to have had relatively little impact on investor expectations even though the policy packages have already made themselves felt in terms of domestic economic recessions and rapid improvements in trade balances because of severe import contraction and sharp real depreciation of the currencies.

The configuration described above, of buyers and sellers in the Southeast Asian currency markets, suggests that IMF resources in themselves, large as they may appear, are simply inadequate to deal with the extent of adverse financial speculation that has affected this region. But the ineffectiveness of the IMF strategy thus far also stems from a perception which is becoming increasingly widespread, particularly among private agents operating in these currency and capital markets, that the IMF strategy is the inappropriate one to adopt in the current circumstances.

There are a number of reasons why the IMF strategy — of exchange rate devaluation combined with domestic credit control — is even more misguided in these countries than it has been elsewhere. The IMF approach to economic stabilisation and balance of payments adjustment has always been remarkable in its total disregard of the differing economic conditions in the countries it is advising. The standard IMF package — which has numerous problems anyway at both theoretical and practical levels — is typically applied to countries experiencing high rates of domestic inflation and unsustainable external deficits, usually resulting from fiscal profligacy. By contrast, these economies of East and

Southeast Asia currently have problems that are primarily related to asset deflation. Indeed, both inflation and government deficits in the region are typically well within norms that are more than healthy by international standards.

Consider, in particular, the three countries which have most recently and most prominently had to approach the IMF for assistance: Thailand, South Korea and Indonesia. All three countries had inflation rates well within single digits, and government fiscal strategy has been remarkably prudent (except in Indonesia to some extent). Domestic savings rates have been high (above 30 per cent in all these countries) and export competitiveness had been varyingly affected by the previously stable nominal exchange rates pegged to the US dollar. In most of the region, the profligacy has been that of the private sector.

Thus, it is clear that the current problems in these countries relate fundamentally to the financial sector, and in South Korea and Thailand, these have been either created or exacerbated by financial liberalisation measures, including a more open capital account. In all these countries, partial liberalisation of domestic and foreign transactions, within financial systems that are relatively under-capitalised and opaque, has created the mess. In such a context, using the blunt deflationary measures for handling problems generated by asset deflation, is both bizarre and certain to exacerbate the problems, rather than alleviate them.

It is easy to see why this is the case. In a situation where over-indebtedness and asset deflation are the problems, economic slowdowns only make these worse. The IMF strategy involves high real interest rates, which add to the sickness potential of both companies and banks, and indeed, to the potential sickness of a highly indebted economy. Further, by imposing such a damaging squeeze on domestic economic activity, IMF-determined policies effectively undermine investor confidence in rapid recovery and future growth, far from restoring it. Most significantly in the current cases, the IMF's insistence on further and faster liberalisation of financial flows actually adds to financial vulnerability and renders these economies even more prone to future crises.

The IMF package for South Korea illustrates this very well. The IMF has insisted on further fiscal tightening by around 1.5 per cent of GDP, as well as control over domestic credit that will further pressurise banks that are already feeling the pinch. The IMF has further demanded that to accommodate a deflationary strategy, the government must revise growth rates over the next year to 2-3 per cent from around 6 per cent. This is contentious, not just because it comes in the wake of long years of growth in excess of 8 per cent, but also because it could take the unemployment rate in South Korea from 3 to almost 9 per cent. The emphasis on containing inflation rates within the target of 5 per cent in 1998 despite the massive (around 40 per cent) devaluation of the won has also involved raising nominal interest rates to more than 21 per cent, implying real rates of interest in excess of 15 per cent. At such high real rates, more and more loans become non-performing and further damage the banking sector. There has been a declared decision to open up domestic money and bond markets to foreign investors, and to open up other financial services to foreign providers as well. This is particularly dangerous at the moment, not only because of the increased external vulnerability involved, but because of the greater likelihood of future scams in the absence of stronger prudential regulation, which in any case cannot really be effective for foreign investors. In addition, there is a proposal to eliminate restrictions on foreign borrowing by domestic corporations — a truly mind-boggling recommendation, which gives domestic companies the enhanced freedom to borrow themselves temporarily out of trouble, at the expense of the economy as a whole.

There is, however, a real problem here. The limitations and mistaken proposals of the IMF are now widely perceived in the region. But attempts by these countries to ignore or deviate from these proposals can bring about even greater calamity. This is precisely what happened to Indonesia after President Suharto's first budget suggested that the government did not plan to keep to the strict deflationary conditions imposed by the IMF. The IMF had asked for a budget surplus of one per cent of GDP, further financial reforms which would allow more entry of foreign providers into financial services, more closures of financial institutions in an already straitened banking sector, along with tighter capital adequacy norms for banks, cutting back of major infrastructure projects and other productive expenditure, and greater emphasis on enforcing private sector 'restructuring', i.e. closing down firms and creating more unemployment.

That these are overly stringent and even mistaken policies in a context of asset deflation and financial collapse, may be widely accepted. That is why there could be some sympathy for a budget that attempted to avoid such a deflationary outcome. The budget Suharto presented was balanced at a higher level of government expenditure, rather than achieving the IMF target of 1 per cent of GDP budget surplus. It is certainly true that the budget was based on wildly optimistic and unrealisable assumptions. Thus, the budget assumed a rate of growth of GDP of 4 per cent (analysts now suggest it will be near zero), only 9 per cent inflation and an exchange rate of Rp4,000 to the US dollar, compared to current value of around Rp10,000 to the dollar (in early March 1998). But more than these numbers, what really seemed to have inflamed the markets was the implicit declaration that the IMF conditionalities were not sacrosanct, and could be played about with, even if not openly flouted.

The result was an immediate and severe speculative attack on the currency, leading to a precipitous fall in one day, and a major battering of the stock market. Subsequently, a chastened Suharto had to declare that his government would abide by IMF conditions. But that did not serve to revive investor confidence — or even the citizenry's confidence — in the government's ability to deal with the crisis. These measures, and the signing of a fresh IMF agreement, failed to stabilise the currency market in Jakarta — the rupiah reached an historic low of Rp16,000 to the dollar in January to recover subsequently to around Rp8,000-11,000 to the US dollar, and the stock market has continued to slump.

The later rescinded declared intention of the Suharto regime to institute a currency board to stabilise the rupiah is another move in an elaborate bargaining game between the regions' rulers and international finance, over stakes which are now becoming more transparently obvious. The movements in capital markets in Southeast Asia have to be seen in conjunction with the reform measures, largely under IMF supervision, that these economies are being forced to undertake. Even as speculative capital flows trigger crises, these countries are now further liberalising capital markets, privatising public companies and increasing foreigners' access to all domestic assets. Whatever the intention, the result of such policies is evident, in terms of providing international investors a chance to pick up major bargains in the form of newly cheapened and available assets in what still remains the most dynamic part of the world economy and potentially the most competitive in terms of exports. Thus, the IMF-style response can only work successfully if it achieves a renewed inflow of foreign capital, based — in this situation — on the easy acquisition of productive assets and stakes in the financial sectors of these economies. This, in turn, requires that the governments concerned must be willing to allow this transfer, which is essentially dependent upon the domestic political and economic configurations in these countries. This question is considered below.

Foreign Finance, Governments and People

Indonesian President Suharto's proposed 'currency board' arrangement to stabilise the volatile rupiah, and the outcry it caused among the international financial community, provide a useful insight into the dynamics of the relations between governments in the region, international finance and the citizenry at the receiving end of these policies. A currency board operates by linking the money supply base in an economy to its foreign exchange reserves at a fixed exchange rate. The IMF, which has not been against a currency board in principle or in the specific instances of Hong Kong, Argentina and Hungary, argued that it is not an appropriate response to Indonesia's problems. Managing the peg with just US$19 billion of reserves and high levels of domestic and foreign debt would, in its view, be impossible. And, since it believes that 'political' factors account for the loss of investor confidence in Indonesia, pegging the currency *per se* is not expected to restore confidence and boost reserves to levels where the board can function successfully.

These arguments conceal the real fear of the IMF that a regulated currency market would be used to avoid attracting foreign capital inflows to buy up cheap domestic assets. Such fears prompted it to threaten to terminate the US$43 billion bail-out package if the government went ahead with the currency board. Similarly, the US and German governments expressed severe displeasure with the idea, and threatened Indonesia with unpleasant consequences if it was pursued. However, while Suharto appeared to backtrack to some extent, it is not certain that the proposal has been definitely shelved. Suharto has strong reasons to want to curb the volatility of the Indonesian rupiah in this dramatic fashion. The massive depreciation experienced by the rupiah has already triggered a sharp increase in the domestic prices of essentials, leading to riots that have culminated in attacks on the Chinese community, which dominates trade in many parts of Indonesia. It also proved damaging to Indonesian firms, many controlled by the family or friends of the president. Having to meet their foreign exchange commitments at the depreciated rate necessitated outlaying large and uncertain amounts of rupiah, with devastating consequences for profits and viability. It was essentially for this reason, rather than any concern for the poor, that the Indonesian president was searching for ways to stabilise the currency immediately at levels close to 5,000 rupiah to the US dollar. Such a scheme would be extremely recessionary and would adversely affect the livelihood of the majority of the Indonesian people, but would preserve more domestic businesses, and keep them under existing (largely national) ownership rather than effecting transfers to foreign ownership.

For the Indonesian government, the alternative to a contractionary currency board regime is the package promoted by the IMF. The IMF policy seeks to restore investor confidence by driving a number of 'family businesses' bankrupt and easing foreign investment regulations so that they can be acquired by foreign interests. This is precisely the route that South Korea has opted for, with some success. The government there has not only eased foreign investment regulations, but has also pushed through labour laws which allow foreign investors picking up bargains to lay-off workers and restructure corporations. Encouraged by such moves, a number of international corporations are rushing in to pick up under-valued assets of cash-strapped companies at dollar prices that are at rock bottom levels because of the massive depreciation of the won. Such acquisitions not only bring in foreign exchange directly, but also restore investor confidence in the short run, which helps stabilise the currency and revive stock markets.

This willingness on the part of the South Korean government to allow foreigners to acquire domestic assets cheap is related to the fact that the new government was elected to power opposing the *chaebols* and their close nexus with previous governments. It is far less squeamish about forcing these *chaebols* to sell out to foreign investors. Suharto, on the other hand, has retained his position despite the crisis and has, in the past, used his position to extend the family empire. He would, therefore, be less amenable to selling out the family jewels in order to restore the stability of the rupiah, which is precisely what the IMF conditionality package had expected him to do. So while he went along, with some reticence, with the IMF's demand for a deflationary budget, he is less willing to ease the process of acquisition of domestic assets by foreign corporations. It is for this reason that he has chosen the 'currency board' as an alternative way of restoring confidence in the rupiah. This may necessitate high interest rates and severe contraction, which would slow down growth and increase unemployment. This would also affect corporate profits in the immediate future. But it would at least ensure that the assets accumulated by his family and friends would remain in their hands, to be appropriately disposed of in the future, rather than handed over at rock bottom prices just now. Indeed, in this scenario, the only area where the regime would immediately have to make a major compromise with regard to foreign acquisition is in banking. Any attempt to make the currency board work requires a restructuring of the banking system, which would have to be more transparent in its functioning as well as meet much higher minimum capital requirements. According to the central bank, only 10 out of the 212 banks in the country would be able to meet these requirements by the end-1998 deadline. If a significant number of the rest have to do so, acquisition by and infusion of funds from foreign banks and institutions seem inevitable.

The real threat to Suharto, however, does not come directly from the IMF. It comes from the Indonesian population, which is probably unlikely to accept the pain of the deep and prolonged deflation that would be needed to stabilise the rupiah at levels that protect the interests of Suharto's family. In the past, when the Suharto regime ruthlessly suppressed internal dissent, it had the support of the US, Japan and other friends from the developed North, who espoused democratic principles but backed authoritarian regimes as long as they kept 'communism' at bay and provided some space for foreign capital. This time around, Suharto and the transnationals are virtually bidding for the same assets. As a result, in a strange twist to history, the IMF and its backers, especially the US, have emerged, on superficial viewing, as the friends of the oppressed in Indonesia, fighting 'shoulder to shoulder' in the battle for democracy. Of course, this is an illusory support, for the consequences of IMF-style deflation would adversely affect the survival and quality of life for most of the citizenry, as well as erode the economic sovereignty of the country. Real economic and political freedom would continue to elude the Indonesian people, even under an alternative political regime if it functioned under IMF dispensation.

The Prognosis

For these countries in East and Southeast Asia, it now appears to be a case of 'damned if you do, damned if you don't,' at least as far as the IMF strategy is concerned. It is obvious that as long as the economies remain dependent upon the goodwill and confidence of investors who have proved themselves to be extremely whimsical, solutions to the current predicament are not easily evident. Yet, it is also obvious that there are urgent areas of policy action which cannot be ignored if the current situation is to be managed in an effective way. Jomo (chapter 1) has highlighted four areas of domestic policy reform challenges that now confront these countries: the need to handle the fact of much greater exchange rate instability, the urgency of financial sector reform, the management of asset price bubbles (and, it could be added, subsequent collapses) and of current account deficits.

Consider the last of these issues. Several analysts have blamed the large and growing current account imbalances for causing the crisis by eroding investor confidence, and have further argued that the resolution of the crisis similarly lies in the achievement of balance or surplus on current account transactions through renewed export growth. This may be the most optimistic interpretation of the present conjuncture: that the current slowdown is no more than a short-term phenomenon reflecting the cyclical changes in international markets in 1995 and 1996. In this view, as soon as international markets of export relevance to Asia revive, as they must given the dramatic real devaluations that have already occurred, they will once again lead these economies to a high-growth trajectory.

The cyclical factors which are most commonly cited are fourfold. The first is the slowdown in demand from rich countries, given the deceleration in industrial production there from the middle of 1995. Since Asian final exports are dominantly directed towards these countries (with intra-regional trade generally reflecting the regional splitting up and diversification of production processes), this has a direct effect on exports, which have been the chief engine of growth for these countries. So, as the US economic growth once again translates into demand for more imports, exports from this region will also recover. Second, the currencies of several countries of this region were effectively linked to the US dollar, which had boosted exports from the region when the dollar was weak in 1994-95, but thereafter had the opposite effect, with the appreciation of the dollar especially *vis-à-vis* the yen. In addition, inflation in several of these countries caused real exchange rates to appreciate despite nominal devaluations. The recent dramatic nominal devaluations in most of these countries — ranging from 40-70 per cent *vis-à-vis* the dollar — have also involved sharp real depreciation since inflation has remained quite moderate so far in most of the region. This means that exports from this region are now super-competitive and extraordinarily cheap. Third, there has been a slump in certain world markets which are of particular interest to this region, especially in semiconductors and in consumer electronic products. But the recent Information Technology Agreement of the WTO means that the potentially large markets of the European Union will now be more open to such exports. Finally, the present crisis is forcing deflationary macroeconomic policies on these countries, but it is fondly supposed that once the stabilisation exercises are completed, these economies will return to their high-growth trajectories.

However, there are several difficulties with focusing simply on these short-term cyclical features to explain the current slowdown, or indeed, with relying on the supposed 'market-friendlines' of policy makers in these countries to explain their earlier high rates of economic expansion. This is the case even if the major effects of the financial failures in terms of real sector depression in these economies are ignored. It is certainly true that much of the past growth in this region has been export-oriented, in that a systematic strategy of export promotion has been adopted by most of these countries to create larger markets than those provided by the domestic economy. This strategy reflected the internal political economy of these countries, but it is important to remember that it was only made possible by geo-political considerations in the second half of this century, which led the US and other Western powers to provide an economic umbrella and accept the rapidly growing manufacturing exports from these countries. The main such geo-political consideration, that is the perceived threat from communism, no longer exists, and it is noteworthy that despite all the grandiose declarations of the last GATT and the WTO, there has actually been an intensification of various forms of protectionism by the rich industrial countries against manufactured exports of Asia in the past two years. This is clearly evident in textiles and consumer electronic goods, for example. This suggests that a strategy which is so heavily based on increasing exports to the US and Western Europe is less likely to be successful than it was in the past. Indeed, the very cheapness of Asian exports may give rise to renewed protectionism, both overt and covert, by the OECD countries.

It should also be remembered that in several of the second-tier NICs, much export production is very import-intensive, and therefore, the costs of such production will be substantially increased by the nominal devaluation. Domestic costs are also likely to increase given the high real interest rates which are the fallout of current adjustment policies. Further, in most of these countries, ˌespecially Indonesia, it is evident that inflationary pressures are on the increase, and this will also be the case in other countries under IMF-led programmes. So, while exports will recover to some extent, it is unlikely that they will quickly go back to the dramatically high growth rates of the previous decade. The fundamental problem of insufficient world markets for very rapidly increasing exports still remains. So the rectification of current account imbalances in these economies may only be possible through massive import contraction and domestic recession, much in the same way as the adjustment of the highly indebted Latin American countries occurred in the 1980s.

Nor is it the case that simply resolving that particular external imbalance will necessarily bring these economies out of crisis, or back on a path of sustained growth. The financial debacle which has already occurred has brought in its train processes which demand major domestic policy changes, which may be difficult given the internal political configuration in these countries. The significant role of the financial class in South Korea, the pressures of the small coterie around the President in Indonesia, the nature of the ruling classes in Malaysia and

Thailand, all suggest that the chosen reform path may be one which is likely to sacrifice the material conditions of the majority of the people to preserve the interests of the domestic élites and foreign investors.

The only ray of hope for the East and Southeast Asian countries in this otherwise rather depressing prognosis may come from the very economic nationalism which has been the region's strength in the past. But if such economic nationalism is to be successful in lifting these economies out of crisis, it cannot be based only on the very rapid export expansion that characterised the past, involving dramatic increases in market share. Nor can it involve relying on clientelist relations with major Western powers to ensure capital inflows. In fact, given the regional nature of both the financial problems and their manner of spread, what is probably called for is something that extends beyond nationalism to regionalism, as well as to a greater recognition of the possibilities of economic co-operation with other developing countries. This involves greater trade dependence on each other and with other developing countries, bypassing dollar-based flows as far as possible, introducing some current account restrictions which would preserve essential imports and reduce material suffering among the mass of people, curbing the volatility of capital flows through regulations and greater use of a regional fund pooling the foreign reserves of the countries to smooth the effects of destabilising speculation, *inter alia*.

Thus, there are alternatives possible. What is still not clear, however, is whether such alternatives will be attempted given the domestic class configurations in these countries, and if so, whether they will be allowed in the current international political environment.

Note

1. These figures are reported in 'Emerging Market Indicators', *The Economist*, 7-13 February 1998. The Institute of International Finance's report was released at the end of January 1998.

Table 4.3
East Asia: Aggregate Net Resource Flows (US$ million)

	1991	*1992*	*1993*	*1994*	*1995*
China					
Long-term Debt	4,536	11,292	12,832	9,808	12,885
Short-term Debt	1,463	2,985	1,531	2,187	4,842
Foreign Direct Investment	4,366	11,156	27,515	33,787	35,849
Portfolio Equity Flows	653	1,194	3,818	3,915	2,807
Malaysia					
Long-term Debt	369	409	2,162	3,362	3,746
Short-term Debt	168	1,565	3,312	-762	1,085
Foreign Direct Investment	3,998	5,183	5,006	4,348	5,800
Portfolio Equity Flows	0	385	3,700	1,320	2,299
Thailand					
Long-term Debt	3,091	1,897	2,479	4,290	5,432
Short-term Debt	4,170	2,235	-1,342	652	4,275
Foreign Direct Investment	2,014	2,113	1,804	1,366	2,068
Portfolio Equity Flows	41	4	3,117	-538	2,154
Indonesia					
Long-term Debt	5,217	5,777	-1,079	3,582	3,529
Short-term Debt	3,180	3,742	-70	-878	5,241
Foreign Direct Investment	1,482	1,777	2,004	2,109	4,348
Portfolio Equity Flows	0	119	2,452	3,672	4,873

Source: World Bank (1997a).

5
TAMING THE TIGERS:
THE IMF AND THE ASIAN CRISIS*

Nicola Bullard with Walden Bello and Kamal Malhotra

This chapter reviews the actions and motives of the International Monetary Fund (IMF) in the ongoing East Asian financial crisis. It begins by describing what actually happened in the three worst-hit countries of Thailand, Indonesia and South Korea and goes on to explore the social impact of the crisis, providing a detailed analysis of the IMF's role, and of the numerous failings in its performance to date. The chapter concludes with recommendations for reform of the Bretton Woods institutions, and the international financial system.

Criticising the solutions imposed by the IMF in no way implies an uncritical endorsement of 'Asian' capitalism. The political and economic development models in these countries have brought some overall improvements in health, education and living standards. But the cost has been high in terms of sharpening the divide between rich and poor, environmental exploitation and loss of community control over natural resources, and growth without economic democracy or expansion of political participation. Rather, this chapter demonstrates that the IMF does not have a monopoly of social or economic wisdom (far from it). If the Fund's neo-liberal crusaders can be reined in, and alternatives explored, the crisis can offer Asia the chance to forge democratic and sustainable alternatives to the ruinous development path of recent years. If not, then ordinary Asians could come to look back on the 1970s and 1980s as a golden era. That would indeed be a tragic testament to the failures of the 'rescue packages' of 1997.

The IMF and Thailand: A Cosy Relationship

Thailand's financial crisis was at least three years old before it dramatically received global attention with the *de facto* devaluation of the baht on 2 July 1997. It cannot be said, however, that the IMF was particularly worried. Indeed, as late as the latter half of 1996, while expressing some concern about the huge capital

---

* An earlier version of this chapter was published jointly by Focus on the Global South in Bangkok and the Catholic aid agency CAFOD in London for the Asia Europe Meeting (ASEM) held in London on 2 and 3 April 1998.

inflows, the Fund was still praising Thai authorities for their 'consistent record of sound macroeconomic management policies' (Chote 1997).

The complacency of the Fund and its sister institution, the World Bank, when it came to Thailand — indeed, their failure to fully appreciate the danger signals — is traceable to several factors. One is that both the Fund and the World Bank had been instrumental in promoting Thailand, with its openness to capital flows and its high growth rate (the highest in the world in the period 1985-95, according to the Bank), as a model of development for the rest of the Third World. It was after all during the IMF–World Bank annual conference in Bangkok in September 1991 that Thailand was officially canonised as Asia's 'Fifth Tiger'.

But probably more important is that the massive capital inflows into Thailand in the form of portfolio investments and loans had not been incurred by government in order to finance deficit spending. Indeed, the high current account deficits of the early 1990s coincided with the government running budget surpluses. As a group of perceptive Indian analysts from New Delhi's Jawaharlal Nehru University's Centre of Economic Studies and Planning noted, '[p]art of the reason for this silence was the perception that an external account deficit is acceptable so long as it does not reflect a deficit on the government's budget but "merely" an excess of private investment over private domestic savings.' In this view, countries with significant budget deficits, such as India in 1991, were regarded as profligate even when their foreign debt was much lower than Thailand's.

The latter's debt, because it was incurred not by government, but by the private sector, was simply reflecting 'the appropriate environment for foreign private investment rather than public or private profligacy' (Ghosh, Sen and Chandrasekhar 1996). In other words, left to its own devices, the market would ensure that equilibrium would be achieved in the capital transactions between private international creditors and investors and private domestic banks and enterprises. So not to worry.

Thailand had, in fact, moved relatively far down the road to the full financial liberalisation that had been urged on it by the Fund and the World Bank throughout the late 1980s and early 1990s. Between 1990 and 1994, under the liberal technocrat government of Anand Panyarachun and its successor, the first government of Chuan Leek-Pai, a number of significant moves to deregulate and open up the financial system were undertaken, including:

- the removal of ceilings on various kinds of savings and time deposits;
- fewer constraints on the portfolio management of financial institutions and commercial banks such as replacing the reserve requirement ratio for commercial banks with the liquidity ratio;
- looser rules on capital adequacy and expansion of the field of operations of commercial banks and financial institutions;
- dismantling of all significant foreign exchange controls;

• the establishment of the Bangkok International Banking Facility (BIBF) (Pakorn 1994).

The BIBF was perhaps the most significant step taken by the Thais in the direction of financial liberalisation. This was a system in which local and foreign banks were allowed to engage in both offshore and onshore lending activities. BIBF licensees were allowed to accept deposits in foreign currencies and to lend in foreign currencies, both to residents and non-residents, for both domestic and foreign investments. BIBF dollar loans soon became the conduit for most foreign capital flowing into Bangkok, coming to about US$50 billion over a three year period.

Thailand's liberalisation was incomplete, but the IMF did not raise a word of protest against the two other key elements of Thailand's macroeconomic financial strategy. The maintenance of high interest rates — about 400-500 basis points above US rates — was probably seen as a necessary inducement for foreign capital to come into Thailand. Besides, in the context of rapid growth, it was the usual IMF formula to contain overheating and inflation.

As for the fixing of the exchange rate at a steady US$1:baht 25 through Bank of Thailand intervention in the foreign exchange market, this was probably seen as a necessary condition for investors to know they could exchange their dollars for baht without fear of being blindsided by devaluations that would drastically reduce their value. Besides, the Fund did not have a reputation of being a partisan of floating exchange rates for developing countries, which could plague them with volatile external accounts that could be quite destabilising.

Thus, when the IMF was requested by the Thai authorities to come in to rescue the economy in mid-July 1997, it was to fix a crisis that had as one of its root causes a Fund prescription (the liberalisation of the capital account) that had led to a problem that the Fund had neither foreseen nor worried about (private sector overborrowing). When Thailand approached the IMF for assistance after the collapse of the baht in early July, it was not unlike a player approaching the coach with a quizzical look that said: 'What went wrong? I was just following your instructions.'

By that time, however, the Fund was busily rewriting history, saying that it had warned the Thai authorities all along about a developing crisis — prompting economist Jeffrey Sachs (1998) to write wryly that 'the IMF arrived in Thailand in July with ostentatious declarations that all was wrong and that fundamental surgery was needed' when, in fact, 'the ink was not even dry on the IMF's 1997 annual report, which gave Thailand and its neighbours high marks on economic management!' It took almost a month for the IMF and the government to nego- tiate the agreement that was announced on 20 August. In return for access to US$16.7 billion — later raised to US$17.2 billion — in commitments gathered from bilateral and multilateral donors, the Thai authorities agreed to a stabilisation and structural adjustment programme with two principal components.

First, a stabilisation programme that would cut the current account deficit through the maintenance of high interest rates, and the achievement of a 'small overall surplus in the public sector by 1998' through an increase in the rate of the value-added tax (VAT) to 10 per cent, expenditure cuts in a number of areas, ending subsidies on some utilities and petroleum products, and greater efficiency in state enterprises via privatisation (IMF 1997a).

Second was structural reform of the financial sector. 'At the heart of the strategy', noted the Fund in its statement, 'has been the up-front separation, suspension, and restructuring of unviable institutions, immediate steps to instil confidence in the rest of the financial system, strict conditionality on the extension of Financial Institutions Development Fund (FIDF) resources, and the phased implementation of broader structural reforms to restore a healthy financial sector'. Part of the financial reform would also 'require all remaining financial institutions to strengthen their capital base expeditiously. This will include a policy of encouraging mergers, as well as foreign capital injection' (IMF 1997a).

Concerns

The main part of the structural reform package was the closing down of insolvent financial institutions. Even before the baht devaluation, the Chavalit government had suspended 16 finance companies, including Finance One, once the country's premier finance company. At the time of the announcement of the agreement, the government declared that another 42 would be suspended, bringing the total to 58 of the country's 92 finance companies. This was a popular move, since the finance companies were widely known to be bankrupt and had absorbed some 17 billion baht in subsidies from the FIDF, which many of them had spent not to restructure their loan portfolios, but to relend, thus expanding their exposure (*AWSJ*, 5-6 December 1997). The IMF wanted a quick government decision to shut down those firms that could not be salvaged. The IMF's question when it came to the stabilisation part of the package was: would the government go through with the agreement to raise taxes, particularly on petroleum?

For others, on the other hand, doubts began to set in on the wisdom of a programme that would exacerbate deflation. With growth already set to slow down owing to the high levels of corporate indebtedness and the depressive effects of skyrocketing baht prices for imports, what was the rationale for drastically cutting back on government expenditure? Government capital expenditures, especially for infrastructure, had been the main factor stimulating growth in 1996 as the private sector lost its dynamism (Bangkok Bank 1997). Eliminating this stimulus would simply kick the economy from slowdown into a severe recession. These fears were related to a larger concern, which was that the IMF was treating the Thai financial crisis with a cure for public sector profligacy, whereas it stemmed from private sector excesses. What was needed was not public sector policies that would speed up the downward spiral of the private sector but a counter-cyclical mechanism to keep the economy afloat.

As Jeffrey Sachs, the main proponent of this view put it, '[T]he region does not need wanton budget cutting, credit tightening and emergency bank closures. It needs stable or even slightly expansionary monetary and fiscal policies to counterbalance the decline in foreign loans' (Vatchara and Thanong 1997). Sachs (1998) went on to claim that the Fund's behaviour in fact worsened what was already a delicate situation in the fall of 1997: '[T]he IMF deepened the sense of panic, not only because of its dire pronouncements, but also because its proposed medicine — high interest rates, budget cuts, and immediate bank closures — convinced the markets that Asia indeed was about to enter a severe contraction.... Instead of dousing the fire, the IMF in effect screamed fire in the theatre. The scene was repeated in Indonesia and Korea in December. By then panic had spread to virtually all of East Asia.'

Another concern that emerged had to do with the actual use of the US$17.2 billion rescue fund. The 20 August agreement stated that this sum would be devoted 'solely to help finance the balance of payments deficit and rebuild the official reserves of the Bank of Thailand' (IMF 1997a). What this meant was that the funds could not be used to bail out local institutions. 'Financing the balance of payments deficit' was, however, a broad canopy that covered servicing the huge foreign debt of the Thai private sector, which in mid-1997 came to US$72 billion, of which over half was short-term debt. The IMF-assembled funds provided an assurance that the government would be able to address the immediate debt service commitments of the private sector, while the government and the IMF sought to persuade the creditors to roll over or restructure their loans. The rescue agreement thus repeated the pattern of the IMF–US Mexican bail-out in 1994 and the IMF structural agreements with indebted countries during the debt crisis of the 1980s, in which public money from Northern taxpayers was formally lent to indebted governments only to be recycled as debt service payments to commercial bank creditors.

To many, there was something fundamentally wrong about a process that imposed full market penalties on Thailand while exempting international private actors — indeed, socialising their losses. As the *Nation* (9/8/97) put it, 'The penalties imposed on foreign creditor banks which have lent to the Thai private sector must be precise and applied equally... Thailand and Thai companies may bear the brunt of the financial crisis but foreign banks must also share part of the cost because of some imprudent lending. It would be irresponsible to lay the blame entirely on Thailand.'

The Chavalit Government Hesitates

It took another two months before the government could come up with the details of the stabilisation programme. On 14 October, the Thai authorities publicly underlined their commitment to the IMF to generate a budget surplus equivalent to 1 per cent of GDP by decreeing a series of taxes, including increases on duties on luxury imports, surcharges on imports not used by the export sector, and, most controversially, a fuel tax of 1 baht per litre of gasoline. On the expenditure side, government spending was cut by baht 100 billion, bringing it down to baht 823 billion. On the financial sector reforms, the authorities announced the creation of the Financial Restructuring Authority (FRA) to oversee the screening of the rehabilitation plans submitted by the 58 suspended companies, which would be the yardstick used to determine whether or not they would be allowed to reopen. Also to be established was an Asset Management Corporation (AMC), with seed money totalling 1 billion baht from the government, which would oversee the disposal of the assets of the finance companies ordered closed. The government also promised to allow foreigners to own up to 100 per cent of financial institutions, to tighten rules for classifying loans as non-performing, to provide full government guarantees for depositors and creditors, and to improve the bankruptcy laws to allow creditors to collect their collateral faster.

At this point, the IMF's main concern was to see promises translated promptly into action. But popular opposition forced the Chavalit government to rescind the petroleum tax just three days after its announcement.

Having presided over the unravelling of the economy, the government simply did not have the legitimacy to make its decision stick. The cabinet also failed to approve the emergency measures that were necessary to put the financial restructuring plans in motion, and procrastinated on identifying the finance companies that would be closed. When Finance Minister Thanong Bidaya resigned over the rescinding of the oil tax, the Chavalit government's credibility hit rock bottom. The rising tension and confusion were captured in the following account: 'In late October and early November, rumours swept regional markets that the IMF might hold back the second phase of stand-by credits due in December. IMF officials reportedly were frustrated by the glacial pace of reforms and the indecisiveness by the government in acknowledging the seriousness of the problems. Foreign creditors began to slash their credit lines and call back outstanding loans to Thai institutions. As the baht slid toward 42 to the dollar, fears emerged that Thailand might declare a debt moratorium' (Soonyuth and Chiratas 1998).

On the other side of the barricades, street demonstrations called for the resignation of the government, and many of the protests were beginning to acquire an anti-IMF flavour. Critics became more vocal in saying that the tight-money, tight-fiscal-policy austerity package was a misguided cure that would only worsen the disease. As two influential analysts put it, 'IMF officials... believed that once its prescription of an austere economic programme was followed strictly, confidence would return and capital would flow back into Thailand to improve liquidity and stabilise the baht. But this wishful thinking has not happened, with the country still paralysed by capital continuously flowing out of the system.' In the meantime, 'without capital, Thai business in general is heading for a breakdown' (Vatchara and Thanong 1997).

Chuan to the Rescue

With its credibility with both the public and the IMF hitting rock bottom, the Chavalit government finally announced on 3 November — just a few hours before the arrival of an IMF team to review government compliance with the agreement — that it would step down and allow a new parliamentary coalition to take power. In the interval between the Chavalit government's announcement that it was stepping down and the formation of the second Chuan government, IMF pressure was instrumental in forcing the National Assembly to pass four emergency decrees that were necessary to get the financial restructuring going.

When the new government was constituted, the Fund did not relax its time-table, demanding that it immediately decide which finance companies should be permanently shut down and which should be rehabilitated. Indeed, it pinned its decision on whether or not the next tranche of US$800 million would be released on the government's announcement. Thai compliance, said Karin Lissakers, US delegate to the IMF, 'would be an important political signal that we had overcome political resistance to action' (Davis 1997). On 7 December 1997, the Chuan government announced that all but two of the 58 finance companies would be closed. The IMF money was released.

But praise for the Thai authorities' demonstration of political will was tempered by the government's admission that the financial crisis and the IMF stabilisation programme would bring about a worse than expected contraction in 1998, with the government and Thai authorities lowering their estimate of economic growth from the 2.5 per cent projected for 1998 at the time of the August agreement to just 0.6 per cent. By the time of the next IMF review, in mid-February 1998, the figure of 0.6 per cent growth had again been revised downward to acknowledge a full-blown recession, with a fall in economic output of 3.5 per cent for the year, and more than 6 per cent for the first two quarters.

This dismal projection, which held out the possibility of an even greater free-fall, prompted the Fund to yield to the government's request that it be allowed to run a budget deficit of 1-2 per cent of GDP rather than be forced to produce a surplus of 1 per cent. Explaining the Fund's concession, Herbert Neiss, the IMF's Asia-Pacific director, admitted that 'the economy had slowed down to such an extent that a continued stringent austerity regime may prompt a new economic crisis' (*Bangkok Post*, 13/2/98). However, the government was   not able to shift the Fund from its insistence on maintaining high interest rates, which were running at 20 per cent and above. The Fund's new understanding with the Chuan administration committed the latter to push a revision of the Alien Business Law to allow foreigners more liberal investment privileges in the non-financial sectors of the economy; to prepare legislation to tighten up the country's bankruptcy laws; and to speed up the total or partial privatisation of key state enterprises such as the Telephone Organisation of Thailand, Thai Airways and the Communications Authority of Thailand.

Finally, the revised agreement committed the government to announce stricter rules on classifying loans as 'non-performing' by the end of March 1998 and to force the banks to recapitalise on that basis. Since it came into office in mid-November, the government had, in fact, been urging the banks to recapitalise along the lines demanded by the Fund ever since the value of their assets had been drastically savaged by the currency plunge. That meant allowing foreign partners to take a big, if not majority, stake in Thai corporations, a step which had been made possible by emergency legislation approved by the National Assembly in October. For some institutions, the choice was between receiving an infusion of foreign money or being brought more directly under the control of the government. Indeed, the government nationalised four near bankrupt banks in order to restructure, sell or dismantle them.

With the legal ground being secured, foreign banks began to work out deals with cash-strapped Thai banks. The Japanese Sanwa Bank announced that it would take a 10 per cent stake in one of the country's biggest banks, Siam Commercial Bank — a move that would bring total foreign shareholding in that bank to 35 per cent. Citibank declared that it would move to gain a 50.1 per cent ownership share in First Bangkok City Bank. While this deal remained suspended as of February 1998, ABN-AMRO, a Dutch financial group, said that it had arrived at an agreement to acquire a majority stake in the Bank of Asia.

By February 1998, after over three months in office, the Chuan government had gained the reputation of being extremely compliant with the IMF, definitely much more so than the preceding Chavalit government and the Suharto government in Indonesia. As IMF representative Neiss put it, 'Thailand has turned the corner, along with Korea... [Thailand has] won a battle or two but not the war yet... Indonesia is still in the intensive-care unit' (*Bangkok Post*, 14/2/98). It would be accurate to say that while there were differences on interest rate policy and government spending, the government and the IMF had achieved a meeting of minds. The key to recovery was winning back the confidence of foreign capital, and the key to winning that confidence was to adhere to the IMF austerity programme. Thais had, however, become disillusioned with a growth pattern based on foreign capital, for that had been after all, what had led Thailand to its current troubles. Moreover, how foreign capital would be induced to come back to an economy in severe recession, where prospects for profits lay quite a few years down the line, was not satisfactorily answered.

The IMF and Indonesia: Under the Volcano

In September 1997, the World Bank was still saying, 'Indonesia has achieved a remarkable economic development success over the past decade and is considered to be among the best performing East Asian economies.' Astonishingly, this view was still on the Bank's public website as late as March 1998. The report continues:

'Indonesia has made great strides in diversifying its economy and promoting a competitive private sector through sound macroeconomic management, increased deregulation and deeper investment in infrastructure services. Today both foreign and domestic investment are booming... Indonesia's investment rates have steadily increased and are now among the highest in the large developing countries. Much of the dynamism can be traced to the government's reform programme which liberalised trade and finance and encouraged foreign investment and deregulation' (World Bank 1997b).

This is the same country that has, since July 1997, seen its stock market drop by 50 per cent, whose currency has plunged more than 70 per cent and whose 'dynamic economy' is being subjected to an amazingly detailed and interventionist set of IMF conditions linked to a US$43 billion bail-out loan. In July 1997, shortly after the Thai baht was unpegged from the US dollar, investors and currency speculators, who were either nervous or opportunistic, started to test the 'fundamentals' in other Asian countries by selling off stocks, calling in debts and dumping currencies, thus triggering the 'contagion' effect which caused currencies and economies throughout the region to collapse. Malaysia, Indonesia and the Philippines were most severely affected, as relentless attacks on their currencies forced each, in turn, to abandon the fixed exchange rate and let the market determine the currency's value.

The weaknesses in the Indonesian economy that made it vulnerable to currency attacks were similar to Thailand's: rising external liabilities, private sector debt problems and poor loan quality, lack of confidence in the government's ability to resolve the problems, excessive amounts of foreign investment inflating an expanding asset bubble and an overvalued currency pegged to the strengthening US dollar. Although most of the macroeconomic indicators were deemed sound, the financial sector was deeply suspect and proved to be the weakest link in the chain (Congressional Report 1997).

Early in the crisis, the Indonesian government attempted to calm the situation by defending the currency, using Central Bank reserves, and loosening its control on the exchange rate. However, by 13 August, just as Thailand was signing a deal with the IMF, the rupiah hit a then historic low of 2,682 to the dollar, from a pre-July level of 2,400. On 14 August, the government abolished the managed exchange rate and the rupiah slid immediately to 2,755. Even though the Central Bank attempted to defend the currency by raising interest rates and the government announced that projects worth 39 trillion rupiah would be postponed to meet the budget shortfall, the situation continued to deteriorate and by 6 October the rupiah was at a new low of 3,845 to the dollar.

Two days later, faced with declining reserves, collapsing financial institutions, and capital haemorrhaging from the country, the government announced its intention to seek IMF assistance. By 31 October, Indonesia had agreed to a US$43 billion loan agreement. Of this, US$23 billion was 'first line financing' made up of US$10 billion from the IMF, US$4.5 billion from the World Bank, US$3.5 billion from the Asian Development Bank and US$5 billion from Indonesia's own international reserves. Second line supplementary financing, totalling about US$20 billion, included US$6 billion from the US, US$5 billion each from Japan and Singapore and US$1 billion each from Australia and Malaysia.[1] The agreement represented about 490 per cent of Indonesia's Special Drawing Rights, just below the 500 per cent threshold requiring special approval.

The objectives of the package were to 'stabilise exchange market conditions, ensure an orderly adjustment of the external current account in response to lower capital inflows, and lay the groundwork for a resumption of sustained rapid growth' (IMF 1997d). The targets set for Indonesia included a current account deficit of 2 per cent of GDP, official reserves worth about five months of imports and a budget surplus of 1 per cent achieved by increasing revenue through excise taxes and removing tax exemptions. The main policy measures to achieve these objectives were tight monetary policy (pushing up interest rates to mop up excess money, to reduce the debt component of financing in favour of equity and to attract foreign investment), closing unviable banks, liberalising foreign trade and investment, dismantling domestic monopolies and expanding the privatisation programme. Specific reforms included reducing tariffs in sectors such as chemicals, fisheries and steel products, an explicit agreement to implement ahead of schedule the WTO ruling on the national car (a case brought by the US) should the ruling go against Indonesia, and postponing or rescheduling major state investments. The Suharto government also agreed to reduce export taxes, open more sectors of the economy to foreign investment and privatise public enterprises under the management of a newly established privatisation board (IMF 1997d).

IMF Causes Bank Run

Rather than restoring confidence, however, the IMF directive to close down 16 insolvent banks caused panic, precipitating a run on two-thirds of the country's banks, further weakening the financial sector and eroding faith in the economy. The Fund itself admitted as much in an internal memo which was reported in the *New York Times* in mid-January: 'A confidential report by the International Monetary Fund on Indonesia's economic crisis acknowledges that an important element of the IMF's rescue strategy backfired, causing a bank panic that helped set off financial market declines in much of Asia.... These closures, far from improving public confidence in the banking system, have instead set off a renewed 'flight to safety'. Over two-thirds of the country's banks were affected, and more than US$2 billion was withdrawn from the banking system' (Sanger 1998).

For the next two months, the IMF bail-out did little to staunch the flow of money out of the country or slow the plunging rupiah. Clearly, the market needed more than the IMF's intervention to convince it that all was well in the state of

Suharto. Neither the IMF nor the investors had confidence in the determination of the Indonesian government to stick to the loan conditions, and confusion resulting from contradictory messages coming from Jakarta exacerbated the situation. At one moment, the 76-year old president was promising to axe a slew of major infrastructure projects, the next he earmarked a select 15 for preferential treatment and continued support.

The fact that several of these projects directly involved or benefited his immediate family highlighted the extent to which the Indonesian economy and its institutions are embedded in a nepotistic system of money-lending and deal-making limited to an inner circle of Suharto's offspring and friends. Estimates of the family fortune vary wildly, from US$6 to US$40 billion, making it one of the world's largest family fortunes and 'Suharto's six children have used political influence to amass holdings that range from airlines, banking and petrochemicals to the Timor, Indonesia's national car. Foreign companies hoping to do business in Indonesia often hire Suharto scions as "consultants" to grease the wheels' (Blank 1998). The inside story of the 17 January issue of *The Economist* (with the cover banner 'Step down, Suharto') commented that: 'Mr Suharto has proved better at promising reform that delivering it. He is, after all, being asked to dismantle an economic structure which has created enormous fortunes for his sons and daughters.... As his relations squeal, he may backslide, setting off a new onslaught on the currency, new bouts of panic hoarding, new hyper-inflationary pressures.'

The crisis in Indonesia started to quicken in early December when rumours of Suharto's ill health and his non-attendance at the Association of South East Asian Nations (ASEAN) meeting in Kuala Lumpur triggered concerns about political and social stability. For anyone who has taken more than a passing interest in Indonesian affairs, the unsustainability of Suharto's regime and the political vacuum he has created is no surprise. Yet it seemed that as long as the ageing autocrat continued to deliver the economic goods, no one was too concerned. However, as the economy started to collapse it became obvious that the rhetoric of national unity and growing prosperity was cloaking a darker reality of dissent, despair, anger and poverty, likely to be translated into violence and chaos. *The Economist* (17-23/1/98) put it succinctly, saying that 'what looked like political stability during a bull market looks like dangerous rigidity when times are tough'.

Suharto Defies the IMF

President Suharto's budget speech of 6 January had a devastating effect. He announced substantial increases in the subsidies for petrol and staples such as rice and fertiliser and an overall 32 per cent increase in government spending, but gave no hint of when and how subsidies and monopolies would be abolished. In addition, the budget figures were based on extremely optimistic assumptions such as 4 per cent growth, 9 per cent inflation and an exchange rate of Rp4,000 to the dollar. (At the time of writing, the growth estimate is -0.5 per cent, annualised consumer price inflation for February 1998 was 32 per cent, and the rupiah is still hovering around 10,000 to the dollar with no improvement in sight.) Faced with massive unemployment, a rapidly contracting economy and potential social unrest, Suharto's budget could be seen as a logical response to the circumstances. However, both the IMF and the markets disagreed.

The market responded by further selling off the currency and by moving more money offshore, sending the rupiah through the critical psychological 10,000 mark on 9 January. By then, the political and economic situation was spinning out of control with food prices soaring and reports of rioting and food hoarding. The government's response was to announce jail sentences for hoarding and to put the army in charge of food distribution – hardly the sort of measures to calm a jittery population and the even more nervous investors.

US Turns up the Heat

The IMF responded by flying in top-level officials to strong-arm Suharto into reneging on his budget promises and to reaffirm his commitment to the IMF deal. Suharto also received phone calls from US President Clinton, Japan's Prime Minister Hashimoto, Australia's John Howard and Helmut Kohl of Germany, all urging him to revise the budget and stick to the IMF conditions. Clinton dispatched two senior members of the administration, Secretary for Defence William Cohen and Deputy Secretary to the Treasury Lawrence Summers to 'deliver messages' to President Suharto. Using tremendous pressure, the IMF was able to extract a new commitment from Suharto on 15 January 1998, powerfully captured in the photograph of IMF managing director Michel Camdessus, arms crossed with the demeanour of an invigilator, imperiously standing over Suharto as he signed on the dotted line.

But the markets were not calmed and stocks fell a further 4 per cent. From a steady 2,400 in July, the rupiah took five months to slide to 4,000 in early December, and thereafter just one month to crash to an astonishing 17,000 to the dollar by 22 January. The details of the second IMF agreement were published in detail, no doubt to put further pressure on Indonesia and to convince the markets that their concerns were being addressed. The agreement acknowledges that, 'The enormous depreciation of the rupiah did not seem to stem from macroeconomic imbalances, which remained quite modest. Instead, the large depreciation reflected a severe loss of confidence in the currency, the financial sector and the overall economy' (*Jakarta Post*, 17/1/98).

In contrast to the first agreement which set quite specific macroeconomic targets, the second realistically asserts that: 'Under current volatile conditions it is difficult to set precise macroeconomic targets. Nevertheless, the programme is designed to avoid a decline in output, while limiting inflation to about 20 per cent' (*Jakarta Post*, 17/1/98). The specific macroeconomic objectives are:

* to achieve a current account surplus;
* keep inflation to 20 per cent, set a balanced budget (a change from the earlier requirement of a budget surplus);
* eliminate subsidies on electricity and fuel (except kerosene and diesel) commencing on 1 April;
* increase excise on various goods, end all VAT exemptions;
* impose a 5 per cent tax on gasoline, improve tax recovery;
* include the investment and reforestation funds in central revenues from fiscal year 1998/99, and ensure that the reforestation fund is used explicitly for the specified purposes.[2]

Specific steps to liberalise trade and investment included:

* reducing tariffs on all imported foodstuffs products to 5 per cent and cutting non-agricultural tariffs to 10 per cent by 2003;
* a major overhaul of the banking system, including opening banks to foreign ownership by June 1998;
* lifting restrictions on foreign banks by February 1998;
* the establishment of the Indonesian Bank Restructuring Agency to dispose of the collateral backing problem loans and oversee the merger or liquidation of weak financial institutions.

But even here, there is 'considerable scepticism… about the ability of the new agency to close down weak financial institutions with strong political connections, particularly those with ties to Mr Suharto's extended family' (Japan Economic Institute, 30/1/98).

Suharto's Interests Under Attack

What the new deal lacks in macroeconomic targets is made up for in microeconomic directives which strike at the very heart of Suharto's economic power, addressing in minute detail the dismantling of cartels, monopolies and taxes which directly benefit Suharto, his family and friends. Twelve megaprojects were cancelled, including several directly linked to Suharto's sons and daughters and all special benefits for the national car project (run by Suharto's youngest son Tommy) and the aircraft project (run by Suharto's 'golden boy', newly appointed Vice-President B.J. Habibie) were stopped (*TAPOL Bulletin*, 1998).

The Fund also demanded liberalisation of trade in agricultural products such as cashews, cloves, oranges and vanilla, removing restrictions on foreign investment in the palm oil industry by 1 February and on wholesale/retail trade by March 1998 and closing the clove marketing board (run by Suharto's son Tommy) by June 1998. Even on this seemingly minor condition, there has been no positive government action. In late February, a cabinet minister made comments 'suggesting that the clove marketing board may be continued, on a different basis' (*AWSJ*, 2/3/98). The clove business is extremely lucrative in Indonesia, since powdered cloves are an essential ingredient of the local cigarettes. The Fund demanded the break-up of formal and informal cartels, monopolies and marketing arrangements (such as those in plywood, paper and cement) whereby producers are required to sell through a central marketing agent, pay commissions, or be allocated production quotas or market shares. It also restricted the monopoly of the state logistics body, Bulog, to rice. Flour had been included in the first agreement but was subsequently dropped, reportedly threatening the ability of Suharto's friend Liem Sioe Liong (the world's biggest manufacturer of instant noodles) to control the price of wheat. Sugar imports will be deregulated and farmers will not be forced to plant sugar cane, allowing land currently used for sugar to be turned over to rice. Social spending will be increased to provide nine years' education and better basic medical services.

Following the new agreement with the IMF, the Indonesian government announced on 27 January a temporary freeze on corporate debt servicing by Indonesian companies, along with plans for a new government agency to oversee bank reforms, including closing down non-viable banks and selling assets. The financial sector in Indonesia is in dire straits. Capital flight, rumoured to have begun as early as March 1997 during violent rioting and looting against the minority ethnic Chinese, has caused many to send their money offshore to safer havens in Singapore and Hong Kong. The capital flight has been so dramatic that Indonesia's very solvency is threatened, with foreign banks severing inter-bank ties to Indonesian banks and refusing to accept letters of credit, preventing importers from bringing in raw materials and other inputs from abroad.

In addition, the collapsing rupiah means that the price of imported goods has more than doubled, supplies are dwindling, people are hoarding, hospitals are having to cut back and even basic medical supplies are now out of reach. The IMF conditions gave momentum to the already rising food prices by ending subsidies on staples such as beans, sugar and flour. Prices were expected to rise again after 1 April when state subsidies on fuel and electricity were due to be lifted. Meanwhile, the Indonesian economy is burdened with a huge foreign debt, estimated at the end of December 1997 at US$140 billion (two-thirds of GDP) of which US$20 billion was short term, and US$65 billion owed by private non-financial institutions (Yamin 1998a). This translates into a debt service ratio of about one-third of exports of goods and services.

Currency Board

In a desperate effort to attract foreign currency President Suharto announced, in mid-February, plans to establish a currency board. The basic principal of a currency board is that every unit of local currency in circulation is backed by foreign reserves at a fixed exchange rate (5,000-5,500 was mooted as the US dollar rate for the rupiah). This put him on a collision course with the IMF, which threatened to withdraw the US$43 billion credit should Jakarta pursue the idea. Suharto, in a grim effort to retain control over economic policy, held on to the last, even dismissing the Central Bank governor who apparently did not support the idea of a currency board. The debate over the currency board is likely to continue. As recently as 11 March, Jakarta was buzzing with rumours that the board would be set up within two days. 'The government is looking for a quick fix and it seems probable that the solution is the currency board,' said an Indonesian analyst at Goldman Sachs in Singapore (*AWSJ*, 11/3/98).

There are several explanations for Suharto's interest in the currency board. Firstly, even if the board was in place for just one or two days, it would allow the Suharto circle to wipe off their foreign debts at Rp5,500 rather than Rp10,000. Secondly, it gave Suharto some breathing space to reassert his control over economic policy after the humiliating acquiescence to the IMF earlier in the year. Whatever his motivation, talk of the currency board has had the effect of sucking foreign exchange into the country from investors eager to get in early just in case the rupiah is re-pegged at a lower rate. Unlike Thailand and South Korea, Indonesia has been a reluctant, even belligerent, recipient of the IMF's largesse.

Clearly, Suharto has vested interests to protect, the very same interests which are being singled out by the IMF in their bid to restore confidence in the Indonesian economy. In the invidious struggle for power between the Fund and the president, no holds are barred. In early March, US President Clinton sent former Vice-President Walter Mondale to have a heart-to-heart talk with Suharto; however Suharto continues to antagonise the West by pushing the currency board plan, brazenly assuming the mantle of President for a seventh consecutive term and even nominating the profligate spender B.J. Habibie as vice-president. In the midst of all this arrogance and intransigence, 200 million Indonesians are suffering.

The impact has been devastating. Estimates of the total number of people who had lost their jobs by the end of 1997 varied enormously, from 2.5 million to 6.6 million. The construction industry in particular has ground to a halt with at least 950,000 workers losing their jobs. Unemployment has jumped from 7.7 per cent to 10 per cent and is expected to climb further during 1998. By late March, the currency devaluation and capital flight had left the financial sector in ruins, causing prices to rise and businesses to crash. Because the Government had dragged its feet on implementing the IMF reforms, it was impossible to assess what impact they would have on the present situation, or indeed on the long-term economic and political future of Indonesia. In any case, political concerns had overtaken the economic crisis, and one could not be resolved without the other.

The IMF and South Korea: Teaching the Tiger a Lesson

On 30 September 1996, South Korea, 'blessed with one of the world's most vibrant economies' (Deen 1997), said goodbye to the developing world and joined the Organisation for Economic Cooperation and Development (OECD). The statistics behind South Korea's promotion are impressive. Korea, which had a per capita GDP less than that of the Philippines in 1965, could by 1995 boast per capita income of US$13,269, compared to the Philippines' US$2,475. This represented a 770 per cent increase in just 30 years (Ahuja *et al.* 1997). Annual economic growth over the same period averaged slightly over 7 per cent and pre-crash figures placed South Korea as the eleventh largest economy in the world. A 1996 United Nation Conference on Trade and Development (UNCTAD) report described South Korea as 'the outstanding example of an "emerging donor" with the potential for making a significant contribution to official development assistance.' The report went on to note that since independence in 1945, South Korea had received aid grants totalling US$4.8 billion and that '(It) is a country that has successfully broken out of aid dependence' (Deen 1997).

Little more than a year later, South Korea is in virtual receivership, having agreed to a US$57 billion rescue package assembled by the IMF — an amount more than ten times the total official development assistance given to South Korea in the previous 40 years. Ironically, membership of the OECD forced financial and other deregulation which were contributing factors to the financial meltdown, by increasing inflows of foreign finance and putting pressure on locally produced goods from less expensive and better quality imports.

What Went Wrong?

Unlike the Southeast Asian economies, Korea, the classic 'NIC' or newly industrialising country, had blazed a path to industrial strength that was based principally on mobilising domestic savings, carried out partly through equity-enhancing reforms such as land reform in the early 1950s. Although foreign capital had played an important part, local financial resources, extracted through a rigorous system of taxation plus profits derived from the sale of goods to a protected domestic market and to foreign markets opened up by an aggressive mercantilist strategy, constituted the main source of capital accumulation.

The institutional framework for high-speed industrialisation was a close working relationship between the private sector and the state, with the latter in a commanding role. By picking priority strategic sectors and industries, providing them with subsidised credit (sometimes at negative real interest rates) through a government-directed banking system, and protecting them from competition from foreign corporations in the domestic market, the state nurtured industrial conglomerates (*chaebol*) that it later pushed out into the international market. This strategy was immensely successful in the 1960s and 1970s, becoming the bedrock of South Korea's 'miracle' industrialisation and export growth. In the early 1980s, the state–*chaebol* combine appeared to be unstoppable in international markets, as the deep pockets of commercial banks that were extremely responsive to government wishes provided the wherewithal for Hyundai, Samsung, LG and other conglomerates to carve out market shares in Europe, Asia and North America. The good years lasted from 1985 to 1990, when profitability was roughly indicated by the surpluses that the country racked up in its international trade account. Yet, even by the early 1980s, the inefficiencies and complacency of what had until then been an extremely successful state-led strategy were becoming evident, as the economy grew and the corruption in the state–bank–*chaebol* nexus multiplied and became evident. Despite this, no action was taken to reform the system by either politicians, economists or government bureaucrats — or for that matter, any of their international backers.

The Squeeze

In the early nineties, the tide turned against the Koreans. Three factors, in particular, appear to be central. The first was distraction from the previous focus on building up industrial and technological capabilities by real estate and other such unproductive investments. The second was the massive trade blitz unleashed on Korea by the US. The third was membership of the OECD, which forced Korea to adopt a more liberal stance towards foreign capital and finance. These factors exposed the government's inability to prevent market failure, the conscious prevention of which had underpinned much of the country's success during the 'miracle' decades.[3] Instead of focusing investments on turning out high-value-added commodities and developing more sophisticated production technologies, Korea's conglomerates went for the quick and easy profits, buying up real estate or pouring money into stock market speculation. In the 1980s, over US$16.5 billion in *chaebol* funds went into buying land for speculation and setting up luxury hotels and golf courses and by 1996, total bank exposure to real estate reached 25 per cent, higher than either Thailand or Indonesia. Most of the machines in industrial plants continue to be imported from Japan, and Korean-assembled products from colour televisions to laptop computers are made up mainly of Japanese components.

For all intents and purposes, Korea has not been able to advance more quickly from labour-intensive assembly with Japanese inputs using Japanese technology. Predictably, the result has been a massive trade deficit with Japan, which came to over US$15 billion in 1996. As Korea's balance of trade with Japan was worsening, so was its trade account with the US. Fearing the emergence of another Japan with which it would constantly be in deficit, Washington subjected Seoul to a broad-front trade offensive that was much tougher than the one directed at Japan, probably owing to Korea's lack of retaliatory capacity. This included a

Plaza Accord-style forced appreciation of the South Korean won. Hemmed in on all fronts, Korea saw its 1987 trade surplus of US$9.6 billion with the US turn into a deficit of US$159 million in 1992. By 1996, the deficit with the US had grown to over US$10 billion, and its overall trade deficit hit US$21 billion. In addition, competition from other East Asian countries with cheaper labour put pressure on Korea. All of these elements, combined with over-expansion and over-specialisation, meant that by 1996 the top 20 listed companies in Korea were earning a mere 3 per cent on assets, while the average cost of borrowing had risen to 8.2 per cent. The average debt to equity ratio was a phenomenal 220 per cent (and up to 300-400 per cent in many cases) and the return on equity a minuscule 0.8 per cent. It is hardly surprising that many companies stopped paying their bills.

Desperate Measures

In a desperate attempt to regain profitability, management tried to ram through parliament in December 1996 a series of laws that would have given it significantly expanded rights to fire labour and reduce the workforce, along the lines of a US-style reform of sloughing off 'excess labour' and making the remaining workforce more productive. When this failed, owing to fierce street opposition from workers, many *chaebol* had no choice but to fall back on their longstanding symbiotic relationship with the government and the banks, this time to draw on ever greater amounts of funds to keep money-losing operations alive.

The relaxation of controls which had accompanied South Korea's compliance with the requirements of OECD membership and the pressures of globalisation led to massive short-term borrowing abroad by the banks and private sector to maintain their profitability by rolling over loans that could not be repaid. Abandoning state controls also resulted in excessive investment in capacity in a few industries by a number of *chaebol*, a problem which was aggravated by increasing autonomy and lack of transparency as the *chaebol* transformed themselves into transnational corporations (see chapter 1).

The domestic banking system was not able to neutralise, or even optimise, the impact of foreign capital flows by directing the funds into productive and safe lending and eventually the excess liquidity spilled over into risky and speculative investments. According to Akyüz (chapter 1), the problem is not necessarily the control and supervision of the banking system, but the absence of instruments to restrict capital inflows to control their impact on the macro economy. As he points out, 'these instruments are usually discarded with the adoption of liberalisation designed to remove "financial repression".'

By October 1997, it was estimated that non-performing loans by Korean enterprises had escalated to over US$50 billion. As this surfaced, foreign banks, which already had about US$200 billion worth of investments and loans in Korea, became reluctant to release new funds to Seoul. By late November 1997, Korea, saddled with having to repay some US$66 billion out of a total foreign debt of US$120 billion within one year, joined Thailand and Indonesia in the queue for an IMF bail-out.

Washington to Seoul, Direct

The IMF wasted no time in responding to Seoul's call for assistance. A team of economists was promptly dispatched with instructions to negotiate the terms of a Mexico-style bail-out to restore 'economic health and stability' (Chossudovsky 1998). An important precedent was being set: for the first time an advanced industrial country would be subjected to the tough IMF conditions usually reserved for developing countries. According to Michel Chossudovsky of the University of Ottawa, the bail-out conditions had been agreed by the US Treasury, the US Chamber of Commerce, Wall Street bankers and key European banks even before the team stepped on the plane. According to one knowledgeable Korean source, the US Chamber of Commerce actually wrote a significant part of the final agreement.[4]

The IMF mission wrapped up the deal on 3 December 1997. In just one week, they had cobbled together US$57 billion in stand-by credits, comprising US$21 billion from the IMF, US$10 billion from the World Bank, US$4 billion from the Asian Development Bank and a total of US$20 billion from leading industrial countries, including US$10 billion from Japan and US$5 billion from the US. For the first time, several European countries promised credit to an Asian country in trouble, signalling the global nature of the crisis (see Table 5.1). In return, the Korean government agreed to a long list of economic, institutional, labour and industrial reforms meant to revive the gasping economy.

But what a week it was: the stock market and currency continued to tumble and twice the Korean finance minister announced that the deal was struck, only to see it unravel. Newspapers reported that the IMF negotiators were nervous about dealing with an advanced economy with notoriously tough negotiators. They were also blamed for the delays, apparently agreeing to terms that had not been approved by their boss Michel Camdessus who, in turn, was under strict instructions from the Fund's most powerful member, the US, to strike a tough deal with Seoul (Burton 1997a). Meanwhile, Korea's foreign currency reserves were dwindling and the government was faced with the prospect of default unless a deal was reached quickly. Korea's negotiating position weakened with each passing day.

What's in the IMF Package?

The IMF nimbly invented a new kind of loan, the 'Supplemental Reserve Facility' to enable it to bypass its normal ruling that financial packages are not allowed to

Table 5.1
Approximate Contributions to IMF Loans (US$ billion)

Source	Indonesia	Thailand	South Korea
International Monetary Fund	10.0	4.0	21.00
Asian Development Bank	3.5	1.2	4.00
World Bank	4.5	1.5	10.00
Australia	1.0	1.0	1.00
Canada			1.25
France			1.25
Germany			1.25
Great Britain			1.25
Italy			
Japan	5.0	4.0	10.00
Singapore	5.0	1.0	
United States	6.0		5.00
South Korea		0.5	
Indonesia	5.0	0.5	
Brunei		0.5	
Hong Kong		1.0	
Malaysia	1.0	1.0	
China		1.0	
TOTAL*	41.0	17.2	57.00

Note: * The figures on the total IMF loan and credit packages vary, and accurate figures for individual countries were not readily available.

exceed five times the recipient country's IMF quota. Its US$21 billion contribution to the South Korea 'rescue package'[5] exceeds the previous record loan of US$17.8 billion to Mexico in early 1995, and is more than 20 times the quota available to South Korea. The deal ensured that South Korea would avoid default on the estimated US$66 billion of the total US$120 billion foreign debt (Japan Economic Institute 1997) which was short term. Sighs of relief were no doubt heard in the board rooms of Japanese banks which had lent US$23.4 billion to South Korea and were in no position to handle defaults given the precarious state of their own banking system.[6] European lenders were also exposed in South Korea — Germany's total lending to Malaysia, South Korea, Indonesia, Philippines, Taiwan and Thailand is greater than that of the US (Congressional Report 1997).

Like all IMF agreements, the details are sketchy, but published information reveals an interesting mix of the traditional IMF formula of fiscal and monetary tightening, combined with some nods to the special interests of foreign bankers and business, such as labour market reform, further opening the financial sector to US banks and fund managers, opening product markets to Japanese goods and clearing the way for majority foreign ownership of Korean companies. According to the publicly available IMF document, the objective of the programme is to 'narrow the external current account deficit to below 1 per cent of GDP in 1998 and 1999, contain inflation at or below 5 per cent, and — hoping for an early return of confidence — limit the deceleration in real growth to about 3 per cent in 1998 followed by a recovery toward the potential in 1999'.[7]

The key elements of the arrangement were:

- tightening monetary policy to 'restore and sustain calm in the markets';
- raising interest rates from 12.5 per cent to 21 per cent to reign in liquidity (interest rates rose to 32 per cent in December);
- controlling money supply to contain inflation at or below 5 per cent;
- floating the exchange rate with minimal interventions;
- maintaining a balanced or slight surplus budget (including the interest costs of financial sector restructuring);
- increasing the VAT and expanding corporate and income tax bases.

In addition to these fiscal and monetary policies, the agreement includes a long list of institutional reforms, including establishing an independent central bank (effectively severing the feed line between the government and the *chaebol*), closing 'troubled' financial institutions, imposing Bank of International Settlements (BIS) debt/equity ratios, and accelerating the approval of foreign entry into the domestic financial sector, including allowing foreign banks to establish subsidiaries. Other key structural reforms include trade liberalisation, capital account liberalisation, reviewing corporate governance and structure, and labour market reform.

Less than a month after the initial agreement, following three weeks of market and currency turmoil fuelled by concerns that the IMF programme would not solve the economic problems and that the government would be unable to meet its short-term debt obligations of US$16.3 billion (with only US$10 billion in foreign reserves), Korea received an emergency injection of US$10 billion to forestall default. Although critics noted that the IMF was too slow in disbursing funds, this was partly because the US in particular was keen to extract additional concessions from South Korea in return for the first tranche of cash.

After the objective was successfully achieved by the IMF and the US, the first instalment of cash was presented as a 'Christmas gift' — provided the government agreed to speed up economic reforms by:

- closing ailing merchant banks and reducing risky assets to make them more attractive for foreign takeover;

- opening the bond market by the end of 1997;
- liberalising interest rates;
- opening domestic markets to cars and other key Japanese industrial goods by mid-1999;
- allowing foreign banks and financial institutions to set up wholly-owned branches ahead of schedule (*The Nation*, 26/12/97).

Far from sharing seasonal goodwill, it seemed that the creditors were using their considerable muscle to squeeze concessions from the down-and-out Korean government, even ones unrelated to the facts of the economic crisis. Criticism of the IMF programme for South Korea has been harsh, prompt and from all directions. Even before the deal was done, an editorial in the *Financial Times* of 27 November said: 'both the government and the IMF must exercise care. Korea faces a private sector financial crisis, not the sort of government-inspired payments problem to which the IMF is traditionally used. Its current account deficit is low and falling, and there is a history of balanced budgets. Stringent fiscal restraint would compound the impact of private sector adjustment. The government can afford to borrow to finance its banks rescue. Insisting on tax increases and spending cuts to meet the cost would smack of overkill.'

Yet, that is precisely what the IMF prescribed: fiscal restraint, tax increases, spending cuts, monetary tightening and more financial liberalisation. Harvard's Institute for International Development director Jeffrey D. Sachs was scathing in his attack on the IMF, accusing the Fund of secrecy, noting that the 'IMF insisted that all presidential candidates immediately "endorse" an agreement they had no part in drafting — and no time to understand.' Outlining the contradictions between the prescriptions and the desired outcome to, in the IMF's own words, 'limit the deceleration in real GDP growth... followed by a recovery toward potential in 1999', Sachs wrote: 'The won has depreciated by about 80 per cent in the past 12 months, from around 840 to the dollar to a (then) record low of 1,565 yesterday (10 December 1997). This currency depreciation will force up the price of traded goods. Yet, despite that the IMF insists that Korea aim for essentially unchanged inflation rates... to achieve unchanged low inflation in the face of huge currency depreciation Korea will need a monetary squeeze. And this is indeed what the Fund has ordered. Short-term interest rates jumped from 12.5 to 21 per cent on the signing of the agreement, and have since risen further' (Sachs 1997b).

These elements together make for a rapidly contracting economy through a surprisingly simple chain reaction: money is in short supply, credit is expensive, companies can't afford credit, companies collapse, people lose their jobs, consumer demand declines and so on. In addition, the troubled financial institutions in their rush to meet BIS debt/equity ratios closed their lending services, refused to rollover existing loans and shored up their reserves in an attempt to push down the ratios. The panic that ensued — as local enterprises (even profitable ones) found their credit drying up and overseas creditors faced the prospect of defaults and a rapid contraction of the economy — did nothing to 'restore and sustain calm in the markets'.

In fact, the IMF's efforts were equivalent to fanning the flames and in the days following the signing of the agreement, almost before the ink was dry, the won tumbled even further. Jeffrey Sachs (1997b) called the IMF's response 'overkill' which made no sense for an economy that 'was (rightly) judged to be pursuing sound macroeconomic policies just months earlier.' He went on to suggest that the IMF could have tried a more behind-closed-doors approach, encouraging Japan, the US and Europe to provide credit to the Bank of Korea and rollover short-term debts. On the other hand, it does seem that the government in Korea was less than forthcoming in their information disclosure, hugely overstating foreign currency reserves when, in fact, they were close to the bottom of the barrel.

Crushing the Chaebol

One of the clear objectives of the IMF package is to dismantle the *chaebol* — the huge family-run conglomerates which have spearheaded Korea's fabulous growth and increasing global presence through household names such as Daewoo, Hyundai and Samsung. As a result of the expansionary policies described above, the *chaebol* are also responsible for the vast majority of Korea's debt. While unpopular with both the public and workers, dismantling the *chaebol per se* is not necessarily the correct solution, especially when the side effects are likely to be massive lay-offs and declining productivity — at least in the short term.

In South Korea, the labour market reforms have created the greatest anti-government backlash. Recalling the protracted battle of 1996 against government legislation to introduce a bill allowing for the sacking of workers (supposedly to increase efficiency), it is possible that this particular clause was introduced with the agreement of both government and the *chaebol* as a way of pushing through unpopular reforms that had been previously tossed out by the parliament and to make the acquisition of Korean firms more tempting for foreign investors. The Korean Confederation of Trade Unions (KCTU) international secretary puts it simply: 'It is the workers, not the government officials or corporate leaders responsible for our economic crisis who will have to bear the brunt of any IMF measures' (Burton 1997b). *Chaebol* officials, for their part, are also angry at the IMF's imperious approach, claiming to 'detect a conspiracy by the US and Japan to use the IMF to weaken their international competitiveness'.

Kim Dae Jung — just days before he was elected Korea's new president — accused the government of surrendering economic sovereignty in return for IMF rescue funds, saying that 'Bowing to pressure, the government opened up the capital market, leaving banks and other healthy firms helpless to foreign takeovers' (*The Nation*, 6/12/97). At the time, Kim promised to renegotiate the terms of the IMF deal if elected. Five days later, it was revealed that the IMF had requested all candidates for the upcoming election to sign a written pledge of support for the IMF package. All agreed, except for Mr Kim who replied saying that he supported the agreement 'in principle but subject to further renegotiations' (Burton 1997c).

Although Kim did not formally take office until 25 February 1998, he and his team have been the main negotiators with the IMF since his election. While he appears to have gone along with the IMF package, his initial caution reflected a strong popular reaction to the IMF deal, based on anger at the government and *chaebol* for reckless expansion which emptied the banks and created a dependency on foreign capital, the perception that economic sovereignty was being handed, on a platter, to the IMF and the US, and that workers would, at the end of the day, bear the brunt of the crisis. Martin Wolf, writing in the *Financial Times* of 16 December 1997, commented: 'The question is not only whether the IMF programme will enable the Korean authorities to ensure short-term foreign liabilities are met. It is also whether it should do so. It is important to remember that the western creditors chose to lend to the chaebol, which they have suddenly noticed are burdened by heavy debt. They chose to lend the money to banks which, they have apparently just realised, are heavily influenced by government.' Despite such criticisms, in late January 1998, US$25 billion of South Korea's short-term debt was restructured into medium-term debt after an agreement was reached with a group of commercial bank creditors in New York City, but not before the South Korean government extended a guarantee to cover US$24 billion of that amount in the case of default by the private sector debtors. Furthermore, despite this government guarantee, the interest rate terms on which the debt was restructured varied between 7 and 9 per cent while the LIBOR international lending rate was only 5.6 per cent, resulting in the very high average spread of approximately 2.5 per cent.

The fears that a rescue package which absolved foreign investors from the consequences of their poor investment decisions would merely encourage such behaviour (otherwise known as moral hazard) has been amply borne out in Korea. Saved from the brink of debtor default, and following a debt moratorium supported by the heavily exposed banks, investors are now pouring money back into the country — more than US$500 million in stocks and bonds entered in January alone and the stock market is the best performer in the world so far this year. Investors have a new spring in their step having achieved labour reforms, effectively dismantled the *chaebol* and gained the radical market and investment openings they have desired for so long.

Yet, the recovery remains extremely fragile and further financial liberalisation runs the risk of turning the South Korean economy into one which exchanges its earlier reliance on domestic savings for a new found addiction to foreign capital, especially portfolio and other short-term capital flows. This is likely to create another crisis, similar to the Thai one, in the near future, a scenario that is already being discussed by some Korean and foreign commentators and economists.

Social Impact of the Crisis

The social impact of the economic crisis and of the measures adopted under IMF pressure is evident in all three countries covered by this case study, although much of the information is anecdotal and inferential at this early stage. Many commentators believe that the main impact of the crisis, in the shape of rising unemployment and poverty, will not be felt until late 1998 in South Korea and Thailand, while few observers are willing to predict when Indonesia will hit rock bottom. Most expect a minimum of several years of economic and social turmoil before any upturn occurs.

While it is extremely difficult to disaggregate the respective social impacts of the original crisis and the IMF-led response to it, it is generally agreed that IMF directives to raise interest rates, raise taxes and cut public expenditure deepened the economic contractions in both Thailand and Korea, although the Fund argues that this was necessary to control inflation and stabilise the currencies. In Indonesia, where the Suharto government has failed to implement many of the promises made to the IMF in two agreements in October 1997 and January 1998, the specific impact of IMF-approved measures is still to be seen. In Thailand and Indonesia, where there is a very large informal and transient workforce, meaningful statistics will be difficult to collect. However, it is likely that this group, in particular, will be badly hit because there is no effective social safety net, and they are generally unskilled and often landless, with few resources or means to seek alternative employment. The situation in Korea is different, given the much higher level of education and employment in the formal sector. Nonetheless, the immediate impact of the currency devaluation, economic recession and the longer-term impacts of the structural reforms prescribed by the IMF are bound to be significant.

Thailand

In the late 1960s, 57 per cent of the Thai population lived below the poverty line. Prior to the crisis, that figure was down to about 13 per cent (World Bank 1997b). Despite tremendous economic growth in the intervening years, around 8 million Thais were still living on less than US$2 a day: they did not benefit from the boom and will now be among the first to suffer from the bust. Almost all sectors of the economy have been effected by the rapid slowdown, the rising cost of imports, the high price of credit, failing businesses and cuts in government expenditure.

Conservatively, unemployment at the end of 1997 was 1.4 million and is expected to rise to 2 million in the first half of 1998, however others estimated that the actual end-of-1997 figure could be as high as 2.9 million out of a workforce of 29 million (*Bangkok Post*, 1/9/97). At the top of the casualty list were the 15,000 employees of the 58 financial firms that had been shut down by the authorities at the urging of the Fund (*Bangkok Post*, 7/12/97). Analysts say up to 200,000 finance employees could be jobless after the restructuring of the sector (Prangtip 1997). Thai Ministry of Labour officials reported at a recent seminar at Bangkok's Rangsit University that 62,000 workers had lost their jobs as a direct result of the economic crisis. However, this figure is bound to be low as it is based only upon companies' monthly reports to the Ministry of Social Welfare on the number of workers laid off, and does not include people working in the informal sector or unofficially (Interview, 13/3/98).

The fallout from the bursting of the bubble economy appeared to be hitting the real economy faster than people anticipated. In the last half of 1997, work on most construction projects ground to a halt in Bangkok, leaving the city with ugly half-finished tower blocks and disgorging thousands of workers onto a contracting economy. An average of five migrants had returned to each of the country's 60,000 villages by December, according to non-governmental organisation (NGO) estimates.[8]

The swarming back into the rural economy was corroborated by, among others, a social researcher in Pichit, a province three hours from Bangkok by bus, who found that considerable numbers of construction workers appeared to be joining the rural workforce. 'To my surprise, I was talking to field labourers that had been recently laid off from construction jobs in Bangkok. They were dispirited and they were hungry' (Interview, 12/1/98).

In a survey of unemployed people in the province of Nan in the far north of the country, the same researcher found that 'about 80 per cent of those interviewed had returned since December (1997) because of the economic crisis' (Interview, 20/2/98).

These findings were in line with data gathered by others. For instance, in the village of Sap Poo Pan in the Northeast — the region that produces the greatest number of internal migrants — World Bank researchers found that out of a total village population of 260, 40 out of the 110 people working outside the village had already returned by late January 1998 (World Bank 1998).

In September 1997 then Finance Minister Thanong Bidaya predicted that about 1 million Thais would lose their jobs in the coming recession. That was an underestimate, according to other sources, which said that 2.9 million out of the country's workforce of 29 million were expected to be unemployed by the end of 1997 (*Bangkok Post*, 1/9/97). Government figures showed that by February, 80,000 workers had been laid off since mid-1997, and this figure, said labour expert Dr Nikhom Chandravithun, must be added to the 2 million unemployed that year owing to causes other than the financial crisis (Interview, 20/2/98).

The explosiveness of the economic contraction was underlined for both Thais and the world at large by what amounted to a mini-uprising by workers at the Thai Summit Auto Parts Factory on 21 January 1998. The protesters blocked the busy Bangna-trat Highway in protest against the company's announcement that it would not give them long-promised bonuses on which they had counted to make ends meet. There followed several hours of pitched battles that pitted workers against police and angry motorists, ending with the wholesale arrest of 54 workers who were herded in prisoner-of-war fashion into police vans. To both the Thais and the international community, the television images of the event were more reminiscent of Korea than Thailand and came across as a harbinger of things to come.

The construction sector, which previously employed up to 1.5 million workers, has been dramatically hit, affecting not only the construction workers themselves, but also the other industries which feed off real estate and property. In January 1998, the Thai government announced its intention to repatriate the estimated 600,000 foreign workers, mostly Burmese, working in low-paid fishing, agriculture and construction jobs to make way for Thai workers displaced from urban-industrial jobs. The government deadline is June 1998, after which the migrant workers' permits will not be renewed. Dramatically, in February (and in front of CNN cameras!) the Thai military forced 100 Burmese men, women and children to make the three hour walk from the provincial town of Karnchanaburi to the Burma border. Whether it will be possible for the government to repatriate migrant workers, and whether indeed Thai workers would be prepared to do the same work for such pitiful pay, remains open to question. There is a decidedly blurred dividing line between those who leave Burma to escape the regime or those who are fleeing poverty. Some end up as refugees, others as migrant workers but all find life back in Burma unbearable.

There is no reliable estimate of the number of construction workers who have been thrown out of work. In addition to the migrant and illegal workers, many construction workers are seasonal, moving to the cities for work during the dry season. During the boom years, more than 6 million rural workers migrated to Bangkok and many are now returning, creating several problems: not only does the family lose the income which was previously sent home but there is an extra person to support. On the other hand, some reports say that people are much happier to be back in their villages, and for those with land there is still a means to make a living. In fact, Thai policymakers are now placing their faith in a resurgence of the rural economy to pull Thailand out of the economic doldrums, mop up hundreds of thousands of unemployed factory and construction workers, and to maintain social stability (Satya 1997).

Although agriculture accounts for less that 20 per cent of the value of Thai exports, more than 50 per cent of the workforce is employed in the agriculture sector. But as Chulalongkorn University economist and labour expert Voravidh Charoenlert comments: 'As in the past, the Thai countryside will absorb surplus labour arising due to industrial recession. But it will leave the villagers much poorer in the long run, as there will be more people sharing the same resources' (Satya 1997). Although Thai agricultural exports should become more competitive due to the devaluation, by the end of March the improved balance of trade was almost entirely due to a drop in imports. A chronic liquidity crisis is slowing down the agricultural sector, which is still heavily dependent on imported inputs. Nonetheless, exports of Thai rice are expected to be the highest for years due to the shortages in countries such as Indonesia, China and Malaysia, which have been affected by El Niño-related droughts. Unfortunately, the high world demand for rice is also pushing up the price in Thailand, increasing the cost of living for the poor, especially in urban areas where food costs are highest.

Budget Cuts Cut Deep

The IMF's insistence on a budget surplus (later revised down to a 1-2 per cent deficit) has cut deep (see Table 5.2), slashing all areas of public sector spending, including health, education, agriculture, industry and labour, and welfare — key government activities especially in times of recession, social dislocation and rising unemployment. The Foundation for Children's Development (1998) surveyed 143 secondary-school-age scholarship recipients from five rural provinces, whose parents were seasonal factory or construction workers. Most were landless and therefore completely dependent on wages. On average, the workers sent home between 1,000 and 3,000 baht per month which covered household expenses, clothes, education, farm inputs and medical expenses. The survey showed that of the 143 students, ten had a family member who had been laid off, 11 had a family member with reduced income and 19 were out of work because the firm they worked for went out of business. The impact on the children was immediate. Bus fares had doubled from 3 to 6 baht and a bowl of noodles had increased from 5 to 7 baht — taking minimum daily expenses from 8 to 13 baht — yet there was less money coming into the family. At the same time, as part of the IMF-imposed budget austerity measures, milk and school lunch subsidies had been cut by between 40 and 50 per cent (Foundation for Children's Development 1998).

The situation for those who have permanently settled in the urban slums of Bangkok is more desperate. These families have no land to return to, and their connection to rural life is tentative or broken. According to anecdotal reports there is an increase in drug use, and in drug sales, evidenced by falling prices as more people turn to selling amphetamines to make money. It is also likely that more women and girls are turning to the sex industry for work.

Table 5.2
Thailand National Budget, January-December 1998 (million baht)

Programme	Projected budget	Actual budget	% cut
Central funds	82,051.6	76,590.0	-6.7
PM's office	7,993.7	6,588.3	-17.6
Defence	105,238.4	80,998.6	-23.0
Finance	44,797.9	42,753.0	-4.6
Foreign Affairs	4,131.9	3,503.2	-15.2
Agriculture	80,864.7	62,580.5	-22.6
Transportation	102,108.1	67,786.4	-33.6
Commerce	4,364.6	3,746.8	-14.2
Interior	178,540.3	132,710.2	-25.7
Labour and Welfare	11,155.2	9,437.2	-15.4
Justice	5,962.5	5,269.1	-11.6
Science and Technology	16,595.7	10,945.6	-34.0
Education	166,308.9	148,577.2	-10.7
Public Health	70,145.5	59,920.9	-14.6
Industries	5,461.7	4,057.3	-25.7
University Affairs	39,337.4	32,900.9	-16.4
Others	5,035.5	4,686.3	-6.9
Government Enterprises	29,660.6	26,932.5	-9.2
Revolving Funds	22,246.0	20,016.0	-10.0
Total	982,000.0	800,000.0	-18.5

Source: *Thai Post*, 26 November 1997.

The overall impression, therefore, is of thousands of families who have lost their livelihood, or whose income has been dramatically reduced, along with an increase in the cost of living due to price hikes in food, fuel and basic services. Rice has doubled in price, from 25 to 50 baht per kilo, mainly due to the global shortage of rice which has pushed up export prices and which has a knock-on effect on domestic prices. The majority of farming households in Thailand are net purchasers of rice, so even landed households will feel the impact of the price rise. In addition, the last rainy season in Thailand was very poor, leaving major irrigation dams only one-third full, and lowering overall rice production. The full impact of the economic crisis and the drought will really only start to be seen in September and October 1998, when families have exhausted their own supplies and have to start buying expensive rice to tide them over to the next harvest. According to the UN's Economic and Social Commission for Asia and the Pacific (ESCAP) (1996), the incidence of poverty increases by 1 per cent for every 10 per cent increase in the price of rice. Conservatively, according to these figures, the number of people living in absolute poverty should increase by at least 5 per cent solely due to the rice factor, without even considering rising unemployment, lower wages and fewer government services.

World Bank to Ease the Pain

Five months after the signing of the IMF agreement, the World Bank sent a team to Thailand to investigate the social impact of the crisis and to identify areas for World Bank involvement. The Bank plans to deal with the social implications of the crisis by establishing the Social Investment Fund, a US$300 million programme to be disbursed partly through the government and the rest directly to communities through the Government Savings Bank. The loans, which attract interest rates of between 7 and 8 per cent, will be used to support existing government programmes which have been affected by budget cuts, such as infrastructure, health, environment and education or projects identified by communities or local municipalities. Communities will receive Investment Funds in the form of a grant, with the government assuming the responsibility of repayments.

The irony of the Social Investment Fund is that it will be used to soften the impact of the savage budget cuts forced by IMF conditions. On the other hand, local and provincial politics in Thailand are riddled with corruption and vested interests, so it is possible that making funds available directly to communities for projects they have identified could redress some of the development imbalances of the past. Forum of the Poor, a mass organisation of farmers' groups from the poorest regions in Thailand, has been sharply critical of the IMF-imposed austerity measures and the socialisation of private debt. But they also see the crisis as an opportunity to go 'back to the village' and slow the seemingly irreversible pattern of urbanisation and industrialisation, bridging the gap between urban and rural populations and re-establishing the traditional values associated with village and agricultural life.

However, there is a concern that the promises made by the Chavalit government last year, as a result of the Forum's three-month 'sit-in' outside the Government House, will not be followed through because of budget constraints. In particular, the government made a commitment to support an innovative national agriculture programme for poor and landless farming families by setting aside 25 million rai (10 million acres) of land for sustainable agriculture (as opposed to export agriculture), providing land, training and other inputs. It is estimated that this could support up to 8 million people, about the same number currently living below the poverty line on between US$1 and US$2 a day. Although there is an urgent need to expand employment opportunities in the rural areas and to redress the damage of more than 20 years of breakneck industrialisation, it seems likely that budget constraints resulting from the austerity programme will make it impossible for the government to address this problem.

Indonesia

Of the three countries included in this study, Indonesia has been worst hit to date, battered by economic and political crises which have become mutually reinforcing, producing a downward spiral of instability, rising poverty and unrest, and government inaction with no end in sight. The social impact of the crisis in Indonesia has been immediate and dramatic, bringing to light underlying social tensions which had previously been obscured by relative economic stability.

Unemployment and lay-off estimates for Indonesia vary wildly, and should be treated with caution. One news report suggested that 6.6 million have lost their jobs since the onset of the crisis, while the official government figure puts it at 2.5 million. An Indonesian labour rights organisation estimates 4 million lay-offs between July 1997 and February 1998, and of a sample of 28,000 workers in 48 factories working with one organisation, 10 per cent had lost their jobs by the end of January. These figures are for jobs lost, and do not include those already unemployed at the start of the crisis, or the roughly 2.5 million new entrants who enter the labour force every year (Green 1998). In early 1998, the Indonesian Muslim Intellectuals Association (ICMI) put overall unemployment at 12 million.[9]

Those still in work complain of a freeze on overtime, leaving them to survive on the Jakarta region's minimum wage of Rp5,700 a day, which has not changed since April 1997. Many more have been sent home from idle factories on a minimum wage, or even less. At current rates, the minimum wage is worth about 63 US cents (40 pence) a day. In dollar terms, this makes Indonesia perhaps the cheapest labour force in the world, although any export boom is likely to be held back by the liquidity crisis in the banking sector and investor nervousness about the ongoing social and political instability.

Prices of basic commodities, such as rice, cooking oil and sugar have increased by 20-100 per cent and gasoline prices are due to rise by 25 per cent if the government follows the IMF directive to lift fuel subsidies on 1 April 1998. Fuel price hikes will have an immediate knock-on effect on food prices, leading to generalised fear of deepening social unrest (Green 1998). In dollar terms, per capita GDP has dropped from US$1,000 to US$230, while year on year inflation for February 1998 was estimated at 32 per cent, well above the IMF-prescribed 20 per cent. Inflation for February alone was 12.7 per cent and the economy is expected to shrink by 2-3 per cent in 1998. The World Bank claims that prior to the crisis, the proportion of the population living below the poverty line had fallen from 60 per cent in 1970 to 11 per cent in 1996 (although others say that the poverty line was lowered to make the statistics more favourable).[10] Since the onset of the crisis, this process has gone into reverse. Local experts are currently reassessing the poverty figures, and are predicting that as many as 30-40 per cent of the population could have fallen below the poverty line by the end of 1998.[11] All this in the country previously held up by the World Bank and the IMF as a paragon of development success.

Shortages Hit the Poorest

Fears of food shortages have proved self-fulfilling, triggering hoarding and speculation, disrupting food supplies and causing shortages. Inevitably, it is the poor who are worst hit as they do not have the cash to buy in bulk when the prices are low, and pay a much higher price to meet their day to day needs. Imported powdered milk has trebled in price since the onset of the crisis. Poor families are being forced to feed their infants sweetened tea rather than milk (Green 1998). The poultry business, an important source of protein, is collapsing as it is heavily dependent on imported feed and medicines which are now completely unaffordable.

Indonesia's problems have been intensified by a 10-12 million metric tonne shortfall in rice due to the El Niño-related drought. Rice prices have doubled in Jakarta since July 1997. Although food shortages could be supplemented by imports, the cost is prohibitive and in any case foreign exporters are refusing to accept letters of credit issued by Indonesian banks, leaving the wheels of trade to grind to a standstill (Japan Economic Institute 1998). Frustration and anger have been directed at the largely Christian Chinese minority. In many towns and villages, the Chinese are the merchants and shopkeepers and are therefore blamed for rising prices and shortages. However reliable sources say the military has deliberately fuelled anti-Chinese sentiments to steer attention away from the government's own failings (Human Rights Watch 1998). In around 30 riots to date, five people have been killed and hundreds of shops, homes and churches destroyed, but the Chinese minority fears that much worse is to come (Green 1998).

The rocketing prices of all imported goods have hit all sectors of the economy and services.[12] Medical supplies and equipment have become prohibitively expensive. About half of the 120-plus health clinics in one part of Greater Jakarta are reported to have closed due to rising prices and fears that patients will sue them for not providing proper services. Seventy per cent of medical drugs are imported and a government source claims that there are only enough medical supplies for four months, while the price of generic drugs, locally produced and partly subsidised by the government, will rise dramatically owing to the increased price of imported chemicals. There is also a shortage of contraceptives. The poor will be hardest hit by this. Hospitals in the rural areas have gone 'back to the basics' using cat-gut for suturing, and re-using all medical equipment. World

Health Organisation officials have expressed fears that the crisis will lead to rising levels of diseases such as measles and tuberculosis (*Associated Press*, 8/3/98).

Food production dropped by 4 per cent in 1997, and for the first time in many years Indonesia started to import rice (Yamin 1998b). All Indonesia's wheat is imported, as is 30 per cent of its sugar and soybeans — both staples. Paper prices have risen four to five-fold, leading some journals to cease operations altogether and others to increase prices, reduce staff and cut pages. There is also a dramatic loss in advertising revenue, leading to an overall reduction in public access to information, vital when the country is going through such deep turmoil.

In a short-term effort to increase export revenues, the government reduced the log tariff from 200 to 10 per cent, leading to increased exploitation of forest timber, rising exports of unprocessed logs and the end of the domestic plywood industry.[13] The World Bank has also weighed into the situation in Indonesia, with a package of up to US$100 million to soften the blow of the crisis by creating '75 million man-days of low-wage jobs during the remainder of 1998'. However, this is just a small part of the Bank's overall plans 'to disburse US$4.5 billion over the next three years for adjustment operations and existing and planned investment loans'.[14]

Critics were unimpressed, pointing to the Bank and the IMF's past record of papering over deep flaws in the economy, and continually boosting Indonesia as a model of development (Yamin 1998a). 'The World Bank tended always to please the government by saying nice things about the Indonesian economy. These judgements then prompted foreign fund managers and donors to pour in loans, most of which were short term', said Rizal Ramli, head of the think tank Econit.

Others who met Bank President James Wolfensohn accused it of ignoring problems of corruption, nepotism and a weak banking system when it heaped praises on Indonesia and continued to lend to the government. The Bank's endorsement discouraged reforms in dismantling monopolies and aided the country's borrowing binge, they said. On 10 March 1998, the World Bank and Asian Development Bank underlined the strings attached to the programme when they announced their decision to delay US$2.5 billion in aid until the Indonesian government met the IMF's reform criteria. This followed hard on the heels of the IMF's decision to delay disbursements of US$3 billion for the same reasons (*Jakarta Post*, 11/3/98).

Indonesia's problems are just beginning. Predictions are almost uniformly pessimistic. One leader of the Nadhatul Ulama (NU), the largest Muslim mass organisation said, 'If the IMF and other governments care for the people, we have hope. If not, unemployment will rise and the people will go hungry and be easy to burn — social unrest, riots and so on. And government must be honest — if corruption continues as it is now, we will see an explosion. We are worried' (Green 1998). It will take more than dismantling the monopolies to restore domestic confidence and stability.

South Korea

The psychological impact of the crisis in Korea was one of shock, followed by an outburst of nationalistic anger. However, the impact was real enough in terms of absolute loss of purchasing power, thousands of small companies going to the wall and a radical transformation in relations between workers and employers. One of the key IMF conditions was 'labour market reform' which would allow companies to lay-off workers. Clearly, this was an overhanging issue from the failed attempt in January 1996 to pass radical legislation which would have dramatically increased employers' rights over workers. Such was the protest that the legislation was quickly withdrawn, only to reappear as part of the IMF reforms.

Unemployment will be the main fallout from the economic crisis, and there is no doubt that job loss and business closure were accelerated by IMF measures which caused a gut-wrenching contraction of the economy. It is estimated that the combined effects of the economic slowdown and industrial rationalisation could dramatically increase (double or triple) the present rate of unemployment, from about 3 per cent in 1997 to a minimum of 6-7 per cent in 1998 (signifying a minimum of 1 million new unemployed). Many observers fear that the actual figure could exceed 2 million by the end of 1998 or about 9 per cent of the workforce. This will require a great deal of psychological and social re-adjustment in a country which has built itself on toil and become accustomed to full employment. Labour research institutes report that women are the first to be laid off, and women with children are likely to be dismissed first because, in the eyes of employers, 'they are needed at home' (Ahn Mi Young 1998).

According to the KCTU (1998), an estimated 200 companies per day have shut their doors since the beginning of the crisis, reaching a peak of 340 on 5 January 1998. This translates into about 4,000 more employees finding themselves on the street every day. The KCTU's international secretary also points out that, while the big conglomerates or *chaebol* have enough 'fat' to see them through the tough times, small to medium enterprises which rely on cash flows and which also employ the majority of workers, are the hardest hit.

On 6 February 1998 a tripartite agreement was reached between government, employers and unions to legalise layoffs through legislation by the National Assembly, paving the way for mass unemployment for the first time. Many workers in South Korea have come to recognise the IMF not as a source of economic relief, but as the driving force behind rising unemployment and job insecurity. In protests and demonstrations, the IMF is often referred to as 'I am Fired'. Under the 6 February agreement, companies will be allowed to lay-off workers only when they face 'emergency situations' such as financial trouble, mergers or acquisitions, but it is widely agreed that this will be left to the sub-jective interpretation of employers, especially in these difficult times. Management is required to give 60 days notice before dismissing workers, however, and employers will be obliged to try to re-hire dismissed workers if business improves, although this is unlikely to be enforceable in practice.

In return for this major concession, trade unions were given the right to engage in political activity for the first time, as from early 1998. Teachers will also be allowed to unionise, again for the first time, from July 1999 and public officials allowed to form a 'consultative body' from early 1999. The employment stability fund, consisting of donations from government, businesses and workers, which is the only 'social safety net' for fired workers, is to be increased to 5 trillion won (US$3.2 billion), an increase from an earlier government proposal of 4.4 trillion won (US$2.8 billion). The effectiveness of the accord, which was signed by the most vocal opposition union coalition, the KCTU, was thrown into some doubt within days of its signature when the union's leadership was ousted by angry members who refused to abide by the agreement. Some members of the National Assembly also cast doubt on its smooth passage through parliament by insisting that the concessions given to labour were too great and were unacceptable in their agreed form.

In early February, a special committee in charge of streamlining the government bureaucracy unveiled plans to reduce the 163,000 strong civil service by 10,000, although the final toll is expected to be higher. At the same time, the cabinet passed 12 new bills designed to speed industry restructuring and enable corporate lay-offs. Budget cuts are unprecedented in the last 25 years, although in Korea they were nowhere near as severe as Thailand's slashing. The budget measures announced in early February included cuts in expenditure on social infrastructure of 13.1 per cent compared with the plans submitted in late 1997, marking a 4.2 per cent decline compared with the previous year. This will put a number of high priority infrastructure projects on hold, including the Seoul–Pusan High Speed Railway, seven new regional expressways and the construction of new subway lines in the capital, in addition to delaying disbursements for the New Port Project. Significant cuts to Korea's infrastructure development could lead to a reduction in international competitiveness in the medium to long term.

The revised budget total announced involved an increase of a mere 3.3 per cent from 1997, the lowest year-to-year rise since 1973. Even the increase in the defence budget, estimated at only 1.8 per cent (15 per cent less than requested) is the lowest in 15 years. Budgets for education and agro-fishery industries were expected to be cut by 5.6 per cent and 10.4 per cent respectively while plans to increase government salaries by 3.5 per cent were abandoned. Inflation in 1998 is expected to be between 10 and 20 per cent, well over the IMF targets and predictions. The economic crisis is seen by some as an opportunity to reconsider and reform social relations and social values. The KCTU, a vehement critic of the IMF, the *chaebol* and government, believes: 'If we can deal with the chaebol system, corruption and collusion of state powers and business, and state-directed financial practices, the current crisis could be a valuable opportunity for a genuine reform and maturation of Korean politics, society and economy' (KCTU 1997).

The Role of the IMF

Following its intervention in Thailand, Indonesia and South Korea, the IMF found itself under attack from all sides. Suddenly NGOs and the progressive left, whose criticism of the IMF dates back to the Fund's stabilisation programmes of the early 1980s, found themselves in unlikely company. The criticisms came from some surprising sources, including former IMF employee and director of the Harvard Institute for International Development Jeffrey Sachs, World Bank chief economist Joseph Stiglitz, conservative journals such as *The Economist* and the *Financial Times*, Republicans and Democrats in the US Congress, and even bone-dry neo-liberals such as former US President Ronald Reagan's chief economic adviser Martin Feldstein and Milton Friedman of the Chicago School. The debates are wide ranging and call into question funda-mentals such as the efficacy and appropriateness of the Fund's economic advice, the way the Fund operates and its relationship with its key shareholder, the US.

The Fund Sometimes Gives Poor Advice

The public sector austerity measures imposed by the IMF, such as budget cuts, pushing up interest rates and raising taxes, were inappropriate for the circum-stances of a private sector debt crisis and in fact deepened and accelerated contraction of the economies they were meant to be helping. As Jeffrey Sachs said 'the currency crisis is not the result of Asian government profligacy. This is a crisis made mainly in the private, albeit under-regulated, financial markets' (Sachs 1997c).

Yet, the IMF applied policy measures designed to rein in government over-spending without addressing the real issue of private sector failure. The Fund's macroeconomic requirements were meant to stabilise currencies and restore market confidence. In Thailand, South Korea and Indonesia, the currencies continued to devalue with gathering momentum even after the IMF's intervention, indicating that their economic policies were neither addressing the real problems nor having the magic effect of restoring market and investor confidence. Of the three countries studied, South Korea is the only one to show any signs of recovery measured by investment inflows (which are still predominantly short term and speculative rather than long-term foreign direct investment) and this occurred only after the main creditor banks agreed to roll over private short-term debts with the government acting as guarantor.

The IMF also stands accused of creating the problem of 'moral hazard', whereby both creditors and debtors who make unwise investment choices are saved from the consequences of their bad decisions, thus making it more likely that they will reoffend in the future.

The Fund has also come under fire for its continued enthusiasm for freeing up capital flows. The crisis in Asia is a crisis of the private sector which engaged in excessive borrowing of easy-to-obtain foreign finance, following liberalisation of capital account regimes from the 1980s onwards. Therefore the IMF's policy response of demanding further liberalisation of the finance sector and financial flows is wrong and actually 'adds to financial vulnerability and renders these economies even more prone to future crisis' (see Chapter 4). Speaking in Helsinki on 7 January 1998, the World Bank's chief economist Joseph Stiglitz went even further, saying that 'financial markets do not do a good job of selecting the most productive recipients of funds or of monitoring the use of funds and must be controlled' (Hanlon 1998).

The Pain of Adjustment is Not Fairly Distributed

There is a double standard at work in the treatment of 'domestic' and 'foreign' interests. Domestic firms are left to the mercy of the market (for example, the IMF insisted that numerous financial institutions in Indonesia and Thailand could not be bailed out). Foreign investors, on the other hand, are given enhanced rights to ownership, the possibility to convert debt to equity in struggling Asian enterprises and the chance of picking up others at bargain basement prices, thanks to changes in foreign ownership rules included in the IMF packages.

IMF bail-outs of the private sector have also been criticised for socialising the debt, leaving the government and the taxpaying public, both in Asia and in the IMF's main contributor nations, to bear the burden of the private sector's failure.

The Fund Has Gone Beyond Its Remit, and Should be Overhauled

Critics argue that the IMF has exceeded its mandate as defined in its Articles of Agreement and has assumed the role of global economic policeman, 'forcing it into a convergence toward the reigning consensus'[15] (in this case, the so-called 'Washington consensus').

Martin Feldstein (1998), Professor of Economics at Harvard University and President of the National Bureau of Economic Research, and former adviser to US President Ronald Reagan, is sharply critical of the IMF. 'Imposing detailed economic prescriptions on legitimate governments would remain questionable even if economists were unanimous about the best way to reform the countries' economic policies. In practice, however, there are substantial disagreements about what should be done'. He goes on to say that the Fund should not use the opportunity of countries being 'down and out' to override national political processes or impose economic changes that 'however helpful they may be, are not necessary to deal with the balance-of-payments problem and are the proper responsibility of the country's own political system'. He continues 'a nation's desperate need for short-term financial help does not give the IMF the moral right to substitute its technical judgements for the outcomes of the nation's political process'.

It is worth going back to the original Articles of Agreement of the Fund to get a rough measure of whether it is achieving its objectives, even in its own terms. The purposes of the IMF are:

- to promote international monetary co-operation through a permanent institution which provides the machinery for consultation and collaboration on international monetary problems;
- to facilitate the expansion and balanced growth of trade, and to contribute thereby to the promotion and maintenance of high levels of employment and real income and to the development of productive resources of all members as primary objectives of economic policy;
- to promote exchange stability, to maintain orderly exchange arrangements among members and to avoid competitive exchange depreciation;
- to assist in the establishment of a multilateral system of payments in respect of current transaction between members and in the elimination of foreign exchange restrictions which hamper the growth of world trade;
- to give confidence to members by making the general resources of the Fund temporarily available to them under adequate safeguards, thus providing them with opportunity to correct maladjustments in their balance of payments;
- in accordance with the above to shorten the duration and lessen the degree of disequilibrium in the international balances of payments of members.[16]

In short, nothing about trade and investment liberalisation, privatisation, foreign investment or public sector austerity measures, all of which have become central to the IMF's demands in Asia. Article II, however, mentions the Fund's role in promoting 'high levels of employment and real income' — purposes which the Fund has clearly failed to achieve in South Korea, Thailand and Indonesia.

While it demands greater transparency from government and financial systems, the IMF has itself been criticised for its lack of transparency and accountability. Again, Jeffrey Sachs (1997c) goes straight to the point, 'Of course, one can't be sure what the IMF is advising, since the IMF programmes and supporting documents are hidden from public view. This secrecy itself gravely undermines confidence.'

The Fund has also been attacked for its intellectual arrogance in applying the same solution, regardless of the problem. According to Joseph Stiglitz the main problem is the belief that 'political recommendations could be administered by economists using little more than simple accounting frameworks', leading to the situation where 'economists would fly into a country, look at and attempt to verify these data, and make macroeconomic recommendations for policy reforms, all in the space of a couple of weeks' (Hanlon 1998).

Finally, there is well-founded concern about the policy and power nexus between the IMF and its major shareholder, the US. In the face of increasing resistance at home to its free-wheeling liberalisation agenda[17] the US government is having to rely even more on bodies such as the IMF and the Asia-Pacific Economic Cooperation (APEC) to push its trade objectives.

Charlene Barshefsky, in her testimony to the House Ways and Means Subcommittee, described how US interests could be furthered by the IMF, 'Many of the structural reform components of the IMF packages will contribute directly to improvements in the trade regimes in those countries. If effectively implemented, these programmes will complement and reinforce our trade policy goals.' To make it clear that the US would brook no competition, Barshefsky continued, 'Support for the IMF... sends the important message that America will continue to lead in the world economy.'[18]

The IMF's first deputy managing director, Stanley Fischer (1998), reinforced this view in a speech when he outlined the primary purpose of the IMF, quoting from its articles of agreement: 'To facilitate... the balanced growth of international trade and to contribute thereby to... high levels of growth and real income' and then added his own words, 'we have consistently promoted trade liberalisation.' There is a seamless congruence between the IMF's world view and that of its biggest shareholder, the US.

The US was also responsible for derailing Japan's proposal, early on in the crisis, to establish an Asian Monetary Fund (AMF) capitalised at US$100 billion and designed to respond quickly to currency and market instability in the region. Japan had good reasons for putting its money on the table: Japanese banks are heavily exposed to Thailand, South Korea and Indonesia and it is in their interests to stabilise volatile currency markets and the Japanese economy is deeply integrated with its neighbours so any slowdown or collapse would have an immediate domestic impact. For some time Japan has promoted an Asia-specific development model in its dealings with international institutions such as the IMF and World Bank. Essentially, Japan has argued that the 'Washington consensus' of rapid deregulation, reducing the role of the state and liberalisation of capital flows may not be the best path for countries such as those in Asia which have followed a state-led development model, and that severing the links between the state and industry of the one hand, and the banks on the other would be politically unpalatable and may not achieve the expected results.

In short, the AMF was conceived as being more flexible, less doctrinaire and 'more Asian' than the IMF deal. It seemed like a good idea if for no other reason than to break the IMF monopoly on economic thought and open the market to new ideas and economic paradigms. In the event, Japan was forced to back down in the face of 'heated opposition from officials at the Department of the Treasury, most notably the Deputy Secretary Lawrence Summers, and the International

Monetary Fund.... They instead reaffirmed the central role of the IMF in the Asian financial bail-out' (Altbach 1997).

The course of the economic crisis might have been quite different had the AMF seen the light of day. The AMF might have been more flexible in its terms whereas the IMF's inflexibility deepened the economic crisis. One should not underestimate the extent to which the IMF is seen in Asia as the instrument of Western neo-liberalism and, for example, an 'Asian' approach might have proved more effective in dealing with President Suharto. The IMF is now cash-strapped and the mobilisation of additional resources is proving difficult. In fact, the US administration is facing tough Congressional opposition, from all sides, in its bid to get approval for additional funding to replenish the IMF's depleted resources. The US Treasury has mounted an all-out campaign to push the bill through Congress and, according to Treasury Secretary Robert Rubin, the stakes are high: 'Failure to provide funding could reduce our leverage in the IMF' (*FEER*, 12/2/98).

Although European shareholders control 29 per cent of the voting rights at the IMF, compared to the US vote of 18 per cent, the European Union has so far taken a back seat in the crisis.[19] However, the current role of the IMF in the Asian crisis appears to contradict stated European Union policy towards the developing world. Article 17 of the Maastricht Treaty sets out the EU's principles for development co-operation, pledging the Community to work for 'the smooth and gradual integration of the developing countries into the world economy'.[20]

This hardly accords with current IMF demands for an extremely rapid and destabilising process of financial and trade liberalisation in return for being bailed out of crises which were themselves the result of over-hasty liberalisation processes. The Maastricht Treaty commits the Union to working for 'sustainable economic and social development' and 'the campaign against poverty in the developing countries', yet IMF measures such as the impending removal of fuel subsidies in Indonesia clearly risk exacerbating poverty and destabilising the economy. Giving greater priority to poverty reduction, or at the very least, avoiding making matters worse, also improves the likelihood of the Fund achieving its stated aim of stabilising the currency and rebuilding investor confidence — food riots and crime waves do not make for economic stability.[21] After discussing the lessons of the Asian crisis at the G7 finance ministers' meeting in London in February 1998, the ministers recommended that, 'A capital account amendment to the IMF Articles should be implemented quickly.'[22] Given the record of such liberalisation in Asia, the appropriate response should be to take stock of the issue of how liberalisation should be managed in order to improve stability and growth, rather than undermine them, and to reduce poverty, rather than increase inequality. This requires discussion and consultation, not the over-hasty push to expand the remit of the IMF that is currently under way.[23]

Thailand

Even before the IMF came to Thailand, Thais themselves had been clamouring for an emergency solution to the unfolding economic crisis, and this had forced the Chavalit government to close down 16 finance companies. But it was known that more Thai finance companies were effectively bankrupt, which is why when 42 more companies were added to the list on 14 August 1997, shortly before the announcement of an IMF deal with Thailand, there was little opposition. In its financial reform policy, the IMF was able to play to the strong feelings among Thais that greedy and irresponsible politicians had brought the country to financial collapse.

Critique of the Stabilisation Package

It was the other part of the IMF package — the stabilisation package — that became the point of contention in the next few months. The Fund's prescription demanded the maintenance of high interest rates to keep further foreign capital from leaving the country and a sharp reduction in government expenditures in order for the government to achieve a budget surplus. Both were expected to combine with the financial crisis to slow down the GDP growth rate, which in August, at the time of the signing of the IMF package, was predicted to fall in 1998 to 2.5 per cent (compared with 8.7 per cent in 1995 and 6.4 per cent in 1996). This figure was revised downwards in November to 0.6 per cent. And it was further revised to (minus) -3.5 per cent at the time of the IMF review in February 1998.

The issue raised by both foreign and domestic critics was: this was not a crisis of the public sector but of the private sector, which had gone on an overborrowing binge. In fact, the Thai government had been consistently running a government surplus until 1996. So why squeeze the public sector, which as private investment slowed down had become the main element of counter-cyclical efforts to prevent a deepening recession? Wasn't the avowed aim of both Thai and IMF authorities — the return of foreign capital — in fact likely to be thwarted by a deep recession? There was no clear response to this except that foreign capital would be reassured by Thailand's willingness to undertake an austerity programme. In any event, when the projections for 1998 foresaw a deeper fall in growth than expected, the IMF agreed that it would allow the Thai government to run a deficit of 1-2 per cent of GDP, an implicit acknowledgment that its original prescription of running a budget surplus had been wrong and may have contributed in fact to a deeper slowdown by affecting business decisions on investment.

The IMF, for its part, countered that the concessions were agreed because the economy was showing signs of recovery due to the Thai government 'resolutely implementing the economic programme in very difficult circumstances', and that the actions taken were 'increasingly being reflected in improved market sentiment' (*Bangkok Post*, 6/3/98). The focus on the government surplus has raised the further question of what the surplus is actually intended for — aside from assuring investors of Thailand's willingness to take bitter medicine and thus in some miraculous way, inspire investors to re-enter the country. The likelihood is that the surplus is destined for the rescue of Thailand's ailing financial sector, on top of the repayments to the IMF and the bilateral donors for the US$17.2 billion rescue fund.

Encouraging 'Moral Hazard'

The IMF has explained that its US$17.2 billion rescue fund is meant 'for balance of payments support and to replenish government reserves'. At least part of the fund will be devoted to servicing the country's foreign debt, most of which was incurred by private borrowers from international private banks. Of course, the hope is the international banks will roll over Thailand's short-term debt, but the multi-billion dollar fund is designed to show that there is cash to back up a substantial part of the debt coming due. The government, in short, is providing a guarantee that the Thai private sector's debt will be repaid, and the IMF has guaranteed international creditors against substantial losses, which lends weight to the criticism that the IMF encourages 'moral hazard' or irresponsible lending because lenders can count on it to act as their ultimate safety net. The IMF can always come back and say that the only way to regain foreign investor confidence is by guaranteeing them against risk.

The strategy for the Thai recovery is extremely narrow — and dangerous — the Thai economy is to rely almost solely on the return of foreign capital rather than to build up a diverse platform for recovery. It is even more dangerous considering that one of the main causes of the financial crisis was the unregulated influx of finance capital and investment.

Interestingly, a fund manager of American Express International, one of the institutions being courted by this strategy, has pointed out that: 'The only card the government has to play right now is the return of foreign investors. It's disconcerting that everything rests on the return of foreign investors' (*Bangkok Post*, 21/2/98). And especially so when the IMF has predicted that Thailand will suffer a US$12-14 billion net capital outflow in 1998 (*Bangkok Post*, 6/3/98).

The IMF and the US Agenda

Some elements of the financial restructuring programme have also come under question. This is especially the case with the IMF's insistence that Thailand's financial institutions, which have suffered big losses from the combination of non-performing loans and escalating foreign debt burdens owing to the precipitous drop of the baht, be re-capitalised mainly through capital infusions from foreign partners in return for greater ownership rights. Mergers among Thai banks and institutions are one alternative, but one that has been frowned on by the Fund. Infusing the banks with state resources in return for greater state ownership is considered a non-starter, given the Fund's anti-statist leanings.

Thailand has already given ground by allowing foreigners to own up to 100 per cent of financial institutions for up to ten years without dilution, and it is also under pressure to concede to the IMF's other demands: to liberalise the Alien Business Law and to allow those foreigners who bring with them substantial investments to own land.

Increasingly, the big push for a more prominent foreign presence in the economy has convinced many Thais that the IMF is really pushing the long-standing agenda of its principal shareholder, the US, which has been to gain a stronger presence in Thailand through more liberal trade, investment and ownership rules. US officials have, in fact, been quite candid about the symbiotic relationship between IMF policy and US trade policy. US trade representative Charlene Barshefsky has admitted that: 'Thailand has made commitments to restructure public enterprises and accelerate privatisation of certain key sectors — including energy, transportation, utilities, and communications — which will enhance market-driven competition and deregulation. We expect these structural reforms to create new business opportunities for US firms' (*Bangkok Post*, 6/3/98).

Indonesia

So few of the IMF conditions have been implemented in Indonesia that it is impossible to know what effect they would have on an already critical situation. The only exception to date has been the disastrous directive to close down 16 banks which, as the Fund itself acknowledged in an internal memo: 'caus(ed) a bank panic that helped set off financial market declines in much of Asia.... These closures, far from improving public confidence in the banking system, have instead set of a renewed "flight to safety"' (Sanger 1998).

However, the war of words between Indonesia's 76-year old President Suharto, who has just entered his seventh consecutive term as its all-powerful president, and the IMF over Suharto's proposed currency board gives a useful insight into just what is at stake. With its blend of belligerence, brinkmanship, self-interest and nationalism, the currency board debate encapsulates the antagonism between President Suharto and the IMF, a power struggle of the highest order in which both sides are playing for the highest stakes.

While the Fund has found compliant partners in South Korea's Kim Dae Jung and Thailand's Chuan Leekpai, whose own liberal democratic aspirations largely fit the Fund's liberalisation agenda, Suharto is another political animal altogether.

The IMF argues that its conditions for Indonesia are designed to root out corruption (the latest passion of the IMF and the World Bank, replacing their previous fixation on Indonesia as the model of successful development) and increase market efficiency and competitiveness. In effect, though, through its explicit attacks on President Suharto's personal interests, the IMF is attempting to dismantle the patrimonial state, a state which is strong, coercive and exclusive, and which protects and promotes highly individualised vested interests in the absence of a strong bureaucracy or effective institutions.

In Indonesia, an attack on Suharto is an attack on the state, and vice versa (MacIntyre 1994). Public statements by members of Suharto's family show the extent to which personal and national interests are perceived as identical: 'if the (IMF) funds sacrifice our nation's dignity, we do not want them', explained Suharto's eldest daughter Siti Hardijanti 'Tutut' Rukmana (*AWSJ*, 11/3/98). In an increasingly nationalistic climate, Suharto is drawing the battle lines between '"liberal" economic principles not in tune with Indonesia's economy' and the '"family principle" as described in the country's 1945 Constitution.' These sentiments clearly resonate with some groups, including Iman Taufik, deputy chairman of Indonesia's chamber of commerce and industry, who called the IMF's decision to suspend the release of bail-out funds a political move. 'You have to question the move, whether it is purely the IMF's or the United States", he said. Since independence in 1945, Indonesia has generally adopted interventionist economic policies and, in spite of poor policy implementation due to nepotism, corruption, bureaucratic weaknesses and lack of capacity, there has been impressive growth in the past 30 years (Yamin 1998c).

However, institutional weaknesses and lack of accountability, combined with Indonesia's highly restrictive political framework, have led to the proliferation of rent-seeking activities, both individually and collectively, through patrimonial networks. That is, special interest groups and individuals are able to pursue their advantage directly with those in power or via those directly connected to power. The process has been supported and reinforced by foreign investors, banks and transnational corporations who have benefited from Indonesia's openness to investment, rapid growth and high profitability. As a result, Suharto's family and friends are tremendously wealthy and powerful. Any attempt by the Fund to undermine Suharto will create a dangerous political vacuum which cannot be filled because, after 32 years of authoritarian and often repressive rule, there is neither an effective bureaucracy nor a strong, well-organised opposition.

The opposition that exists, centred on NGOs and independent trade unions, has mixed views of the IMF's role, summed up in one activist's description that it is 'politically good and economically bad'. In interviews, NGO activists have identified the positive elements of the programme as better management of banking and financial sectors, pressure for transparent and clean government and the elimination of monopolies and cartels.

The negative aspects are seen as the cuts in the government's fuel subsidy and other subsidies, moves to make the labour market more flexible by reducing workers' rights and a wage freeze. Most interviewees take a short-term view that the most pressing need is to get rid of Suharto, and that the IMF could help in that. Few show interest in longer-term issues of sovereignty or whether the Anglo-Saxon development model espoused by the IMF is the best for Indonesia (Green 1998).

The possible outcomes for the Indonesian people are invidious, boiling down to little more than a choice between the devil you know and the devil you don't. Firstly, Suharto and the IMF could reach some *rapprochement*, in which case Indonesia is stuck with the Suharto regime (at least until age or infirmity forces him from power), but loses economic sovereignty, as the economy is opened up to foreign interests. This could ensure some degree of stability, but will only defer the necessary political transformation of Indonesian society. At the time of writing, such a scenario looks increasingly unlikely given the line-up of Suharto's newly-appointed cabinet, which includes golfing-buddy Mohamad 'Bob' Hasan, a prime target of the IMF reform programme, as minister of trade and industry, and Suharto's daughter Siti Hardiyanti Rukmana as minister of social affairs. This will do nothing to smooth relations between Indonesia and the IMF.

Secondly, the IMF could pull out of Indonesia. IMF withdrawal is widely expected to lead to the mass flight of capital and a slide into political and economic chaos. However, there are some indications that Indonesia has some real options apart from the IMF. A consortium of Japanese and German banks has offered to establish a stabilisation fund of between US$10 to US$15 billion dollars, which would allow cash-strapped Indonesian firms to borrow at R5,000 and repay one year later at the same rate. In addition, the Suharto family fortune, thought to be safely invested overseas, is rumoured to be as much as US$40 billion — enough for Suharto to personally bank-roll the currency board. It has even been suggested that Suharto's wealthy friends, whose interests are threatened by the IMF reforms, would be prepared to back the currency board with their personal fortunes, provided the 'IMF is shown the door'. And, as one Singapore-based banker commented, 'They may even make some profit out of it' (*AWSJ*, 11/3/98).

Third, external and internal pressures could force Suharto out, but this possibility seems to have passed with his unchallenged 'election' in March 1998 by the National Assembly to a further five year term. With the high-spending B.J. Habibie only a heart-beat from the presidency, the West may be wishing Suharto a long and healthy life.

Behind the political theatre of Suharto and the IMF, lie the profound problems of poverty, exclusion, and the lack of popular participation and economic democracy which continue to hamper Indonesia's progress. Neither Suharto nor the IMF has a solution to this wider developmental problem, and in the absence of an organised opposition or an alternative agenda, Indonesia's future may come to resemble its past.

South Korea

South Korea, more than any other country, shows the role of the IMF as an instrument of its major shareholders and main contributors to the bail-out package. In many ways, the IMF has served as a modern-day Trojan horse, bringing in a whole range of trade, security and commercial interests on the coat-tails of its 'rescue package'. This explains, perhaps, why criticism of the IMF reached its most intense in South Korea.

For more than 30 years, South Korea had been the master of its own economic destiny, an attitude which had galled the US, but filled Koreans with a nationalistic pride at having transformed themselves from pauper to prince in just one generation. Therefore, the immediate public reaction to the IMF was one of anger, rejection and insistence that this was just another back-door way for the US to prise open Korean markets. And, there is some evidence to support this theory.

In a telling testimony to the House Ways and Means Subcommittee, US trade representative Charlene Barshefsky said that: 'Policy driven rather than market-driven economic activity... meant that the US industry encountered many specific structural barriers to trade, investment and competition in Korea.'[24]

Rolling back the interventionist state and breaking the state–industry link (which was weakening of its own accord in any event) is a high priority for the US and it is perhaps no coincidence that an important part of the IMF conditions is a set of measures aimed to dismantle the *chaebol* and weaken the links between the state and industry. The specific barriers mentioned by Barshefsky include import clearance and certification, import licensing for agricultural products, and opening the financial services sector to foreigners. According to the IMF agreement, Korea has agreed to liberalise rules for import licensing and certification requirements for, amongst others, agricultural products and to open the financial sector radically to foreign ownership and foreign firms. Clearly satisfied with the outcome, Barshefsky says that the IMF package should 'improve market access in Korea and correct the over-capacity and aggressive exporting patterns of the Korean chaebols'.[25]

IMF Backs Off Conditionalities

Even after the IMF agreement was announced in early December, the Seoul stock market continued to tumble and the won collapsed even further. It seemed that the IMF magic was not working, either to restore investor confidence, calm the markets or stabilise the currency. In fact, the tight fiscal requirements of the IMF deepened the crisis by squeezing domestic credit and pushing up interest rates, turning what had thus far been a crisis of the financial sector into a crisis of the real economy. Real people with real jobs started to feel the pinch. As discussed earlier, the deteriorating situation put the government at the risk of default unless there was an immediate injection of cash, ahead of the IMF schedule. According to reliable sources,[26] the US insisted on a *quid pro quo* on several key points before they would liberate the funds. These included closing ailing merchant banks and reducing risky assets to make them more attractive for foreign takeover, opening the bond market by the end of 1997, liberalising interest rates, opening domestic markets to cars and other key Japanese industrial goods by mid-1999, and allowing foreign banks and financial institutions to set up wholly owned branches ahead of schedule (*The Nation*, 26/12/97). Thus, Korea was subjected to a second round of conditions, before they even received the money.

Security interests are never far from the surface in any discussion about South Korea. It is reliably reported[27] that when it was suggested that the government might cut the defence budget to meet IMF targets, there was a timely call from the US Pentagon suggesting that significant commercial contracts were at stake, and that it would not be a good idea to pursue that particular budget cut. Within a month of its bail-out programme, the IMF had eased some of its conditions. These included revising the inflation target upward from 5-9 per cent, allowing monetary growth to rise from 9-14 per cent, dropping its insistence on a budget surplus and extending the deadline for banks to meet BIS capital adequacy standards. This last measure in particular has caused banks to freeze all lending to meet the BIS standard (see Chapter 10).

Not only was the stabilisation package in practice *destabilising*, but the prescribed opening of the finance sector is the opposite of what is required, given that unregulated borrowing was one of the key factors in the crisis. There is no reason to believe that investors who acted incautiously in the past will be *more* responsible with *less* regulation. Further, the criticism that the IMF promotes 'moral hazard' by protecting investors against the risks of their decisions appears particularly true in Korea. Although the debtors and creditors have agreed to roll over approximately 95 per cent of its US$22.5 billion in short-term debt for one, two or three years (at interest rates averaging 2.5 per cent above the LIBOR international rate), this was not before the government agreed to put up a guarantee for the total amount (*AWSJ*, 16/3/98).

Finally, as in Thailand, the IMF and its major shareholders have found a compliant and willing partner in Kim Dae Jung: his democratic credentials are sound, having been a brave and relentless opponent of the military and quasi-military regimes that ruled South Korea for decades. He is also trenchantly opposed to the all-powerful *chaebol* and is able to bring the union movement on board due to an earlier alliance (although this dates back to the years when the union movement was the only voice of opposition in Korea). However, Kim's economic credentials are less impressive, and the risk is that South Korea will lose the unique elements of its development strategy, which allowed it to achieve both growth and a degree of economic democracy, in its over-eager efforts to satisfy the IMF, the US and Japan.

Conclusions and Recommendations

Thailand, Indonesia and South Korea have all been dubbed 'Asian tigers' on the basis of their impressively high growth rates over the past ten or more years. Although each has adopted an economic development strategy based on export-oriented industrialisation, there are significant differences in other aspects of their economic policies, including the role of the state, industrial policy, the degree and nature of trade and financial liberalisation, and the openness of their markets. One thing that they do have in common, though, is that the private sector has become increasingly dependent on foreign finance, an addiction made possible by rapid capital account liberalisation and the inexorable expansion of global financial flows.

In many ways the Asian crisis is not an 'Asian' crisis at all, but a global crisis which has shown the inadequacies of markets, governments and inter-national institutions in coping with rapid financial liberalisation. In particular, the high levels of now unserviceable private sector debt show that the capital market is incapable of efficiently allocating resources, that national governments have not developed the necessary levels of transparency, institutional strength and regulation to keep pace with the rapidly changing external environment, and that fast-track liberalisation is incompatible with sustainable and equitable development.

Nor is the Asian crisis simply a financial crisis. It is above all a human crisis. Already millions of people have been thrown out of work, and poverty and hunger are on the increase, as decades of social progress have been thrown into reverse. Worse is to come in the rest of 1998, and perhaps beyond. In Indonesia, the long-term viability of the nation is at stake as the Suharto regime clings grimly to power while the economy collapses and food riots and protests spread.

The crisis has tested the effectiveness and relevance of the IMF, finding it wanting on both counts. The IMF-prescribed policies accelerated economic contraction, did not stabilise currencies, and did not restore market confidence.

Further, the public sector austerity measures demanded by the Fund were the wrong response to what was fundamentally a private sector crisis. In effect, the Fund socialised private sector debt and compounded the already devastating impact of the crisis on workers and the poor.

The pain of adjustment has not been fairly distributed. It has hit the poor hardest, through job losses and price rises. It has also hit local companies who borrowed during the days of easy money, rather than the foreign banks and financial institutions which also profited from the speculative investment which precipitated the crisis. This raises the issue of moral hazard — bailing out investors in this way makes it more likely that they will reoffend in the future.

The IMF-imposed conditions have gone far beyond its mandate by demanding structural and policy reforms unrelated either to its role, as laid out in its Articles of Agreement, or to the causes of the economic crisis. In particular, the Fund has become a major proponent of capital account liberalisation, and the G7 governments are currently seeking to change the Articles to make this a central part of its mandate. Indeed, they see this move as part of their response to the Asian crisis. Given that over-hasty financial deregulation was one of the main causes of the crisis, putting the Fund in charge of speeding up the process is rash, to say the least. When the train is leaving the rails, the answer is not to speed up.

Both the Fund's performance and public statements by senior US government officials demonstrate that the IMF can reasonably be criticised as promoting the interests of its major shareholders — in particular the US — over and above the interests of the countries in trouble. Finally, as a public institution the Fund has failed to adopt reasonable standards of accountability and transparency.

Criticising the solutions imposed by the IMF in no way implies an uncritical endorsement of Asian development models. Economic development in these countries has brought some overall improvements in health, education and living standards. But the cost has been high in terms of sharpening the divide between rich and poor, environmental exploitation and loss of community control over natural resources, and growth without economic democracy or expansion of political participation.

In this sense, the crisis is a moment of opportunity to re-assess the economic and political directions taken in the past and to devise a development model based on economic democracy, political participation and environmental sustainability. Certainly, this is what the peoples' organisations in Thailand, Indonesia and South Korea are demanding. Sadly, the impetus is in the opposite direction, and it seems likely that the pressure to export their way out of debt will simply deepen the inequities of the existing model.

There is growing agreement, even from within, on the need critically to evaluate, and if necessary, to overhaul the Bretton Woods institutions. A crucial role should be played by the governments of the EU, which together make up the largest voting bloc on the IMF board. These governments should ensure that their voting and lobbying records at the Fund are fully coherent with their stated policy goals of furthering poverty eradication and sustainable social and economic development around the globe. So far, however, the European governments have stayed on the sidelines, only emerging as a chorus line to support Washington in urging the Asian governments to comply with the demands of the IMF.

World Bank senior economist Joseph Stiglitz has called for a 'post-Washington consensus' which 'cannot be based on Washington'. 'One principle of the emerging consensus', he says, 'is a greater degree of humility, the frank acknowledgement that we do not have all the answers' (Hanlon 1998).

Humility notwithstanding, at least two key issues need urgent attention: reviewing the role, policies, accountability and suitability of the IMF as presently constituted and establishing a global mechanism for the governance of inter-national financial transactions.

Recommendations

On the International Monetary Fund

- There should be an immediate and thorough review of the Bretton Woods institutions to assess their relevance to present global economic conditions with the possibility of either replacing the IMF and World Bank or rewriting their constitutions.

In the meantime, some immediate measures must be taken, including:

- Strictly limiting the role of the IMF to preventing a breakdown in trade caused by exchange rate volatility or balance of payments difficulties (Unger 1996).
- Opposing any changes to the IMF's Articles of Agreement, such as extending their remit to include capital account liberalisation, pending a full review of the Fund's role and performance.
- Clearly separating the short-term 'clearing' or stabilisation mission of the IMF from the long-term development mission of other institutions, such as the World Bank or Regional Development Banks.
- Eliminating cross-conditionalities between the IMF and the World Bank.
- De-linking all trade and investment liberalisation and democratisation and good governance conditions from IMF funding.
- Restructuring the IMF to increase transparency, accountability and equality between members, regardless of their level of contribution to the Fund.
- Ensuring the neutrality and impartiality of the advice given by the IMF so that it cannot be used to 'police national economic policies and force them into a convergence toward the reigning consensus' (Unger 1996: 23).
- In particular, the EU and Asian governments should play a more proactive role at the Fund, using their vote on the board to press for the reforms out-lined above.
- Unless and until the IMF can be reformed along these lines, regional initia-tives such as the AMF should be encouraged in order to mobilise additional resources of capital and offer alternatives to the IMF's narrow policy pre-scriptions.

On Financial Flows

- Mechanisms to monitor, regulate and if necessary control, international finan-cial flows, especially of speculative short-term capital, are urgently needed to prevent further crises.

On Debt

• IMF funds should not be used to bail-out the private sector. Instead, a system should be established for the effective resolution of private sector debt crises, based on clear rules and bankruptcy procedures. These should govern international debtor-creditor relations, providing an alternative to the state assuming full responsibility for unrecoverable private sector debts (see Chapter 1).

Notes

1. Although the widely publicised figure is US$43 billion, the figures available add up to US$41 billion. The source of the other US$2 billion is not clear.
2. The Reforestation Fund, which reportedly runs to billions of dollars drawn from timber taxes, was intended to replant and protect Indonesia's tropical forests. However, it was revealed that the funds were not able to be used to fight last year's forest fires because they had been earmarked for the national car project, see Richardson (1998).
3. For more details of the Korean economic crisis, see Walden Bello's "Korea: Travails of the Classic Tiger Economy" and Ha Joon Chang's "Korea: The Misunderstood Crisis.".
4. Interview, anonymity requested, 15 February 1998.
5. Although this sounds like a Red Cross parcel, it is in fact an interest-bearing loan with strict conditions attached. No country has ever defaulted on an IMF loan.
6. It has been suggested that one of the reasons Japan backed down so easily on their proposal for an Asian Monetary Fund is because they realised they could soon need the cash at home to bolster their own economy.
7. IMF Stand-by Agreement Summary of the Economic Program, 5 December 1997 (downloaded from IMF website).
8. Figure from Wanida Tantiwitthayaphitak, spokesperson for Forum of the Poor, Bangkok, 21 January 1998.
9. Estimate by the Secretary General of the Indonesian Muslim Intellectuals Association reported in the *Indonesian Observer*, 27 January 1998.
10. Taken from World Bank website, 3 March 1998.
11. Siddho Deva, Oxfam UKI, personal communication, 13 March 1998.
12. I am grateful for Nurina Widagdo who provided much of the information on the social impact of the crisis in Indonesia.
13. Ending the plywood cartels was one of the IMF's objectives. It would be unfortunate if IMF conditions led directly to unsustainable resource exploitation.
14. Taken from World Bank website, 13 March 1998.
15. This article by Unger (1996: 23) is an extremely interesting and constructive analysis of how the Bretton Woods Institutions should be reformed, animated by the impulse that 'the world economy needs more, not less, of all the benefits Bretton Woods was designed to provide through international coordination and supranational institutions'.
16. IMF Articles of Agreement, Article 1, Purposes (IMF website).
17. Late in 1997 Congress failed to renew the President's 'fast-track' trade negotiating authority responding to an all-out public campaign opposing further liberalisation.
18. Testimony of Ambassador Charlene Barshefsky US Trade Representative before the House Ways & Means Trade Subcommittee, 24 February 1998 (USTR website).
19. IMF website, 18.3.98.
20. Maastricht Treaty, Title XVII, Article 130u.

21. Britain currently holds the EU presidency and here too, there are differences between the government's stated development policy of focusing on poverty eradication and coherence between the different arms of government's relations with developing countries ('Eliminating World Poverty: A Challenge for the 21st Century', White Paper, November 1997), and its behaviour in the Asian crisis. To its credit, the British government has, along with the World Bank, launched a Trust Fund to help countries assess the poverty impact of the crisis ('UK Initiative to Help Asia', HM Treasury Press Release, 17 February 1998). However, the British Government is also leading moves within the G7 to change the IMF's Articles of Agreement to give it more authority to pursue capital account liberalisation.

22. 'Statement by the G7 Finance Ministers and Central Bank Governors', February 1998.

23. Joint UK aid agency letter to Gordon Brown, 19 February 1998.

24. Testimony of Ambassador Charlene Barshefsky US Trade Representative to the House Ways & Means Trade Subcommittee, 24 February 1998 (USTR website).

25. *Ibid.*

26. Interview, anonymity requested, 15 February 1998.

27. Interview, anonymity requested, 16 February 1998.

6
THAILAND:
CAUSES, CONDUCT, CONSEQUENCES

Laurids S. Lauridsen

In the past, the main preoccupation of the Thai political élite was territorial integrity, national independence and regime maintenance. This stability-oriented strategy was instrumental in advancing conservative financial and monetary management in the country. The public sector developed restrictive budgetary procedures and a monitoring system to manage and control the size and maturity structure of public sector debt. Moreover, the Ministry of Finance and the Bank of Thailand (BoT) co-operated in keeping the current account in balance and inflation under control. Compared with most less developed countries, Thailand was a relatively open economy with 'mild' protection of domestic industries and with a 'hands-off approach' to credit allocation and to economic development more generally.

Therefore, it is ironical that Thailand, reputed for its financial orthodoxy and macroeconomic stability, and once regarded — in the World Bank's 1993 East Asian Miracle Report — as a model for economic development, should emerge as 'the weak link in the Asian financial chain', triggering a serious financial crisis throughout the East Asian region.

Thailand became the epicentre of the financial meltdown in Asia. Why did the financial crisis start in Thailand? How was a loss of confidence in the baht transformed into a loss of confidence in the whole financial system? What did the Thai state do? What did the IMF do? What are the costs and consequences of the financial crisis in Thailand so far, and how will that impact upon medium- and long-term prospects for socioeconomic development in the country? These are the questions addressed in this chapter.

Political instability, indecisiveness and mismanagement at the political and administrative level certainly contributed to the financial meltdown in Thailand, but classical macroeconomic problems — such as fiscal imbalances and excessive money supply — were of minor importance. As we shall see, capital market liberalisation during the early 1990s as well as the pegging of the baht against the US dollar, which was increasing in value, turned out to be unwise. Nonetheless, the financial crisis in Thailand was not fundamentally a case of 'state failure' originating in the alleged 'statism' and 'cronyism' of Asian capitalism. On the contrary, private sector failure partly expresses itself in increasing current account problems, but mainly in careless lending/borrowing, resulting in the accumulation of non-performing loans in the financial sector.

Excessive Short-term Borrowings and Casino Capitalism

Basically, the financial crisis in Thailand was due to excessive investments — many of which turned out to be too optimistic and too unproductive. During the 1990-96 period, the investment ratio (gross domestic investment as a percentage of GDP) was between 40 per cent and 44 per cent, compared to average investment ratios of 25 per cent and 30 per cent during the 1980-84 and 1985-89 periods respectively.[1]

Many investments were based on money borrowed abroad. Due to high interest rates in Thailand and a fixed exchange rate policy linking the baht to the US$, foreign investors were eager to place their money in Thailand, preferring to lend on a short-term basis (typically for three or six months), for which they could obtain 10-11 per cent interest rates. Domestic borrowers were also eager to borrow offshore because such money was cheaper (lower interest rates) and the 'virtually pegged' exchange rate encouraged borrowers to think that there was no currency risk. Corporate borrowers discovered they could thus borrow at an interest rate of 5-8 per cent, instead of paying more than 13 per cent when borrowing domestically. They could even earn money simply by borrowing from abroad and depositing baht in Thailand.

In 1992, as part of a broader financial liberalisation package, the Anand government deregulated foreign exchange. The Bangkok International Banking Facility (BIBF) was established in 1993 to attract more foreign funds to cover the increasing current account deficits, to turn Thailand into a regional financial centre, and to ensure a greater degree of competition in the banking sector. The BIBF made it possible for local and foreign commercial banks to take deposits or to borrow in foreign currencies from abroad, and to lend the money, both in Thailand and abroad (Naris 1995: 172).

As a consequence, Thailand undertook too much offshore borrowing. The external debt increased from almost US$40 billion in 1992 to US$80 billion in March 1997. Therefore, total outstanding debt as a share of GDP increased from 34 per cent in 1990 to 51 per cent in 1996, an increase generated almost exclusively by the private sector. Of the total debt stock, 80 per cent was private debt and almost 36 per cent was short term, i.e. maturing in 12 months or less. In August 1997, the BoT revealed that the foreign debt was about US$90 billion, of which US$73 billion was by private companies with US$20 billion falling due by the end of 1997. In January 1998, the Thailand Development Research Institute (TDRI) showed that the ratio of short-term debt to foreign reserves increased from 0.6 in 1990 to 1.0 in 1995 (and 1996), implying that the ability of the country to service short-term debt had deteriorated during the first half of the 1990s.[2]

Through its access to foreign credit via the BIBF and the Eurobond market, the private sector had obtained large amounts of foreign credit. The figures show that the Thai financial crisis is primarily a 'private sector' crisis.

The massive inflow of money tripled the amount of loans in the financial system, causing a *misallocation of investment resources*. An investment bubble was thus created by careless lending. A substantial part of the money was channelled into already inflated assets in the *real estate sector*. Between 1992 and 1996, a total of 755,000 housing units were built in Bangkok, double the national plan estimate. Loans from financial institutions to property developers also increased. In 1993, loans totalled 264 billion baht, but by March 1996, they had increased to 767 billion baht, of which 45 per cent stemmed from finance companies and 54 per cent from commercial banks. By 1996, it became apparent that the supply of housing was outstripping effective demand, and in the following year, Thailand had residential vacancy rates of 25-30 per cent and vacancy rates for offices in Bangkok of 14 per cent.[3] Moreover, many property owners artificially inflated the value of their assets and kept borrowing against them, while most real estate companies had poor cash flows. Lester Thurow (1998) describes the problem of inflated commercial land values which did not reflect their underlying earnings capacity in the following manner: 'Bangkok, a city whose per capita productivity is about one twelfth that of San Francisco, should not have land values that are much higher than those of San Francisco. But it did — as did other Southeast Asian cities. Grossly inflated property values had to come down.'

The Thai experience saw a boom-bust cycle involving property and stock markets.[4] When the economic recession started in 1996 and the buying power of the middle and upper classes began declining, the property bubble burst and left substantial bad debts on the balance sheets of the finance companies, which had financed their investments by borrowing abroad. In February 1997, Somprasong Land missed payment on a euro-convertible debenture worth US$80 million. In March 1997, the BoT had classified Bt100 billion of the loans owned by real estate developers as non-performing (i.e. not having been serviced for 12 months), but the amount of bad property loans was estimated by financial agencies at Bt300 billion (about US$7.5 billion) (Krissana Parnsoonthorn 1997, Thammavit Terdudomtham 1998). Part of the borrowed money went into large industrial complexes in steel, pulp and paper, cement and petrochemicals.

Misallocation of loan funds was one problem. A second problem was *vulnerability*. First, most of the loans — even those going to the industrial sector — were *not hedged* against currency fluctuations. Second, a *currency mismatch* arose as much of the foreign money went into non-tradable sectors of the economy, i.e. with no foreign exchange receipts. Third, there was a *term mismatch* as short-term borrowing was utilised to finance long-term projects with longer-term returns. Finally, financing of equity purchases by loans without taking the foreign exchange risk into account was not unusual.[5]

Financial Institutions and the Financial Crisis in the 1980s

The present financial crisis in Thailand is not the first economic downturn since 1980. Thailand went through a serious financial crisis in 1983-85, involving a substantial bail-out and a *de facto* 25 per cent devaluation of the baht. In 1986-87, Thailand's recession turned into an impressive export-driven economic boom as the cheapening of Thai exports due to devaluation was succeeded by an appreciation of East Asian currencies, leading to a massive flow of direct investments from Japan, Taiwan and South Korea to Southeast Asia, including Thailand. This new optimism and the stronger presence of financial technocrats in the Anand and Chuan governments (1991-95) paved the way for financial liberalisation.

Thailand's organised financial system has long been dominated by the commercial bank sector, which in 1990 accounted for 71 per cent of financial assets. The second largest group of financial institutions includes finance and securities companies which accounted for almost 14 per cent of financial system assets in that year (Robinson, *et al.* 1991: 20-21).

The commercial bank group is divided into 15 local commercial banks — with extensive branch networks — accounting for 95 per cent of bank assets in 1990, and 14 foreign banks, which are disadvantaged by a number of restrictions and only accounted for 5 per cent of bank assets. The local commercial banks were originally set up by business groups and trading houses to finance their operations and, despite government attempts to diversify ownership, are still dominated by no more than 16 Sino-Thai families. The state is involved in the commercial banks through ownership of the second largest bank (Krung Thai Bank) and via military ownership of the sixth largest bank (Thai Military Bank), while the royal family, through the Crown Property Bureau, controls the fourth largest bank (Siam Commercial Bank) and has shares in the Siam City Bank (Suehiro 1985 and 1992, Hewison 1989).

Moreover, the commercial banking sector is highly concentrated, with the five largest banks (Bangkok Bank, Krung Thai Bank, Thai Farmers Bank, Siam Commercial Bank and Bank of Ayudhya) accounting for more than two-thirds of bank assets. The concentration ratio of these five banks increased from 56 per cent in 1962 to almost 70 per cent in 1980. In 1990, the top five banks had 69 per cent of assets, 73 per cent of deposits and 64 per cent of branches.[6]

In reality, the top five commercial banks formed a powerful cartel. Peter Warr (1993: 24) describes the broader structure of the commercial banking industry 'as a cartel-like structure with 16 banks organised loosely under the Thai Bankers Association, whereby they collectively set the standard rates of service charges and loan rates. This oligopolistic practice makes interest rates (loans and deposits) respond relatively slowly to market conditions as it takes time for all banks to agree on the same adjustment, particularly in the downward direction.'

Finance and security companies emerged in the early 1960s as affiliates of commercial banks and expanded rapidly during the 1970s. They were originally set up 'either to provide services that the parent bank could not undertake directly or to engage in higher-margin but higher-risk consumer finance, and subsequently expanded into certain types of corporate finance' (Robinson, *et al.* 1991: 20).

The second oil shock led to a deterioration of the trade balance and accumulation of foreign debt, and Thailand entered a period of economic stabilisation and adjustment programmes under the supervision of the Bretton Woods institutions. The economic recession was succeeded by a financial crisis starting in October 1983. From the perspective of the present financial crisis, it is worth emphasising that the 1983 crisis was also triggered by large losses of a finance company and its affiliates. The financial crisis in 1983-86 affected one-third of all financial institutions, accounting for one-fourth of financial assets. 'The crisis, which was aggravated by a slowdown in growth and a tightening of monetary policy, brought to the fore widespread pressures in the banking system and particularly among the more loosely controlled finance companies.... The pressures included weak management practices (notably the extension of credit and guarantees to businesses with which bank directors and shareholders were involved, and an over-concentration of lending to a few large-scale and interrelated industries) together with weaknesses in supervisory and regulatory frameworks' (Robinson; *et al.* 1991: 22). During the 1983-86 financial crisis, 15 finance companies collapsed and 32 companies were given liquidity injections through various schemes, including the so-called 'lifeboat' scheme set up in April 1984. One particular rescue mission for the commercial bank sector involved five banks.

Exposure of cases of financial mismanagement in 1978-79 had led to tougher banking regulations and the first formal controls of finance companies through the 1979 Commercial Banking Act. The more serious 1983-86 financial crisis led to further state initiatives. One was the establishment of a Fund for the Rehabilitation and Development of Financial Institutions receiving interest-free contributions from all financial institutions. Moreover, the 1985 amendment to the Commercial Banking Act empowered the BoT 'to enforce compliance with regulations through direct intervention, to order an increase in bank capital, and to remove bank directors and officers when deemed necessary in the public interest; restrictions on transactions between financial institutions and their directors were tightened; and the Bank's powers to conduct on-site examinations were strengthened' (Robinson, *et al.* 1991: 22. See also Doner and Unger 1993: 115-116).

The financial crisis was soon forgotten as Thailand began an export-led economic boom in the second half of the 1980s. Speculation in real estate and stock markets led to a doubling of the average value of these assets during the 1986-90 period. But the main focus of government policy at the time was not on control and regulation, but rather on deregulation and competition (Naris 1995: 163).

Financial Liberalisation in the 1990s

In the period 1989-93, the financial sector went through a process of financial reform aimed at boosting domestic savings and foreign capital inflows, improving the capability of the financial sector to compete internationally, and eventually developing Thailand into a regional financial centre. The reform process was accelerated when the military installed Anand Panyarachun as prime minister in February 1991. During his 13 month interim government (the first Anand government), the BoT and the Ministry of Finance utilised their renewed independence and autonomy to pass 20 financial reform bills (Doner and Unger 1993: 121). Interest rate ceilings, which had been lowered during the 1980s, were abolished on the deposits side in 1990 and on the lending side in 1992. Foreign exchange transactions were also liberalised, first with respect to current account transactions (1990), and later for capital account transactions (1991) as well, ostensibly to enhance confidence among investors and to improve Thailand's creditworthiness.[7] The scope of business of commercial banks and finance companies was widened, and in order to promote competition and introduce a variation of universal banking, finance companies were allowed to expand into business areas previously reserved for commercial banks, e.g. the foreign exchange business (for details, see Jaruwan 1992: 51-52 and Naris 1995: 171-174). The Anand government also decided to support the 1990 BoT plan for setting up offshore banking institutions under the BIBF to promote Thailand as a regional financial centre, to ensure more (but not excessive) competition for domestic commercial banks and to enable Thai business to have greater and cheaper access to foreign loans. The BIBF was introduced during the Chuan government in 1993 and business in foreign currencies was unrestricted, which intensified competition in out-in lending (acquiring foreign loans for the domestic market), which had been dominated by the major Thai commercial banks before 1993.[8]

In the field of foreign exchange policy, the guiding policy principle in Thailand has always been stability, while monetary policy has been utilised to defend the exchange rate when external balance problems arose. For more than 20 years (1963-84), the Thai baht was fixed to the dollar, and monetary policies were utilised to maintain low inflation and to avoid balance of payment imbalances. In 1981, as the value of the dollar increased rapidly, two minor devaluations (roughly 10 per cent altogether) were executed. During 1984, a particular political conjuncture made it possible for Prime Minister Prem to devalue the baht by almost 15 per cent and to link the baht to a basket of currencies in which the dollar remained the major component, thus leading to further *de facto* devaluation of the baht when the dollar fell against the yen and other currencies from 1985.[9] During the post-1984 period, the baht was again stable against the US dollar, pegged to the above mentioned basket of currencies.

During the early 1990s, portfolio investment and short-term private borrowing grew. Portfolio investments increased from 23.5 billion baht in 1992 to 138 billion baht in 1993, a six-fold increase.[10] The virtually pegged exchange rate constrained monetary policy, though some economists pointed to the potentially destabilising influence of short-term inflows.

'While the authorities may wish to keep the Thai baht fixed to the US dollar in keeping with past practice, they will find the supply of money increasingly difficult to control. For example, attempts to tighten the domestic money supply, leading to increases in domestic interest rates, will only induce greater capital inflows, which will eventually restore the differential between domestic and foreign interest rates. In the extreme case, monetary policy will not be able to influence domestic money supply and price levels if interest rates are exogenously determined and the exchange rate is fixed.... Shielding the domestic economy from external instability and restoring the effectiveness of monetary policy can be attained only by greater willingness on the part of the Thai authorities to accept increased fluctuations in the exchange rate' (Naris 1995: 177-178).

The recent economic meltdown in Thailand was a mixture of a financial and currency crisis. After 12 years (1984-96) of a virtually pegged exchange rate policy, the currency issue became a problem again during 1996.

Economic Slowdown, Loss of Competitiveness and Currency Crisis

During 1996, it became clear that the Thai economy had lost its momentum. The economy was slowing down to the lowest rate of GDP growth in a decade. Thailand suddenly experienced negative export growth and export sales of labour-intensive goods such as footwear, textiles, garments and plastic products.[11] As imports kept growing, the current account deficit increased. Meanwhile, the stock exchange lost around one-fifth of its value during the first nine months of 1996, implying a stock market collapse prior to the currency crisis, as suggested by Krugman (1998). Finally, the Board of Investment registered a downward trend in foreign investments.

It was also generally believed that the instability and incompetence of the Banharn government (1995-96) and then the Chavalit government (1996-97) repeatedly undermined the confidence of both foreign and domestic investors. The poor economic performance lead to increasing widespread awareness that Thailand — due to the stronger baht, higher wages and competition from low-cost producers such as China — was losing its traditional competitiveness in labour-intensive industries. Consequently, it became obvious that a transition to more sophisticated, higher technology industries was required and that some kind of structural reform was needed to address among other things, issues such as the low-skilled labour force, low technological capability and inadequate infrastructure.

Moreover, the technocrats in the Ministry of Finance and the BoT became worried about the large inflow of 'hot money' and the fact that Thailand's system of pegging the baht against a basket made up of US dollars, Japanese yen and German marks made such short-term speculative investments 'too secure'.[12] Nonetheless, the stable baht was considered crucial for attracting the investments needed to finance the country's current account deficit just as there were strong vested interests (i.e. large corporations with high external indebtedness) that would lobby against a more flexible exchange rate regime.

In the second half of 1995, the US dollar began to appreciate sharply *vis-à-vis* the yen and other major currencies. As a result, the Thai baht and other Southeast Asian currencies pegged to the dollar followed that trend. During 1996, there were repeated rumours that the baht would be devalued. Instead, the BoT continued the tight monetary policy it had already introduced in 1995, but the policy proved ineffective due to high domestic interest rates and the free flows of capital through the offshore banking facilities established in 1993. Therefore, in the middle of 1996, the BoT imposed a requirement for bank and finance companies to hold higher cash reserves on short-term deposits by foreigners. The tight monetary policy also led to a further deterioration of the quality of assets held by the financial sector (*Bangkok Post Year-end 96 Economic Review*, 1997; *Asia 1997 Economic Yearbook*, p. 218).

However, many analysts kept on predicting at least a widening of the band within which the baht was allowed to fluctuate. Gordon Fairclough of the *Far Eastern Economic Review* drew the following conclusion in May 1996: 'In the long-term, however, the problem remains. With the baht pegged so firmly, the central bank's hands are largely tied when it comes to trying to control the money supply, and thereby rein in inflation, and the current account deficit. Eventually, change must come' (*FEER*, 16/5/96). Furthermore, the investment-rating company Moody's downgraded Thailand's rating on short-term debt, arguing that Thailand's over-reliance on short-term funds from overseas made it vulnerable to a Mexico-style financial shock. In June, the IMF warned about the large and increasing current account deficit and suggested more exchange rate flexibility.[13] In mid-July, bankers and financial analysts warned that the failure to lower the high current account deficit and the heavy reliance on short-term financing might shake the confidence of foreign investors in the Thai economy (*Bangkok Post*, 23/7/96).

In its October 1996 cover story on Thailand, *Asiaweek* pointed to Thailand as the region's worst performer in 1996 noting: 'Between 1994 and 1996, the current account deficit was ballooning at an average of 40 per cent every six months. As the share of GDP, the deficit may well top 8 per cent this year, as it did in 1995, causing observers to draw unfavourable comparisons with Mexico's 1994 currency meltdown, which occurred when the current account deficit passed 8 per cent of GDP' (*Asiaweek*, 4/10/96, p. 25).

Therefore, it was hardly surprising that currency traders made some preliminary attacks on the baht in November–December 1996. After the Mexican crisis in 1995, currency traders had become obsessed by the 8 per cent current account deficit (as a percentage of GDP), a limit which Thailand had exceeded in 1990 when the deficit amounted to 8.5 per cent of GDP without currency problems (OBI, May 1996: 3). While currency traders became fixated on the current account deficit, corporations with unhedged borrowings had a crucial interest in retention of the quasi-pegged foreign exchange rate, while the BoT persisted in defending the pegged baht by keeping interest rates high.

The currency crisis hit Thailand in early March 1997 after a speculative attack on the baht in February had driven up inter-bank rates and made liquidity tighter. Speculators realised that the Thai currency was overvalued, and there was growing reason to believe that speculative attacks would lead to a lowering of the baht's value. Similarly, some local investors began selling baht for US dollars in order to hedge against a possible devaluation, while exporters increasingly delayed converting their export earnings into baht. As a consequence, there was a huge supply of baht in the money market.

In May 1997, with severe problems in the financial sector unsolved and with no sign of economic recovery, a new series of attacks on the baht took place and the central bank spent billions of dollars defending the baht. There were reports that international hedge funds and currency speculators were betting up to US$10 billion on a devaluation of the baht. The BoT spent US$4 billion in the spot market and, as came to light later, also accepted more than US$23 billion in forward obligations.[14] Furthermore, the government introduced currency controls by limiting offshore trading involving the baht to deter speculation; a 50 billion baht stock market rescue fund was set up in co-operation with the banking sector. During May and June, it seems that economic tsar Amnuay tried to convince the cabinet to introduce a 'managed float' foreign exchange system, a radical financial sector reform and some minor tax increases, but failed, particularly due to resistance from the Chart Pattana (CP) party. As a consequence, Amnuay, who was considered the most capable member of the economic team, resigned on 19 June (*EIU Country Report: Thailand*, 1997: 3; *FEER* 29/5/97).

The Politics of the Financial Crises

The political conjuncture in 1996/97 was also quite different from that in 1984, when Prime Minister General Prem and the economic technocrats succeeded in depreciating the baht. In the meantime, parliamentary democracy, under the strong influence of provincial business interests, had replaced an authoritarian Bangkok-based semi-democracy as political instability prevailed. The Banharn government had renewed attacks on some bastions of military-technocratic power and given more voice to provincial businessmen — two processes which had been initiated by the Chatichai government (1988-91). In September 1996, however, Prime Minister Banharn Silpa-archa was forced to resign under pressure from both inside and outside the coalition government. Banharn had mostly chosen provincial bosses as his ministers while the shifting short-term policies of the government were mainly driven by the logic of patronage and particularistic connection. Besides not being able or willing to address the problem of the current account deficit, the Banharn government was involved in two developments which came to affect the financial crisis in 1997. The first development was the declining autonomy of, and the increasing interference in, the working of the macroeconomic agencies, particularly in the activities of the BoT. The second related development was the Bangkok Bank of Commerce (BBC) scandal.

During the Banharn administration's 16 months in office, there was much political turmoil. Of particular importance here is the firing of the heads of three core macroeconomic agencies — the BoT, the Securities and Exchange Commission (SEC) and the Ministry of Finance. In fact, there were, in all, three finance ministers during this period. It started with the firing of Ekamol Khiriwat, the popular secretary-general of the SEC and deputy governor of the BoT in December 1995. The head of the BoT, Vijit Supinit, probably influenced by Finance Minister Surakiat, gave his consent to sacking Ekamol.

While the Ekamol affair was still going on, the Democrat party raised the Bangkok Bank of Commerce (BBC) issue. The BBC had run into deep financial troubles with 78 billion baht of doubtful debts, mostly caused by the provision of loans with insufficient collateral to companies owned by the bank's top executives and top advisers as well as to the so-called 'group of 16' faction of Banharn's Chart Chai party. The BoT was criticised for not taking appropriate action in the BBC case. When BoT Governor Vijit's professional ethics were questioned due to his close personal links to the BBC's chief executive, and the central bank's economic forecasts suddenly became rather inaccurate, the BoT head was forced to resign, as was Finance Minister Surakiat, who was accused of having used his political influence with the BoT governor to fire Ekamol and in the BBC affair.[15]

As a consequence, the independence and credibility of the central bank eroded as some of the banking sector's doubtful practices were revealed. It has been argued that the BBC scandal was the starting point of the financial crisis in Asia as it suggested that the Thai banking sector was seriously out of control. 'The scandal, at the Bangkok Bank of Commerce, involved billions of dollars in questionable loans. The bank's managers disguised their malfeasance using financial shell games, such as backing loans with vastly overvalued property. The mess at the Bangkok Bank exposed the weakness of Thailand's banks and the lack of government oversight in a deregulated financial system run amok' (*International Herald Tribune*, 5/1/98).

The November election in 1996 brought another representative of old-style Thai politics to power. After a total expenditure on vote-buying in the range of US$700-1,000 million, the majority of which was spent by the New Aspiration Party (NAP) in the northeastern and central regions, the NAP leader Chavalit Yongchaiyudh finally took over as prime minister heading a six party coalition. In late 1996, non-MPs who were believed to be able to restore investor confidence — Dr Amnuay Viravan and Dr Narongchai Akrasanee — were appointed ministers, with the former taking the posts of finance minister and deputy prime minister with responsibility for finance. The CP party which wanted to be in charge of economic policy, tried to block this arrangement but failed in the first instance. However, in May 1997, after realising that, as a non-MP, he had no negotiating power, Amnuay resigned and the Chavalit government began to look more like the Banharn government, unable to address longer-term social and economic development issues or solve the credibility crisis.

Financial Crisis and Breakdown of Investor Confidence

During the first quarter of 1997, the property bubble burst. Somprasong Land became the first real-estate company to default on an interest payment on a Euro-bond in early February, but soon after, it was reported that several other property companies had difficulty servicing their debts. Although the central bank had assured the public in mid-February that no financial institutions under its supervision faced liquidity problems it was suddenly obvious that several of Thailand's finance companies (fincos), including the largest — Finance One — were over-extended in the property and hire-purchase sectors.

The Ministry of Finance and the central bank reacted fairly rapidly. Finance One was ordered to merge with Thailand's twelfth largest commercial bank, the Thai Danu Bank. Meanwhile, the Finance Institutions Development Fund (FIDF) injected 40 billion baht into Finance One.[16] Nine other finance companies and a credit foncier (housing loans broker) with high exposure to property loans were ordered to raise their registered capital. The remaining finance companies were asked to find a further 26 billion baht as debt cover while the banks were asked to raise provisions against bad loans.

The main strategy of the BoT involved mergers among Thailand's 91 finance companies and 18 banks. In early March, the central bank also announced the setting up of a Property Loan Management Organisation (PLMO) to provide 100 billion baht in five year loans to ailing property firms. The funds were to be raised by issuing seven-year, zero-coupon bonds guaranteed by the government. Finally, the cabinet accepted a 106 billion baht down-sizing in the 1996/97 budget. Through these initiatives, the government seemed to have averted devaluation of the baht and a deep financial crisis (*EIU Country Report: Thailand*, 1997: 2).

Implementation of these initiatives was not easy. Lacking clear guidelines for the chosen merger strategy and with Chart Pattana ministers as major shareholders in some of the worst performing finance companies, merging and closing finance companies was difficult. When the Finance One/Thai Danu merger, considered a model for further mergers, collapsed in late May, the strategy collapsed with it. Finance One was the largest and most well-known finance company with involvement in real estate, hire purchase and stock margin lending. The fate of Finance One was a striking indicator of the state of finance companies in general, but it was still believed that the BoT would act as a lender of last resort. However, the BoT itself had been weakened when three senior officials (including a deputy governor) were suspended because the BoT failed to act in the BBC case within the 12 month limit and therefore had to drop charges against BBC executives. Finally, the PLMO initiative failed because of lack of interest in the zero-coupon bonds needed to finance the scheme (*EIU Country Report: Thailand*, 1997: 2; *EIU Country Report: Thailand*, 1997: 3).

After a month of indecisiveness and unsuccessful implementation of measures aimed at restructuring the financial and property sectors, the new finance minister (and former president of the Thai Military Bank) Thanong Bidaya investigated deeper into the matter. When he personally looked into the arrangements of the central bank's Banking Department, he discovered that US$8 billion had been lent out to debt-ridden finance companies through the FIDF and that foreign reserves were seriously low, probably below the legally required level (total reserves had, according to a 1940 statute, to be equal to the value of currency in circulation).

On 27 June, 16 finance companies (including Finance One) were suspended for 30 days, and ordered to come up with merger plans or close. On 1 July, the prime minister declared, 'I will never allow the baht to devalue. We will all become poor', but the following day (2 July), the finance minister announced the introduction of a 'managed float' system, allowing the baht to slip from 26 to 32 for US$1 in just two weeks.

The financial sector initiatives did not restore confidence in the finance sector. Firstly, questions were raised as to whether vested political interests had affected the selection of the 16 suspended fincos, leaving some even more troubled companies out. Secondly, the government did not stick to its own deadline and extended the suspension instead. This was linked, in the press, to the presence of senior cabinet members among the major shareholders. Thirdly, the BoT sent contradictory signals as to whether it was backing the finance companies as it had done with the largest finance company — Finance One — since 1996. Finally, financial analysts did not believe the government's insistence that only the 16 suspended fincos were unsound (*EIU Country Report: Thailand*, 1997: 3; *FEER*, 26/6/97; *FEER*, 3/7/97; *FEER*, 10/7/97; *FEER*, 31/7/97; *FEER*, 25/9/97).

It became clear when it suspended the operations of a further 42 finance companies on 5 August, after negotiations with the IMF, that the government initiatives were 'too-little-too-late', leaving only 33 finance companies open. This time, the conditions were clear — creditors and debtors would be protected while shareholders would lose their investments.

The gravity of the situation and the uselessness of the policy responses became clear when it was revealed that the BoT had utilised a substantial part of Thailand's foreign reserves saving the baht and had committed more than US$23 billion to forward contracts defending the baht against speculators. Furthermore, it was disclosed that through the FIDF, the BoT had extended more than US$8 billion or, more precisely, 430 billion baht (or 10 per cent of GDP) through the FIDF to rescue troubled finance companies.[17]

In late July, the two pillars of investor confidence which had kept the baht and the financial sector afloat during the first half of 1997 broke down. The stable baht was history, and the BoT was no longer a safety net for the leading financial institutions, just as confidence in the BoT itself had fallen. In early August, with alarmingly low foreign reserves and a private sector weighed down with foreign debt, it was obvious that some kind of foreign assistance was needed, and when the Japanese were not willing to provide this alone, the IMF was called in (*EIU Country Report: Thailand*, 1997: 3; *FEER*, 14/8/97; *FEER*, 21/8/97; *FEER*, 4/9/97; *Bangkok Post*, 11/8/97; *Bangkok Post*, 12/8/97; *Bangkok Post*, 13/8/97; *Bangkok Post*, 14/8/97).

The IMF Medicine

The IMF rescue package was approved by the Fund's board on 11 August. Under the umbrella of the IMF, a US$17.2 billion stand-by credit facility was made available mainly by East Asian governments for balance of payment support, and with disbursement made quarterly over almost three years and contingent on Thailand meeting IMF performance requirements. The total sum included US$2.7 billion from the World Bank and the Asian Development Bank to be used to enhance industrial competitiveness, improve capital markets and mitigate social problems arising from the austerity programme. It is worth mentioning that China decided to deploy US$1 billion of its foreign exchange reserves for this purpose, while the US, in contrast, did not make any direct contribution. In contrast with the Mexican crisis (1994-95) which resulted in a US-led IMF US$50 billion bail-out, the Thai crisis was left to the IMF and Japan, which contributed US$4 billion each. According to the Bank of International Settlements (BIS), Japanese banks accounted for more than half of the Thai debt to foreign commercial banks (US$37.5 billion). In this light, the Japanese contribution appears modest (for more information on contributions from individual countries, see *EIU Country Report: Thailand*, 1993: 3; *Bangkok Post*, 12/8/97 and *Bangkok Post*, 13/8/97).

The IMF demanded that Thailand adopt an *austerity programme*, which included an increase in the national value-added tax from 7 per cent to 10 per cent; a 1 per cent surplus in the public budget to cover restructuring costs in the financial sector, implying a cut in fiscal spending (in all sectors apart from education and health) of 100 billion baht in the 1997-98 budget; the ending of subsidies to state companies; tight monetary policy to keep inflation at 9.5 per cent in 1997 and 5 per cent in 1998; reduction of the current account deficit to 5 per cent in 1997 and 3 per cent in 1998, as compared with the 8.2 per cent deficit in 1996; continuation of the 'managed float' system; maintaining reserves at a level that would provide over three months' import cover (US$23 billion in 1997 and US$25 billion in 1998); a clean-up of the finance industry and discontinuation of the rescue of ailing finance companies (*FEER*, 14/8/97; *FEER*, 21/8/97; *Bangkok Post*, 12/8/97; *EIU Country Report: Thailand*, 1997: 3, pp. 18-19).

The BoT followed the IMF conditions and, as mentioned earlier, suspended 42 more debt-ridden finance companies in addition to the 16 already suspended in June. The *plan for restructuring the financial sector* was worked out with technical assistance from more than 15 IMF and World Bank officials and was finally announced on 15 October — two weeks after the original IMF deadline. The financial restructuring package contained the following main elements: a) setting up two new agencies, the Financial Restructuring Agency (FRA) to supervise the 58 suspended fincos and to evaluate the rehabilitation plans submitted by these firms before the end of October, and the Asset Management Corporation (AMC) to buy bad assets and to then manage, restructure and sell them under the direction of the FRA; b) tightening loan classification by reducing the period after which a loan is considered non-performing from 12 to 6 months and requiring higher capital-to-risk assets ratios (12-15 per cent compared to the international norm of 8.5 per cent) in order to 'gradually bring the sector into line with international standards by 2000'; c) new rules allowing foreigners to take majority stakes in all financial institutions for a ten year period, after which their shares have to be lowered to less than a majority through capital increases only available to Thais; d) a full government guarantee to both depositors and creditors in the country's 15 local banks and remaining 33 finance companies; e) acceptance of equal claims of all creditors to the collateral of finance companies, i.e. requiring that the government remove FIDF's declared preferential claim to this collateral (FIDF had extended 430 billion baht to the 58 fincos against collateral); f) enactment of new laws allowing the BoT to take control of troubled financial institutions, order changes in management, and 'write down' shares to pay for losses, improve bankruptcy laws so that debtors can collect their collateral faster, and ensure that the BoT announces its forward foreign currency commitments every month (*Bangkok Post*, 14/10/97; *Financial Times*, 15/10/97; *EIU Country Report: Thailand*, 1997: 4, pp. 15-17, pp. 31-34).

In addition to the six royal decrees containing the financial reform package, the government also announced further cuts in public spending and new taxes so that it could achieve the 1 per cent surplus in the 1997/98 budget as agreed to with the IMF in August 1997.

The new loan classification made it almost impossible to save the 58 finance companies. The suspended companies had loan assets of 1.3 trillion baht, the majority of which were non-performing under the new classification standards and collectively had US$16 billion in loans from foreign lenders (*Bangkok Post*, 8/12/97). The new policies were not implemented promptly due to indecisiveness and government instability. A coalition partner, CP utilised Chavalit's weakness to take over responsibility for economic affairs. CP party leaders were known to have considerable interests in the financial sector, including some of the suspended finance companies. Hence, CP was eager to gain control over the FRA and the AMC, and the issue of six royal decrees was delayed. Soon after, the CP party pushed for a government reshuffle, but the composition of the new government was not sufficient to restore confidence. On the last day of October, the baht passed the US$1 to 40 baht threshold, and on 3 November, Chavalit announced that he would resign three days later (*FEER*, 6/11/97; *FEER*, 13/11/97; *EIU Country Report: Thailand*, 1997: 4, pp. 13-17).

The Chuan Government: Financial Clean Up and Sticking by the Terms

Under the leadership of former prime minister Chuan Leekpai, a new government took office on 15 November. Chuan, who leads a six-party coalition, installed his own economic team headed by two highly esteemed technocrats from his own party (the Democrats) — Supachai Panitchpakdi (a former central bank governor) as deputy prime minister and minister of commerce, and Tarrin Nimmanahaeminda (a former finance minister) as finance minister.

The new government sent a *letter of intent* to the IMF confirming that it would adhere to the earlier IMF conditions besides specifying further measures that would be taken to re-establish confidence in the economy. The letter of intent stipulated that the new government will work towards a 1 per cent surplus in the 1997/98 budget by increasing indirect taxes, cutting the investment programmes of state-owned enterprises, raising utility prices, and lowering real wages in the public sector, just as further expenditure cuts were announced. Other measures included an accelerated and extensive privatisation programme, improving the financial system's regulatory framework, which would include more liberal rules for foreign investors, and accelerated and in-depth financial restructuring following the October guidelines (for details, see MOF Press Release Regarding Second Letter of Intent No. 69/1997).

Financial restructuring 'was done according to the strongest possible criteria'; it was announced on 8 December that only two of the 58 suspended finance companies had had their rehabilitation plans approved while the remaining 56 companies would be permanently closed. Their good assets would be transferred to one or two new banks while bad assets would be managed by the FRA and the AMC. Bad assets would be sold to the state-supported AMC for gradual market liquidation. The FRA had to complete the disposal of all assets by the end of 1998. Creditors (including foreigners) were assured that all creditors (i.e. also the FIDF) would be treated equally and that the assets disposal process would be orderly and fair. In August, creditors of the 42 finance companies were guaranteed by the government and could either take equity stakes in the good bank(s) or exchange their claims for negotiable certificates of deposit issued by the Krung Thai Bank at an interest rate of 2 per cent per annum over five years. By contrast, creditors of the 16 finance companies suspended in late June 1997 had to negotiate debt repayment schemes with the FRA and the FIDF. The liquidation scheme was announced in February 1998, and in the final scheme, assets were not classified into good and bad assets as evaluation of the quality of assets was left to bidders at auctions. However, assets were split into core assets (outstanding loans) and non-core assets (company assets, cars, etc.) with auctioning of the latter starting in late February. The book value of the assets was 866 billion baht, of which 30-60 per cent was expected to be retrieved from auctions and shared among creditors. In order to ensure that asset values 'are not unduly eroded by the dumping of assets' and to 'assure bids for each asset', the AMC was also meant to participate in auctions, as was the newly established Radhanasin Bank (RAB). During the auction process, the AMC was to focus on the lowest-quality assets and to serve as buyer of last resort, while the RAB was to bid for the highest quality assets and to be guided by commercial principles.[18]

The minister of finance further announced that the government and the BoT would 'take firm action against any institutions that endanger the public interest', that legal changes in the banking act would take place in 1998, and that a committee would be set up to restore the credibility of the BoT. The committee would also investigate the role of the BoT in the events leading to the collapse, i.e. into things such as the BBC scandal and the granting of 430 billion baht to the 58 suspended finance companies.[19]

Finally, the Chuan government took radical action when it *nationalised four medium-sized banks* — Bangkok Metropolitan Bank (BMB), First Bangkok City Bank, Siam City Bank and Bangkok Bank of Commerce — in order to prepare them for sale to foreign financial institutions. The action appeared to be inspired by the saving and loans industry bail-out in the US in the 1980s, as the BoT first wrote down shareholder capital to almost nothing and then converted short-term loans (through the FIDF) into equity, whereby the FIDF obtained almost total ownership of the banks. As a bail-out arm of the BoT, the FIDF had channelled more than 500 billion baht into the banking sector by late January (in addition to the 430 billion baht that had gone to the suspended finance companies). The BMB, which had more than 43 per cent of its loans considered non-performing at the end of November 1997 and more than half its funding reported to depend on short-term liquidity provided by the FIDF, was taken over by the central bank in late January 1998. The takeover included a write-off of 11 billion baht in bad loans, while the Techapaibul family, one of the Sino-Thai families controlling private commercial banks and finance companies, had to register a 3.8 billion baht loss. The BMB model was then utilised for the three other banks subjected to similar conditions.[20]

These measures and signals neither stopped the large net outflow of capital from Thailand nor stabilised the foreign exchange rate. When the exchange rate passed the US$1 to 50 baht threshold in early January 1998, talk of reviewing the IMF terms came up again. Prime Minister Chuan Leekpai stressed that the IMF had been too optimistic about economic recovery when it had drawn up the austerity measures, and identified the high interest rate policy and economic growth predictions as issues for discussion with the IMF. A downward revision of the latter would make it easier for Thailand to achieve the 1 per cent fiscal surplus goal in spite of an expected revenue shortfall of about 100 billion baht in 1998. Similar reservations about certain aspects of the IMF programme were expressed by Deputy Prime Minister Supachai and Finance Minister Tarrin (*Bangkok Post*, 7/1/98). After a visit by Tarrin to Washington, during the second IMF quarterly review of Thailand's performance under the rescue package, the IMF Asia-Pacific Director Hubert Neiss announced that the IMF would ease the economic bail-out conditions. Thailand would be allowed to run a budget deficit of about 1-2 per cent of GDP in the financial year ending 30 September 1998, instead of the previously stated 1 per cent surplus target. When the IMF decided to change its conditions, the baht was fluctuating in the range of US$1 to 41-47 baht, while an ease in the high interest policy was postponed to 'sometime after the currency market stabilises'. The new conditions (which included a more flexible interest rate policy) was stipulated in the Third Letter of Intent from the Royal Thai Government, which in turn led to IMF approval of the third tranche in early March 1998.[21]

From Financial Crisis to Socioeconomic Crises

The immediate effects of currency depreciation, capital flight, closing down 56 finance companies and cuts in the budget have been recessionary and a decline in imports, which has improved the balance of trade. During the last quarter of 1997, Thailand had a current account surplus, and a sizeable surplus is also expected in 1998 and 1999, providing foreign exchange for debt repayment. However, while the financial crisis might seem to be over, the economic and social crises have barely begun. According to official estimates, Thailand is expected to experience negative growth in 1998 (-3.0 to -3.5 per cent), with gross fixed investments expected to decline by 21 per cent, while capital outflow of US$12-14 billion is forecast for the same year (*Letter of Intent No. 3 from the*

Royal Thai Government, 24 February 1998). Some sectors have been, and will be, hit more than others.

Problems in the property market are still there and defaults by more property developers are expected. In the financial sector, the restructuring of the 56 finance companies through the FRA is proceeding. While Thai small and medium-sized commercial banks (some of which also faced severe difficulties during the mid-1980s financial crisis) have seen their deposits moving to foreign banks and the larger Thai commercial banks, some of them have been taken over by state or foreign banks. Thai Danu Bank was bought by the Development Bank of Singapore, while the writing down of equity and the nationalisation of the four medium-sized banks with liquidity problems and relatively greater exposure to property loans have taken place. Thus, the financial crisis has tended to favour the top five Thai commercial banks so far. But even these banks have opened their doors to foreign investors in their re-capitalisation efforts.

The Chuan government has promised the IMF that it will prepare a restructuring and privatisation strategy for the four nationalised banks by the end of June 1998. As Thai private bankers and some members of the cabinet are against the foreign takeover of the four banks, it is too early to rule out the possibility of the original owners buying assets back cheaply at future auctions (*FEER*, 5/3/98, p. 53).

Financial sector restructuring has seen further disintermediation as well as huge public costs. In addition to the write-off of shareholder equities, the costs of financially restructuring loans in finance companies and banks are expected to be in the range of 12-15 per cent of GDP, to be funded by the state budget (i.e. tax payers' money) and by the banks through their (higher) contributions to the FIDF. But the capacity of the fund is weak after its rescue operations in both the finance company and bank sectors. More specifically, the government will incorporate the interest costs of the debt of the FIDF into the public budgets, while the amortisation of the principal is expected to be paid through proceeds from the privatisation of state enterprises (*EIU Country Report: Thailand*, 1997: 4; *FEER*, 4/12/97; *Letter of Intent No. 3 from the Royal Thai Government*, 24 February 1998). Re-capitalisation of the financial sector will require US$10 to 25 billion over the next several years, and as local funds are tight, increased sale of equity to foreign financial institutions, even allowing foreign investors to take a majority stake, has been the strategy chosen.

In manufacturing industry, some sectors and some types of enterprises have been more affected than others. One major problem is the high import-intensity of much manufacturing. The lower value of the baht makes Thai exports more competitive, but the costs of imported components and raw materials have gone up too. Import content is high in 'sunrise' industries, such as computers, electronics and the automotive industry, which were expected to be the future backbone of Thai industry. The large Japanese automobile producers who rely on the domestic market have suffered and closed plants, while auto-makers from the US — Ford, GM and Chrysler — that had decided to use Thailand as their regional platform have 'postponed' their plans. A study showed that the decline from 26 baht to a US dollar to the new expected equilibrium exchange rate of 32 baht to a dollar (in early January 1998, the exchange rate was 56 baht to a dollar) (*Bangkok Post*, 25/10/97; *Bangkok Post*, 11/1/98; *Bangkok Post*, 13/1/98) would raise production costs of 20 export products by almost 15 per cent. In 1997, exports of automobiles and auto-parts as well as of some types of electrical and electronic products expanded in baht as well as dollar terms, but long-term prospects will depend on the extent to which assembly firms can increase local content.

In contrast, more 'sunset' industries — traditional export industries such as paper and pulp, textile, garment, footwear and food products — are expected to benefit from the baht devaluation, but that again will depend on the extent of competitive devaluation in other East Asian countries and trade policy in the EU and the US. Garments exports, which declined in 1996, improved substantially in 1997.

The baht's depreciation has also had a severe impact on the profits of large companies and conglomerates with unhedged foreign loans. A study of the impact of foreign exchange losses on corporate earnings in October 1997 revealed that companies in construction and petrochemicals were most vulnerable. Among the big losers were giants such as Thai Petrochemical Industry (TPI) and Siam Cement Company (which belongs to the Crown Property Bureau, i.e. the royal family). Some of the large companies have stopped paying back the principal, but continue to pay interest. However, the extent of bankruptcy in the corporate sector will probably be limited as the present (not yet amended) bankruptcy law makes it very difficult for collapsed companies to go bankrupt. Therefore, debt restructuring — involving debt-to-equity swaps combined with discount trading with so-called 'distressed corporate debt' — is more likely (*Bangkok Post*, 24/10/97; *EIU Country Report: Thailand*, 1997, 3; *Financial Times*, 14/1/98).

Generally, credit is drying up in Thailand and the liquidity problem is not only found among large enterprises. The suspension and later closure of 56 finance companies has particularly affected *small and medium-sized enterprises* (SMEs) that have obtained their working capital from these sources. 'Closing the finance companies imposed a heavy strain on the Thai economy, which relied on the non-collateralised loans they issued for working capital. "They were the lubricating mechanism for the trading sector all over Thailand" says a senior economic advisor to the government' (*FEER*, 4/9/97. See also *EIU Country Report: Thailand*, 1997, 3, p. 32).

Thailand's economic crisis might, to some extent, be cushioned by other sectors such as *agriculture and tourism*. Tourism is still the largest foreign exchange earner but the increase in arrivals in 1997 was less than 1 per cent (well below the 7 per cent forecast earlier), partly because travel from East Asia was affected by the financial crisis. Few believe that the 'Amazing Thailand' campaign for 1998-99 will achieve its tourism revenue target of 600 billion baht (*Bangkok Post*, 4/12/97; *Bangkok Post*, 2/1/98; Peerawat 1998). Although weather conditions were not very good in 1997, high prices and regional demand for tapioca and rice gave Thailand higher export earnings than in the year before.

Broader socioeconomic consequences have also appeared. Many once *nouveau rich* Thai entrepreneurs and middle class people operating in the local investment markets have become *nouveau poor*, and expensive cars and luxury items are now sold cheap in order to obtain hard cash.[22] Cases of suicide as a consequence of the financial crisis have also been reported. Even middle class consumers are changing their spending habits, cutting back on luxury items, particularly on imported goods. In October, Marks & Spencer reported that their sales had dropped by over 30 per cent. The retail market is generally expected to have declined in 1997 (for details see *Bangkok Post*, 26/10/97; *FEER*, 11/12/97).

The main factors affecting ordinary people's living standards are inflation and unemployment. Due to slow growth in the economy and available stocks of imported goods, *inflation* was just 5.7 per cent in 1997, but is expected to increase to 11-18 per cent in 1998. The final level of inflation will depend on whether the exchange rate stays grossly undervalued and whether or not the government introduces suggested increases in taxes on gasoline. Vegetable oil and rice price increases have already affected living conditions of poor families, and the World Bank has responded with a US$300 million social safety net programme (*Bangkok Post*, 6/2/98; *Bangkok Post*, 10/2/98; Chalongphob 1998). Unemployment is growing too, mainly in the finance and real estate sectors, construction and industries that manufacture goods with a high import content. It is estimated that around 600,000 people have already lost their jobs. More specifically, it is estimated that 20,000-30,000 workers have lost their jobs in the financial sector, and that there are 300,000-400,000 fewer construction workers. The car industry has reported almost 29,000 lay-offs. Further, it is estimated that small businesses have lost around 70,000 workers and that another half million people can expect to become unemployed in 1998. Generally, public data on unemployment are highly unreliable as there is no reporting system for job losses. The urban centres have been hit most. More than half of the labour force in Thailand is still engaged in agriculture, but the rural areas are affected by the decline in the flows of income from relatives working in Bangkok, while some unemployed workers survive by returning to the homes of their parents. Service and manufacturing enterprises outside Bangkok have also been affected by the closure of the 56 finance companies and the drying up of SME financing (*FEER*, 23/10/97; *FEER*, 30/10/97; *EIU Country Report: Thailand*, 1997, 4, p. 22; *The Nation*, 8/12/97).

Foreign workers are a particularly vulnerable group. In January 1998, Thailand's labour minister declared 'This is our country and we want to take it back', when he announced that the government planned to repatriate almost a million illegal foreign workers, mostly from Myanmar, and to refrain from renewing the work permits of almost 300,000 legally registered workers (*Financial Times*, 13/1/98; *FEER*, 22/1/98).

Concluding Remarks

The roots of Thailand's financial crisis date as far back as the early 1990s. Boosted by financial liberalisation, a second wave of foreign capital entered Thailand then. The first wave of East Asian direct investment had been pushed by the currency appreciations in Japan, South Korea and Taiwan after the Plaza Agreement, and pulled by cheap labour and land costs in Southeast Asia. The second wave of investments came predominantly from Europe, Japan and the US, pushed by declining returns in the stock market and low real interest rates in depressed Europe and recession-bound Japan, and pulled by high profit margins, high interest rates and low risk due to dollar-pegged currencies in Southeast Asia. In Thailand, net capital inflows (mostly in the form of short-term loans) increased from about 8 per cent of GDP in 1990 to 14 per cent of GDP in 1995. These capital inflows contributed to over-investment, especially in property, and eventually led to a property bubble (Bello 1998, Chalongphob 1998). The public sector was able to control its own debt creation, but after liberalisation of the capital account in 1993, it was unable to control a private sector that lacked discipline in its debt creation.

As the real economy weakened in 1996 with sluggish export growth and an increase in the current account deficit, even more 'hot money' flowed in to cover the deficit, but also encouraging more reckless investments and further asset price inflation.[23] The gradual loss of competitiveness during the 1990s was aggravated by the foreign exchange regime which tied the baht to a strengthening US dollar. The current account deficit widened and reached a level that worried currency traders in the post 'tequila crisis' period. When the creditors realised that 'the party was over', they over-reacted, as did local firms desperately trying to hedge their foreign exchange liabilities. As a consequence, the booming inflow of short-term funds turned into a panicky outflow of capital.

The BoT (as well as the Ministry of Finance), once reputed for its autonomy from politicians and its macroeconomic prudence, had gradually lost much of its autonomy since 1988, and had become increasingly controlled by politicians during the Banharn and Chavalit governments. The bank responded to the unfolding currency crisis by spending almost all its reserves defending the baht and by tightly controlling money supply to keep interest rates high. When it became clear that the property sector had left banks and finance companies with substantial bad debts on their balance sheets, the BoT — through its FiDF — pumped huge amounts of funds into weak financial institutions. Both the defence of the baht and the 430 billion baht pumped into the finance companies — not just to rescue depositors and creditors, but also investors — proved to be both costly and useless.

The Banharn and the Chavalit governments were fundamentally unstable and unable to offer credible macroeconomic policy. When the government intervened, it was in a 'too-little-too-late' fashion, with strong policy formulation usually followed by weak policy implementation. The political crisis aggravated the financial crisis by undermining investor confidence. The Banharn and Chavalit governments — like the governments before them — proved to be unable to implement more long-term strategies that could improve productivity and upgrade the industrial sector by restructuring away from low-cost assembly towards higher value-added production. Major issues — such as the low level of basic education, the shortage of skilled labour and technical skills, high interest rates and the power of commercial banks, the inefficient bureaucracy, insufficient infrastructure and low technological capability in private companies — were never addressed in any consistent manner by the state. 'Short-termism' also prevailed in the private sector, where investors went for 'easy profits' in the financial and property sectors or invested in joint ventures with foreign capital in manufacturing.

In the second half of 1997, an IMF-driven austerity and financial sector restructuring programme was introduced and implemented. So far, Thailand has stuck to the IMF prescriptions and has been commended by Michel Camdessus, 'for resolutely implementing the economic programme in very difficult circumstances' and for taking actions 'increasingly being reflected in improved market sentiments' (*Bangkok Post*, 6/3/98). The IMF has, as in South Korea, accepted some changes in the bail-out programme. More generally, the US and the IMF leaderships have gradually realised that the roots of the Asian financial crisis have been of a different nature than they had presumed. US Deputy Treasury Secretary Lawrence Summers expressed this new insight in the following manner: 'This crisis is profoundly different because it has its roots not in improvidence, but in economic structures. The problems that must be fixed are much more micro-economic than macroeconomic, and involve the private sector more and the public sector less' (*Financial Times*, 20/2/98).

In Thailand, as elsewhere in the region, IMF policy aims to restore foreign investor confidence, and if this policy works out, Thailand could, in some years, return to the economic growth pattern — based on relatively cheap labour and abundant natural resources — which fuelled growth during the decade prior to 1996. The devaluation of the baht will make it easier to exploit static comparative advantage, and increasingly, international banks, the Japanese government and the Asian Development Bank are injecting loan funds into the export sector to relieve the damaging shortage of liquidity there. In the long term, economic development will still depend on its ability to develop dynamic competitive advantages, just as its broader social and political development will depend on its ability to solve its problems of regional and social inequality in the country. In the medium term, Thailand is facing falling output, declining investment, bankruptcies, falling real wages and higher unemployment. The World Bank and the Asian Development Bank have approved social programmes for US$430 million and US$500 million respectively, but the effects of these programmes on the livelihoods of ordinary Thais are still to be seen. Also, these programmes cannot conceal the strategy chosen by the Chuan government and the IMF which focuses narrowly on the financial side of the crisis.

Notes

1. The investment ratio was also above 40 per cent during the 1990-92 period. Domestic savings increased too. The domestic savings ratio went up from 23 per cent in 1985 to 32 per cent in 1990 and 36 per cent in 1995 (Bank of Thailand data). See Muscat (1994: 294), OBI (September 1993, 3), OBI (May 1996, 3).

2. *EIU Country Report: Thailand* (1997: 4), *Bangkok Post* (12/8/97), *The Nation* (3/10/97), Sussangkarn (1998). TDRI included foreign liabilities of commercial banks in short-term debt, while total reserves included currency assets of commercial banks.

3. Warnings about over-supply in the property sector came as early as 1992-93. See, for instance, Kenneth Ywin, 'Beware of the Boom', *The Nation, Year in Review 1992*, January 1993.

4. Krugman's (1998) approach to the Asian crisis seems to highlight certain aspects of the economic collapse in Thailand. According to Krugman, the prices of assets (stocks and land) as well as the particular role played by financial intermediaries can explain financial excesses and financial collapse, and constitute the core of the Asian crises. 'The problem began with financial intermediaries — institutions whose liabilities were perceived as having an implicit government guarantee, but were essentially unregulated and therefore subject to severe moral hazard problems. The excessive risky lending of these institutions created inflation — not of goods but of asset prices. The overpricing of assets was sustained in part by a sort of circular process, in which the proliferation of risky lending drove up the prices of risky assets, making the financial condition of intermediaries seem sounder than it was. And then the bubble burst. The mechanism of crisis, I suggest, involved that same circular process in reverse, forcing them to cease operations, leading to further assets deflation.'

   As will be shown in a later section, Krugman's argument concerning the working of moral hazard problems in over-guaranteed, but under-regulated financial intermediaries certainly makes some sense in the Thai case. Financial intermediaries — in banks and, particularly, finance companies — became involved in excessive and speculative investments which can partly be explained with reference to moral hazard. These actions also have to be partly explained by the greed of the upper classes and the new middle classes. Finally, as Krugman himself mentions, access to the world capital market allowed the vicious spiral 'to translate into real excess capital accumulation', just as overseas investors provided all these credits, often without demanding any real security.

   Moreover, Krugman (1998) argues that the Asian crisis is only incidentally about currencies and that 'the boom-bust cycle created by financial excess preceded the currency crisis because the financial crisis was the real driver of the whole process, with the currency fluctuations more a symptom than a cause'. Although Krugman's contribution deserves much attention, it appears to underestimate the role played by the exchange rate, at least in the case of Thailand. Excessive and careless investments certainly were a major factor in the Thai financial crisis, but the virtually pegged exchange rate was another.

5. *Bangkok Post*, 6 October and 7 October (1997); *EIU Country Report: Thailand* 1997, 3; *EIU Country Report: Thailand*, 1997, 4. It should be noted that the debt–equity ratio was substantially lower than in South Korea for instance. According to Paribas Asia Equity, the debt–equity ratio for all unlisted non-financial companies was 139 per cent in 1995, but increased to 170 per cent in 1996 (*EIU Country Report: Thailand*, 1997: 3, 35-36). Although financing of equity through loans was not unusual in the corporate sector and although the debt–equity ratio went up, the Thai financial crisis does not conform to the 'Asia High Debt Model' suggested by Robert Wade and Frank Veneroso. The debt–equity ratio was not particularly high, and Thailand has developed through a fairly open economy

in which government-directed credit has played a very limited role as the state chose a hands-off stand and left credit allocation to the powerful private banks (Veneroso and Wade 1998).

6. Richard Doner and Daniel Unger (1993: 106). By the end of October 1997, the top five banks accounted for 70 per cent of bank assets, 75 per cent of bank deposits and 68 per cent of bank loans (Cholada Ingsrisawan and Parista Yuthamanop, January 1998).

7. The remaining restrictions covered capital outflows by Thais in the form of portfolio investments and real estate investments abroad.

8. For business in baht, the BIBF was not allowed to lend in baht to the domestic market (out-in) (Jaruwan 1992: 52, and Naris 1995: 172).

9. See Richard F. Doner and Anek Laothamatas (1994: 423-24). For details on the politics of devaluation during this period, see Doner and Unger (1993: 113-114), Robert Muscat (1994), Pasuk Phongpaichit and Chris Baker (1995: 149-51, 346-49).

10. Office of the Board of Investment (May 1996: 3). The intrinsic instability of the portfolio investments was demonstrated the following year when the net flow of equity securities (due to large negative net flows to the United Kingdom and the Netherlands) was minus 10 billion baht compared to plus 68 billion baht in 1993 (Bank of Thailand 1996: 83).

11. Thai exports declined by 1.3 per cent in 1996, compared to 24 per cent growth in 1995.

12. This complaint about the foreign exchange peg being 'too secure' was publicly stated by Finance Minister Surakiart Sathirathai at the Asian Development Bank meeting in Manila at the end of April 1996. He explicitly warned speculators: 'We want to send the message to speculators that there is some risk' (*FEER*, 16/5/96, p. 76). The weight of US dollars in the basket was 80 per cent, while the Japanese yen and the German mark had 12 per cent and 8 per cent weights respectively.

13. 'The stability of the baht had served the Thai economy well in the past, but directors recommended a greater degree of exchange rate flexibility to improve monetary autonomy and to reduce the incentive for short-term capital inflows.' IMF paper quoted here from Soonyuth Nunyamanee and Chiratas Nivatpumin (January 1998). The IMF suggested more flexibility, but did not suggest a free floating baht. During a Bank Indonesia–IMF sponsored conference in the Autumn of 1996 on macroeconomic issues in ASEAN countries, IMF managing director Michel Camdessus explicitly warned against the risk stemming from the large inflow of volatile short-term capital to ASEAN countries, as many of these inflows 'can be suddenly reversed, either because of changes in market sentiment about the recipient country, contagion effects, or changing financial market conditions in other countries.' According to Michel Camdessus (1998), 'Globalization has clearly put new strains on domestic financial systems, especially banks. Large capital inflows often lead to rapid expansion of domestic credit which can set the stage for problems in the financial sector, especially if prudential supervision and capital adequacy requirements are insufficient.... In many countries, increased inflows and domestic demand have stimulated excessive lending for consumption and real estate. At the same time, the risks in the region's financial markets have also increased owing to, among other factors, the many new incentives and instruments for domestic enterprises to borrow in foreign currency.' After having praised the ASEAN governments for the steps they had taken to reduce overheating and macro-economic imbalances, he suggested that further measures be taken to reduce current account deficits and strengthen the domestic financial sector, but that direct quantitative controls on private capital inflows would run against the thrust of external liberalisation and were therefore not advisable (*IMF Survey*, 25 November 1996, pp. 379-380).

14. When Amnuay testified before the Finance Committee in February 1998, he insisted that he had no knowledge about the disastrous build-up of foreign exchange contracts. He

explained that the currency deal occurred in the banking department of the Bank of Thailand and not in the exchange equalisation fund responsible for daily setting of the value of the baht. Amnuay also stated that 'the central bank is too independent. The central bank did (swap contracts) without the knowledge of the Finance Ministry, which only learnt about the matter afterwards when everything was too late' (*The Nation*, 10 February 1998).

15. *Bangkok Post Year-end 96 Economic Review* (January 1997); *Asia 1997 Yearbook*, Far Eastern Economic Review, p. 216. The autonomy was also eroded by the Economic Stability and Security Committee that tried to interfere in BoT interest rate policy and tried to change the way housing loans were categorised, probably in a move to bail-out troubled, but well connected investors in the property sector (*Bangkok Post*, 23 July 1996).

16. On the rise of Pin Chakkaphak and his Finance One as the leading finance company in Thailand and on its growing problems in 1996 and 1997, see *Financial Times*, 12 January 1998, pp. 6-7.

17. The FIDF had injected 200 billion baht in the first group of 16 suspended fincos (including Finance One) and 230 billion baht in the second group of 42 fincos (Nuntawan Polkwamdee 1998).

18. *Bangkok Post*, 14 February 1998 and Letter of Intent no. 3 and Memorandum on Economic Policies of the Royal Thai Government, 24 February 1998. The liabilities of the finance firms amounted to 430 billion baht to the FIDF and 855 billion baht to local and overseas investors.

19. *Bangkok Post*, 8 December 1997, and speech of the FRA chairman Dr Twatchai Yong-kittikul and speech of Minister of Finance, Mr Tarrin (1997); *Bangkok Post*, 21 December 1997. The new committee was the second appointed in 1997 to investigate the procedures of the Bank of Thailand. In July 1997, then Finance Minister Thanong appointed the so-called Suthee Committee to evaluate the central bank's supervisory and examination procedures (Cholada Ingsrisawan and Parista Yuthumanop 1998).

20. *Financial Times*, 22 January 1998; *Financial Times*, 24 January 1998; *Bangkok Post*, 26 January 1998; *Bangkok Post*, 27 January 1998; *Bangkok Post*, 28 January 1998; *Bangkok Post*, 6 February 1998; *Bangkok Post*, 10 February 1998; *Bangkok Post*, 14 February 1998. Siam City Bank also had to write down capital during the 1983-86 financial crisis. For details on the Techapaipul (Tejapaipul) family, its investments in the financial sector and its links to other major Sino-Thai families, see Hewison 1989, pp. 104-109.

21. *Far Eastern Economic Review*, 22 January 1998, p. 21; *Bangkok Post*, 13 February 1998; *Bangkok Post*, 14 February 1998; *Bangkok Post*, 6 March 1998; Letter of Intent no. 3 and Memorandum on Economic Policies of the Royal Thai Government, 24 February 1998. The IMF explained its new policy by referring to the danger that the continued austerity regime might induce a new economic crisis. While the softening of conditions did 'save' the Chuan government, which was unable to cut public sector expenses and raise taxes sufficiently to reach the previous target, increasing protests from the business community against high interest rates did not initially change the IMF position on that issue. It should also be noticed that the revised IMF approach came after the Chuan government had firmly moved to clean up the four mid-sized banks and had eased the foreign exchange controls it introduced in May 1997 to protect the value of the baht on 30 January 1998.

22. In 1995, new Mercedes Benz sales in Thailand ranked third in the world. Nuntawan Polkwamdee (1998).

23. As suggested by Krugman (1998), a boom-bust cycle of property and stock markets preceded the financial crisis. Although Krugman's analysis points to a crucial aspect, other factors also contributed to Thailand's economic crisis.

7
INDONESIA:
REAPING THE MARKET

Manuel F. Montes and Muhammad Ali Abdusalamov

The Indonesian economy found itself in a state of near collapse in January 1998, in the midst of the Asian economic crisis that had been triggered by the devaluation of the Thai baht in July 1997. There is no shortage of explanations for Indonesia's crisis: from instabilities in international currency markets to unsound macroeconomic management to domestic corruption.

This chapter attempts to sort out the roles of these different explanations. It develops the following thesis. When the currency crisis erupted in Asia, Indonesia had an excessively expanded and weak banking system as a result of the imprudent financial liberalisation process it had been undertaking since the 1980s. Such imprudent and unsustainable processes have been known to occur in episodes in other countries (Chile before its 1981 crisis, Norway, Sweden and Finland before 1992, Mexico before 1995); all of these cases, and Indonesia's, abounded with aggressive lending practices, poor prudential supervision and insider exploitation of the process.

As the crisis erupted, Indonesia carried out classic adjustment policies of tight credit and higher interest rates that exacerbated the weakness in the banking system. The impact of credit constriction on the real sector is to reduce expected profits in companies and the banking system. These abetted further attacks on the equity and other asset markets, worsening the performance of the rupiah. The worsening rupiah further weakened the economy's prospects and encouraged investment withdrawals.

We situate the crisis squarely in the asset markets, stemming from the interaction between a weak financial system and volatile international capital markets, instead of in the real flow markets. We take the position that Indonesia's 'fundamentals', meaning the state of the commonly measured flow deficits, were sound, but that these are being subsequently undermined by policies in response to the crisis.

Interpreted this way, Indonesia's experience raises strong cautionary signals in regard to economic liberalisation with ballooning dependence on international finance. These have been evident not only after the crisis erupted but were also particularly deleterious to Indonesia in setting the stage for its crisis.

Setting the Stage

When the Indonesian financial system began to be liberalised in 1983, the capital markets had been under a dense set of regulatory restrictions and practices. These restrictions have to be understood in the context of Indonesia as a major world exporter of oil. The oil boom of the 1970s resulted in enormous inflows of foreign exchange into Indonesia affecting domestic spending and inflation. The central bank imposed credit ceilings in order to control credit growth and money supply. These credit ceilings, coupled with the availability of cheap funding through the central bank's liquidity credits, left no motivation for domestic banks to attract deposits and extend credits; ceilings on interest rates kept both deposit and loan rates below the inflation rate. At the same time, low deposit rates, the open capital account, stable exchange rates and credit ceilings encouraged the investment abroad of excess funds of domestic banks, creating an outward flow of foreign exchange (Cole and Slade 1996: 19), which had salutary effects for a country that espoused the export-oriented development model of keeping the rupiah weak and restraining the onset of 'Dutch disease'.

The attention of the central bank during the period 1970-82 was focused generally on credit controls of banks. Central bank management has always put great stress on controlling inflation after the experience of the mid-1960s. In this regard, the policy had been quite successful. Table 7.1 shows that since the 1970s, inflation has generally been kept at below two digits. If all the export inflows had been monetised, either inflation would have been higher or the rupiah would have been appreciating more strongly. However, credit controls could be criticised for not being market-oriented and for being prone to corruption.

In 1977, the continuing inflows of foreign exchange forced the government to reduce the required reserve ratio from 30 to 15 per cent. This measure, along with credit ceilings, encouraged banks to increase their foreign assets abroad, i.e. to increase the overall foreign exchange reserves of the economy (Nasution 1994: 134). As a measure to defend the producers of exportable goods against the continuing inflationary processes, the central bank made a 'surprise' devaluation of the rupiah by more than 50 per cent against the US dollar in 1978. This has to be understood as a signal event, since at that juncture, the rupiah should have appreciated with the second oil shock.

It is important to recognise the role of the Indonesian financial system before liberalisation. Economies that eventually found themselves in a banking-cum-balance of payments crisis had undertaken the 'twin liberalisations', the liberalisation of the domestic financial system and the capital account (Reinhart and Dunaway 1996; Montes 1998). By conventional standards, Indonesia had opened its capital account by 1970; Indonesians have been free to purchase financial assets denominated in foreign currencies. They could open bank accounts in Singapore and US dollar accounts in Indonesian banks in Jakarta.

Table 7.1
Indonesia: Inflation and Monetary Aggregates

Year	Inflation Rate	M1/GDP	M2/GDP
1966	635.30	3.219	3.262
1967	154.00	3.701	3.831
1968	125.20	5.437	6.009
1969	17.90	6.769	8.608
1970	12.40	7.542	9.946
1971	4.00	8.715	12.745
1972	6.70	10.408	15.228
1973	30.60	9.906	14.615
1974	41.00	8.750	13.560
1975	18.80	9.887	15.646
1976	20.00	10.364	17.011
1977	11.00	10.540	16.450
1978	8.20	10.938	16.746
1979	20.60	10.570	16.306
1980	18.50	10.991	16.923
1981	12.20	12.003	17.984
1982	9.60	11.941	18.572
1983	11.70	9.751	18.890
1984	10.50	9.547	19.955
1985	4.70	10.417	23.870
1986	5.90	11.372	26.938
1987	9.20	10.163	27.148
1988	8.10	10.128	29.554
1989	6.00	12.031	35.114
1990	9.50	12.096	42.977
1991	9.50	11.597	43.612
1992	4.90	11.190	46.289
1993	9.80	11.161	44.031
1994	9.20	11.871	45.658
1995	8.60	11.644	49.215
1996	6.50	12.116	54.566

Notes: M1 = currency and demand deposits; M2 = M1 plus savings deposits.
The inflation rate is the percentage change in the Consumer Price Index
(CPI) based on 1988-89 = 100.

Sources: David C. Cole and Betty F. Slade (1996); Bank Indonesia, IFS.

Banking-cum-balance of payments crises follow on a lending boom fed by foreign exchange inflows. However, because of its oil revenues, Indonesia was quite practised in absorbing foreign exchange inflows — through the administered credit ceiling programme. As explained above, this programme put a ceiling on the liquidity injections from the foreign exchange inflows and helped to keep the rupiah weak by encouraging the outward investment of these same flows. These administered ceilings were, in effect, controls on capital inflows; at the same time, Indonesia did not have any controls on capital outflows. When Indonesia liberalised its domestic financial system, it was, in effect, dismantling its controls on capital inflows, setting up the infrastructure for the boom-to-bust process. When the bust period came, Indonesia, unlike China, did not have controls on capital outflows. As in other economies in which the financial system was both narrow (a limited number of financial instruments in the market) and shallow (limited secondary markets for financial assets), almost all portfolio realignments of Indonesian financial asset holders became withdrawals from rupiah-denominated assets.

Financial Liberalisation

In 1982, declining oil prices resulted in sharp decreases in government revenues, which forced the government to cut spending by curtailing a number of investment projects. The rupiah was further devalued by 38.5 per cent in March 1983, and major financial sector deregulation was announced by the government, called PAKJUN 1, 1983.

The liberalisation of the domestic financial sector began as part of Indonesia's response to the 1982 crisis, triggered by the sharp decline in international oil prices. This programme: 1) abolished the credit ceiling system as a means of monetary control and introduced indirect monetary instruments; 2) reduced the injections of liquidity into the market through the liquidity credits of the central bank; 3) permitted state-owned banks to fix their own interest rates and encouraged all banks to mobilise deposits from the public and to extend credits. In other words, banks were free to establish loan rates at the levels they thought feasible for a particular project and to pay deposit rates at the levels necessary to attract money from the public.

In light of the fact that the credit ceiling system restricted capital inflows, as explained in the previous section, by dismantling these controls, the liberalisation programme injected new resources into the economy.

Private banks took on more risky projects and used the flexibility to extend credit quickly, while state banks, hampered by cumbersome procedures in granting loans, were more successful in attracting deposits, as they were considered less risky by the public and had better developed and spread networks of branches. Private banks were in constant shortage of funds while state banks were in surplus, which resulted in dynamic development of the inter-bank money market, with initially high fluctuating interest rates. Higher interest and deposit rates encouraged foreign currency inflows, including banks' repatriated foreign exchange, which significantly affected the amount of funds being exchanged on the inter-bank market. It also contributed to overall confidence in the stability of the rupiah. In 1984, the central bank introduced the Sertifikat Bank Indonesia (SBI), a short-term liability of the bank, to manage overall liquidity and the Surat Berharga Pasar Uang (SBPU), a banker's acceptance instrument which could be sold to Bank Indonesia at a discount.

The October 1988 package (PAKTO 27, 1988) constituted Indonesia's most ambitious financial reform effort. It introduced measures to foster competition, such as:

a) the removal of most restrictions on entry of foreign banks and the establishment of branches of domestic banks;
b) permitting public sector entities to place up to 50 per cent of their deposits outside state banks;
c) permitting non-bank financial institutions (NBFIs) to issue certificates of deposit;
d) permitting banks and NBFIs to raise equity capital in the stock markets;
e) easing entry to leasing, insurance, venture capital, cònsumer finance, factoring and securities activities;
f) drastically reducing bank reserve requirements from 15 to 2 per cent;
g) instituting improvements in other aspects of bank soundness requirements.

These reforms also provided for the setting up of a privately owned parallel stock market with less strict listing requirements, with permission, in principle, for the establishment of other private stock exchanges.

The package provided the basis for the explosive growth of banks and new branches in 1988 and 1989; the total number of banks increased from 124 (with 2,044 branch offices) in 1988 to 158 in 1989. By 1994, there were 244 banks, with 6,090 branch offices. The unleashed competitive pressures required each of Indonesia's large private conglomerates to own at least one bank; pension funds of state-owned enterprises established their own banks. Chart 7.1 dramatically illustrates the sharp rise in the number of banks after 1988, while the number of state banks stays constant at seven banks. The weakening of differentiation by function in the financial sector encouraged all the NBFIs to become fully-fledged commercial banks in 1993. The rapid growth in the banking and branching network was already raising concerns about the minimal level of prudential regulation.

In September 1989, foreigners were given the right to buy up to 49 per cent of all issued securities of firms listed on the stock exchanges. Banks were permitted to operate more actively in foreign exchange and open branch offices abroad, while foreign banks enjoyed eased entry into the Indonesian economy. Indonesian

Chart 7.1
Indonesia: Growth and Type of Banks, 1979-96

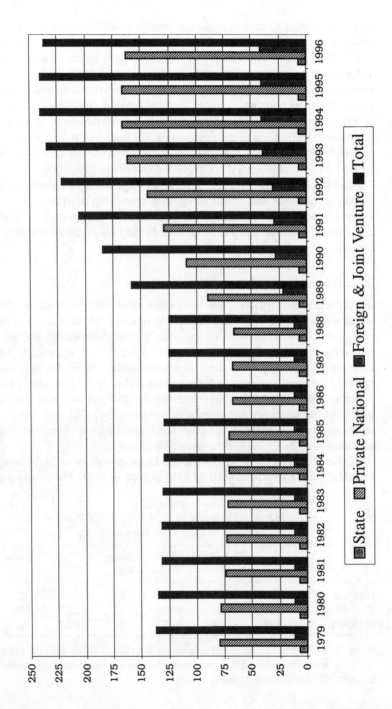

banks authorised to deal in foreign exchange established branches in 14 foreign countries, including tax havens such as the Cayman and Cook Islands (Nasution 1996: 9). Japanese, American, and later, European banks established offices in Indonesia to serve transnationals from their countries locating operations in Indonesia. Foreign-owned banks also increased their activities in arranging private sector loans to both government and Indonesian companies, and serving as conduits for official development assistance from their own governments and multilateral institutions to the government. Ceilings on offshore borrowings were replaced by a system of Net Open Positions (NOPs),[1] and limits for inflows of foreign direct investments were abolished (Nasution 1996: 11).

The Banking Law of 1992 unified the regulations governing the banking system in Indonesia and further deregulated ownership restrictions in the financial system. It permitted commercial banks to issue shares through stock exchanges and allowed foreigners to purchase up to 49 per cent of the shares of commercial banks at the stock exchange.

Success in Increasing Financial Intermediation

By conventional measures, the Indonesian financial liberalisation effort was a signal success. The number of banks and NBFIs more than doubled in the first two years. Their repatriation or any other inflow from abroad and the decrease in reserve requirements led to an enormous increase in the size of funds intermediated in the financial system, an amount called 'TAFI' for total assets of all types of financial institutions by the main architects of the reform programme (Cole and Slade 1996). Both increases in the numbers of banks and NBFIs and growth of M1 (currency and demand deposits) and M2 (M1 plus savings deposits) increased the concentration of assets in financial institutions and the level of intermediation by them in the system (Wardhana 1995: 88).

Table 7.2 captures the growth of the financial system of Indonesia, with the M2/GDP ratio rising from 0.10 in 1970 to 0.40 in 1991. The slowing growth of

Table 7.2
Indonesia: Ratios of M2 and TAFI* to GDP and to
Each Other, 1970-91 (selected years)

	1970	Growth (%)	1982	Growth (%)	1988	Growth (%)	1991
M2/GDP	0.10	47	0.19	36	0.30	25	0.40
TAFI/GDP	0.26	50	0.52	35	0.81	21	1.03
M2/TAFI	0.38	(0.02)	0.37	0	0.37	0.05	0.39

Note: * TAFI is a measure of all financial assets, but excludes the assets of the central bank or capital market instruments held by non-financial institutions.

Source: Cole and Slade (1996).

the TAFI/GDP ratio suggests that banks still possess a significantly larger portion of the total financial system. This is proved by the decrease between 1970 and 1982 of the M2/TAFI ratio, representing the share of the financial system controlled by institutions other than banks, and almost no further growth since. As can be seen from above, banks still play a significantly more important role than other institutions in the development of the financial system of Indonesia.

Vulnerable Domestic Financial and Capital Markets

As in other countries, financial liberalisation sparked a lending boom in Indonesia, which progressively involved lending for property development and an increasing proportion of bad loans. The liberalisation process left a weakened banking system and domestic capital markets that would be highly vulnerable to falls in the international value of the rupiah in its wake.

To be accurate, the financial reforms in the 1980s were also meant to reduce problems inherent in the state-dominated financial system. On the other hand, the reasons could be traced even further in the past to when large state-owned banks were the conductors of central bank subsidised credits. Later, they became the first targets for implementation of the so-called 'Sumarlin shocks', in which state deposits were transferred to the central bank in order to quickly reduce domestic liquidity. The portfolios of state banks were traditionally weaker as practices used by the state banks in evaluating projects, assessing collateral, etc. came as a legacy of the old system, i.e. state banks, with their cumbersome procedures, were not flexible enough to adjust to the new situation. Bad debts were also the result of a number of malpractices involving various fraud schemes and overall corruption in which credits were extended on the basis of personal contacts and recommendations.

After liberalisation, the problems of poor lending practices in the public sector did not subside; with the inflow of foreign financing, there were more resources to lend out. In 1993, newly-appointed minister of finance Mar'ie Muhammad discovered that six out of seven state-owned banks were technically insolvent and urgently needed re-capitalisation up to 8 per cent in accordance with the 1991 prudential regulations (Cole and Slade 1996: 138-139). Through a merger programme, only completed on 31 July 1998, the seven state banks were reduced to three; by then, the Thai crisis had already broken out.

Liberalisation of the domestic financial system added private players to the game and saw an enormous increase in foreign financiers' interest in providing resources to the system. But private domestic banks did not necessarily fare better in terms of their loan performance. According to initial estimates in April 1995 and April 1996, state-owned banks accounted for 72.0 per cent and 65.9 per cent of all bad debts in the banking sector respectively (Table 7.3). Table 7.3 indicates that 5.08 per cent of the total credit of state-owned banks and 5.82 per

Table 7.3
Indonesia: Status of Bank Credit, 1993-1995

	Amount (Rp trillion)				Composition (percentages)			
	Oct. 93	Dec. 93	Mar. 94	Dec. 94	Oct. 93	Dec. 93	Mar. 94	Dec. 94
All banks								
Total credit	170.6	177.5	185.8	217.0	100.0	100.0	100.0	100.0
Current	143.5	152.3	159.4	190.9	84.1	85.8	85.8	88.0
Classified[a]	27.1	25.1	26.4	26.2	15.9	14.2	14.2	12.1
State-owned banks[b]								
Total credit	92.4	94.1	96.9	104.1	100.0	100.0	100.0	100.0
Current	72.8	75.5	77.5	84.7	78.8	80.2	80.1	81.4
Classified	19.6	18.6	19.3	19.4	21.2	19.8	19.9	18.6
Private banks								
Total credit	74.6	79.8	85.4	108.7	100.0	100.0	100.0	100.0
Current	68.2	74.0	79.1	102.8	91.4	92.1	92.6	94.6
Classified	6.8	5.8	6.3	5.9	8.6	7.3	7.4	5.4

Memorandum: Non-Performing Loans by Bank's Ownership, April 1995 (as percentage of)

	Total Assets	Total Credit	Capital, Reserves and Profit & Loss
State-owned banks (including Bapindo)	7.38	8.84	103.80
State-owned banks (excluding Bapindo)	4.24	5.08	59.59
Private National Forex Banks	1.04	1.16	10.39
Private National Non-Forex Banks	5.13	5.82	32.54
Foreign and Joint Venture Banks	2.03	2.88	20.21

Notes: a Classified loans consist of three categories, namely: 'sub-standard', 'doubtful' and 'loss'.
b Includes Bapindo and Bank Tabungan Negara, but excludes Regional Development Banks.
Sources: Nasution (1996: Table 4).

cent of the total credit of private non-foreign exchange banks were non-performing by 1995.

This meant that banks would have needed a margin of about 6 per cent on their loans in order to absorb the losses on their existing loans. Because of financial liberalisation, banks had to compete for deposits, and deposit rates went up. The high domestic interest rates also encouraged domestic corporations to borrow externally, putting a cap on the interest rates that could be charged on the lending side. Table 7.4 provides estimates that the interest differential between lending and deposit rates for domestic banks was at the maximum of 6 per cent in 1993, but declined to 2 per cent by 1996.

The Indonesian financial system therefore approached the 1997 Asian currency crisis with a banking system heavily in need of re-capitalisation (in anticipation of the write-offs of non-performing debt). The private corporate sector and the banking system had heavy unhedged external liabilities mostly denominated in US dollars. A fall in the international value of the rupiah would immediately impose debt servicing difficulties on the corporate and banking sectors. A strategy of tight liquidity to defend the rupiah had the potential of causing a crash in the banking system, already teetering on the verge of bankruptcy. This is what happened next.

Asian Crisis Erupts

When Thailand secured IMF credit after devaluing the baht on 2 July 1997, Indonesia and South Korea, both subsequently victims of the crisis, participated in the Thai rescue package, finalised on 5 August 1997, both pledging half a billion US dollars each.

State of the Economy

When the Asian crisis began in mid-1997, Indonesia's macroeconomic situation was sound. While this interpretation is contrary to the position taken by other economists in Indonesia's politically charged situation (for example, see Nasution 1998), it is difficult to interpret the data otherwise. Of course, any macroeconomic configuration can certainly be sounder, at the cost of a lower economic growth rate. Table 7.5 shows that GDP had been growing at nearly 8 per cent per year in the previous two years while the current account deficit hovered at 4 per cent.

Reisen (1997) argues that current account deficits even higher than 8 per cent of GDP could be sustainable if account is taken of a country's existing external debt, advantages in productivity growth and the extent to which its capital inflows are of the more stable variety, such as direct foreign investment. Table 7.5 suggests that of the 3.7 per cent current account deficit in 1995, 2.2 per cent was financed by (net) direct foreign investment; this suggests that current account deficits of over 4 per cent, as in 1996, would have been sustainable. With the breakdown

Table 7.4
Indonesia: Monetary and Banking Data, 1990-96

	1990	1991	1992	1993	1994	1995	1996
Rate of Growth Money Supply (% per year)							
M1 (Narrow Money)	15.9	12.1	7.9	27.8	23.3	16.1	21.7
M2 (Broad Money)	44.6	17.5	21.1	21.5	20.1	27.5	29.6
Rate of Growth Bank Credit (% per year)							
State Foreign Exchange Banks	54.2	16.3	8.9	22.3	25.7	24.2	24.9
Private National Banks	35.2	11.8	14.0	4.8	11.8	16.8	16.5
Foreign National Banks	88.1	19.6	1.2	42.8	42.8	29.4	34.3
Foreign & Joint Venture Banks	98.3	37.8	9.6	57.9	24.7	32.0	13.8
Regional Development Banks	41.7	13.6	15.3	17.9	18.2	24.8	23.2
Memorandum items:							
1. Dollar deposits at DMB as % of M2	17.3	20.2	19.1	17.5	17.5	17.4	17.2
2. Credit in dollar as % of total credit	12.2	15.6	17.9	18.8	19.1	19.5	20.2
3. % of total excess liquidity of DMBs held in US$	3.5	3.6	6.9	13.6	9.3	6.8	2.7
4. The role of SBI in total market instrument (%)	100.0	71.6	88.0	94.4	79.7	73.8	78.7
5. Deposit rates (3 month, % p.a.)	21.0	23.4	19.5	14.5	12.6	16.8	17.2
6. Lending rates (working capital, % p.a.)	21.0	25.2	24.1	20.5	17.8	18.9	19.2
7. Interest differential (6-5) (%)	0.0	1.8	4.5	6.0	5.1	2.1	2.0

Note: DMB – Deposit Money Bank;   SBI – Sertifikat Bank Indonesia.
Source: Nasution (1998: Table 2).

Table 7.5
Indonesia: Macroeconomic Fundamentals, 1990-96
(percentages of GDP, unless otherwise indicated)

	1990	1991	1992	1993	1994	1995	1996
Real GDP growth rate (%)	9.0	8.9	7.2	7.3	7.5	8.1	7.8
Inflation Rate (CPI, %)	9.5	9.5	4.9	9.8	9.2	8.6	6.5
Fiscal Balance	0.4	0.4	-0.4	-0.6	0.1	0.8	0.2
Current Account Balance	-2.8	-3.7	-2.2	-1.6	-1.7	-3.7	-4.0
Net Capital Inflows	4.9	5.0	3.8	1.9	2.4	4.6	5.0
of which:							
Net Portfolio Investment	-0.1	0.0	-0.1	1.1	2.2	2.0	n.a.
Net Direct Investment	1.0	1.3	1.4	1.3	1.2	2.2	n.a.
Other Capital	3.3	3.6	3.5	1.4	-0.9	1.3	n.a.
Net Error and Omissions	0.7	0.1	-1.0	-1.9	-0.1	-0.9	n.a.
Consumption	63.3	64.1	61.8	64.7	65.6	65.9	66.0
Private	54.4	55.0	52.3	55.7	57.4	57.8	58.3
Government	9.0	9.1	9.5	9.0	8.1	8.1	7.7
National Savings	27.5	26.9	26.9	27.0	28.4	28.0	28.5
Private	19.1	19.8	20.5	20.4	22.0	22.4	22.8
Public	8.4	7.1	6.4	6.6	6.4	5.6	5.7
Investment	30.1	29.9	29.0	28.3	30.3	31.3	32.1
Private	23.5	21.7	20.9	20.9	24.0	25.8	26.9
Public	6.6	7.7	7.8	7.4	6.3	5.5	5.3

(continued...)

Table 7.5 (continued)

Indonesia: Macroeconomic Fundamentals, 1990-96

(percentages of GDP, unless otherwise indicated)

	1990	1991	1992	1993	1994	1995	1996
Reserves (in months of imports)	4.7	4.8	5.0	5.2	5.0	4.4	5.1
Ratio M2 to Reserves (%)	514.0	505.7	497.4	557.1	602.9	657.4	633.3
Total External Debt (percentage of Exports of Goods and Services)	222.0	236.9	221.8	211.9	195.8	205.0	194.0
Short-term Debt (percentage of Total External Debt)	15.9	17.9	20.5	20.1	17.7	20.9	24.8
Short-term Debt (in US$ billion)	11.1	14.3	18.1	18.0	17.1	24.3	29.3
Debt Service Ratio (percentage of Exports of Goods and Services)	30.9	32.0	31.6	33.8	30.0	33.7	33.0
Exports (% of GDP)	26.6	27.4	29.4	25.9	26.0	26.0	26.2
Exports (% of growth rate)	15.9	13.5	16.6	8.4	8.8	13.4	9.7
Oil Price (US$ per barrel)	28.64	20.06	18.71	14.14	16.11	18.02	22.78

Source: Nasution (1998).

of Indonesia's financial system, maintaining its previously high level of direct foreign investment inflows has become problematic.

Trends between 1995 and 1996 suggest the strengthening of Indonesia's fundamentals; figures for 1997 are unavailable and in any case, would also be tainted by the crisis response. Table 7.5 suggests reserves (measured in months of imports) improved to five months in 1996, while the ratio of M2 to the level of reserves declined in 1996. The debt service ratio stayed steady at 33 per cent in 1996 while total external debt as a proportion of exports declined in 1996. The total amount of Indonesia's foreign debt underwent revisions as the crisis unfolded since data on the extent of private external borrowing were not readily available. The most recent estimate at the time of writing (March 1998) is that Indonesia's foreign debt is US$137.4 billion; of this, private corporate debt is US$73.96 billion.

The only disturbing item in Table 7.5 is the increase in short-term debt, which jumped from 17.7 per cent of total debt in 1994 and 20.9 per cent in 1995 to 24.8 per cent in 1996. As in Thailand (Montes 1998), the increase in short-term debt was due to a complicated set of factors, mostly related to the financial liberalisation process. High domestic interest rates, brought about by the authorities' efforts to maintain modest increases in money supply in the face of persistent capital inflows, encouraged further capital inflows into short-term instruments. In this situation, the alternative would have been to let the rupiah appreciate even more, which would certainly have weakened the fundamentals.

The main point here is that the breakdown between short and long-term debt is not as easily susceptible to influence by standard macroeconomic instruments. This problem needs to be addressed, either with controls or taxes — as Chile has been doing (Agosin and Ffrench-Davis 1997). But installing capital controls and taxing capital inflows run contrary to the overall liberalisation stance. Hence, while the fundamentals were relatively sound, it was the weakened banking sector, resulting from the liberalisation process, which explains the crisis.

Crisis Response

When the crisis began in Thailand, Indonesia had already been implementing a tight credit stance, but for contrary reasons — to prevent the continued capital inflow from expanding domestic money supply. In April 1997, for example, it raised bank reserve requirements from 3-5 per cent. With the crisis, Indonesian authorities responded by continuing to tighten credit in order to fend off attacks on the rupiah. On 2 July 1997, banks were completely prohibited from increasing credit to property development except for low-cost housing.

Withdrawals from rupiah-denominated assets started and soon gained strength. Chart 7.2 chronicles the rupiah-dollar exchange rate from 1 July to 27 November 1997, while Chart 7.3 shows the exchange rate from 1 December 1997 to 6 February 1998. On 11 July, Indonesia widened the intervention band for the

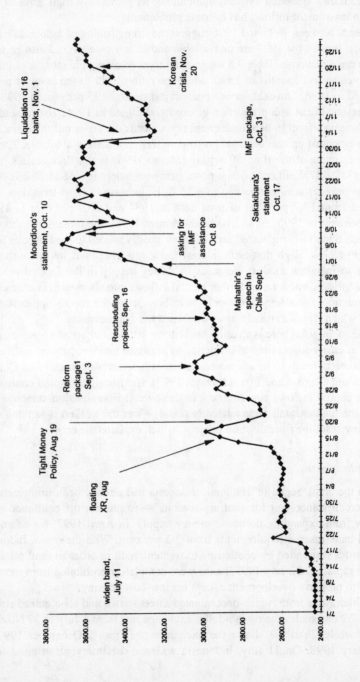

Chart 7.2
Rupiah/US Dollar Movements, 1 July–27 November 1997

Source: Presentation Notes of Mari Pangestu, 9 March 1998.

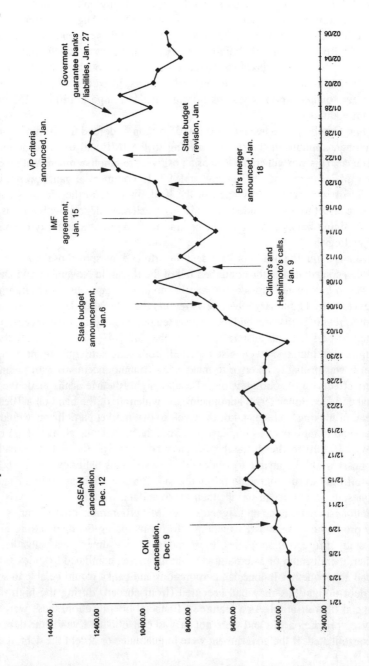

Chart 7.3
Rupiah/US Dollar Movements, 1 December 1997–6 February 1998

Source: Presentation Notes of Mari Pangestu, 9 March 1998.

exchange rate from 8 to 12 per cent. Between 20 and 22 July, Indonesia used US$1 billion to support the currency. Between 22 July and 18 August, interest rates were raised from 7 per cent to 30 per cent. On 14 August, Indonesia abandoned the crawling peg and installed a managed floating currency system; it also withdrew Rp12 trillion from liquidity by instructing banks to transfer public sector deposits to the central bank. In September, Indonesia announced the postponement of US$37 billion of public sector-related projects, lifted the 49 per cent ceiling on foreign ownership in new stock offerings and cut import tariffs on 153 groups of commodities.

On 6 October, Indonesia used US$0.65 billion to defend the currency, and on 8 October, announced that it was turning to the IMF and external donors for assistance. This was generally seen as a positive, pre-emptive move. With the start of the IMF programme on 31 October 1997, 16 commercial banks were closed. Instead of improving confidence in the banking system, the closures had the opposite effect to that intended; the closures accelerated deposit withdrawals from the remaining banks and forced the central bank to provide liquidity beyond the IMF ceilings.

Doubts about the health of President Suharto and the spread of the Asian crisis to Korea contributed to the continued fall of the rupiah in November and December. When Indonesian President Suharto announced a new budget programme on the evening of 11 January 1998, news reports the following day were dominated by interpretations that the budget represented defiance of the IMF because it was judged to be not at all austere. Rumours that the IMF was cutting off its programme with Indonesia were also reported. Both were subsequently proven to be false. It was probably an error to make such an announcement, with potentially strong effects on the currency, on a Tuesday night (the Mexicans made the same mistake in December 1994, announcing the widening of the band on a Tuesday), instead of making it at the end of the week so that market participants would have a weekend to mull over its implications. Still, the precipitous plunge of the rupiah to over 10,000 to the dollar began on Wednesday as the belief spread that Indonesia would be unable to work with the IMF. This belief eventually became self-fulfilling as the continued fall in the rupiah made it increasingly difficult for Indonesian companies to service their external debt.

Indonesia negotiated and signed a new IMF programme on 15 January 1998. This programme contained sweeping reforms including the dismantling of state and state-enforced monopolies, the removal of consumer price subsidies, and further liberalisation of external trade. But the rupiah continued to slide as doubts spread as to whether Indonesian corporations and banks would be able to service the debt obligations they had accepted (from abroad) during the high tide of financial liberalisation. As a feature of financial liberalisation, these were debts between private parties and were not easy to consolidate. Even if the debt could be consolidated, if the government were to guarantee or accept the debt, it would create enormous moral hazard, and permanently characterise financial liberalisation programmes as efforts to create private wealth from public finances for external creditors and favoured Indonesian parties.

The continued fall in the rupiah had rendered the IMF programme irrelevant to economic stabilisation; the 15 January 1998 programme had assumed an exchange rate of Rp5,000 to the dollar while the exchange rate hovered around Rp8,000. Indonesia took the initiative of preparing to install a currency board system as a response to its situation of clear distress. A currency board, however, only restores stability when it has the features of a 'classic currency board', that is, in 'auto-pilot' as far as possible, with the government's ability to determine domestic money supply totally restricted.

Where credible currency boards have been put in place (in many past instances, in areas devastated by war or riots), they have generally led to the strengthening of the currency, restarting trade and economic activities, and, as long as the value of the reserve backing is stable, the quick disappearance of inflation. Would the installation of a classic currency board solve Indonesia's currency problem in this time of stress? The unequivocal answer would have to be: if Indonesia installed a classic — and the word 'classic' is important — currency board, it would work. There would be no arguments against it based on principle and past experience.

The issue of whether a currency board would succeed in Indonesia does not depend on whether or not a currency board is appropriate at this juncture. The question to ask is what kind of currency board would most likely emerge in Indonesia. How would Indonesia implement such a system? If it did not install a credible system, the answer would be equally unequivocal: it would fail very quickly, and at the end of the day, Indonesia would have run out of reserves.

Conclusions: Understanding the Political Economy

Identifying the causes of Indonesia's economic crisis will be subject to contentious debate in the years to come. It is not just that there is a rich variety of explanations, or that the available data and existing tools of analysis will always be inadequate to discriminate among these explanations. Political considerations also intrude. To emphasise the external as opposed to the internal sources of Indonesia's crisis, for example, would be to minimise the government's role in causing it. To emphasise the weakness of fundamentals would be to absolve the financial liberalisation process for preparing the ground for the crisis.

In spite of the surfeit of funds flowing in after liberalisation, Indonesia consistently failed to strengthen its banking system by recognising the losses incurred. Many of the losses were in state banks, requiring injections of public funds. In 1994, Indonesia accepted a US$307 million World Bank loan to help re-capitalise the banks. However, significant losses had also been experienced in the private sector. At about the same time, in 1993, the capital injection into PT Bank Duta (a small private bank by comparison with other banks), as a result of losses — mainly from foreign exchange speculation — came to US$419 million. The liberalisation process was clearly generating significant losses, but the leading participants in the process were not themselves experiencing losses in wealth. Indonesia had an *ad hoc* bail-out programme for the banking system, mainly rewarding and maintaining political connections and alliances.

It has now become common wisdom that Indonesia pursued a financial liberalisation programme but did not undertake adequate prudential protection of its system. This statement sounds wiser than it actually is since the same kinds of failures have happened in Thailand, in Japan's financial liberalisation process, in the US savings-and-loan crisis and in the Scandinavian countries in the late 1980s. Indonesia pursued a classic financial liberalisation programme in that the programme walked into the same boom-to-bust pattern as the other programmes. The political economy of these liberalisation programmes rewards behaviour that causes the boom, unmindful of the ensuing bust. Wealth through credit creation and increases in stock and property values characterise the boom period. Besides the rewards from corruption in such a process, government officials are reluctant to dampen private sector efforts to expand and diversify the financial system.

When the crisis began, Indonesia implemented a classic tight liquidity regime to defend the currency. This further weakened the banking system and encouraged more capital withdrawals. Indonesia approached the IMF early, and by January 1998, had promised to completely restructure its economy, supposedly to elicit the return of investor confidence.

The political events leading to President Suharto's resignation in May 1998 have cast a harsh light on the consequences of the standard liberalisation approach to structural reform. Suharto had been 're-elected' in early March after signing on to an IMF programme that contained promises to carry out thoroughgoing trade liberalisation, dismantle government-created private monopolies, and speedily remove consumer subsidies. Food shortages and price increases grew as trade financing dried up and the rupiah fell in value. The government removed fuel price subsidies on schedule in a bid to secure the release of an IMF tranche and to signal that it would indeed carry out the incredible set of reforms it had agreed to.

Eventually, riots by the poor and middle class demonstrations in Jakarta forced Suharto to resign. Clearly, the imposed programmes were inappropriate, untimely, as well as destabilising. Without political support and economic credibility for such programmes, the rupiah will continue to be excessively weak and unstable, and this will certainly obstruct efforts at economic recovery.

Note

1. NOP requirements state that commercial banks must keep long and short positions in different currencies within 20 per cent of their equities.

8
MALAYSIA: FROM MIRACLE TO DEBACLE

Jomo K.S.*

Since mid-July 1997, the Malaysian ringgit has fallen precipitously, reaching RM4.88 to the US dollar in early January 1998, its lowest level ever. This represented a collapse by almost half within half a year from a high of RM2.47 in July 1997. The stock market has fallen more severely, with the main Kuala Lumpur Stock Exchange (KLSE) Composite Index (KLCI) dropping to less than 500 in January 1998 from over 1,300 in the first quarter of 1997.

While rapid growth and structural change, initially led by export-oriented industrialisation, with low inflation for a decade was very impressive, not all macroeconomic fundamentals were alright. Although high growth had been sustained for a decade, during most of which fiscal balances were in order, monetary expansion was not excessive and inflation was generally under control, some other indices have been awry. Export-led growth since the late 1980s has been followed by a construction and property boom, fuelled by financial sectors favouring such 'short-termist' investments — involving loans with collateral which bankers like — over more productive, but often, also more risky investments in manufacturing and agriculture. The exaggerated expansion of investment in such 'non-tradables' has worsened current account trade deficits. Financial institutions and other big corporations in East Asia became increasingly exposed to the real estate sector. The asset price bubble first burst in Thailand with declining export-led growth in the face of a sharply missing property glut.

At least two major macroeconomic concerns had emerged by the mid-1990s from the rapid growth of the last decade:

First, the *savings–investment gap*, which was 5 per cent of GNP in 1997, *lay behind the current account deficit*, which has exceeded RM12 billion since 1994 and remained among the highest in the region in the nineties. The gap had been bridged historically by heavy reliance on foreign direct investment (FDI). But high FDI and foreign debt have, in turn, caused growing investment income outflows abroad.[1]

* I am grateful to Al Alim Ibrahim and Din Merican for their useful critical feedback, but implicate neither of them.

With the encouragement of emerging stock markets by the International Finance Corporation, the World Bank subsidiary, the government's determination to promote the KLSE after its split with the Stock Exchange of Singapore (SES) at the beginning of the nineties, and the establishment of the Securities Commission (SC) after passing enabling legislation in 1992, foreign funds and easy credit fuelled the expansion of the market in 1993 before collapsing in early 1994, and then again after that to exceed five times annual national income by early 1997. Malaysia has one of the highest levels of stock market capitalisation in the world, and far higher than most of its East Asian neighbours with their more bank-based financial systems.

It has been estimated that by mid-1997, half the stock on the KLSE was held by retail traders, another quarter by Malaysian institutions and the remaining quarter in the hands of foreigners, mainly institutions. However, it is generally agreed that more than the other two groups, foreign institutions made the market, shifting their assets among stock markets as well as among different types of financial investment options all over the world. In the face of limited transparency, the regional nature of their presence and the nature of fund managers' incentives and remuneration, foreign financial institutions were much more prone to herd behaviour and contributed most to the regional spread of contagion.

So-called *reverse investment*, i.e. Malaysian FDI abroad (around RM6 billion in 1996), has exacerbated the problem in recent years. Such investments were often encouraged by the government and sometimes involved the abuse of inter-government relations to favour Malaysian investors, who became the object of much resentment, especially when many failed to deliver on expectations.[2]

In recent years, the current account gap has been temporarily bridged by short-term capital inflows, as in 1993 and since 1996, with disastrous consequences upon the subsequent reversal of such flows. Many recent confidence restoration measures seek to induce such short-term inflows once again, but they cannot be relied upon to address the underlying problem in the medium to long term.[3]

Second, as in the rest of the region, there was a *recent explosion of private sector debt, especially from abroad*, in recent years. The official policy of privatisation contributed a great deal to increased demand for credit to finance share purchases. The ratio of loans to GNP had risen rapidly in recent years to at least 160 per cent of GNP. In Malaysia, government-owned non-financial public enterprises (NFPEs) have been very much part of this other-wise largely private sector debt growth phenomenon.

Banks and big companies in Malaysia borrowed heavily from abroad. Commercial banks' net foreign liabilities increased from RM10.3bn at the end of 1995 to RM25.2bn in June 1997, while their net external reserves position declined from -RM5.3bn to -RM17.7bn over the same period. However, compared to Thailand and Indonesia, a lower share of foreign borrowings was of a short-term nature and a higher proportion was hedged, given the lower costs of hedging in Malaysia.

The foreign borrowings of Malaysia's largest listed companies have been estimated at around RM35bn, with the three biggest borrowers accounting for three-quarters of this total. Malaysia's medium and long-term borrowings as a percentage of net external reserves rose over two and a half years from 102 per cent at the end of 1994 to 176 per cent in mid-1997 after declining since the mid-eighties crisis.

The explosion of private debt from abroad was due not least to the efforts of 'debt-pushers' associated with the growth of 'relationship' and 'private banking' facilities in the region and the establishment of the Labuan International Offshore Financial Centre (IOFC) in Malaysia. Encouraged by the virtual peg of the ringgit and other regional currencies to the US dollar, especially in recent years, much of the foreign debt was dollar-denominated, short term and unhedged. Meanwhile, commercial banks' foreign liabilities more than tripled between 1995 and 1997 as they seized the opportunities for profitable arbitrage, ignoring the downside risks involved.

According to the Bank of International Settlements (BIS) (*Asian Wall Street Journal*, 6 January 1998), 56 per cent of foreign borrowings *from commercial banks* were short term in nature, i.e. coming due soon. In response to this report, the Malaysian central bank announced that only 30 per cent of *all* foreign borrowings in Malaysia were short term in nature, with another 9 per cent due in the next year, i.e. 39 per cent in all.

Although the Banking and Financial Institutions Act (BAFIA) of 1989 provided a good legal framework for prudential regulation, there has been a growing perception of less effective prudential regulation by the central bank since the replacement of the second governor of Bank Negara Malaysia (BNM), Aziz Taha, apparently for taking positions independent of the political authorities (Gomez 1991).[4]

Increased political interference, lack of experience due to high staff turnover and the reduced scope for effective regulation in the face of reorganisation, devolution and financial liberalisation, both globally and domestically, have all reduced the efficacy of the central bank in ensuring sound national monetary management. For example, the establishment of the IOFC on the East Malaysian island of Labuan is believed to have greatly enhanced domestic investors' access to foreign funds while reducing effective BNM surveillance of flows of funds as well as banking practices more generally.

Meanwhile, only slightly over a quarter of total Malaysian commercial bank lending goes to manufacturing, agriculture, mining and other productive activities (Chin and Jomo 1996). The percentage is likely to be even smaller with foreign borrowings, most of which have been collateralised with assets such as real property and stock. The stock market boom in recent years does not seem to have more effectively raised funds for productive investment, while less than 30 per cent of commercial bank lending in the mid-nineties went to productive investments besides construction financing. While financial intermediation has shifted in the early nineties from debt to equity financing, a growing portion of bank credit went to share purchases.

The economic pain due to the crisis has been exacerbated by the combination of currency depreciation, stock market collapse and rising interest rates. Meanwhile, investment of funds, especially from abroad, in 'non-tradables' has made things worse, especially for the current account. Raising domestic interest rates in response to the crisis is, arguably, quite misleading as much of the recent increase in corporate borrowings has come from abroad. In Malaysia, as elsewhere in the region, financial liberalisation in combination with lucrative abuses of the domestic financial system have combined to exacerbate the crisis. Perhaps more so than elsewhere in region, with the probable exception of Indonesia, official policy and other responses have actually exacerbated the situation.

Policy Responses: Solution or Problem?

The initial Malaysian government reaction to the 'attack' on other Southeast Asian currencies after the floating of the Thai baht on 2 July 1997 was to rush to its defence, with the ringgit rising to RM2.47 against the US dollar from RM2.53 in mid-July before the authorities gave up ringgit support operations after hefty losses of at least 8 billion US dollars. It appears that the main reason for such currency support operations and losses was the apparent desire of the authorities to defend its 'quasi-peg' against the US dollar, and thus the interests of those involved in the tremendous recent growth of unhedged short-term borrowings in US dollars from abroad by politically influential business interests.

There was widespread consensus that the ringgit and other Southeast Asian currencies had become overvalued by their 'quasi-peg' against the US dollar as the US economy and dollar had strengthened significantly in recent years. This was reflected, for example, by the yen depreciation from 76¥ to the US dollar in April 1995 to over 130¥ in 1997, or the 1997 float of the Deutschmark against the US dollar.

Hence, it was expected that the ringgit would depreciate to around RM2.7-3.0 against the dollar, the supposed 'equilibrium' exchange rate based on calculations taking account of purchasing power parity, etc. Instead, it 'overshot' to RM4.88 in early January 1998, i.e. over 2 ringgit or 70 per cent more than the anticipated 'correction' of RM0.3 from RM2.5 to RM2.8. This raised serious questions about the market instability inherent in the international monetary system.

Thus, the ringgit fell from around RM2.5 in early July to about RM2.7 before the end of July 1997, when Prime Minister Mahathir returned from a two-month working holiday abroad. The rate seemed to hold for the first week after the prime minister's return, but then began to tumble, ironically often in response to new official pronouncements and policy responses. After that, it went through the 'bottom', long thought to be the pre-1973 rate of RM3 to the dollar, almost as if in free fall.

The prime minister's attacks on the international financier Georg Soros, and the various conspiracies implied by his attacks, sent confusing signals. On the one hand, they contributed to the impression that the authorities were continuing to deny the gravity of the crisis which had befallen the region and/or were trying to distract attention from their own culpability by blaming foreign conspiracies. Some specific statements especially affected sentiment about the Malaysian economy adversely, giving the impression that the Malaysian authorities might unilaterally change the rules of the game, e.g. for foreign exchange trading. The establishment of a RM60 billion bail-out facility and subsequent 'bending of the rules' to enable cash-rich toll operator United Engineers Malaysia (UEM) to execute a reverse takeover of its heavily-indebted parent firm, Renong, only served to reinforce this impression. The 'designation' of the hundred KLCI counters — ostensibly to check short-selling — adversely affected liquidity, causing the stock market to fall further. Designation also indicated the authorities' willingness to change the rules in mid-game, thus inadvertently undermining confidence and adversely affecting sentiment about Malaysian markets.

Denial and Distraction

The ringgit's collapse was portrayed by Prime Minister Mahathir as due to speculative attacks on Southeast Asian currencies after the fall of the baht on 2 July 1997. Contagion — partly due to herd behaviour by investors — is believed to have exacerbated the situation, involving stock markets. Both currency and stock markets are also believed to have fallen further than might otherwise have been the case due to international market reactions to Prime Minister Mahathir's various statements, including his tough speech in Hong Kong on 20 September at a seminar before the joint World Bank–IMF (International Monetary Fund) annual meeting. Arguing that 'currency trading is unnecessary, unproductive and immoral', Mahathir argued that it should be 'stopped' and 'made illegal'. Coupled with an interview in Hong Kong's *South China Morning Post* which appeared the following day, this was widely seen as signalling an imminent ban on foreign exchange purchases unrelated to imports.

Despite subsequent denial and clarification by Deputy Prime Minister and Finance Minister Anwar Ibrahim, the market reaction was swift and painful, pushing the ringgit even lower — which can only be explained by market sentiment, rather than any serious reference to economic fundamentals. Subsequent Mahathir remarks in faraway Chile on the last day of September plunged the ringgit to a new all-time low, casting a long shadow halfway round the world on the Malaysian financial sector the next morning.

Even before his Hong Kong speech, Mahathir had railed against George Soros and international speculators for weeks, suggesting dark Western conspiracies. Instead of analysing the consequences of international financial liberalisation,

Mahathir repeatedly accused Soros of manipulating the recent currency movements in Southeast Asia, offering no evidence for his latest conspiracy theory. Soros's claim that he was only involved up to 10 million US dollars in Thailand was greeted with derision in Thailand and elsewhere in the region, where it was well known that fund managers from his Quantum Fund were heavily involved in the attack on the weak Thai baht from May 1997. While Soros may have been right in terms of his own personal investment, his personal credibility was badly affected in Southeast Asia.

Not surprisingly, Soros, in turn, accused the Malaysian prime minister of using him as a scapegoat for the consequences of Mahathir's own economic mismanagement. Mahathir's call for an end to international foreign exchange markets and currency speculation only seemed to confirm Soros's claim that he had become a 'menace to his own country' as 'interfering with the convertibility of capital at a moment like this is a recipe for disaster'. Soros added that Mahathir's appeal 'does not deserve serious consideration' and was, not surprisingly, endorsed by US Treasury Secretary Robert Rubin, a former Wall Street trader himself.

All this actually obscured, rather than enhanced understanding of what was actually happening. In fact, both Mahathir and Soros have been critical of the operations of the international financial system. Soros has even warned that if left unregulated, financial anarchy threatens the future viability of the capitalist system as a whole.

Thus, the Malaysian prime minister's partly — but not entirely — ill-founded attacks, invoking various conspiracy theories against George Soros, financial speculators and manipulators, the international Jewish community and the IMF, further reinforced the impression of official denial, with blame for the crisis conveniently attributed abroad. The fact that there was some basis for Mahathir's complaints was hardly enough to save his reputation in the face of an increasingly hostile Western media. Thus, Mahathir and Malaysia were seen as the regional 'bad boys' while other governments in the region went 'cap in hand' to the IMF and others in desperate efforts to restore confidence and secure funds to service the fast-looming foreign debt liabilities, albeit privately held.

Bail-outs for 'Cronies'

Meanwhile, the post-cabinet meeting announcement on 3 September 1997 of a special RM60 billion fund for selected Malaysians seeking to unload stock was seen as a bail-out facility designed to save 'cronies' from disaster. It is unclear how much has actually been deployed for such purposes. It is widely believed that the Employees Provident Fund (EPF) as well as other government-controlled institutions have been instructed to buy certain stocks in an effort to prop them up, and presumably the stock market as well. In so far as such massive purchases may well have stemmed stock price declines, such purchases seem to have succeeded, strengthening the usual official justification that such purchases have largely been at attractive prices. Nevertheless, a Singapore *Business Times* (8 September 1997) report, widely circulated in Malaysia, immediately raised questions about the possible vested interests involved. For example, it claimed that, of Malaysia's billionaires, Mahathir's oldest son Mirzan was the most adversely affected *in percentage terms* by the stock market collapse, having lost more than 69 per cent of the value of his stock.

In so far as it is aware, the public has become increasingly outraged about having to bail-out the politically connected or influential with government-controlled public (EPF, Permodalan Nasional Berhad (PNB) and Khazanah) funds as well as diverted private resources. Meanwhile, Malaysian employees contributing to the EPF will not be pleased by another year of yet lower returns, especially as they will be seen to be due to bail-out operations to rescue the well-connected rich as with the EPF's purchase of UEM shares at four to five times their price in mid-January 1998.

The prospect of government funds being used to compensate Ekran — for 'giving up' the Bakun project — has caused outrage. Awarded to Ekran in dubious circumstances in late 1994 after Mahathir had publicly called off the project in 1990, the government is considering paying compensation to Ting Pek Khiing's company for delaying and taking over the project. In fact, the delay had come about even before the government announced postponement of some 'megaprojects' due to the crisis from September 1997. The delay was due to Ting's apparent change of mind over the contract he had signed with the Swiss–Swedish concern (ABB), the principal contractor for construction of the dam. Meanwhile, Pacific Chemicals, another firm controlled by Ting, has already gained handsome profits from logging the area likely to be inundated by the dam's reservoir, as well as downstream. The apparent government willingness to compensate Ting raises many complex issues, and underscores the impression that special consideration is being given to a long-time favourite of the prime minister.

The most damaging bail-out was probably the first, involving the protracted UEM–Renong saga. After a two-month saga from mid-November, the authorities allowed the reputedly cash-rich listed company, UEM, to undertake a reverse take-over of the presumed United Malays National Organisation (UMNO) holding company, Renong, to save the latter and its Chairman Halim Saad, who are reputedly deep in debt. This 'bail-out' to the tune of RM2.34 billion, at the expense of minority shareholders, gravely undermined public confidence in the Malaysian investment environment in several ways. Stock market rules, including the mandatory general offer required after exceeding the 33 per cent ownership trigger point, are seen to be manipulable to serve the interests of the politically influential.

Halim is believed to have been in serious trouble for various reasons associated with the officially sanctioned business practices of the last decade, involving cronyism, government patronage of private businesses and investments abroad, especially in the South or Third World. Halim is believed to have acted on a supposed Mahathir instruction — after a complaint from Filipino President Fidel Ramos — for Renong to take over the Philippines National Steel Corporation (NSC) from Wing Tiek Holdings, controlled by ruling coalition Member of Parliament Joseph Chong. The funds came from a syndicated loan for US$800 million from Malayan Banking, Bank Bumiputra, Bank of Commerce and Rashid Hussein Bank, all of which breached their single customer limits of RM450, RM250, RM150 and RM250 million respectively.

In the first three days after the initial 17 November 1997 announcement of UEM's reverse takeover of Renong, stock market capitalisation fell by RM70 billion, or 20 per cent. Subsequent slides as the authorities dithered over the following eight weeks suggest that between a fifth to a third of stock market decapitalisation since July 1997 can be attributed to this episode and its implications. The conclusion of the affair seemed to suggest that the newly-appointed executive director of the yet to be formally established National Economic Action Council (NEAC), UMNO treasurer and government economic adviser, former Finance Minister Daim Zainuddin, is in a position to overrule Finance Minister and Deputy Prime Minister Anwar, who had publicly announced his opposition to UEM's exemption from the rules.

In early March 1998, the *Asian Wall Street Journal* reports of two more bail-outs did not have quite the same impact as the UEM–Renong saga. First, it was reported that the otherwise reputedly well-run national petroleum company, Petronas, would buy the prime minister's son's stock in a shipping firm at a price believed to be considerably higher than its current worth after having earlier bought over the Malaysian International Shipping Corporation (MISC) when Mirzan Mahathir was no longer able to afford to take it over owing to the financial crisis. Second, the ruling party UMNO's co-operative, Koperasi Usaha Bersatu (KUB) is expected to get the lion's share of the proceeds of the sale of the virtually bankrupt Sime Bank, in which it only had a 30 per cent stake. It is expected to then take over lucrative assets from the government-controlled Malaysian Mining Corporation (MMC) at an attractive discount and thus cut its losses from the Sime Bank collapse, and perhaps even turn a handsome profit to placate its and UMNO's members.

There are several possible explanations for the more muted response to these bail-outs. Some have suggested that since the market has come close to rock bottom, there was little more to fall, whereas the UEM–Renong saga began in different circumstances. Second, the latter two bail-outs largely involve public funds in companies which are clearly government-controlled; hence, the impact on private investors is said to be more limited, and the response has been correspondingly less. Third, the bail-outs do not so far involve any changing of rules, which tends to be more destabilising. Fourth, some also suggest that bail-outs of the Prime Minister's son and the ruling party's co-operative were only to be expected after the UEM–Renong bail-out given the family and political stakes involved; for some, there is no indication yet that cronies further removed will be similarly saved. Fifth, it is said that private investors have already 'factored in' such bail-outs after the cabinet's announcement of the bail-out facility and the UEM–Renong episode. The muted response may well encourage the authorities to allow more such bail-outs in view of the apparently high level of market and public tolerance.

Thus, concerns about abuse, including nepotism, caused by the cabinet's controversial RM60 billion facility to 'rescue' selected businessmen by utilising funds held by the EPF, Petronas, Khazanah and other major financial institutions have not been allayed. The government has not even tried to ensure some transparency and accountability in the use and deployment of the facility. Although the authorities have conveyed the impression that use of the facility has been suspended, there continues to be evidence to the contrary. Furthermore, the apparent willingness of the government to consider and condone bail-out operations has adversely affected confidence.

Other government responses to the rapidly emerging downward spiral of the currency and stock markets did not help. Besides the disastrous 'designation' of the top 100 KLCI stocks and the RM60 billion 'bail-out' facility, the government's threat to use the notorious Internal Security Act (ISA) and other repressive measures against financial analysts and other commentators for making unfavourable reports about the Malaysian economy only strengthened the impression that the government had a lot to hide from public scrutiny.

The Changing Budget as a Reflection of Changing Stance

The negative reaction of the foreign exchange and stock markets to the 1998 Malaysian Budget, announced on 17 October 1997, has been variously interpreted and may be attributed to several factors.[5] As it turned out, the Budget was somewhat predictable and had largely been anticipated and factored in by players.[6]

In so far as it was much milder than expected, probably to avoid damaging the real economy by over-reacting to the financial crisis, the financial community was generally disappointed because the minister did not raise interest rates, as they wanted him to. In fact, interest rates had been going up, but probably not as much as they wanted, especially for the medium term. Many critics point out that interest rates in Malaysia have been much lower than in most neighbouring countries, neglecting to acknowledge that this has long been the case, even well before the crisis. They also neglect to mention that despite raising interest rates and otherwise contracting liquidity, Malaysia's neighbours have continued to be in trouble.

However, the Budget did not do enough on the fiscal front,[7] inadvertently sustaining the macroeconomic conditions — particularly the current account deficit — which have allowed currency speculators and others to drive down the ringgit (and other Southeast Asian currencies). Most significantly, the government missed an opportunity to send a clear message by cancelling most of the postponed 'mega-projects', particularly the economically indefensible ones which had not begun. Such a measure would have sent a stronger signal about the government's seriousness of intent. The apparent official reluctance to reduce growth rate expectations and to cancel economically unfeasible projects — such as the Genting–Camerons highland highway, the proposed Kansai-style new Northern Regional International Airport in the sea off Mahathir's home state and the (world's longest) Malacca Straits bridge to Sumatra — did not help to inspire confidence in the Malaysian government's response to the crisis.[8]

More significantly, Finance Minister Anwar's October 1997 Budget was viewed as only the latest of a series of official reactions and policy measures by the Malaysian government from July 1997 which were seen by many observers as being tantamount to 'denial' of the gravity of the crisis and its ostensible causes. However, 'denial' is an inappropriate metaphor to some extent because it is not as if the government did not respond at all, but rather that it did not respond in the manner desired by 'the market', i.e. mainly the Western financial community.

Finally, the Tide Turns

Mahathir's announcement in early December 1997 that the 'land bridge' project over the Isthmus of Kra in southern Thailand would proceed seemed to further undermine the Finance Minister's attempts to exercise fiscal discipline. However, the supplementary Budget for 1998 announced the following day on 5 December 1997 managed to reassert Anwar's leadership in economic management, at least for the time being. He announced cuts of up to 18 per cent of public expenditure as well as other measures intended to restore market confidence.

The central bank seems to have followed up by drastically raising interest rates and otherwise contracting liquidity, which is expected to have severe deflationary consequences. Since more than 70 per cent of bank lending in Malaysia has not been for productive investments in manufacturing, agriculture and mining, but for other purposes, especially real property as well as share purchases and consumption credit, which should have been rationed a long time ago, such a measure would not adversely affect the real economy too much if matched by adequate compensatory measures. After tightening bank credit from December 1997, special funds for investment in food production and for small and medium industries (SMIs) were established. There continues to be much scepticism about the actual availability of these funds however. Meanwhile, credit for car purchases (especially for the 'national cars' after the 1998 Budget increased tariffs on imported cars and components for assembly) has been increased, and borrowing for tertiary education has been designated 'productive' and therefore to be encouraged. The contractionary consequences of tighter credit are nevertheless bound to otherwise slow down the economy fairly indiscriminately.

Meanwhile, the authorities seem to be pushing for the rapid merger of financial companies, a particularly difficult process in these turbulent times. This strategy has only limited chances of success, especially in light of the recent failure of a similar Thai attempt. For several years, the central bank had encouraged the merger of banks by offering inducements in the form of additional types of financial transactions only available to banks of a certain minimum size. Such mergers had been encouraged in anticipation of facing the challenges of financial liberalisation. While the consolidation of the financial sector may be desirable to achieve economies and other advantages of scale in anticipation of further financial liberalisation, the rapid and drastic merger process — reducing over 40 firms to half a dozen by the end of March 1998 — being forced upon the finance companies in response to the crisis seems to be less well conceived.

The situation has been worsened by the perception that Mahathir and Daim were taking over economic policy making from Anwar, causing ambiguity about who is in charge and what to expect. Some of the measures introduced by the Finance Ministry and the central bank since early December 1997 have been perceived as pre-empting the likely role and impact of the NEAC, chaired by the prime minister with Daim as executive director. The NEAC is widely seen as an attempt to over-ride the finance minister, who arguably has much stronger support within the ruling UMNO and among the public at large. His supporters are suspected to be aspiring to accelerate the political succession in the wake of the crisis, which is seen to have badly damaged the prime minister's reputation and popularity. However, there appears to be far greater co-operation between Anwar and Daim than originally anticipated, with Daim expected to pursue his own reform agenda quite independently of Mahathir.

Some of the IMF conditionalities undermining crony capitalism in South Korea and Indonesia have raised the question of the desirability of IMF intervention even though the relatively smaller size of Malaysia's foreign (including private) debt does not really necessitate an IMF credit facility with its accompanying conditionalities. Since the relative significance of foreign borrowings is lower in Malaysia compared to the three other East Asian governments which have sought IMF credit recently, Malaysia is less likely to need IMF credit facilities. However, it appears that the Malaysian authorities have been more than willing to adopt IMF-prescribed policies without getting IMF credit. During his visit to Malaysia on 16 January 1998, IMF Managing Director Michel Camdessus said:

> I believe that there is a need to strengthen policies further — particularly on the monetary side — to achieve a better policy mix, underpin the restoration of market confidence, and thereby ensure a rapid return to exchange rate stability and sustainable growth. Malaysia does not necessarily need an IMF-supported programme to achieve this. Our efforts, rather, are directed at providing whatever advice and technical assistance we can to support the

Malaysian authorities in putting together their own comprehensive economic programme, including measures in such areas as financial sector reform and structural policies. To this end, an IMF team has started the annual Article IV consultation, and will discuss formulation of a comprehensive package.

Hence, the recent official policy measures are close to what the IMF would like to see. In Malaysia, the possibility of IMF intervention enjoys a certain mystique and considerable wishful thinking as various different parties have rather different perceptions of the IMF's actual record and motives. Instead, for many critical of Malaysian government policy, not just in response to the crisis, IMF intervention is expected to put an end to all or at least much of what they consider wrong or wish to be rid off, e.g. Malaysia's ethnic redistributive New Economic Policy (NEP). Mahathir has focused on this popular perception of a likely IMF recommendation to galvanise support against the IMF. As in neighbouring Indonesia, the pro-IMF lobby in Malaysia sees the IMF as the only force capable of bringing about desired reforms which domestic forces cannot bring about on their own. Ironically, most of those in favour of IMF intervention fail to recognise that the recent contractionary measures — which have ensured the translation of the financial crisis into a crisis of the real economy — are what the IMF would like to see.

Confidence Restoration

In so far as the financial crisis has been precipitated by 'irrational pessimism' writ large by herd behaviour and contagion, the principal policy challenge now is obviously one of *confidence restoration*, but hopefully, *not* to restore the *status quo ante*. Before December 1997, it was not yet clear whether the Malaysian government had overcome 'denial' to respond adequately to the crisis. As noted earlier, Malaysia's 17 October 1998 Budget tax measures did not help, while expenditure proposals were not tough enough, especially on mega-projects. The finance minister had not then succumbed to pressures to tighten liquidity and precipitate the 'cleansing recession' desired in some circles.

Unfortunately, successful official promotion of the stock market has meant greater vulnerability to its volatility. Malaysia's greater financial intermediation by the share market compared to the banking system as well as the degree of stock market capitalisation has meant a much bigger impact of its share market collapse than in the rest of the region. Most worryingly, recovery and confidence restoration is primarily understood and measured in terms of attracting the short-term capital inflows which precipitated this crisis in the first place. Such inflows would undoubtedly raise the ringgit exchange rate as well as stock market indices, but would eventually also pave the way for another collapse.

To make matters worse, the 1998 Commonwealth Games in Kuala Lumpur and various government efforts to prop up the real property market, especially its residential component, may eventually only delay its apparently inevitable collapse. Given the heavy exposure of so many companies to the property sector, especially among the KLCI's top 100 counters, this could drag out the crisis in the country much longer than in the neighbouring countries where the property markets have already collapsed.

Yet, one has to acknowledge that in some ways, Malaysia and Malaysians are relatively better off than our neighbours affected by the crisis. Although prudential regulation has been weakened in recent years by the pressures of financial liberalisation, it remains better than in most other countries in the region after Singapore and the Philippines, thus saving Malaysia from some of the worst excesses witnessed in the region. Lower domestic interest rates also limited the extent of foreign borrowings, which had been encouraged by official promotion of Labuan as an IOFC, limiting its relative significance in the crisis. Given the greater strength of Malaysian macroeconomic fundamentals as well as prudential regulation of its banking system, it seems likely that there will be less pressure on the Malaysian authorities to bring about more drastic reforms, especially as they do not need to seek IMF credit and thus be forced to accept IMF conditionalities.

Nevertheless, the currency and financial crises have contributed to new macroeconomic problems besides undermining economic development efforts more generally in the following ways:

- with the massive ringgit devaluation, imported inflation is inevitable, especially for Malaysia's very open economy;
- over-zealous efforts to check inflation would exacerbate deflationary tendencies;
- business failures, growing unemployment and reduced incomes will contribute to a vicious deflationary cycle;
- the stock market collapse is bound to adversely affect both consumption and investment;
- credit restraint policies will further dampen economic activity;
- the flight of foreign funds cannot be easily replaced by domestic funds, which would have to be diverted from alternative uses;
- loan recovery difficulties will further constrain the financial system and economic activity;
- the depreciated ringgit has increased the relative magnitude of foreign borrowings as well as the external debt servicing burden;
- despite the massive ringgit devaluation, there has not been a commensurate export boom for many reasons;
- technological progress is slowing down with the greater costs of foreign technology acquisition as well as the greater attraction of cheap labour and production costs.

The recent currency and financial crises suggest that Malaysia's economic boom was built on some shaky and unsustainable foundations. Recent growth has been increasingly heavily reliant on foreign resources, especially immigrant labour. It is now abundantly clear that Malaysia's future economic progress can no longer be secured by continued reliance on its previous economic strategy emphasising cheap labour and other production costs, e.g. by allowing the continued inflow of foreign workers willing to accept lower wages and poorer working conditions by Malaysian standards. Limited and inappropriate investments in human resources have held back the development of greater industrial and technological capabilities throughout the region. Malaysia's resource wealth and relatively cheap labour sustained production enclaves for export of agricultural, forest, mineral and, more recently, manufactured products, but much of the retained wealth generated was captured by business cronies of those in power. They, in turn, who contributed to growth by re-investing such captured resource and other rents in the 'protected' domestic economy in import-substituting industries, commerce, services and privatised utilities and infrastructure.

Despite various weaknesses, this Malaysian brand of ersatz capitalism — dominated by *crony rentierism* — has sustained rapid growth for three decades, but has come unstuck as it is forced by the forces of economic liberalisation to interface competitively with the rest of the world economy. Failure to recognise the nature of the processes of accumulation and growth in the region has prevented the design and implementation of an adequate pro-active strategy of well-designed and sequenced liberalisation in the face of the apparently inevitable. In contrast, Malaysian central bank-guided consolidation of the banking sector has helped ensure its greater robustness and readiness compared to its neighbours.

Political Fallout

In the region, although there has been lingering resentment of Mahathir's perceived role in exacerbating the problem, Malaysia's gesture of lending a billion dollars each to both Thailand and Indonesia reflects a serious commitment to try to bring about East — including Southeast — Asian regional co-operation on the monetary front, with Japanese support and possibly patronage. This is in spite of US opposition. By the end of 1997, the Asian Monetary Fund idea as well as milder versions involving some autonomous regional facility had been killed by US and European resistance, partly through the IMF.

Not surprisingly, especially after Indonesian President Suharto was forced by the IMF in mid-January 1998 to dismantle several lucrative monopolies controlled by his children and cronies, there has been a growing domestic constituency for IMF intervention in Malaysia to restore confidence and dismantle political as well as economic arrangements, policies and practices. The tightening of bank credit and higher interest rates, especially since December 1997, have strengthened the perception that Malaysia has begun to adopt policies prescribed by the IMF without having to do so as conditions for receiving an IMF credit facility.

After almost three years of unprecedented popularity in Malaysia culminating in a decade of growth exceeding 8 per cent per annum and a resounding electoral victory in April 1995 with 65 per cent of the vote (and 85 per cent of parliamentary seats, compared to only 52 per cent of the vote and 70 per cent of the seats in October 1990), Mahathir's reputation at home and within the region has taken a beating, ironically not least because of what has elevated his stature elsewhere in the South, namely his bold, but sometimes almost quixotic tilting against the windmills of Western dominance.

Domestically, Mahathir has been badly wounded, not only by the financial crisis, but also by some imprudent criticisms of the Muslim *ulama*' at the 1997 UMNO General Assembly. Stung by foreign media suggestions that he should go, he has come fighting back in typical style, though some of his opponents would like to believe that he has finally been mortally wounded politically. For the time being, however, it appears that heir apparent Finance Minister Anwar Ibrahim will be hemmed in by the Mahathir-dominated NEAC, with Mahathir loyalist Tun Daim Zainuddin appointed executive director. However, insiders claim that Daim's importance to Mahathir has declined in recent years while Daim has taken private positions quite independent of Mahathir's and seems to have reconciled with Anwar after drifting apart after Anwar won the deputy leadership of the party in late 1993. Nevertheless, as principal architect of 'Malaysia Incorporated' — now cynically referred to as 'crony capitalism' — of the last dozen years, which arguably bears much of the responsibility for the current crises in Malaysia, Daim's appointment did not inspire the market confidence his 'can-do' and 'market-savvy' reputations were expected to generate (*FEER*, 19/2/98).

The imminent collapse of much of the property market, its repercussions on financial institutions and the stock market, as well as the still unknown consequences of recent and forthcoming government policy initiatives still loom large on the Malaysian economic horizon. Those who expect salutary reforms to emerge from the crisis in East Asia are nonetheless less hopeful for Malaysia, ironically partly because the crisis has not been as severe and the economy is much more sound. Hence, the consociationalist regime presiding over ethno-populist political mobilisation seems more than likely to continue to sustain some variation of the crony capitalism which now dominates Malaysia's political economy.

To its credit, however, the Malaysian political leadership — both in government and in the opposition — has wisely resisted the ethno-populist tendencies they have so successfully mobilised and gained from in the past. This is in stark contrast with the Indonesian regime's seeming tolerance for anti-Chinese actions in an apparent bid to secure further concessions from the IMF's conditionalities. While the NEP's success in creating a Bumiputera business community and the privatisation policy's success in consolidating executive patronage of politically influential rentiers have undoubtedly undermined simplistic ethnic identification of business interests, the continued popularity of such ethnic stereotypes has been checked by responsible political leadership on the part of leaders of the ruling coalition as well as the opposition.

Notes

1. Of course, the availability of cheap foreign funds — e.g. due to a low real interest rate — can help to temporarily close both domestic savings-investment as well as foreign exchange gaps, especially if well invested or deployed.
2. In some instances, e.g. logging, Malaysian investors have often been distinguished by poor practices no longer permissible for loggers from the North facing more vigilant civil societies.
3. In this connection, it is interesting to note that the Chicago school-influenced Chilean government has maintained strict controls on the capital account. Portfolio investments in Chilean stock are permitted in the New York Stock Exchange, rather than in the Santiago stock market, while unlike FDI, portfolio capital inflows into Chile are subjected to conditions which inhibit easy exit.
4. It is widely believed that complaints were made internationally that BNM subsequently used privileged information available to central banks for trading on currency, gold, junk bonds and other markets in the West. Such investments are believed to have been quite successful in the second half of the eighties and the early nineties until BNM lost tens of billions of ringgit after taking sterling positions before its collapse in September 1992 under selling pressure from George Soros and other currency speculators.
5. The Budget is primarily an instrument of fiscal, not monetary policy, and should not have been expected to address the currency and stock market crises frontally, as many apparently expected it to. Hence, there were unrealistic expectations of the Budget, which were not met even though Finance Minister Anwar Ibrahim announced some monetary measures in his Budget Speech.
6. Despite media hype about a tough Budget, it was surprisingly mild, with little evidence of belt-tightening as far as government expenditure was concerned. Although operating expenditure for 1998 was expected to go down, development expenditure was expected to continue to rise despite huge increases in the mid-1990s. This was probably seen as necessary to offset the anticipated private sector slowdown. Of course, some expenditures are contractually 'locked in', while others are necessary or socially desirable (e.g. most educational or public health expenditures), but this is unlikely to be a sufficient explanation. Anwar's tax initiatives were primarily to influence economic behaviour, rather than for revenue purposes. Unfortunately, however, many of the instruments were blunt and, arguably, unlikely to be either effective or equitable. For example, the reduced corporate income tax is unlikely to translate into reduced consumer prices, which is the justification offered. Although the rate is lower in Singapore, there is no need to lower the rate for those companies which have to locate in Malaysia because of the nature of their businesses, whereas other incentives have been successfully used to attract companies which have a choice in locating.
    True to form, neo-liberal economists have protested the increase in trade taxes and the re-introduction of non-tariff barriers. In fact, the measures are probably unnecessary in view of the much cheaper ringgit and the slowdown in construction and car sales. The higher taxes on imported cars and completely knocked-down (CKD) units will mainly favour

Proton and Perodua, the government's national cars which have yet to make much of a dent in terms of overseas sales. The structure of the taxes also does not encourage other car assemblers to increase local content. Nor do the higher taxes address the larger problem of an excessively high car-to-population ratio, which the minister claimed they were supposed to address.

7. The main reason the government has been running a fiscal surplus in recent years is because of its sale of public assets as part of the privatisation policy, often in dubious circumstances or at heavily discounted prices, both with negative consequences for economic welfare. Now that the privatisation policy has been suspended, partly in response to the growing public outcry about some consequences of the policy, the government should encourage discussion of alternative public sector reforms which might be instituted in the public interest. There is even a real possibility of 're-nationalisation' being invoked to use public funds to bail-out businessmen in serious trouble.

8. Not surprisingly then, many would argue that citizens should not be forced to suffer the consequences of such government actions by being allowed to buy foreign exchange, as it were, to protect themselves.

Table 8.1
Malaysia: Key Macroeconomic Variables, 1989-96 (percentages)

	1989	1990	1991	1992	1993	1994	1995	1996
GDP Growth Rate	9.2	9.7	8.7	8.0	9.0	9.1	10.1	8.8
Share of GDP								
Gross National Savings	29.0	29.1	28.4	31.3	33.0	34.0	34.7	36.0
Consumption Expenditure	65.2	66.6	66.5	63.5	62.3	61.2	60.5	58.1
Private	50.8	52.6	52.6	50.5	49.2	48.6	47.9	46.9
Public	14.4	14.0	13.9	13.0	13.1	12.6	12.6	11.2
Gross Capital Formation	29.3	32.4	36.4	36.0	38.3	40.1	43.0	41.8
Private	18.5	20.9	25.9	24.8	26.7	27.2	30.5	29.2
Public	10.8	11.5	10.5	11.2	11.7	13.0	12.6	12.6
Balance of Payments								
Current Account	-0.7	-2.1	-8.8	-3.8	-4.8	-6.3	-8.5	-5.2
Official Long-term Capital	-2.4	-2.5	-0.5	-1.9	0.6	0.3	2.7	0.3
Private Long-term Capital	4.4	5.5	8.3	8.9	7.8	6.0	4.7	4.5
Long-term Capital, Net	2.0	3.0	7.8	7.0	8.4	6.2	7.4	4.8
Basic Balance	2.7	0.9	-1.0	3.2	3.6	-0.1	-1.1	-0.4
Private Capital: Net	1.5	1.2	3.9	8.0	8.4	-4.5	1.1	4.5
Private Capital: Commercial Banks	1.1	2.0	2.7	6.2	6.6	-7.0	0.1	3.4
Private Capital: Others Private	0.4	-0.8	1.2	1.8	1.8	2.5	1.0	1.1
Errors and Omissions	-1.0	2.6	-0.3	0.1	5.7	0.2	-2.0	-1.6
Overall Balance	3.2	4.6	2.6	11.3	17.7	-4.3	-2.0	2.5
Implicit Capital Inflows	3.9	6.8	11.4	15.1	22.5	2.0	6.5	7.7
Short-term Capital Inflows	1.9	3.8	3.6	8.1	14.1	-4.2	-0.9	2.9

Source: Montes (1998).

9

THE PHILIPPINES AND THE
EAST ASIAN ECONOMIC TURMOIL

Joseph Y. Lim

The Philippines missed out on the last 'takeoff' of its Southeast Asian neighbours, particularly during the late eighties and early nineties. Just when growth turned respectable in the mid-nineties, the currency turmoil rocked the region and continued to drag the economy down for the whole of 1998 and perhaps beyond.

To really assess where the Philippines stands in its path towards economic development, especially in the light of the latest financial and economic turmoil in East Asia, one has to study the economic history of the Philippines in the past two decades. This period was a volatile period of stabilisation, structural adjustments, opening up of the economy to both goods and capital flows, alternating periods of political and economic stability and instability. Influences and effects of domestic policies and conditions need to be juxtaposed against external influences and conditions.

The Philippines is also the only country in East Asia that suffered a foreign debt crisis in the eighties similar to Latin America. Especially with the linking of 'crony capitalism' to the current financial and economic woes, the experience of the Philippines rings a bell suggesting similarities to circumstances in the other Southeast Asian tigers (and perhaps South Korea), .

Economic Phases in the Last Two Decades

In our discussion of the Philippines in the last two decades, we categorise the era into the economic collapse period of 1983-85, the recovery period of 1986 to 1990, the slowdown and recession period of 1990-92, and the recovery and growth period of 1993-96. The economic crisis in 1997 and 1998 will be presented in a later section.

Economic Collapse, 1983-1985

The extremely difficult years of 1983-85 were marked by:

1) an unsuccessful expansionary and counter-cyclical policy (rife with 'cronyism' and corruption) to offset adverse external conditions from 1981-83;

2) the foreign debt crisis and stoppage of foreign loans and external inflows of 1982-84;

3) the political upheaval brought about by rising mass opposition to the Marcos government in the aftermath of the 1993 Aquino assassination.

The collapse was aggravated by massive capital flight from the Philippines, allegedly by Marcos cronies, as instability mounted. The stabilisation during this period included a series of sharp currency devaluations (more than 100 per cent in 1982-85), massive monetary contraction and high interest rates (effected by issuing high-yielding — 50-60 per cent interest rates — Central Bank bills). From the fiscal side, the sharp drop in income reduced tax revenues; the sharp increase in foreign and domestic interest rates increased debt service, and squeezed capital outlays and public investment. At the same time, extreme monetary contraction and high interest rates killed private investments (which fell more than 30 per cent per annum in 1984 and 1985) and substantially reduced the level and share of the industrial and manufacturing sector (which fell by more than 10 per cent per annum in 1984 and 1985). (See Table 9.1 for some statistics.) The fall in incomes substantially reduced savings, especially household savings.

The series of sharp devaluations as well as sharp monetary and supply contraction led to high inflation (47 per cent and 23.5 per cent in 1983 and 1984 respectively). The overall effect of all this involved extreme tightening in both the external and fiscal constraints, bringing the economy down to a deep depression as GNP declined by 9 per cent and 7 per cent in 1984 and 1985 respectively. On a per capita basis, the Philippines retarded to levels achieved a decade earlier. There were massive lay-offs, excess capacity in the industrial sector, and de-capitalisation as gross investments were less than the amount needed to replace the depreciated stock. The effect of the sharp economic decline was beneficial to external accounts as imports declined sharply (even as exports stagnated or fell slightly), so that current account deficits fell sharply and balance of payments turned positive from 1984 to 1986.

The Philippine situation during this period has several similarities to that of Indonesia in 1998. First of all, the large foreign borrowings (denominated in dollars), supposedly led by 'cronies' of an authoritarian government investing in the 'wrong' sectors, bear a striking resemblance that is hard to ignore. This brings to the forefront the strong links between the role of the state and the financial crisis of the corresponding periods. The authoritarian political structure, including strong arm tactics against the political opposition, intertwined with the economic woes of the country to galvanise strong opposition against the government. In the Philippine case, this led to the downfall of the long-running dictatorship, but not after more than two years of political and economic instability from the start of the economic crisis.

Second, the strong austerity measures imposed by the IMF deepened the economic decline, but allowed the economy to build international reserves (at the

Table 9.1
Some Macro Indicators for the Philippines, 1981-97

Year	GDP Growth Rate	GNP Growth Rate	GDP per capita (1985 prices)	GNP per capita (1985 prices)	Growth in GNP per cap. (1985 prices)	Exchange Rate P/US$	Change in Exchange Rate	Unemploy- ment Rate (%)	Inflation Rate (%)	Treasury Bill Rates (91 days)
1981	3.42	3.24	12,730	12,643		7.90			17.30	12.55
1982	3.62	2.84	12,869	12,633	-0.08	8.54	8.10		8.58	13.78
1983	1.87	1.51	12,787	12,526	-0.85	11.11	30.13		5.34	14.26
1984	-7.32	-8.83	11,564	11,110	-11.30	16.70	50.27		47.06	28.24
1985	-7.31	-7.02	10,461	10,086	-9.22	18.61	11.43		23.45	25.87
1986	3.42	4.15	10,561	10,205	1.18	20.39	9.56		-0.45	15.63
1987	4.31	4.62	10,755	10,476	2.66	20.57	0.89		3.03	11.51
1988	6.75	7.71	11,216	10,971	4.73	21.10	2.56	9.55	8.93	14.67
1989	6.21	5.61	11,638	11,385	3.77	21.74	3.04	9.13	12.20	18.64
1990	3.04	3.69	11,722	11,661	2.42	24.31	11.84	9.53	14.17	26.67
1991	-0.58	0.41	11,397	11,456	-1.76	27.48	13.03	10.50	18.66	21.11
1992	0.34	1.29	11,188	11,382	-0.65	25.51	-7.15	9.82	8.95	16.02
1993	2.12	2.76	10,961	11,151	-2.03	27.12	6.30	9.27	7.61	12.45
1994	4.39	5.25	11,168	11,456	2.74	26.45	-2.47	9.48	7.06	12.71
1995	4.76	4.96	11,425	11,743	2.51	25.70	-2.84	9.52	8.10	11.76
1996	5.70	6.90	11,800	12,275	4.53	26.21	1.98	8.58	8.50	12.34
1997	5.10	5.80	12,125	12,693	3.41	29.47	12.44	8.70	5.10	12.89

Source: National Statistical Co-ordination Board.

expense of imports), partly to pay off foreign loans. This, most likely, will be the effect of the IMF package on Indonesia. The failure of many firms and banking institutions and the assumption of their liabilities by the government will saddle the fiscal account for many years to come.

Third, the crisis in the Philippines was precipitated by both external and internal factors. Externally, the defaults of Mexico and Brazil on their foreign loans transmitted the foreign debt crisis to the Philippines. For Indonesia, the Thai financial crisis precipitated the depreciation of the rupiah and exposed the financial vulnerability of the economy (in the end, the Indonesian vulnerability was revealed to be much worse than that of the Thai economy). Internally, the lack of succession to an ailing dictator and the regime's stifling of political dissent has worsened Indonesia's economic decline and financial instability.

The experience of 'crony capitalism' in the Philippines should have been a strong warning to other authoritarian East Asian governments of the dangerous links, especially in the financial sector, between vested interests promoted by the government, on the one hand, and financial and economic mismanagement, on the other.

Economic Recovery, 1986-1990

Strong stabilisation measures, though partly to blame for the sharp inflation in 1984-85, were able to bring inflation down to zero in 1986, as aggregate demand declined sharply. With inflation tamed, the balance of payments displaying a positive balance and the installation of the new Aquino government, the severe stabilisation measures were relaxed and the economy underwent economic recovery between 1986-90. The relaxation of stabilisation measures brought growth rates back to high positive levels as the economy easily filled in large excess capacities in 1987-89. Investment rates rose from 16.9 per cent of GDP in 1986 to 23.7 per cent in 1990. Industry and manufacturing as well as services also recovered from their slump in the previous period.

Still, this period was marked by significant structural adjustments and painful debt restructuring and payments as the spectre of the foreign debt overhang continued to haunt the economy. The debt overhang brought zero, and sometimes negative, net inflows of medium and long-term loans. Foreign debt interest payments shot up to more than 6 per cent of GDP. Initially, this had little macro impact as international reserves were still high between 1986 to 1988. But as the recovery brought higher trade and current account deficits (through increased imports and large foreign interest payments), this situation became extremely difficult in 1989 and 1990.

Problems also persisted on the fiscal front. Even with the higher tax and non-tax revenues due to tax reforms and the privatisation effort, the assumption of the government of many of the debts of the private and government corporate sector during this period created fiscal pressures during most of the period, especially in 1989 and 1990. Specifically, interest payments shot up, starting in 1987, as the government assumed much of the foreign debt of failed government companies. Interest payments increased even further between 1989 and 1991 as higher treasury bill rates and high issuances of treasury bills (effected to slacken the growth of an overheating economy) increased the domestic debt payments of the government. The fiscal pressure squeezed capital outlays as infrastructure deteriorated. Eventually, another stabilisation measure had to be effected from 1990 to 1992.

Important structural adjustments during 1986-1990 were:

1) Import liberalisation that lifted almost all quota restrictions. Many quota restrictions were converted into tariffs, but tariff reduction schemes were also drawn up.
2) Financial liberalisation, which had started in the early eighties, were implemented in earnest. This effectively lifted all interest rate ceilings, substantially reduced credit subsidies and allowed banks and financial markets to operate using market processes.
3) Tax reforms, which included a shift towards more global taxation and value-added taxation.
4) Rehabilitation of many state enterprises and privatisation of a sizeable share of them.

Though the above reforms were praised for bringing the Philippines closer to market-friendly policies that would make the economy more efficient and competitive, it must be pointed out that the strong impact of trade liberalisation and the slow real appreciation of the peso (a conscious policy of the Central Bank and an offshoot of its high interest rate and ultra-conservative monetary policy) started to make imports very cheap, and there was a marked increase in the import intensity of the economy — a tendency that would continue until the currency turmoil. (See Table 9.2b — the share of imports and trade deficits to GDP.) This aggravated the current account deficit and net external outflows during 1986-1990.

In summary, the stabilisation measures of the previous period succeeded in decreasing inflation and the balance of payment deficits. This allowed some relaxing of the external and fiscal constraints in 1986 to 1988. However, the continued debt overhang and government assumption of the liabilities of the private and government corporate sector implied a quick return to tight fiscal binds. The import liberalisation and slow real appreciation of the peso, the higher import needs of a recovering economy and high interest payments outflows, and little infusion of medium and long-term loans made sure that the external constraints again become strongly binding. This paved the way for another stabilisation effort in 1990-92.

Based on the foreign debt experience of the Philippines, the lesson learnt here which is relevant to the Southeast Asian crisis now is that for countries that have huge foreign borrowings, the 'overhang' effects will last several years unless sufficient debt relief is given early on in the crisis. The lingering effects will constrain the external and fiscal sectors. We shall return to this point later.

Another important point is that parallel to the volatility and instability of economic growth (due to the foreign debt overhang) was the series of right-wing coups directed against the Aquino government on the political front. Because of the economic and political instability during 1986-1990, the Philippines completely missed out on the massive Japanese investments that flowed to Thailand, Malaysia and Indonesia in the aftermath of the Plaza Accord and the yen appreciation. Thus, the eighties was a decade of missed opportunities towards 'tigerhood' for the Philippines.

Recession Revisited, 1990-1992

The stabilisation measures from 1990-92 again consisted of tight monetary and fiscal policies and currency devaluation. The tight monetary policy began in earnest in 1990 as inflation approached 15 per cent and current account deficits surpassed 6 per cent of GDP. This time, high yielding treasury bills were used to reduce money supply. The consolidated public sector deficit reached close to 5 per cent of GDP in 1990 (the national government deficit itself was 3.5 per cent of GDP) and the government decided this ratio should fall.

Devaluation was effected naturally as a result of the Iraq–Kuwait crisis. The result of these stabilisation measures was that GDP growth started to sputter in 1990 and remained nil in 1991 and 1992. In the worst year, 1991, inflation shot up to near 20 per cent. The results were reminiscent of the 1984 to 1985 period, though smaller in magnitude. Investment and domestic savings (both the levels as well as their shares of GDP) fell significantly from 1990 to 1991. In terms of industrial origin, the hardest hit was the industrial sector as construction, manufacturing and mining and quarrying all posted significant declines.

By 1992, the stabilisation measures and recession were able to bring down inflation to single-digit levels again. Current account deficits were reduced substantially so as to increase the balance of payments and international reserves in 1991 and 1992. The stage was set again for a relaxation of macro policy from 1993 onwards.

The stabilisation of 1990-91 was small compared to 1984 and 1985. Its effects, however, dragged on till late 1993 as political instability (aftershocks of the near successful coup against the Aquino administration in December 1989) and a crippling power shortage (up to ten hours of 'brown-outs' daily) precluded any earlier recovery.

The recession in the early nineties was another major setback for the Philippines as per capita GNP became lower than that achieved 15 years earlier. The gap between the Philippines and its successful Association of South East Asian Nations (ASEAN) neighbours widened even more.

Integration with the World Economy and Growth, 1993-1996

The period 1993 to 1996 saw monetary and fiscal policies relaxed. This was facilitated by the debt restructuring agreement (based on the Brady Plan, which converted the loans into long-term bonds) made in 1992, which substantially reduced principal and interest payments on foreign debt, and the liberalisation of foreign exchange restrictions, also done in 1992. The foreign exchange liberalisation — removal of practically all obstacles to the inflow and outflow of foreign exchange — brought about a substantial rise in remittances of Filipino workers abroad (already a growing item in the second half of the eighties and early nineties) and increased both direct equity foreign investments and portfolio investments. These portfolio investments initially went to high-yielding treasury bills in 1992, but as monetary policy relaxed and interest rates fell, the portfolio investments shifted into the stock market — as 'hot money' and the 'emerging market' syndrome started. These portfolio investments have caused a lot of volatility, not only in the stock market, but in external funds outflow and inflow, as both increased tremendously (Table 9.2a). The supposedly market-determined exchange rate had to be perennially managed by the central bank to avoid wild fluctuations and to implement the central bank bias for a stable, undepreciating currency. The peso actually experienced nominal appreciation during this period.

This period saw many important developments. Exports and imports share of GDP rose rapidly from 30 and 37 per cent respectively in 1990 to 49 and 61 per cent respectively in 1996 (see Table 9.2b). The rise of imports can be explained by tariff reduction schemes, implemented earnestly in the nineties, and the appreciating peso, facilitated by the inflows of dollars resulting from foreign exchange liberalisation. Starting from 1995, very significant tariff reductions were effected to 'lock in' trade liberalisation in line with the General Agreement on Tariffs and Trade (GATT) and the Asia-Pacific Economic Cooperation (APEC) agreements. The Philippines have taken these agreements seriously and implemented tariff reductions ahead of schedule, pledging that by the year 2004, all products, with the important exception of rice, will have a uniform tariff of 5 per cent.

Exports defied textbooks as nominal and real appreciation of the peso saw exports climb up continuously through the nineties. The high growth in exports can be explained mainly by high growth in semiconductor and electronic exports, which by 1996 accounted for more than 50 per cent of the nominal dollar value of merchandise exports. This rise in exports of semiconductors and electronic parts can be explained by rising world prices and Japanese firms' medium-term decision to expand their semiconductor and electronic production and exports from the

Table 9.2a
Philippines: Balance of Payments, 1990-97 (US$ millions)

	1990	1991	1992	1993	1994	1995	1996	Jan. – Sept. 1996	1997
I. Current Account									
A. Merchandise Trade, Net	-4,020	-3,211	-4,695	-6,222	-7,850	-8,944	-11,342	-8,760	-8,252
(As percentage of GNP)	-9.12	-7.03	-8.71	-11.25	-11.94	-12.20	-13.02	-14.10	-12.40
Exports	8,186	8,840	9,824	11,375	13,483	17,447	20,543	14,926	18,363
Imports	12,206	12,051	14,519	17,597	21,333	26,391	31,885	23,686	26,615
B. Non-merchandise Trade, Net	739	1,515	3,020	2,507	3,964	4,765	6,839	5,500	4,704
Receipts	4,842	5,624	7,443	7,497	10,550	14,374	19,006	13,778	17,015
Payments	4,103	4,109	4,423	4,990	6,586	9,609	12,167	8,278	12,311
of which: net investment	-1,942	-1,848	-1,629	-1,339	-1,146	-1,524	-928	-577	-604
net personal income	1,198	1,640	2,215	2,263	2,996	3,869	4,306	3,383	4,117
interest expense	2,026	1,993	1,703	1,518	1,579	2,179	2,167	1,555	1,840
C. Transfers, Net	714	827	817	699	936	882	589	515	386
Inflow	717	828	826	746	1,041	1,147	1,185	751	1,215
Outflow	3	1	9	47	105	265	596	236	829
Current Account, Net	-2,567	-869	-858	-3,016	-2,950	-3,297	-3,914	-2,745	-3,162
(As percentage of GNP)	-5.82	-1.90	-1.59	-5.45	-4.49	-4.50	-4.49	-4.40	-4.70
II. Capital and Financial Account									
A. Medium and Long-term Loans, Net	674	835	633	2,455	1,313	1,276	2,690	2,159	3,295
Inflow	4,575	3,622	7,432	5,205	4,369	3,927	6,329	4,367	5,171
Outflow	3,901	2,787	6,799	2,750	3,056	2,651	3,639	2,208	1,876

(continued...)

Table 9.2a (continued)

Philippines: Balance of Payments, 1990-97 (US$ millions)

	1990	1991	1992	1993	1994	1995	1996	Jan. – Sept. 1996	Jan. – Sept. 1997
B. Foreign Investments, Net	480	654	737	812	1,558	1,609	1,168	1,281	-2,316
Non-res. Investments in the Philippines	498	681	931	2,135	2,492	2,944	3,621	2,910	771
Resident Investments Abroad	18	27	194	1,323	934	1,335	2,453	1,629	3,087
of which: net direct investments	528	529	675	864	1,289	1,361	1,338	1,210	1,016
non-res. investments	550	556	776	1,238	1,591	1,459	1,520	1,377	1,093
residents investments abroad	22	27	101	374	302	98	182	167	77
net portfolio investments	-48	125	62	-52	269	248	-170	71	-3,332
inflows	156	242	588	2,369	3,685	4,488	8,007	5,705	6,435
outflows	204	117	526	2,421	3,416	4,240	8,177	5,634	9,767
C. Purchase of Collateral			-469						
D. Short-term Capital, Net	19	349	660	-148	1,002	-56	540	378	366
E. Change in Commercial Banks' NFA	603	40	289	-299	674	1,574	4,211	3,962	3,010
Capital and Financial Account, Net	1,776	1,878	1,850	2,820	4,547	4,403	8,609	7,780	4,355
III. Others									
A. Monetisation of Gold	218	245	130	113	154	177	198	158	61
B. Revaluation Adjustments	800	387	527	431	100	-96	-203	-138	-239
Others, Total	1,018	632	657	544	254	81	-5	20	-178
IV. Errors & Omissions, Net Unclassified	-320	462	-157	-514	-49	-556	-583	-1,306	-2,223
V. Overall BoP Position	-93	2,103	1,492	-166	1,802	631	4,107	3,749	-1,208
(As percentage of GNP)	-0.21	4.61	2.77	-0.30	2.74	0.86	4.72	5.74	-1.85

Table 9.2b

Philippines: Balance of Payments, 1990-97 (percentages)

	1990	1991	1992	1993	1994	1995	1996	Jan. – Sept. 1996	1997
I. Current Account									
A. Merchandise Trade, Net	-9.07	-7.07	-8.86	-11.44	-12.25	-12.53	-13.54	-13.94	-13.22
Exports	18.47	19.46	18.54	20.92	21.04	24.45	24.52	23.75	29.42
Imports	27.55	26.53	27.41	32.37	33.29	36.98	38.05	37.69	42.65
B. Non-merchandise Trade, Net	1.67	3.34	5.70	4.61	6.19	6.68	8.16	8.75	7.54
Receipts	10.93	12.38	14.05	13.79	16.46	20.14	22.68	21.92	27.26
Payments	9.26	9.05	8.35	9.18	10.28	13.47	14.52	13.17	19.73
of which: net investment	-4.38	-4.07	-3.07	-2.46	-1.79	-2.14	-1.11	-0.92	-0.97
net personal income	2.70	3.61	4.18	4.16	4.68	5.42	5.14	5.38	6.60
interest expense	4.57	4.39	3.21	2.79	2.46	3.05	2.59	2.47	2.95
C. Transfers, Net	1.61	1.82	1.54	1.29	1.46	1.24	0.70	0.82	0.62
Inflow	1.62	1.82	1.56	1.37	1.62	1.61	1.41	1.20	1.95
Outflow	0.01	0.00	0.02	0.09	0.16	0.37	0.71	0.38	1.33
Current Account, Net	-5.79	-1.91	-1.62	-5.55	-4.60	-4.62	-4.67	-4.37	-5.07
II. Capital and Financial Account									
A. Medium and Long-term Loans, Net	1.52	1.84	1.19	4.52	2.05	1.79	3.21	3.44	5.28
Inflow	10.32	7.97	14.03	9.57	6.82	5.50	7.55	6.95	8.29
Outflow	8.80	6.14	12.83	5.06	4.77	3.71	4.34	3.51	3.01

(continued...)

Table 9.2b (continued)

Philippines: Balance of Payments, 1990-97 (percentages)

	1990	1991	1992	1993	1994	1995	1996	Jan. – Sept. 1996	Jan. – Sept. 1997
B. Foreign Investments, Net	1.08	1.44	1.39	1.49	2.43	2.25	1.39	2.04	-3.71
Non-res. Investments in the Philippines	1.12	1.50	1.76	3.93	3.89	4.13	4.32	4.63	1.24
Resident Investments Abroad	0.04	0.06	0.37	2.43	1.46	1.87	2.93	2.59	4.95
of which: net direct investments	1.19	1.16	1.27	1.59	2.01	1.91	1.60	1.93	1.63
non-res. investments	1.24	1.22	1.46	2.28	2.48	2.04	1.81	2.19	1.75
residents investments abroad	0.05	0.06	0.19	0.69	0.47	0.14	0.22	0.27	0.12
net portfolio investments	-0.11	0.28	0.12	-0.10	0.42	0.35	-0.20	0.11	-5.34
inflows	0.35	0.53	1.11	4.36	5.75	6.29	9.56	9.08	10.31
outflows	0.46	0.26	0.99	4.45	5.33	5.94	9.76	8.97	15.65
C. Purchase of Collateral	0.00	0.00	-0.89	0.00	0.00	0.00	0.00	0.00	0.00
D. Short-term Capital, Net	0.04	0.77	1.25	-0.27	1.56	-0.08	0.64	0.60	0.59
E. Change in Commercial Banks' NFA	1.36	0.09	0.55	-0.55	1.05	2.21	5.03	6.30	4.82
Capital and Financial Account, Net	4.01	4.13	3.49	5.19	7.10	6.17	10.27	12.38	6.98
III. Others									
A. Monetisation of Gold	0.49	0.54	0.25	0.21	0.24	0.25	0.24	0.25	0.10
B. Revaluation Adjustments	1.81	0.85	0.99	0.79	0.16	-0.13	-0.24	-0.22	-0.38
IV. Errors & Omissions, Net Unclassified	-0.72	1.02	-0.30	-0.95	-0.08	-0.78	-0.70	-2.08	-3.56
V. Overall BoP Position	-0.21	4.63	2.82	-0.31	2.81	0.88	4.90	5.97	-1.94

Philippines. Current account deficits shot up in the 1993 to 1996 period compared to 1991 and 1992. The current account deficit would have been higher if foreign debt interest payments had not declined (relative to GDP) and if remittances of Filipino overseas workers had not increased so rapidly. The years 1994 to 1996 actually saw current account deficits' share of GDP decline from 1993 largely due to these two items.

Trade deficits, however, went up from 9 per cent of GDP in 1992 to 12 per cent in 1994 and 1995 and to 13 per cent in 1996. Furthermore, some observers believe that overseas remittances, exports and net investments in the current account table have all been overestimated since 1994 because they are partly estimated from foreign currency deposit units (FCDUs), which do not distinguish their sources (whether resident or non-resident) or their breakdown. When this was corrected in 1997, the data for exports, net investments, merchandise exports and, especially, exports of services all declined, indicating possible overestimation of these data and therefore underestimation of the current account deficits in previous years.

Even with the alarmingly large trade deficits, the balance of payments was positive in 1994 to 1996 due to the large inflows of remittances of overseas workers, the smaller debt burden, the larger net inflows of medium and long-term loans and, most especially, higher levels of net foreign investments. By early 1997, gross international reserves had risen to more than US$12 billion. A paradoxical situation had arisen, with trade deficits unprecedentedly high, but international reserves bountiful. The appreciation of the peso in real terms continued to hurt the real prices of tradables even further.

Economic growth rates accelerated during this period. GDP growth rates accelerated from 4.4 per cent in 1994 to 5.5 per cent in 1996. GNP growth was even more spectacular, reaching 6.8 per cent in 1996, mainly due to the fast rise in net factor income from abroad, made up of remittances of overseas workers and improvements in net investments, both of which might have been exaggerated in the 1993-1996 period. Investments recovered during this period, reaching 25.6 per cent of GDP, a percentage almost equal to that achieved in the early eighties. Domestic savings also increased, but at a lower and slower pace.

Industry and services posted high growth rates as agriculture continued to lose its share of GDP. Before the currency turmoil, the government was able to realise fiscal surpluses for 1995 and 1996. As treasury bill rates declined and as monetary policy relaxed, interest payments by the government, as a share of GDP, also declined significantly. One victim of fiscal conservatism was infrastructure. Government construction, which has suffered massive declines since the foreign debt crisis of the eighties, is still nowhere near the levels achieved in the early eighties, and capital outlays are only 3.3 per cent of GDP. The financial sector boomed, spurred on by continuing financial liberalisation, culminating in the easing of bank entry to both domestic and foreign banks. Numerous banks opened, including many owned by foreign banks or with foreign equity. Because of optimism with recent growth (founded partly on greater political stability), a classic overlending and overborrowing syndrome emerged, with credit expanding phenomenally.

Thus, before the currency and financial crisis hit East Asia, the Philippines was enjoying a spate of economic growth and low inflation (with excellent fiscal balances) which it direly needed after two significant recessions. The growth, however, occurred in a situation of very high trade deficits and import dependence. It therefore relied a lot on foreign capital inflows and remittances of overseas workers. Furthermore, the appreciating peso, combined with tariff reduction, made tradables unusually cheap, providing impetus to investments in non-tradables. This aggravated the boom-oriented tendency for asset prices to soar — particularly real property and stock market prices. Investments in the financial, trade (particularly department stores and 'megamalls') and property sector (reflected in the un-precedented growth in construction) outpaced investments in manufacturing. Property and financial bubbles were created and became ripe for bursting on the eve of the currency and financial turmoil.

Economic Slowdown, Currency and Financial Turmoil since 1997

It would be worthwhile at this juncture to summarise the important trends that had a direct bearing on the currency crisis that hit the country starting July 1997.

1. Foreign exchange and capital liberalisation had led to increases in net foreign investments and remittances of overseas workers to the Philippines. This allowed growth to be sustained for several years even as trade deficits became very large.
2. Capital liberalisation, however, led to massive portfolio inflows and outflows that increased volatility on the external account as short-run money ('hot money') came in and turned around very quickly.
3. The net external inflow of capital led to a paradoxical situation where the currency was appreciating in real terms (sometimes in nominal terms) as trade deficits became very large and current account balances continued to be in the red.
4. The appreciation of the currency in real terms hurt the export sector (with the exception of semiconductors), and, in conjunction with significant tariff reduction, increased tremendously the import intensity of the economy. Furthermore, this bias against tradables encouraged the fast-growing economy to shift to non-tradables, particularly, the real property, financial and trade sectors. This, together with the overlending syndrome in the financial sector, created asset bubbles that would aggravate the financial crisis.
5. Financial liberalisation and easing of bank entry allowed the overborrowing and overlending syndrome to unfold in full force without sufficient prudential regulation by the central bank. This regulation should have focused on reducing

exposure to risky assets and loans, especially real estate loans, foreign borrowings and expansion of consumer lending to high risk groups.

6. Financial liberalisation, together with the central bank's sterilisation of monetary inflows and the policy of a stable currency, made sure that domestic interest rates[1] were above foreign interest rates, particularly the dollar interest rates.

As the growth rate approached 7 per cent of GNP in 1996, optimism in the Philippine economy increased, culminating in the first two months of 1997 when the growth numbers for 1996 were revealed. The picture changed suddenly in the next few months. First, the Thai crisis was looming as the property and financial bubble in Thailand became publicised. Then came a realisation that things were not as rosy as everyone thought. Growth rates for the first and second quarters of 1997 declined, particularly in the manufacturing sector. The export sector also declined, with merchandise exports growing more slowly and exports of services declining by a large amount. The slower growth was revealed exactly at the time of the currency crisis and brought the stock market down to unprecedented depths (by January 1998, the stock market was below 50 per cent of its level in February 1997).

When the currency crisis struck in July 1997 with the baht devaluation, the portfolio inflows that had exploded in the past few years suddenly left, facilitated by electronic and computer technology. The central bank Banko Sentral Pilipinas (BSP) tried to defend the peso vainly with almost US$2 billion worth of reserves. When the peso exchange rate finally caved in, the BSP initially tried to stem the peso depreciation by high interest rate policies (a combination of increasing liquidity reserves, higher loan loss provisions,[2] higher overnight borrowing and lending rates and open market operations). High interest rates persisted, even when the BSP tried to bring them down towards the end of 1997. The banks themselves have been keeping deposit and lending rates higher than what the BSP wants because of high risk exposure to loan defaults and continuing depreciation and volatility of the peso (as expected devaluation and expected inflation keep going up). Strict monetary targets, agreed upon by the government and the IMF, as well as their strict implementation by the central bank closed all avenues to reducing interest rates. Financial sector vulnerability began to become a major cause of worry.

There was a slow revelation that due to the past stability and appreciation of the peso and the higher peso interest rates compared to dollar interest rates, many commercial banks and large and medium-sized firms borrowed heavily in unhedged dollars. With the sharp devaluation that has occurred in the second half of 1997, these banks and firms have suddenly found themselves burdened with expensive unhedged dollar-denominated debts which, in turn, have contributed to the continuing speculation (in fact panic by unhedged dollar borrowers) and depreciation of the peso as other East Asian countries continue to become more deeply enmeshed in financial trouble.[3] The currency depreciation during the first few months of the crisis — July to October 1997 — was mainly caused by portfolio investors moving out of the country coupled with speculators, many of whom were saddled with unhedged dollar debt. This brought the exchange rate from P26.3 per dollar in July 1997 to around P35 per dollar in early 1998. From November 1997 to the first quarter of 1998, most speculation on the peso has been made by local players exposed to dollar borrowings. It is this set of speculators that have brought the peso from around P35 to as high as P45 to the US dollar during the worst period in January 1998.[4]

Furthermore, with the sharp rise in interest rates, many loan exposures to the property sector (which were so attractive from 1994 to the first half of 1997) were now in jeopardy. Construction firms suddenly found themselves unable to finish existing projects as interest rates skyrocketed. Many property developers started selling their unfinished units at 20-30 per cent discounts in desperate attempts to get additional financing. Real property prices dropped significantly, bursting the bubble in the property sector just as the stock market bubble had burst.

Firms that are import-dependent, those that are highly leveraged and those that branched out to the property sector found themselves close to default, threatening to cause a domino collapse in the banking sector. Rising defaults in consumer and car loans caused past due ratios to rise. Rumours of bank runs and withdrawals continue to hound the financial sector. A vicious cycle has arisen. The peso is constantly being threatened by unending depreciation and interest rates continue to rise as unhedged foreign borrowings and the threat of more defaulting firms continue to become more serious. At the same time, increasingly more expensive foreign borrowings, constantly increasing import costs (both due to peso devaluation) and rising interest rates create more impetus for loan defaults and further hedging and speculation in dollars by indebted and import-dependent firms. The reduction in bank profits and, in many cases, outright bank losses have kept lending rates far above deposit and treasury bill rates as banks try to recoup part of their losses by keeping the spreads high.

Given the turmoil in the second half of 1997, the growth rate for that year was rather respectable: 5.1 per cent for GDP and 5.8 per cent for GNP — only 1 per cent short of that achieved in 1996. The inflation rate was 5.1 per cent — the lowest since 1987. The inflation rate, based on the consumer price index, however, is well-known to be biased, with food accounting for almost 60 per cent of the basket, and import-intensive goods having a low share in the basket. Still, the inflation rate jumped to an annual rate of 7.4 per cent in February 1998, signalling many more hard times ahead.

Analysis of the Causes of the Crisis

After going through the above story, it is worthwhile to consider the important factors (both domestic and external) contributing to the vulnerability of the

Philippine economy when the economic and financial crisis hit East Asia. We will also consider the factors that may be aggravating the crisis in the Philippines.

Dependence on Foreign Savings and External Flows

The Philippines has the lowest domestic savings rate among the ASEAN countries — around 22 per cent to 23 per cent of GDP in 1996 compared to well over 30 per cent in the other countries. This has made the Philippines more dependent on foreign savings and foreign inflows to sustain its growth. It was able to grow substantially for a long period in the seventies because of the foreign debt inflow from petro-dollars stored in foreign commercial banks. In the mid-nineties, it was portfolio investments, foreign direct investments, remittances of overseas workers and foreign borrowings that allowed the high trade deficits to continue without affecting growth and inflation. Once the external conditions become unfriendly, however, the economy goes into a downward trend. Without substantial external inflows for a significant period of time, the economy goes into short-run bust-boom cycles. Booms lead to unsustainable external outflows and recessions, followed by recovery, growth and high external deficits and downturn. It is therefore to the detriment of some East Asian countries — such as Thailand and South Korea — that with higher savings rates, they still incurred much higher current account deficits (in terms of percentage of GNP) than the Philippines. A main cause of some of the East Asian woes is an attempt to grow too fast too soon using foreign (including borrowed) money.

Blanket Foreign Exchange and Capital Liberalisation

In terms of external financing, there is the option of incurring external debt (and this could be sub-categorised further as public or private debt), portfolio investments, foreign direct investments and remittances of overseas workers. The result of the policy in the mid-nineties has been a blanket opening up of capital inflows and outflows, without recognising the positive and negative effects of different types of capital inflows and differentiating among them accordingly. It must be pointed out that, based on the experiences of the past, foreign debt is quite unreliable, not only because world interest rates may rise but also because the currency might devalue substantially and the supply of funds may dry up (as it did in the eighties). Further, investments by a private sector facing 'distorted' prices and economic incentives, or dominated by vested interests supported by a corrupt government, or by a public sector compromised by 'crony capitalism' (which also happened in the eighties), may result in unsound and unproductive use of the borrowed money. This leads to a financial crisis and repayment problem.

The experience of the nineties is that portfolio investments have a fickle and unreliable streak determined by uncontrollable factors such as crises in Mexico and Thailand. Furthermore, portfolio investments also follow a 'herd' mentality that encourages mass entry and exit to entire regions based on psychological sentiments. This aggravates the volatility, uncertainty and speculation that have been key to the currency turmoil in Southeast Asia.

It would seem therefore that direct foreign investments which enter a country with medium to long-term perspectives would be superior to short-run portfolio investments and foreign borrowings. A more liberal allowance of foreign direct investments and more taxes or regulation on the entry and exit of the latter types of external flows would therefore be a more appropriate policy than blanket foreign exchange and capital liberalisation.

Furthermore, foreign exchange and capital liberalisation brought about an influx of external net inflows crucial to the appreciation of the peso. The distortion of relative prices — making tradables relatively cheap compared to non-tradables — allowed capital (both domestic and foreign) to invest in the property and stock markets, thus creating the speculative bubbles. In terms of sequencing of reforms, even for neo-classical economists, capital liberalisation should be the last to be effected (if at all) once all relative price distortions are eradicated.

As it is, capital liberalisation increased the volatility of external inflows and outflows culminating in the massive exodus from the region when the Thai crisis occurred.

The Strength of Globalisation

One feature of the present trends in trade and capital liberalisation is that most countries in the region and in other parts of the world undertook, to various degrees, the liberalisation and the opening up of their economies at the same time.[5] Thus, all countries compete with each other for portfolio and direct investments as capital flows almost instantaneously from one developed or developing economy to another. The participation of most countries in the World Trade Organisation (WTO) and regional blocs has also heightened competition in the trade of goods.

When the currency turmoil hit the region, capital flowed out of the region almost instantaneously. Simultaneous with this, speculation on the currencies heightened as economic troubles in one country were transmitted to other competitor countries via speculation by portfolio investors and unhedged dollar debtors. This speculation was spurred on by the fact that these are similar countries in close proximity, competing with their exports. Further, the countries had pursued similar policies and made similar mistakes such as borrowing unhedged dollars, overinvesting in overpriced real property and stock market assets, encouraging long periods of nominally stable and appreciating (in real terms) currency while incurring large current account deficits, and allowing deteriorating prudential regulation of the banking and financial system. In a way, globalisation had resulted in linking the economies in East Asia in such a way that the economic woes in one country were passed on to the others via speculation on their currencies.

Thus, we see a spiralling free-fall of currencies during the worst periods of the crisis as one currency depreciation fed back on the other currencies and vice versa. This phenomenon is quite new and strange even to policymakers and bankers. As a result, conspiracy theories which blame individuals (e.g. Soros), other governments (e.g. the US or China) or sets of institutions (e.g. European banks) are earnestly formulated and believed.

Financial Liberalisation and Lack of Prudential Regulation:
The Role of the Central Bank

As was made clear in the previous sections, financial liberalisation, easing of bank entry and advances in bank technologies involving automatic tellers and credit cards, had facilitated the 'overborrowing syndrome'. Too much credit, given in too lax a way, led to rising past due ratios and default rates of loans both before and during the financial turmoil. More importantly, without proper regulation, credit was provided for 'wrong' investments in the overpriced property, trade and import-dependent sectors — since economic incentives and relative prices were biased towards these sectors (as explained earlier). Equally important was the allowance of voluminous unhedged foreign borrowings by domestic banks and private firms. These unhedged borrowings were later to be one of the causes of speculative attacks on the currency during the crisis.

All these issues point to a common feature among the East Asian countries hard-hit by the financial crisis: the lack and inadequacy of prudential regulation by the central banks of these economies. In fact, the role of the BSP in contributing to and aggravating the crisis has been a point of bitter contention among some economists in the University of the Philippines, on the one hand, and the Central Bank itself and its allies on the other. The other controversial issues are:

1) Was the Central Bank responsible for the overvaluation of the peso that made it so vulnerable to the speculative attacks? The critics of the Central Bank claim that in the over-enthusiasm to provide a stable exchange rate, the Central Bank had defended the peso by sterilisation of monetary inflows and high interest rates. The resulting overvaluation of the peso and high domestic interest rates *vis-à-vis* foreign interest rates were directly responsible for creating the climate ripe for the crisis. The Central Bank claims that it had actually done the opposite by stemming the appreciation of the peso with interventions in the foreign exchange market during times of high external inflows. Furthermore, money supply expanded significantly and interest rates declined from 1993-96 — the crucial years of the latest growth. Whatever the details of each side's arguments, one should acknowledge that the main cause of the

overvaluation of the peso was precisely the positive net external inflows from abroad as trade deficits and current account deficits were in the red.

2) The critics claim that the Central Bank was foolish to defend the peso wasting at least US$2 billion, which in effect subsidised the outgoing portfolio investors and speculators when the peso did cave in to the pressures for depreciation. This, of course, was also done by other central banks in the region, with the Bank of Thailand being the biggest loser so far.

3) After the initial depreciation of the peso, the Central Bank tried to defend the peso further by increasing liquidity reserve requirements (bringing required reserves to more than 20 per cent), and increasing the Central Bank's overnight borrowing and lending rates. The high interest rates and very tight monetary and credit policy contributed to aggravating the crisis by threatening further defaults from credit-dependent sectors, particularly the property sector. Because the main causes of the currency depreciation were the financial troubles of Thailand, South Korea and Indonesia as well as the unhedged dollar borrowers who became natural speculators, the high interest rate defence of the peso was futile and unnecessary. The Central Bank, of course, claims that the initial high interest rate policies were temporary (implemented till November and December of 1997) and required to stem the free-fall of the peso.

4) At a later stage (starting in 1998), the Central Bank provided the non-deliverable forward cover (NDF) to buyers of dollars at a future date in order to stem speculation on the peso. The scheme, in effect, insured dollar purchasers (at a future date) from fluctuations in the exchange rate. It made sure that payment of the differential between market and contracted prices be made in pesos rather than dollars at the future date, thus avoiding further depletion of international reserves. So far, it is hard to say whether the scheme worked for it came just when other regional currencies began to stabilise (thus also stabilising the peso). But critics of the Central Bank claim that it is again unnecessarily subsidising dollar purchases of big banks since the period of many of the forward cover contracts is more than six months. In effect, this makes the Central Bank bear all the risk of the foreign exchange transactions in favour of the big commercial banks.

5) The Central Bank has also been criticised heavily for lack of transparency of data on the financial sector. This has contributed to uncertainty, volatility and speculation in the entire system as it refuses to reveal the extent of financial trouble besetting both firms and commercial banks. The latest information on the foreign liabilities of banks, firms and non-performing assets and loans dates back to June 1997, the last pre-crisis month.

The above issues point to the complicated nature of the system of regulations and interventions in the financial sector. It may be easy to point to 'prudential regulation' and interventions in the financial sector as one answer to the present crisis. So far, everybody — from left-wing thinkers to the IMF — agrees on the need for prudential regulation. What is difficult and more controversial is whether the Central Bank has the expertise, sophistication and relative autonomy from vested interests (especially from commercial banks and the powers-that-be) to do it correctly and competently.

The Pro-Market Versus the Anti-Market Arguments

Undoubtedly, those explaining the crisis will have their own bents or biases. On one end would be those geared to market reforms (sometimes called neo-liberal economists) who will concentrate on the policies that led to price distortions against tradables and the relative inexpensiveness of dollar credits during the period right before the crisis. Capital liberalisation as implemented in the Philippines, although part of the scheme of opening up the economy to the world market, is mainly viewed as a wrong policy, most likely, as it has involved wrong sequencing of reforms which ultimately distort the prices of tradables. Complete capital restrictions will, of course, be frowned upon. A middle course which gives more incentives (complete opening up) to foreign direct investments and penalises (via taxation or regulation) portfolio investments (especially outflows) and foreign borrowings will be the best course. It is also now accepted by some neo-classical economists (Stiglitz 1992, McKinnon and Pill 1996) that financial and credit markets may be characterised by market failure — e.g. 'moral hazard', especially if banks feel they will be bailed out by the central bank. This leads to the 'overborrowing syndrome' and the need for strong prudential regulation of the financial sector.

The thrust of the anti-market arguments will undoubtedly blame the series of trade and capital liberalisation measures and easing of foreign bank entry as opening up the economy to globalisation and international volatility, which finally brought about this financial and economic crisis. There would be some persuasive arguments here, particularly regarding the volatility and strength of globalisation, that have been underestimated by most neo-liberal economists. But the blanket condemnation of all policies opening up the national economy to the world market in this period of intense world integration and interlinkages is unrealistic. One can look at China and Chile as two economies that have opened up their economies tremendously (compared to their starting point, say, two decades ago) to the world market. They are, so far, very successful. One thing they have in common, though, is capital regulation that discriminates between foreign direct investments, portfolio investments and foreign borrowings. Hence, both neo-liberal and anti-market positions would accept the need to be very carefully selective about areas to be opened up to the world economy. If increased risks and greater volatility are expected with opening up certain sectors, compensating measures should be adopted (e.g. if it is decided to open up the financial sector to foreign banks and to undertake financial liberalisation strong prudential regulation should be implemented).

A blanket attack on opening up to market processes ignores the positive contribution to efficiency, productivity and economic welfare of some initiatives in competition, deregulation and import liberalisation. Wholesale condemnation of capital, trade and financial liberalisation without taking into consideration distortions in economic incentives (perhaps through market pricing) would over-simplify the analysis and explanation of the crisis. Because many anti-market thinkers are against devaluation of the currency, they refuse to consider possible overvaluation of a currency in the period immediately prior to the crisis. This completely ignores the fact that the tariff reduction and capital liberalisation together cheapened imported and tradable goods. Similarly, an aversion to consider relative prices will ignore why so many banks and firms borrowed in dollars, rather than pesos, in the immediate pre-crisis period.

Finally, many anti-market thinkers correctly point to corruption and weak institutions as contributing to the present crisis. This, of course, raises problems for those who argued that developmental state policies were key to the success of most of the East Asian newly industrialising countries. This tension between market failures — usually used to justify strategic state interventions — and government failures — usually used to attack government interventions associated with inept policies or in favour of certain vested interests — becomes a crucial arena of debate.

Prospects for the Future

The Philippine government has, time and again, proclaimed that the East Asian crisis has not hit the Philippines as badly as the other countries, as evidenced by the smaller depreciation of the currency and the smaller number and magnitude of loan defaults and bank insolvencies. This may be the case, but it is most likely due to the fact that the Philippines grew much more slowly (roughly 6 per cent GNP growth in 1995 and 1996) compared to the other affected East Asian countries (whose growth rates were generally above 8 per cent). It is also true that the other East Asian countries had been growing faster for a longer period of time and that foreign inflows were much greater elsewhere than in the Philippines. There is also the belief that Philippine firms and banks did not incur large foreign borrowings until well into 1996 because of the traumatic foreign debt experience of the eighties. Instead, many waited until the exchange rate was very stable and foreign inflows were very large before borrowing from abroad.

Still, the crisis has caused very considerable damage. First is the shattering of business confidence.[6] This happened especially towards the end of 1997 and in early 1998, when the exchange rate went up from P35 to P40 and hit P45 to the US dollar in January 1998. The severity of the crisis finally forced business firms to stop expansion plans and scale down their operations, with lay-offs starting in earnest in early 1998. Government bureaucrats agreed that continuing to say that the 'fundamentals are still alright' and 'this is just temporary' would ultimately be counterproductive. They finally admitted that growth rates would decline (to 3 per cent, at most) and that inflation would go up (to at least 7 per cent).

Credit tightness and exceedingly high interest rates are stifling investments and scaling down the operations of many plants, while the peso depreciation has increased costs for firms using imports. In fact, export expansion — widely expected as a result of the currency depreciation — may not be very large due to the unavailability and high costs of credit as well as the widespread expectations of continued instability.

Further, the Philippines, as mentioned earlier, had the lowest savings rate among the countries hit by the currency turmoil. It therefore has the biggest need (in the medium and long term) for such funds. Hence, in order to grow rapidly, tremendous increases in export earnings, remittances of overseas workers, and medium- and long-term public debt will have to be effected in the medium and long term. Finally, the sustainable growth of the Philippines in the medium to long term is now jeopardised as foreign inflows may not be forthcoming for some time to come. With Japan deeper in recession than in the past, foreign direct investments will not be very large. This trend is further aggravated by the regional perceptions of international capital which now views this part of the world as seriously unstable and mismanaged.

Crises can be useful only if we learn from them and can make a fresh start. On the first count, it is now clear that more care should be given to policies concerning capital inflows and outflows in the future. Policies discriminating against short-term fly-by-night portfolio capital and short-run foreign borrowings will have to be instituted. Furthermore, the crisis has shown that ASEAN countries cannot easily overcome their own economic crises on their own. If the countries learn to co-ordinate their financial, foreign exchange and capital flow polices over time (perhaps even in conjunction with other East Asian countries) and negotiate with the IMF and other foreign entities in a more united and hence stronger manner, the results should be more conducive to long-run sustainable growth for the entire region.

Finally, the recent growth of the Philippines has been driven by non-tradables (real estate, mega-malls) and asset bubbles, leading to growth being concentrated in a limited number of centres at the expense of other regions, particularly the rural areas. This aggravates regional disparities and does not contribute to alleviating poverty in the rural areas. As economic downturn occurs and a new administration takes over, it is a good time to call for and consider an alternative development strategy — one that should prioritise rural and agricultural development, an approach neglected by the Philippines. By concentrating on rural development and rural–urban linkages, economic development can become more equitable, less import-dependent and, ultimately, more sustainable.

Notes

1. The domestic interest rates had actually been falling substantially since 1993, but the levels were still above foreign interest rates.
2. Prudential regulation for loan loss provisions is actually very necessary.
3. Every time the currency of some other country in East Asia depreciates, these local speculators panic and try to buy dollars (which they predict will become more expensive with continuing devaluations).
4. As of early March 1998 — the time of the writing of this chapter — the exchange rate was roughly P40 to a dollar.
5. This was, of course, a result of the participation of most countries in the World Trade Organisation (WTO) and in regional agreements such as the ASEAN Free Trade Area (AFTA) and the APEC forum. Even countries that are not yet members of WTO, such as China and Vietnam, have opened up their economy significantly compared to the past.
6. The author who is a rabid Keynesian would prefer to use the term 'animal spirit'.

10
SOUTH KOREA:
THE MISUNDERSTOOD CRISIS

Chang Ha-Joon*

When the South Korean crisis first broke in November 1997, many commentators argued that it was proof that its famous state-led economic system had reached its limits.[1] The medicine to cure the country's economic ills, it was widely argued, was to ditch the inefficient and corrupt state-directed economic system, and to create, in its place, a 'genuine' market economy through extensive liberalisation of finance, international trade and the labour market. The IMF bail-out programme implemented in December 1997, and the series of structural 'reforms' that followed, were supposed to provide this medicine.

Is this analysis correct? Was the Korean crisis really one of over-regulation based on corrupt state–business relations? Is institutional reform in an 'Anglo-American' direction going to enable the country to overcome the current crisis and get back on a more robust growth path? While it is difficult to provide satisfactory answers to these questions with the crisis still unfolding, this article offers some evidence and analyses questioning some of the conventional wisdom about the current Korean crisis.

Understanding the Crisis

Contrary to the conventional wisdom, the current Korean crisis is largely 'financial' in origin, rather than a crisis of the 'real economy'. However, the financial crisis has turned into a crisis of the real economy.

Most of South Korea's manufacturing firms make products that sell even in the most demanding markets — if the exchange rate is right. It is widely agreed that, during the last couple of years, the South Korean won was overvalued by

---

* A preliminary version of this chapter was presented at a conference on the Asian crisis held at the University of Oslo, 23-24 January 1998. The chapter draws on collaborative work in progress on the issue with Hong Jae Park and Chul-Gyue Yoo. In writing this chapter, I have benefited from discussions with Jan Kregel, Peter Evans, Lance Taylor, Richard Kozul-Wright, Chalmers Johnson, Meredith Woo-Cumings, Soo Haeng Kim, Un Chan Chung, Tae In Jung, Yilmaz Akyuz, Chung H. Lee, Gary Dymski, and Robert Pollin. The participants at the conference also provided useful comments.

10 to 20 per cent. Nevertheless, on the eve of the crisis, the current account deficit was just over 3 per cent of GNP. By way of comparison, current account deficits equivalent to over 8 per cent of GNP emerged in Thailand and Mexico before their recent crises; in previous downturns, for example in 1980, Korea had current account deficits approaching 9 per cent of GNP.

Furthermore, most Korean foreign borrowings are believed to have financed investments in tradable sectors, rather than real estate developments or imports of consumer goods, as in Mexico and Southeast Asia. The Korean annual budget has been largely in balance and gross public debt amounts to only 3 per cent of GDP — described as the second best budgetary position in the Organisation for Economic Cooperation and Development (OECD) by an influential British financial journalist (Wolf 1997). Now, if Korea's real economy was relatively sound, why did it crash?

Immediate Causes

The first obvious suspect is the accumulation of non-performing loans in the domestic banking system, which many commentators argue is the inevitable outcome of state direction of credits. And indeed, according to information from the Bank of Korea (the central bank), the share of non-performing loans to total loans increased from 4.1 per cent at the end of 1996 to 6.8 per cent in September 1997, at the eve of the crisis.

While this may sound high, it is not particularly high by Korean historical standards. It was only marginally higher than the average for the 1990-95 period (6.4 per cent), and lower than in 1990 (7.5 per cent) and 1993 (7 per cent). Therefore, the accumulation of non-performing loans in the domestic banking system alone cannot explain the current crisis.

What about the accumulation of foreign debt? After all, the current Korean crisis is a debt crisis of sorts. At a superficial level, this is correct, but the reality is much more complex.

In Korea, foreign borrowing had increased very quickly during the last few years. Foreign debt nearly trebled from US$44 billion in 1993 to US$120 billion in September 1997, before falling slightly to US$116 billion by November 1997.[2] This debt build-up was almost twice as fast as during 1979-85, i.e. before the country's earlier near debt crisis. Korea's foreign debt grew at an average of 17.8 per cent per annum during 1979-85, and by 33.6 per cent per annum during 1994-96.

While certainly large and fast-growing during the last few years, Korea's foreign debt was *not* at an obviously unsustainable level. The World Bank defines a country as 'less indebted' when its debt/GNP ratio is under 48 per cent. In 1996, Korea was well below this threshold at 22 per cent, and on the eve of the crisis, it could not have been much more than 25 per cent (the data for 1997 are not yet available).[3] In contrast, the corresponding figures at the end of 1995 were 70 per cent for Mexico, 57 per cent for Indonesia, 35 per cent for Thailand, 33 per cent for Argentina and 24 per cent for Brazil (World Bank 1997a). Korea's debt service ratio (total debt service to exports of goods and services), another common indicator of the debt burden, was well below the World Bank's 'warning' threshold (18 per cent) at 5.4 per cent in 1995 and 5.8 per cent in 1996. Thus, Korea's situation compared very favourably with those of countries like Mexico (24.2 per cent), Brazil (37.9 per cent), Indonesia (30.9 per cent) and Thailand (10.2 per cent) in 1995 (World Bank 1997a).

Moreover, the main debt build-up was between 1994 and 1996, when growth of Korea's foreign debt averaged 33.5 per cent per annum. By 1997, growth of Korea's foreign debt was already slowing down. Its foreign debt increased from US$105 billion at the end of 1996 to US$120 billion in September 1997 — an annualised growth rate of 19 per cent — and, as already seen, actually decreased to US$116 billion by the end of November 1997.

However, even though the overall debt level was not very high, Korean foreign debt had a poor maturity structure. The share of short-term debt (defined as debt with less than a year's maturity) in total debt rose from an already high 43.7 per cent in 1993 to 58.2 per cent at the end of 1996. In contrast, on the eve of the 1980s debt crisis (between 1980 and 1982), the average ratio of short-term to overall debt for non-OPEC (Organisation of Petroleum Exporting Countries) developing countries was only 20 per cent (Koener *et al.*, 1986: 8, Table 1.1). However, even in this regard, things were not getting any worse for Korea in the build-up to the crisis, as the share of short-term debt actually fell marginally from 58.2 per cent at the end of 1996 to 58.0 per cent at the end of June 1997.

Thus seen, the Korean foreign debt situation was almost as bad at the end of 1996 as it was on the eve of the crisis, hence it is difficult to say that the worsening debt situation sparked off the crisis. What then shook the confidence of foreign lenders in the economy, making them suddenly withdraw their loans, thus prompting a debt crisis? This brings us to two high-profile corporate bankruptcies, which undermined confidence in the economy during 1997.

In January 1997, Hanbo, a major new steel company went bankrupt. It was subsequently revealed that a web of high-level corruption — involving some very close associates and the second son of then President Kim Young Sam — surrounded Hanbo's entry into the steel industry and continued loan extension despite its known problems. Since the biggest conglomerate, Hyundai, had been consistently denied entry into the steel industry in the preceding years, securing the licence and continued financing for a minor conglomerate (*chaebol*) with a dubious record of manufacturing capability could not be explained otherwise.

In contrast to the currently popular perception, the corruption involved in the Hanbo case was *not* typical of what was going on in Korea under its state-led model of development. Admittedly, large sums of money had flowed from big business to powerful politicians and top bureaucrats. Such flows were often tied to particular projects in areas like urban planning and government procurement, but they rarely directly relate to specific projects *in the main manufacturing sectors*. Moreover, under the Kim Young Sam government, for the first time in Korean history since the 1960s, the names of particular *chaebols*, such as Samsung, were talked of as being particularly 'close to the regime'. Previously, the *chaebols* as a group were treated preferentially, but rarely was any one or a few of them regarded as being closer to the government than the others. The Hanbo scandal thus reflected this fundamental transformation in the state-business relationship in Korea, which meant that the major manufacturing sectors were no longer as insulated from corrupt political practices as before.

As significant as the Hanbo case may have been, foreign confidence in the economy was really battered by the saga surrounding the fate of the third (once the second) biggest automobile producer, Kia, the eighth largest *chaebol* in the country. When Kia first showed signs of trouble in June 1997, then Finance Minister Kang Kyung Shik argued that the Korean economy needed more market discipline and therefore, he did not mind showing that 'even the *chaebols* can fail'.

Given Kang's well-known connection with Samsung, the second biggest conglomerate, many observers interpreted this as a coded message that he would let Kia be taken over by Samsung. At the time, Samsung's new automobile venture was looking increasingly doubtful without the acquisition of an existing firm with solid manufacturing capability, as Samsung had already spent an inordinate amount of money buying and strengthening expensive, but unsuitable reclaimed land in then Korean President Kim Young Sam's hometown of Pusan.[4] When the Kim Young Sam government found out that a takeover of Kia by Samsung was not going to go down well with public opinion, it changed its policy stance about Kia's fate many times, undermining international confidence in the economy.

As is well known, the Kia saga unfolded during an especially unfortunate time, i.e. when the Southeast Asian financial crises broke out, starting in Thailand. The Southeast Asian crisis contributed to the Korean crisis in a number of ways. First of all, 'contagion' meant that confidence in all Asian economies, not just the Southeast Asian economies first affected by the crisis, was shaken. Of course, this is not to say that the effect was purely psychological. Falling demand in Southeast Asia meant reduced Korean exports while some Korean financial institutions which had invested in the region were hard hit by the collapsing stock and, especially, bond markets; it is estimated that Korean financial institutions lost at least US$2 billion, and possibly more, in Southeast Asian financial markets with the outbreak of the crisis. Some commentators claim that the fall in the Southeast Asian asset values prompted some Japanese banks, which had heavily invested in the region, to withdraw loans from Korean debtors in order to improve their balance sheets, although this is hard to verify, given the unwillingness of Japanese banks to reveal the extent of their exposure in Southeast Asian markets for fear of adverse effects on their share prices.

Deeper Causes

It is all very well to say that the high ratio of short-term foreign debt and certain high-profile bankruptcies, combined with the fallout from the Southeast Asian crisis, prompted the crisis. However, how did Korea's foreign debt situation and corporate problems get to where they were in 1997? To answer this question, we need to consider the changes in government policies during the few years preceding the crisis. We examine three policy areas — financial regulation, exchange rate management and investment co-ordination.

Previously, the Korean government had controlled all (internal and cross-border) financial flows very tightly (Chang 1993). And despite some liberalisation in the 1980s, the system remained tightly monitored until the early 1990s (Amsden and Euh 1990). However, from the early 1990s, the Korean government started significantly relaxing its control over the financial sector. The liberalisation process was accelerated under the Kim Young Sam government.

Liberalisation was considerable, especially in relation to foreign borrowing, an area which had traditionally been most tightly controlled by the government, with virtually no restrictions left. To be fair, this was not entirely a matter of policy choice, as the biggest Korean firms and banks now had sufficiently good credit ratings to gain easy access to international financial markets. However, the Kim Young Sam government relaxed controls on foreign borrowing more than it needed to, and, more importantly, failed to adequately supervise the financial institutions involved in such borrowings.

The merchant banks newly licensed by the Kim Young Sam government — nine by 1994, and 15 by July 1996, in contrast to the 6 that existed before 1994 — took full advantage of this new situation. Supervision of these merchant banks was virtually non-existent, to the extent that the government was apparently not even aware of the huge mismatch in maturity structures between their borrowings (64 per cent of the US$20 billion total were short term) and lendings (85 per cent were long term).

Exchange rate management was another policy area in which abandonment of previous practices was detrimental. The country had been known for its quick actions against currency overvaluation in order to maintain export competitiveness. However, under the Kim Young Sam government, this started changing.

The current account surplus of US$0.4 billion in 1993 turned into a deficit of US$4.5 billion in 1994, which grew to US$8.9 billion in 1995, and to a record US$23.7 billion in 1996 (equivalent to over 5 per cent of GDP), although it had fallen to US$12.5 billion or so by November 1997. Of course, this current account deficit of this magnitude was not the worst that Korea has seen. As pointed out earlier, the current account deficit in 1980 was equivalent to more than 9 per cent of GNP. More recently, the current account deficit was US$8.7 billion in 1991, which was around 3 per cent of GNP, i.e. proportionately *bigger* than US$8.9 billion in 1995, equivalent to about 2 per cent of GNP.

The 1991 deficit quickly fell back to US$4.5 billion in 1992 and then turned into a small surplus in 1993, whereas the 1994 deficit continued to grow until 1996, and although it started falling in 1997, it was still substantially higher than in 1995. The collapse in the price of memory chip, the country's biggest export item, from a high of nearly US$50 to under US$4 at one point, was a major reason for the persistence of this deficit. But the failure to take timely action to reverse currency overvaluation, especially when the Japanese yen and the Chinese renminbi massively depreciated from 1995 and 1994 respectively, proved fatal.

The relative importance of the various reasons behind such a policy shift is not easy to establish, but a few can be singled out as important. First, the increasing dominance in Korean and international policy-making circles of the monetarist idea that inflation control should be the most important policy objective and that the exchange rate should be used to 'anchor' that policy. Second, having already built up a large foreign debt stock, the Korean government feared that significant depreciation would make the foreign debt repayment burden unbearable. Also, the Kim Young Sam government did not want devaluation as it would have set the country's per capita income back below the symbolic US$10,000 benchmark achieved in 1995.

The third change from the previous policy regime saw abandonment of investment co-ordination. With the rise of a pro-market ideology and the consequent loss of legitimacy for centralised co-ordination, the five-year plan process, which had provided the overall policy co-ordination framework since its introduction in 1962, was abandoned in 1993, shortly after the Kim Young Sam government took office, in favour of a poorly devised '100-day Plan for the New Economy'. At the same time, in the name of government administrative 'rationalisation', the planning ministry, the Economic Planning Board (EPB), was merged with the Ministry of Finance (MOF) to form a super-ministry, the Ministry of Finance and Economy (MOFE), which symbolised the demise of 'planning' in Korea.

At the same time, the Kim Young Sam government accelerated the dismantling of selective industrial policy, that had started in the late 1980s. Already in 1986, the Chun Doo Hwan government introduced the Industrial Development Law (IDL), which emphasised a 'functional', rather than sectoral, approach to industrial policy, in response to long-standing domestic and international criticisms of the latter approach. However, the IDL, through its provision for rationalisation programmes, allowed enough room for selective industrial policy, if the government had the will. And indeed, in the early days of the IDL, this was the case — several major rationalisation programmes were implemented throughout the late 1980s and the early 1990s, covering, among others, industries such as automobiles, heavy construction machinery, heavy electrical machinery, ferro-alloys, naval diesel engines, dyeing, textiles and coal mining (for more details, see Chang 1993: 142-4).

However, from the late 1980s, the will to conduct selective industrial policy started to decline with the rise of neo-liberal ideology and the growing power of the *chaebols* which wanted to be free of government regulations. In 1989, the government, for the first time, openly refused to co-ordinate investments in the petrochemical industry despite the looming threat of massive over-capacity, although it later had to intervene when the industry got into trouble due to over-capacity — for example, by imposing compulsory export quotas.

The Kim Young Sam government went even further and basically gave up on industrial policy other than involvement in R&D projects in some high-technology industries. The most symbolic in this regard was the previously mentioned decision to allow Samsung into the already over-crowded auto industry in 1993. Lack of investment co-ordination led to over-capacity, which resulted in falling export prices, falling profitability due to low capacity utilisation, and the accumulation of non-performing loans in a number of leading industries, including semi-conductors, automobiles, petrochemicals and shipbuilding.

The above-mentioned policy shifts were at one level, due to certain structural forces. First, the *chaebols* have become more independent of the government, as they started gaining direct access to international capital markets and acquired controlling stakes in certain minor regional banks (ownership of large national banks continued to be subject to strict ceilings) and non-bank financial institutions such as merchant banks. With their increasing financial independence, the *chaebols* became more aggressive in recent years in calling for withdrawal of the government.[5] Second, during the 1990s, there have been various multilateral and bilateral attempts by advanced economies, especially the US, to pry open formerly closed markets in developing countries. With its newly-acquired wealth and wide array of interventionist policies, Korea became a target for such pressures. Third, there has been a rise of neo-liberal ideology throughout the world since the 1980s, and it became difficult for a country like Korea, with a relatively weak intellectual tradition of its own, to resist such global intellectual trends.

However, these policy shifts did not simply reflect structural forces beyond the strategic control of Korean policymakers. For example, the demise of five-year plans and sectoral industrial policy under the Kim Young Sam government were the results of a deliberate strategic choice by the government, rather than something imposed by a strong private sector or by an overwhelming external force. The country's application to join the OECD (which it eventually joined in 1996) intensified external pressure to liberalise the economy.

Moreover, following the abolition of five-year planning and the serious weakening of sectoral industrial policy, well-publicised 'rational' criteria for intervention disappeared, making it easier to 'bend rules' for political reasons. This meant the end of the 'generalistic' state–business relationship that characterised the Korean model and the rapid rise of 'particularistic' (or 'cronyistic', to use the currently popular expression) relationships, and more importantly, its spread into the major manufacturing industries which were previously largely insulated from corruption — as exemplified by the Hanbo corruption scandal and Samsung's entry into the auto market. In this sense, it may be said that, contrary to the common perception, it was under the Kim Young Sam government that full-blown 'crony capitalism' emerged in Korea.

The above discussion shows that, while there may have been some inevitability in the policy shifts that contributed to the crisis, the Kim Young Sam government did not need to go as far as it did in dismantling the existing system. In other words, it made a number of important strategic choices which were crucial in generating the crisis.

What Future for Korea?

Within a month of the launch of its Korean bail-out programme in December 1997, the IMF had backed off from its earlier conditionalities. Although this was not publicised very much outside Korea, by mid-January, the inflation target was revised upward (from 5 to 9 per cent), and so was the monetary growth target (from 9 to 14 per cent). At the same time, the IMF dropped its insistence on a budgetary surplus, and admitted the seriousness of the credit crunch its policies were causing by extending the deadline by which Korean banks should meet the Bank of International Settlement's capital adequacy standard (allowing them to extend more loans), and allowing the Korean government to expand credit to exporting firms, which could not take advantage of the weak currency because of credit shortage. While even these revised targets are going to create unprecedented levels of corporate bankruptcy and unemployment — at the time of writing (mid-February 1998), more than 100 firms were going bankrupt *daily* — implying that the initial debate on the IMF programme for Korea had been settled in favour of its critics.

However, the more serious problem is with all the institutional changes that the IMF has been pressing for — although, to be fair to the IMF, many of these things had already been contemplated by the Kim Young Sam government and were enthusiastically embraced by the new government of Kim Dae Jung, at least initially.

First of all, the IMF's recommendation for rapid financial liberalisation is almost exactly the opposite of what it should have done, given that poor financial regulation was an important cause of the Korean crisis. The unstated logic behind it seems to be that by opening up the financial market, more able foreign financial institutions would come in to put the house in order. However, since these same foreign financial institutions had lent so much money to 'badly-managed' Korean financial institutions and had subsequently openly defied market logic (which they now insist the Koreans should accept) by asking the Korean government to assume a large amount of the private sector debt, it does not seem all that promising.

The proposal to restrain reckless corporate expansion through greater exposure to the threat of domestic and international takeover has a certain rationale, but evidence from the advanced countries suggests that the takeover mechanism has serious downsides as well. It can shrink investment horizons and even encourage reckless corporate expansion by allowing inefficient large firms or professional corporate raiders to take over efficient small firms (e.g. see Singh 1975, Dertouzos *et al.*, 1989).

Making redundancy easier by changing the labour law may actually be desirable, if combined with a well-managed unemployment insurance programme and re-training schemes, as the current system of quasi-lifetime employment and company-based welfare provision tends to favour workers in large firms. However, this requires sea changes in Korean attitudes and institutions regarding job security, taxation, the welfare state, corporate recruitment, remuneration structure and industrial training — which cannot be achieved without a careful consensus-building process and a well-designed programme for institutional reform.[6]

While the new government of Kim Dae Jung has certainly taken this process of consensus-building seriously by setting up a new tripartite committee involving the government, business and unions, it was not clear at the time of writing (mid-February 1998) whether its initial success in forging some broad agreements on the reform of labour law and corporate restructuring will be sustained over time with mounting unemployment, which is predicted to rise to at least 1 million by the end of the year and possibly to 2 million.

And as for the 'crony capitalism', which the IMF 'reforms' are supposed to eliminate by reducing the power of the government and making corporate accounts more transparent, the ultimate solution lies in strengthening, not weakening, the co-ordinating function of the government — albeit in a more consensual and sophisticated way than before. It will also require reforms in the civil service in order to reduce the incentives to take bribes and furthering changes in the political funding system (for some discussion of these issues, see Chang 1998b).

The current Korean crisis has been misunderstood in many ways as its 'miracle' was for a long time. While it is unwise to suggest that a return to the traditional model is possible and desirable, the country's headlong dash towards the Anglo-American institutional model, half voluntary and half under IMF pressure, does not seem particularly desirable, especially given the rather poor record that such reform programmes have produced in many developing and transition economies in the last two decades (see Taylor 1987 and Banuri 1991 for developing countries, see Chang and Nolan 1995 for transition economies).

Notes

1. The very existence and achievements of this model were hotly debated during the last two decades. A review of the earlier phase of this debate can be found in Chang (1993). The more recent phase of the debate has been prompted by the publication of *The East Asian Miracle* report by the World Bank (World Bank 1993). Criticisms of the latter can be found

in the special symposium that featured in the pages of *World Development* (1994, vol. 22 no. 4), Fishlow *et al.* (1994) and Akyüz, Chang & Kozul-Wright (1998, forthcoming).

2. The definition of foreign debt here follows the World Bank definition, and is therefore different from the concept of 'external liabilities', which include offshore borrowings of Korean banks and overseas borrowings of foreign branches and subsidiaries of Korean banks. The IMF and the Korean government started using this definition following their accord on 28 December 1997. At the end of November 1997, Korea's external liabilities amounted to US$157 billion, of which US$92 billion was of less than a year's maturity.

3. A country is 'moderately indebted' when this ratio is between 45 and 80 per cent, and 'severely indebted' when it is over 80 per cent. For exact definitions, see World Bank (1997a), vol. 1, pp. 49-50.

4. It is widely believed that the Kim Young Sam government gave a go-ahead to Samsung's proposed automobile venture after it decided to build the factory in the then president's home town, Pusan, instead of its initial choice of Taegu, the group's home base. In the build-up to this decision, Kang Kyung Shik, a native son of Pusan, then a former minister working as a private sector consultant, led the local campaign for Samsung's automobile factory to be located in his home town.

5. Symbolic of this was a document prepared in 1997 by the research institute affiliated to the large employers' association, Korea Federation of Industries, which called for, for example, the abolition of all government ministries except the foreign ministry and the ministry of defence. When the document was leaked in advanced, it created such an uproar it had to be withdrawn before publication.

6. The current debate on Korean labour market reform shows how misinformed the earlier literature on the labour market in Korea (and in East Asia generally) has been. For a criticism of this literature, see You and Chang (1993).

AFTERWORD

THE EAST ASIAN AND OTHER FINANCIAL CRISES: CAUSES, RESPONSES AND PREVENTION*

G.K. Helleiner

The East Asian crisis, unlike previous developing country financial crises, had its origins within the private sector. This crisis has been a market phenomenon. Governments of the crisis-stricken countries had managed their budgets prudently and there was little prior indication of severe macroeconomic mismanagement.

Causes

It is well-known that financial markets, indeed all asset markets, are different in their functioning and behaviour from the text-book markets for goods and services in which we all are so thoroughly schooled. Because of the importance of information in asset markets and its imperfect and asymmetric availability, participants in financial markets respond to 'signals' in sometimes herd-like and apparently perverse fashion. The available information is always subject to interpretation by these market participants and interpretations can and do alter at short notice. It follows that asset markets can settle at multiple equilibrium points in consequence of participants' alternative interpretations of available information about the future. These markets are therefore highly vulnerable to fluctuations in 'animal spirits' and, as in the recent East Asian case, to self-fulfilling losses of confidence. 'Bubbles' in asset prices and crises are inherent in financial markets. No amount of increased information, transparency or supervision can prevent recurrent 'runs', panics and crises in stock and bond markets, property markets or currency markets. The best that policymakers may be able to achieve is some reduction in their frequency and greater preparation for the modification of their consequences.

The fact that this most recent financial crisis originated within private markets and was driven by private international capital flows must not lead us to forget that crises will, at times, continue to originate in macroeconomic mismanagement as well. Public sector debt crises will recur. Nor does the world yet have a solid system for the prevention and management of these more 'traditional' crises either.

---

* An earlier version was presented at the UNCTAD Seminar on 'The East Asian and Other Financial Crises', Geneva, 1 May 1998.

Not to speak of the continuing 'non-stop' debt crisis of the low-income countries on which the HIPC initiative has yet to make much of an impact.

Issues in Crisis Management

Let me note three principal issues that have figured in the management of the East Asian crisis and then consider two further issues that are likely to arise in future crises. The main issues in the management of the recent crisis were as follows.

The Distribution of the Burden of Adjustment as between Residents of the Debtor Country and the External Creditors

Crisis response has typically taken the form of the immediate application of austerity measures to the borrowers and, more generally, the residents of the crisis-stricken countries. This involves real adjustment downward in economic activity — real GNP, employment and investment. In the case of the five most-affected East Asian countries, a turnaround in the current account balance of roughly 11 per cent of GDP was accomplished between 1996 and 1997 — involving an enormous real (downward) adjustment.

If, as most observers now believe, the crisis was a matter of short-term liquidity difficulties and panic, the timely provision of significant further external credit could easily have overcome the need for such draconian adjustment measures. Rather than permitting external private creditors to 'take off', by failing to roll their short-term credits over, the financial 'system' should have encouraged them or forced them to maintain their previous exposures. Just as a bank should close its doors temporarily during a liquidity crisis, to prevent further runs on the bank, external creditors should be prevented from leaving precipitately and thereby creating an unnecessary economic collapse. Instead of bailing them out, international financial institutions should have bailed these private creditors 'in' by demanding, as a condition for their assistance, that private creditors impose a standstill on their exposure and restructure their short-term credits over a longer term. (In some circumstances, the official 'rescuers' might even demand *expanded* private credits as a condition of official assistance.) The official response to such crises should involve the early 'pushing' of *both* sides to the credit relationship, the creditors as well as the debtors, rather than only imposing tough measures upon the latter. If it is truly a liquidity crisis, the creditors will suffer no long-term harm from such official pressures, which are simply overcoming a collective action problem.

If the problem really is one of solvency, in which there will be a problem in future debtor payments, the sooner that the creditors 'take a hit' and begin the initiation of a debt workout, the better. In these circumstances, official action will again be needed to stop the creditors from each running for a 'piece of the action' immediately. Official co-ordination and compulsion will be needed for orderly debt workout in cases of insolvency as well as of liquidity crisis.

Such a balanced approach to the distribution of the real adjustment burden implies that the IMF and other official institutions involved in the response to a financial crisis will be encouraging a moratorium on external payments at a fairly early stage and will be lending into arrears. There is a precedent, of course, in the 1980s debt crisis for IMF lending into commercial arrears. Early and significant official measures to ensure equity and balance in the burden of adjustment to crisis can reduce both the real costs at present borne by crisis-stricken countries and the real costs of financial crises to the entire global system.

Appropriate Domestic Macroeconomic Policy and, in particular, the Distribution of the Burden of Domestic Adjustment in the Crisis-stricken Country

Whatever the degree of real restraint that is still required, after better balance between external creditors and the debtor country is achieved, there remain important domestic policy choices in the debtor country. A key objective should always be the protection of the most vulnerable to domestic macroeconomic restraint — the poorest and those most affected by cutbacks. Pursuit of this objective is likely to involve either a reordering of the government budget, or increased tax revenues to finance the necessary expenditures, or a degree of fiscal loosening. (It is important to recognise that fiscal loosening is not the only way to finance officially-provided safety nets for the most vulnerable.)

More broadly, there is the matter of the appropriate fiscal-monetary policy mix, given the required degree of macroeconomic policy restraint. Current approaches emphasise the role of monetary restraint and sharp increases in interest rates to restore confidence in the currency. Sharp interest rate increases failed, however, to restore confidence in the recent East Asian experience. Rather, they seemed to be taken by investors as a signal of the extreme seriousness of underlying problems. Confidence was certainly *not* furthered by declarations by the IMF and others that the problems of the affected countries were deep and structural rather than of a short-term (liquidity) nature. Interest rate increases, of course, generate enormous negative side effects in the form of increased bankruptcies and reduced asset values, whatever their signalling effects upon operators in currency markets. Reasonable people may differ as to the details of the appropriate monetary and fiscal policy response to crisis; but there is little doubt that the monetary measures taken in the recent East Asian crises failed in their primary intent.

Other policy measures, associated with IMF conditionality, are also at issue:

- *Inappropriate Issue Linkage.* External sources of support should not intrude into policy spheres unrelated to the financial crisis, as they have done in Korea and Indonesia. Longer-term development policy relating to the role of the

State, governance questions, competition policy, openness to foreign direct investment, and trade protectionism should not be conditions attached to external finance intended to address crisis situations. This point has recently been forcefully argued by Martin Feldstein in *Foreign Affairs*.

- *Timing of Reforms.* Major structural reforms should, in any case, not be introduced at the height of a financial crisis. Widespread bank closures, with only limited provision for depositor protection, constitute, at such a time, a major further blow to confidence. Most fundamental reforms take considerable time and should be introduced with due caution. Certainly, as the Chief Economist of the World Bank, Joseph Stiglitz, has recently argued, the worst time for the introduction of structural reforms in the financial sector is in the midst of a financial crisis.

- *Capital Account Policies.* Since most now assign some responsibility for the crisis to premature financial liberalisation and, in particular, liberalisation of the external capital account, the conditioning of finance upon the *further* liberalisation of the capital account is surely inappropriate. At the very least, it is extremely controversial! Most would describe it as foolhardy.

Size and Nature of External Financial Support

It is clear from the Mexican and East Asian experiences that the size of the external financial inputs required for the resolution of financial crises in developing countries may be very large. It is far from obvious that the IMF will have the resources to supply the necessary amounts in the future. Even in these recent experiences, it was necessary to find a variety of other complementary sources of official finance.

No less important, however, is the manner in which such finance is to be supplied. In order to address a liquidity crisis it is necessary to insert liquidity, i.e. finance that is available at very short notice, in large amounts, and virtually unconditionally. Finance that is supplied only on the basis of negotiated conditions and which is released only on the basis of compliance with them, through successive tranches, is *not* liquidity. It may be very helpful in the resolution of the crisis. In some circumstances, it may even be sufficient. But future liquidity crises will require a liquidity response. It is striking that the amounts quickly supplied to Mexico during its crisis far exceeded the amounts only slowly being made available to the East Asian countries in response to their crisis. Only about 20 per cent of the financial package put together for East Asia has so far been disbursed.

Two further issues that are likely to arise in future crises deserve advance attention:

- *How will the system respond to financial crises,* including those originating within the private sector, in countries too small to constitute a threat to the international monetary and financial system? Sharp reversals in private capital flows have already created havoc in some African countries — generating massive required turnarounds in the current account, just as large, relative to GDP, as those required in recent East Asian experience. There is no reason, on the face of it, why official support from the IMF and others should not be provided to 'less important' countries in the same way as it is provided to 'systemic threats' when they face identical difficulties. But no such agreements are yet in place. They need to be put in place.

- In times of financial crisis, there is likely to be a flight to large foreign financial institutions within the crisis-affected countries, whatever other directions the flight may take. In these circumstances, the 'national treatment' required under the terms of the financial services agreement within the WTO *may be quite inappropriate*. It may be sensible and should be legitimate for the national authorities to devote particular attention to the problems of domestic financial institutions which are usually smaller and less internationalised. While there is some recognition of this potential problem in the WTO agreement on financial services, it is somewhat ambiguous in its formulation and will have to be tested through particular cases. It is important to prepare for such cases in advance.

Crisis Prevention and Damage Control

In developed market economies, steps have been taken to reduce the frequency and size of financial crises, and to limit the damage they are likely to cause. Appropriate institutions have been created — central banks, banking and financial supervisors, deposit insurance, etc. — and rules, incentive systems and resources have been deployed in their support. Yet, the increasingly globalised international economy does not yet have much of a comparable character. Let me highlight four issues that arise in this connection.

Discouragement of Short-term Private Capital Flows

In the aftermath of the East Asian crisis, there has been greatly increased interest in the problem of volatile short-term private capital flows. Most discussion now revolves around the question of *how* to reduce surges in short-term capital flows, rather than, as before, *whether* to. The current debate about the appropriate international capital account regime for countries at different stages of financial development is a healthy one.

It is important that the developing countries to develop a coherent response to the OECD push for across-the-board capital account liberalisation — a push which is found within the IMF, as it discusses its new purposes and jurisdiction in the capital account; in the WTO, as it completes its negotiations on financial services and discusses the initiation of discussions on foreign direct investment;

and in the OECD, as it continues its work on a multilateral agreement on investment. Developing countries have yet to put together their own consistent and coherent approaches to capital account issues, and they need to do so as a matter of urgency. For the present, their emphasis on caution and order in capital account liberalisation is entirely appropriate. It will also be in everyone's interest if the turf struggles between the IMF, WTO and MAI can be quickly resolved.

In this connection, it is also worth noting that direct bilateral co-operation among central banks can be very helpful. The degree of such co-operation among G-10 or BIS central bankers is much greater than that between any central bankers in the North and their counterparts in the South. How is it that Northern financial authorities can be both so demanding and so co-operative with their Southern counterparts in the sphere of money laundering, but not in the sphere of short-term capital flows?

The Financing of External Crisis Responses

It is clear that the resources of the IMF are quite inadequate to provide sufficient liquidity to address future financial crises of the East Asian kind. The IMF Managing Director has already appealed for a significant increase in IMF quotas, but to little effect. There is little prospect that developing countries can acquire sufficient reserves or access to sufficient credit lines to protect them adequately against such future crises. The IMF will therefore have to develop its role, less as a financier than as a 'leader' and 'signaller' for other sources of finance, notably central banks and the members of the BIS. New forms of regional co-operation, such as were mooted in response to the East Asian crisis, but discouraged by the US and the IMF, should also be explored further. Direct central bank co-operation through swap arrangements and similar devices will also have to be expanded. Again, if central banks can work so closely in co-operation against money laundering, it is difficult to see why they cannot act similarly in other spheres.

Regulation, Supervision, Transparency

Both within the developing countries and at the international level, the search is on for new rules and institutions that can function more effectively in the provision of information, supervision and, where appropriate, regulation. These efforts should be encouraged, but they will take some time to bear fruit. There are also limits to the degree to which they can prevent further financial crises.

The Roles of the IMF and World Bank

I have argued above that financial crises in the future will require larger and earlier insertions of liquidity and that the IMF should lead in its provision. It is the World

Bank, however, that plays the major role in structural reforms in the financial sector. The IMF and the Bank must work co-operatively. During the Asian crisis, significant policy disagreements have arisen between IMF and Bank advisors. This is not inherently undesirable or surprising. What *is* undesirable is the effort to suppress such professional disagreements in the interest of the creation of a consistent Washington position.

What the recent experience most clearly underlines is that the IMF (and the international community) still suffers from the fact that it has no independent evaluation and assessment unit. The recent IMF experiment with external assessment of its ESAF programme, which uncovered significant differences of view as between the IMF staff and the external assessors, illustrates the potential importance and value of such independent assessments. A recently-released report by Jacques Polak and others, done for the Washington-based Center of Concern also makes a persuasive case for increased IMF transparency and independent evaluations of IMF activities.

BIBLIOGRAPHY

Agosin, Manuel R. and Ricardo Ffrench-Davis (1997). 'Managing Capital Inflows in Chile', manuscript, United Nations University/World Institute for Development Economics Research (UNU/WIDER), Helsinki, June.

Ahn Mi Youg (1998). 'Women Go First as Firms Shed Jobs', *Inter Press Service*, 3 February.

Ahuja, Vinod, Benu Bidani, Fransisco Ferreira and Michael Walton (1997). *Everyone's Miracle? Revisiting Poverty and Inequality in East Asia*, Washington: World Bank.

Akyüz, Y. (1995). 'Taming International Finance', in J. Michie and J.G. Smith (eds), *Managing the Global Economy*, Oxford: Oxford University Press.

Akyüz, Y. (1998). 'New Trends in Japanese Trade and FDI: Post-industrial Transformation and Policy Challenge', in R. Kozul-Wright and R. Rowthorn (eds), *Transnational Corporations in the Global Economy*, London: Macmillan.

Akyüz, Y., Chang Ha-Joon and R. Kozul-Wright (1998, forthcoming). 'New Perspectives on East Asian Development', *Journal of Development Studies*.

Altbach, Eric (1997). 'The Asian Monetary Fund Proposal: A Case Study of Japanese Regional Leadership', Japan Economic Institute Report, No. 47A, 19 December.

Amsden, A. (1989). *Asia's Next Giant: South Korea and Late Industrialization*, New York: Oxford University Press.

Amsden, A. and Y. Euh (1990). 'Republic of Korea's Financial Reform: What Are the Lessons?', Discussion Paper, No. 30, United Nations Conference on Trade and Development (UNCTAD), Geneva.

Andrews, Edmunds S. (1998). 'Banks Shut Off Capital to Asia Last Fall as Greed Turns to Fear', *New York Times*, 30 January.

Asia 1997 Economic Yearbook, Far Eastern Economic Review.

Asiaweek, 4 October 1996.

Associated Press, 'Health Crisis Feared in Indonesia', 8 March 1998.

AWSJ — Asian Wall Street Journal, 'Finance Firms in Thailand Express Regret', 5-6 December, 1997.

AWSJ — Asian Wall Street Journal, 'Currency Board Rumours Elevate Asian Currencies', 11 March 1998.

AWSJ — Asian Wall Street Journal, 'Habibie Gets Set to be Named Vice-President', 11 March 1998.

AWSJ — Asian Wall Street Journal, 'Korea Wins Agreement for Major Debt Rollover', 16 March 1998.

Bangkok Bank (1997). 'The Economy in 1996 and Trends in 1997', *Annual Report 1996*, Bangkok: Bangkok Bank.

Bangkok Post Year-end 96 Economic Review, January 1997.

Bangkok Post, '2.9 Million Thais Risk Losing Their Jobs by December', 1 September 1997.

Bangkok Post, 'Most of 58 Firms Will Not Survive', 7 December 1997.

Bangkok Post, 'IMF Agrees to Relax Conditions', 13 February 1998.

Bangkok Post, 'Discipline Must be Maintained Despite Breathing Space: Supachai', 14 February 1998.

Bangkok Post, 'SET Maybe the Bet in the World, but Reform Still Needed', 21 February 1998.

Bangkok Post, 'Austerity Drive Begins to Rekindle Confidence', 6 March 1998.

Bank of Thailand (1996). *Quarterly Bulletin*, June.

Banuri, T. (ed.) (1991). *Economic Liberalisation: No Panacea*, Oxford: Oxford University Press.

Bello, Walden (1995). 'Government, Markets and Countryside Development in the Asian NICs: Myths, Realities and Lessons for the Philippines', *Issues and Letters*, Quezon City: Philippine Center for Policy Studies, November-December.

Bello, Walden (1997). 'Addicted to Capital: The Ten-year High and Present-day Withdrawal Trauma of Southeast Asia's Economies', *Issues and Letters*, Philippine Center for Policy Studies, September-December.

Bello, Walden (1998). 'The Rise and Fall of Southeast Asia's Economy', *The Ecologist*, 28(1), January/February: 9-17.

Bergsten, Fred (1997). 'The Asian Monetary Crisis: Proposed Remedies', Testimony to the US House of Representatives Committee on Banking and Financial Services, 13 November.

BIS — Bank for International Settlements (1995). *International Banking and Financial Market Developments*, Basle, May.

BIS — Bank for International Settlements (1997). *67th Annual Report*, Basle, 9 June.

BIS — Bank for International Settlements (1998a). *The Maturity, Sectoral and Nationality Distribution of International Bank Lending, First Half 1997*, Basle, January.

BIS — Bank for International Settlements (1998b). *The Transmission of Monetary Policy in Emerging Market Economies*, Basle, January.

Blank, Johan (1998). 'Suharto's Family has Prospered, but Indonesians Suffer', *Inter Press Service*, 24 January.

Brennan, Michael J. and H. Henry Cao (1997). 'International Portfolio Investment Flows', *The Journal of Finance*, LII(5), December: 1851-80.

Burton, John (1997a). 'Bruising Battle at Korea IMF Talks', *Financial Times*, 3 December.

Burton, John (1997b). 'Painful Prospect', *Financial Times*, 8 December.

Burton, John (1997c). 'Anger at IMF Terms May Boost Korean Opposition', *Financial Times*, 11 December.

Camdessus, Michel (1998). 'The IMF and Its Programs in Asia', Remarks by the Managing Director of the IMF at the Council on Foreign Relations, New York, 6 February.

Chalongphob Sussangkarn (1998). 'Thailand's Debt Crisis and Economic Outlook', Paper presented at the 1998 Regional Outlook Forum, ISEAS, Singapore, Thailand Development Research Institute, 16 January, http://www.info.tdri.or.th.

Chang Ha-Joon (1993). 'The Political Economy of Industrial Policy in Korea', *Cambridge Journal of Economics*, 17(2): 131-57.

Chang Ha-Joon (1994). *The Political Economy of Industrial Policy*, London: Macmillan.

Chang Ha-Joon (1998a). 'The Korean Crisis: A Dissenting View', *Third World Economics*, 16-31 January.

Chang Ha-Joon (1998b). 'An Alternative View on Regulatory Reform in Korea', a paper presented at the conference on 'Korea's Transition to a High-productivity Economy', 6-7 February, held at the Center for Korean Studies, University of Hawaii at Manoa, Honolulu.

Chang Ha-Joon and P. Nolan (eds) (1995). *The Transformation of the Communist Economies — Against the Mainstream*, London: Macmillan.

Chin Kok Fay and Jomo K.S. (1996). 'Financial Liberalisation and Intermediation in Malaysia', in Jomo K.S. and Shyamala Nagaraj (eds), *Globalisation and Development: Heterodox Perspectives* (forthcoming).

Cholada Ingsrisawan and Parista Yuthamanop (1998). 'Troubling New Era Awaits', *Bangkok Post Year-end Economic Review 1997*.

Chossudovsky, Michel (1998). 'The IMF Korea Bailout', *Third World Resurgence*, 89, January.

Chote, Robert (1997). 'Thai Crisis Highlights Lessons of Mexico', Survey, *Financial Times*, 19 September.

Claessens, Stijn and Thomas Glaessner (1997). *Are Financial Sector Weaknesses Undermining the East Asian Miracle?*, IBRD/World Bank, Washington, D.C.

Cole, David C. and Betty F. Slade (1996). *Building a Modern Financial System: The Indonesian Experience*, Cambridge: Cambridge University Press.

Congressional Research Service Report for Congress (1997). No. 97-1021 E, 'The 1997 Asian Financial Crisis', 25 November.

Daim Zainuddin (1997). 'I Was Taken By Surprise', *Asiaweek*, 7 November.

Davis, Bob (1997). 'Thailand Tests IMF's Resolve on Reform', *Asian Wall Street Journal*, 8 December.

Deen, Thalida (1997). 'South Korea Leaves Developing World', *Inter Press Service*, 30 September.

Dertouzos, M., R. Lester and R. Solow (1990). *Made in America*, Cambridge, MA: The MIT Press.

Diaz-Alejandro, Carlos (1985). 'Good-bye Financial Repression, Hello Financial Crash', *Journal of Development Studies*, September-October.

Doner, Richard F. and Daniel Unger (1993). 'The Politics of Finance in Thai Economic Development', in Stephan Haggard, Chung H. Lee and Sylvia Maxfield (eds), *The Politics of Finance in Developing Countries*, Ithaca: Cornell University Press.

Doner, Richard F. and Anek Laothamatas (1994). 'Thailand: Economic and Political Gradualism', in Stephan Haggard and Steven B. Webb (eds), *Democracy, Political Liberalization and Economic Adjustment*, New York: Oxford University Press.

Eatwell, John (1997a). *International Financial Liberalisation: The Impact on World Development*, Discussion Paper Series, Office of Development Studies, United Nations Development Programme, New York, May.

Eatwell, John (1997b). Selected extracts in John Eatwell, 'International Financial Liberalisation: The Impact on World Development', *International Journal of Technical Cooperation*, 3(2), Winter: 157-162.

Einzig, Paul (1937). *The Theory of Forward Exchange*, London: Macmillan.

EIU — Economist Intelligence Unit Country Report: *Thailand 1997: 2*.

EIU — Economist Intelligence Unit Country Report: *Thailand 1997: 3*.

EIU — Economist Intelligence Unit Country Report: *Thailand 1997: 4*.

ESCAP — Economic and Social Commission for Asia and the Pacific (1996). 'Economic Liberalisation and Rural Poverty: A Study of the Effects of Price Liberalisation and Market Reforms in Asian Developing Countries', United Nations, New York, p. 170.

FEER — *Far Eastern Economic Review*, 'Dollars and Sense', 12 February 1998.

Feldstein, Martin (1997). 'The Political Economy of the European Economic and Monetary Union: Political Sources of an Economic Liability', *The Journal of Economic Perspectives*, 11(4), Fall.

Feldstein, Martin (1998). 'Refocusing the IMF', *Foreign Affairs*, March/April.

Fischer, Stanley (1997). 'IMF — The Right Stuff', *Financial Times*, 17 December.

Fischer, Stanley (1998). 'The Asian Crisis: A View from the IMF', address by the First Deputy Managing Director of the IMF to the Midwinter Conference of the Bankers' Association for Foreign Trade, Washington, D.C., 22 January.

Fishlow, A., C. Gwin, S. Haggard, D. Rodrik and R. Wade (1994). *Miracle or Design? Lessons from the East Asian Experience*, Washington, D.C.: Overseas Development Council.

Foundation for Children's Development (1998). 'Voices of the Disadvantaged Amidst the Economic Crisis', No. 1: Data on the Situation of Children and the Family, February (in Thai).

Ghosh, Jayati, Abhijit Sen and C.P. Chandrasekhar (1996). 'Southeast Asian Economies: Miracle or Meltdown?', *Economic and Political Weekly*, 12-19 October.

Goeltom, Miranda S. (1995). 'Indonesia's Financial Liberalisation: An Empirical Analysis of 1981-1988 Panel Data', Institute of Southeast Asian Studies, Singapore.

Gomez, E.T. (1991). *Money Politics in the Barisan Nasional*, Kuala Lumpur: Forum.

Gomez, E.T. and Jomo K.S. (1997). *Malaysia's Political Economy: Politics, Patronage and Profits*, Cambridge: Cambridge University Press.

Green, Duncan (1998). 'The Indonesian Economic Crisis', CAFOD, London, March.

Greenspan, Alan (1997). 'Statement Before the U.S. House of Representatives Committee on Banking and Financial Services', Washington D.C., 13 November.

Greider, William (1997). *One World, Ready or Not: The Manic Logic of Global Capitalism*, New York: Touchstone, Simon & Schuster.

Guttmann, Robert (1994). *How Credit-Money Shapes the Economy: The United States in a Global System*, New York: M.E. Sharpe.

Hanlon, Joseph (1998). 'Bank Admits HIPC Conditions Wrong', *Debt Update*, March.

Helleiner, G.K. (1997). 'Capital Accounts Regimes and Developing Countries', in UNCTAD, *International Monetary and Financial Issues for the 1990s*, Vol. VIII Geneva: UNCTAD.

Hewison, Kevin (1989). *Power and Politics in Thailand: Essays in Political Economy*, Manila & Wollongong: Journal of Contemporary Asia Publishers.

Hormats, Robert D. (1997). 'Testimony Before the U.S. House of Representatives Committee on Banking and Financial Services', Washington D.C., 13 November.

Human Rights Watch Asia Division (1998). 'Economic Crisis Leads to Scapegoating Ethnic Chinese', 24 February.

IIF — Institute of International Finance (1998). 'Capital Flows to Emerging Market Economies', Washington D.C., 29 January.

IMF — International Monetary Fund (1997a). 'IMF Approves Stand-by Credit for Thailand', Press Release No. 97/37, 20 August.

IMF — International Monetary Fund (1997b). *World Economic Outlook*, Washington D.C., October.

IMF — International Monetary Fund (1997c). *International Capital Markets*, Washington, D.C., November.

IMF — International Monetary Fund (1997d). 'IMF Approves Stand-by Credit for Indonesia', Press Release No. 97/50, 5 November.

IMF Survey, 25 November 1996.

International Herald Tribune, 5 January 1998.

Interview, Dr Angkarb Korsieporn, Bangkok, 12 January 1998.

Interview, Dr Angkarb Korsieporn, Bangkok, 20 February 1998.

Interview, Jaran Ditapichai, 13 March 1998.

Interview, Professor Nikhom Chandravithun, Bangkok, 20 February 1998.

Iwan J. Azis (1997). 'Currency Crisis in Southeast Asia: The Bubble Finally Bursts', paper presented at the 45th Annual Conference on the Economic Outlook, organised by Research Seminar in Quantitative Economics (RSQE), University of Michigan, USA, 20-21 November.

Jakarta Post, 'Indonesia — Memorandum of Economic and Financial Policies', 17 January 1998.

Jakarta Post, 'WB, ADB Delay Aid to Indonesia, Japan Goes Ahead', 11 March 1998.

Japan Economic Institute (1997). 'IMF, Japan to Aid South Korea in Record Bailout', *Japan Economic Institute Report*, No. 46B, 12 December.

Japan Economic Institute (1998). *Japan Economic Report*, No. 4B, 30 January.

Jaruwan Lertwinyu (1992). 'The Money's Rolling In', *The Nation, Year in Review 1992*.

Johnson, R. Barry, Salim M. Darbar and Claudia Echeverria (1997). 'Sequencing Capital

Account Liberalization: Lessons from the Experiences in Chile, Indonesia, Korea and Thailand', IMF Working Paper No. 97/157, November.

Jomo K.S. (ed.) (1990). *Undermining Tin: The Decline of Malaysian Pre-eminence*, Sydney: Transnational Corporation Research Project.

Jomo K.S. *et al.* (1997). *Southeast Asia's Misunderstood Miracle: Industrial Policy and Economic Development in Thailand, Malaysia and Indonesia*, Boulder: Westview.

Kaminsky, G. and C.M. Reinhart (1996). 'The Twin Crises: The Causes of Banking and Balance-of-Payments Problems', Working Paper No. 17, Center for International Economics, University of Maryland at College Park.

KCTU (1997). 'IMF Bailout and Employment Crisis: The Labour Response', Korean Confederation of Trade Unions, 11 December.

KCTU (1998). 'Unbridled Freedom to Sack Workers is No Freedom at All', Korean Confederation of Trade Unions Report of KCTU-IMF Dialogue, 13 January, downloaded http://kctu.org.news8.htm.

Koener, P., G. Maass, T. Siebold and R. Tetzlaff (1986). *The IMF and the Debt Crisis*, London: Zed Books.

Krissana Parnsoonthorn (1997). 'Greed Reaps Grim Reward', *Bangkok Post Year End 96 Economic Review*.

Krugman, Paul (1994). 'The Myth of Asia's Miracle', *Foreign Affairs*, November-December.

Krugman, Paul (1997a). 'Bahtulism', *Slate Magazine*, 14 August.

Krugman, Paul (1997b). 'What Ever Happened to the Asian Miracle?', *Fortune*, 18 August.

Krugman, Paul (1997c). 'Currency Crises', prepared for NBER conference, October.

Krugman, Paul (1998a). 'What Happened to Asia', Available from: URL: http://web.mit.edu/krugman/www/disinter.html.

Krugman, Paul (1998b). 'Firesale FDI', Available from: URL: http://web.mit.edu/ krugman/www/disinter.html.

Le Fort, G. and C. Budnevich (1997). 'Capital Account Regulations and Macroeconomic Policy: Two Latin American Experiences', in UNCTAD, *International Monetary and Financial Issues for the 1990s*, Vol. VIII Geneva: UNCTAD.

Letter of Intent No. 3 and Memorandum on Economic Policies of the Royal Thai Government, 24 February 1998, http://www.bot.or.th.

Lim, J. (1996). *Philippine Macroeconomic Development: 1970-1993*, Quezon City: Philippine Center for Policy Studies.

Lim, J. (1998). 'The Philippine Economy in a Globalized Setting', Quezon City: Action for Economic Reforms (forthcoming as one paper in a collection of essays).

Liu Li-Gang, Marcus Noland, Sherman Robinson and Zhi Wang (1998). 'Asian Competitive Devaluations', Working Paper Series, No. 98-2, Washington, DC: Institute for International Economics.

Long, Simon (1997). 'The Limits to Golf: Regional Implications of the Southeast Asian Currency Depreciations of 1997', paper presented at the ISIS/CSIS Conference on 'Political Change and Regional Security in Southeast Asia', Bali, 7-10 December.

MacIntyre, Andrew (ed.) (1994). *Business and Government in Industrialising Asia*, Sydney: Allen and Unwin.

Malhotra, Kamal (1996). 'Globalisation, Trade and Financial Integration: The Case of Thailand', paper presented at the Social Research Institute, Chulalongkorn University, Bangkok.

Malhotra, Kamal (1997). 'Celebration of "Miracle" Turns into Damage Control by IMF', *Focus on the Global South*, 3 October.

Mander, Jerry and Edward Goldsmith (eds) (1996). *The Case Against the Global Economy and For a Turn Toward the Local*, San Francisco: Sierra Club Books.

McKinnon, R. and H. Pill (1996). 'Credible Liberalizations and International Capital Flows: The Overborrowing Syndrome', in T. Ito and A. Kreuger (eds), *Financial Deregulation and Integration in East Asia*, Chicago: Chicago University Press.

McLeod, Ross H. (ed.) (1995). *Indonesia Assessment 1994: Finance as Key Sector in Indonesia's Development*, Research School of Pacific and Asian Studies, Australian National University and Institute of Southeast Asian Studies, Singapore.

Ministry of Finance, Thailand (1997), Press Release Regarding Second Letter of Intent, No. 69/1997, 25 November, http://www.mof.go.th.

Minsky, H. (1982). *Inflation, Recession and Economic Policy*, Armonk, New York: Wheatsheaf.

Minsky, H. (1986). *Stabilizing an Unstable Economy*, New Haven: Yale University Press.

Montes, Manuel F. (1998). *The Currency Crisis in Southeast Asia*, Singapore: Institute of Southeast Asian Studies (ISEAS).

Montes, Manuel F. and J. Lim (1996). 'Macroeconomic Volatility, Investment Anemia and Environmental Struggles in the Philippines', *World Development*, 24(2).

Montgomery, John (1997). 'The Indonesian Financial System: Its Contribution to Economic Performance and Key Policy Issues', IMF Working Paper 97/45, Washington D.C.: International Monetary Fund, April.

Muscat, Robert (1994). *The Fifth Tiger: A Study of Thai Development Policy*, New York: M.E. Sharpe.

Naris Chaiyasoot (1995). 'Industrialization, Financial Reform and Monetary Policy', in Medhi Krongkraw (ed.), *Thailand's Industrialization and Its Consequences*, London: Macmillan.

Nasution, Anwar (1994). 'An Evaluation of the Banking Sector Reforms in Indonesia, 1983-1993', *The Asia Pacific Development Journal*, 1(1), Bangkok: UN-ESCAP.

Nasution, Anwar (1995). 'Banking Sector Reforms in Indonesia, 1983-93', in Ross H. McLeod (ed.), *Indonesia Assessment 1994: Finance as Key Sector in Indonesia's Development*, Research School of Pacific and Asian Studies, Australian National University and Institute of Southeast Asian Studies, Singapore, pp. 130-157.

Nasution, Anwar (1996). 'The Banking System and Monetary Aggregates Following Financial Sector Reforms: Lessons from Indonesia', United Nations University/World Institute for Development Economics Research (UNU/WIDER), Helsinki, Finland, Research for Action No. 27.

Nasution, Anwar (1998). 'Lessons from the Recent Financial Crisis in Indonesia', paper presented at the AT10 Researcher's Meeting of the Tokyo Club Foundation for Global Studies, Tokyo, February.

Nation. 'IMF Package No Free Lunch for Thailand', 9 August 1997.

Nuntawan Polkwamdee (1998). *Bangkok Post Year End 1997 Economic Review*.

OBI — Office of the Board of Investment (1993). *Key Investments Indicators in Thailand*, Royal Thai Government, September.

OBI — Office of the Board of Investment (1996). *Key Investments Indicators in Thailand*, Royal Thai Government, May.

Ostrey, Jonathan D. (1997). 'Current Account Imbalances in ASEAN Countries: Are They a Problem?' IMF Working Paper No. 97/51, Washington D.C.: International Monetary Fund, April.

Pakorn Vichyanond (1994). *Thailand's Financial System: Structure and Liberalization*, Bangkok: Thailand Development Research Institute.

Pasuk Phongpaichit and Chris Baker (1995). *Thailand: Economy and Politics*, Kuala Lumpur: Oxford University Press.

Peerawat Jariyasombat (1998). 'Tourism — Still Waiting to be Amazed', in *Bangkok Post Economic Review, Year End 1997*, January.

Prangtip Daorueng (1997). 'Crisis Promises More Pain for Workers', *Inter Press Service*, 26 December.

Radelet, Steven and Jeffrey Sachs (1997). 'Asia's Re-emergence', *Foreign Affairs*, Nov/Dec: 44-59.

Raghavan, C. (1998). 'BIS Banks Kept Shovelling Funds to Asia, Despite Warnings', *Third World Economics*, 16-31 January.

Reinhart, Carmen M. and Steven Dunaway (1996). 'Dealing with Capital Inflows: Are There Any Lessons?', Manuscript, University of Maryland, June.

Reisen, Helmut (1997). 'Sustainable and Excessive Current Account Deficits', United Nations University/World Institute for Development Economics Research (UNU/WIDER) Working Paper No. 151, Helsinki, May.

Richardson, Michael (1998). 'Renewed Indonesia Fires Worry Southeast Asia', *International Herald Tribune*, 13 February.

Robinson, David, Yangho Byeon and Ranjit Teja with Wanda Tseng (1991). *Thailand: Adjusting to Success, Current Policy Issues*, Washington: IMF, August.

Sachs, Jeffrey (1997a). 'Secretive Workings of the IMF Call for Reassessment', *New Straits Times*, 23 December.

Sachs, Jeffrey (1997b). 'IMF is a Power Unto Itself', *Financial Times*, 11 December.

Sachs, Jeffrey (1997c). 'The Wrong Medicine for Asia', *New York Times*, 3 November.

Sachs, Jeffrey (1998). 'The IMF and the Asian Flu', *The American Prospect*, March-April: 17.

Sanger, David E. (1998). 'IMF Now Admits Tactics in Indonesia Deepened the Crisis', *New York Times*, 14 January.

Satya Sivaraman (1997). 'Farmers Come to the Rescue', *Inter Press Service*, 17 December.

Singh, Ajit (1975). 'Take-overs, Economic Natural Selection and the Theory of the Firm: Evidence from the Post-war U.K. Experience', *Economic Journal*, 85(3).

Singh, Ajit (1996). 'Financial Liberalisation and Globalisation: Implications for Industrial and Industrialising Economies', in Jomo K.S. and Shyamala Nagaraj (eds), *Globalisation and Development: Heterodox Perspectives* (forthcoming).

Soonyuth Nunyamanee and Chiratas Nivatpumin (1998). 'The Year They Sank the Baht', *Bangkok Post Economic Review Year End 1997*.

Soros, George (1994). *The Alchemy of Finance: Reading the Mind of the Market*, New York: John Wiley.

Soros, George (1997). 'Avoiding a Breakdown', *Financial Times*, 31 December.

Soros, George (1998). 'Toward a Global Open Society', *The Atlantic Monthly*, 281(1), January: 20-32.

Soros, George with Byron Wien and Krisztina Koenen (1995). *Soros on Soros: Staying Ahead of the Curve*, New York: John Wiley.

Stiglitz, J. (1992). 'Banks Versus Markets as Mechanisms for Allocating and Coordinating Investment', in J. Roumasset and S. Barr (eds), *The Economics of Cooperation, East Asian Development and the Case for Pro-Market Intervention*, Boulder: Westview.

Stiglitz, J. (1996). 'Some Lessons from the East Asian Miracle', *The World Bank Research Observer*, 11(2).

Suehiro Akira (1985). *Capital Accumulation and Industrial Development in Thailand*, Social Research Institute, Chulalongkorn University, Bangkok.

Suehiro Akira (1992). 'Capitalist Development in Postwar Thailand: Commercial Bankers, Industrial Elite and Agribusiness Groups', in Ruth McVey (ed.), *Southeast Asian Capitalists*, Southeast Asia Program (SEAP), Cornell University, Ithaca, New York.

TAPOL Bulletin, Number 145, February 1998.

Tarrin Nimmanahaeminda, Minister of Finance (1997). 'Speech', http://www.mof.go.th, 8 December.

Taylor, L. (ed.) (1987). *Varieties of Stabilisation Experience*, Oxford: Oxford University Press.

Thammavit Terdudomtham (1998). 'The Bubble Finally Burst', *Bangkok Post Year End Economic Review 1997*, January.

The Economist, 'And Now the Political Fall Out', 17-23 January 1998.

The Nation, 'Koreans Ask "Who's to Blame?"', 6 December 1997.

The Nation, 'Seoul gets Christmas Day Surprise of US$10 billion Loans', 26 December 1997.

Third World Resurgence, 'Financial Crisis Deepens', No. 87/88, Nov/Dec 1997.

Thurow, Lester (1998). 'Asia: The Collapse and the Cure', *The New York Review of Books*, 14(2), 5 February: 22.

Turner, Anthony G. and Stephen S. Golub (1997). 'Towards a System of Multilateral Unit Labor Cost-based Competitiveness Indicators for Advanced, Developing and Transition Countries', IMF Working Paper No. 97/151, Washington D.C.: International Monetary Fund, November.

Twatchai Yongkittikul, FRA chairman (1997). 'Speech', http://www.mof.go.th, 8 December.

UNCTAD (1996). *Trade and Development Report*, Geneva: United Nations.

UNCTAD (1997). *Trade and Development Report*, Geneva: United Nations.

Unger, Roberto Mangabeira (1996). 'The Really New Bretton Woods', in Marc Uzan (ed.), *The Financial System Under Stress: An Architecture for the New World Economy*, New York & London: Routledge.

Vadarajan, S. (1998). *Times of India*, 30-31 January.

Vatchara Charoonsantikul and Thanong Khantong (1997). 'Is the IMF Mistreating its Thai Patient?' (quoting Jeffrey Sachs), *Nation*, 11 November.

Veneroso, Frank, and Robert Wade (1998). 'The Asian Financial Crisis: The Unrecognised Risk of the IMF's Asia Package', *Public Policy*, January.

Wade, R. (1990). *Governing the Market: Economic Theory and the Role of Government in East Asian Industrialization*, Princeton: Princeton University Press.

Wain, Barry (1997). 'Let's Not Bury Asian Values', *Asian Wall Street Journal*, 5-6 December.

Wardhana, Ali (1995). 'Financial Reform: Achievements, Problems and Prospects', in Ross H. McLeod (ed.), *Indonesia Assessment 1994: Finance as Key Sector in Indonesia's Development*, Research School of Pacific and Asian Studies, Australian National University and Institute of Southeast Asian Studies, Singapore, pp. 79-93.

Warr, Peter (ed.) (1993). *The Thai Economy in Transition*, Cambridge: Cambridge University Press.

White, G. (ed.) (1988). *Developmental States in East Asia*, London: Macmillan.

Wolf, M. (1997). 'Korea's Big Chance', *Financial Times*, 16 December.

Woo-Cumings, Meredith (1997). 'Bailing Out or Sinking In?: The IMF and the Korean Financial Crisis', paper presented at the Economic Strategy Institute, 2 December.

World Bank (1993). *The East Asian Miracle*, New York: Oxford University Press.

World Bank (1997a). *Global Development Finance*, vol. 2, Washington, D.C.: World Bank.

World Bank (1997b). *Thailand Country Brief*, September (downloaded from World Bank website).

World Bank (1998). 'Social Aspects of the Crisis: Perceptions of Poor Communities', Draft report, February.

World Development (1994). 22 (4).

WTO (1997) *World Trade Organisation*, 2: 63.

Yamin, Kafil (1998a). 'World Bank Brings Aid for Jobs, Gets Flak Instead', *Inter Press Service*, 5 February.

Yamin, Kafil (1998b). 'Medicine, Food Become Luxuries in Crisis', *Inter Press Service*, 23 February.

Yamin, Kafil (1998c). 'Suharto's New Mandate Does Little to Ease Uncertainty', *Inter Press Service*, 10 March.

Yergin, Daniel and Joseph Stanislaw (1998). *The Commanding Heights: The Battle Between Government and the Marketplace That Is Remaking the Modern World*, New York: Simon & Schuster.

You, J.I. and Chang Ha-Joon (1993). 'The Myth of Free Labour Market in Korea', *Contributions to Political Economy*, 12: 29–46.

Ywin, Kenneth (1993). 'Beware of the Boom', *The Nation: Year In Review 1992*, January.

Periodicals

Asian Wall Street Journal
Asiaweek
Bangkok Post
Business Times
Business Week
The Economist
Far Eastern Economic Review
Financial Times
Fortune
International Herald Tribune
Jakarta Post
Korean Times
The Nation (Bangkok)
New Straits Times
New York Times
Third World Economics

INDEX

ABN-AMRO, 92
accountability, 133, 134
Aquino, 200, 202, 204
Agosin, Manuel R., 175
Ahn Mi-Young, 118
Ahuja, Vinod, 100
Akyuz, Yilmaz, 22, 36, 38, 69, 102
Alien Business Law, 91, 127
Altbach, Eric, 124
American Express International, 126
Amnuay Veeravan, 145
Amsden, A., 226
Anand Panyarachun, 86, 140, 142
Andrews, Edmunds S., 67
Anwar Ibrahim, 185, 186, 188, 190, 191, 195
Argentina, 36, 224
Asia 1997 Economic Yearbook, 144
Asia Pacific Economic Cooperation (APEC), 123
Asiaweek, 144
Asian Development Bank (ADB), 94, 103, 117, 149, 158, 162
Asian Monetary Fund (AMF), 123, 124, 134, 194
Asian Wall Street Journal (*AWSJ*), 5, 88, 98, 99, 128, 129, 131, 183, 188
asset markets, 37, 59, 60, 162, 232
asset prices, 7, 9, 11, 14, 15, 17, 18, 38, 58, 76, 77, 152, 211, 220, 232
Asset Management Corporation (AMC), 151, 152
Associated Press, 117
Association of South East Asian Nations (ASEAN), 47, 94, 95, 205, 220
Australia, 94
Aziz Taha, 183

baht-dollar, 6, 37, 51, 70, 85, 86, 88, 90, 93, 112, 113, 127, 137, 138, 139, 140, 142, 147, 149, 153, 154, 155, 157, 158
bail-out, 21, 135, 139, 152, 153, 185-9, 229

Bakun Dam project, 187
balance of payments (BoP), 2, 16, 19, 23, 34, 45, 51, 52, 57, 59, 63, 73, 75, 122, 126, 142, 149, 165, 200, 202, 203, 204, 210
Bangkok, 86, 87, 110, 111, 112, 139, 145, 156
Bangkok Bank of Commerce (BBC), 146, 152
Bangkok Bank, 140, 156, 158
Bangkok International Banking Facility (BIBF), 51, 87, 138, 139, 142
Bangkok Metropolitan Bank, 152
Bangkok Post Year-end 96 Economic Review, 144
Bangkok Post, 91, 110, 126, 127, 144, 149, 150, 151, 153, 155, 156
Bangna-trat Highway, 111
Banharn Silpa-Archa, 143, 145, 146, 147, 157, 158
Bank Bumiputra, 188
Bank Negara Malaysia (BNM), 183
Bank of Asia, 92
Bank of Ayudhya, 140
Bank of Commerce, 188
Bank of International Settlements (BIS), 5, 35, 48, 58-9, 106, 131, 149, 229, 237
Bank of Japan, 51
Bank of Korea, 107, 223
Bank of Thailand, 50, 51, 87, 89, 137-52, 157, 217
Banuri, T., 230
Barshefsky, Charlene, 123, 127, 130
Bello, Walden, 23, 157
BIBF, *see* Bangkok International Banking Facility
Blum, George, 69, 165, 169, 180, 181, 183, 193
boom-bust cycle, 14, 39, 180, 214
Brady Plan, 205
Brazil, 202, 224

Bretton Woods, 9, 10, 11, 12, 15, 33, 42, 45, 52, 133, 134, 141
budget surplus, 77, 157
Budnevich, C., 35
Bullard, Nicola, 23
Burma, 111
Burton, John, 106, 108

Camdessus, Michel, 96, 103, 158, 191
capital
    account, 6, 9, 17, 18, 19, 23, 24, 66, 69, 70, 71, 76, 87, 105, 121, 124, 132, 133, 134, 142, 157, 163, 235
    flight, 17, 68, 98, 99
    flows, 23, 41, 47, 57, 66, 67, 75, 76, 83, 86, 109, 121, 157, 199, 215, 220
    inflows, 6, 9, 11, 12, 13, 16, 17, 22, 34, 35, 39, 41, 45, 48, 50, 51, 57, 60, 68, 69, 85, 86, 94, 102, 123, 143, 157, 165, 171, 175, 214, 220
    liberalisation, 211, 215, 218, 219
    market, 12, 23, 36, 50, 51, 66, 68, 69, 75, 76, 78, 107, 132, 137, 149, 163
    outflows, 75, 126, 153, 165
    regulation, 218
chaebol, 53, 68, 71, 79, 100, 101, 102, 105, 107, 108, 118, 119, 130, 131, 224, 225, 228
Chalongphob Sussangkarn, 156, 157
Chandrasekar, C.P., 22, 86
Chang Ha-Joon, 24, 72, 188, 226, 227, 230
Chart Thai Party, 146
Chart Pattana, 145, 147, 151
Chavalit Yongchaiyudh, 89 - 92, 114, 125, 143, 147, 151, 157, 158
Chicago, 6, 120
Chile, 6, 36, 52, 162, 175, 185, 218
Chin Kok Fay, 183
China, 3, 24, 39, 41, 53, 66, 112, 143, 149, 165, 213, 218
Clinton, Bill, 96, 99
Cohen, William, 96
Cole, David C., 163, 168, 169
commercial banks, 4, 5, 70, 72, 108, 138-42, 149, 153, 154, 158, 166, 168, 182, 183, 212, 217, 218
commercial borrowing, 70, 72
Commonwealth Games, 192

consociationalist regime, 195
conspiracy, 6, 185, 186, 216
contagion, 4-8, 10, 15, 18, 37, 41, 68, 74, 93, 82, 185, 192, 225
Cook Islands, 168
corruption, 24, 162, 163, 169, 199, 219, 224
counter-cyclical policy, 199
crony, 137, 186, 187, 191, 194, 195, 199, 200, 214, 228, 229, 230
currency board, 1, 11, 53, 78, 79, 80, 98, 99, 127, 129, 179
currency speculation, 6-9, 68, 90, 145, 190
currency trading, 10, 13, 15, 145, 147
current account, 2-9, 10, 13, 16-9, 34, 46, 51, 54, 63, 66-7, 70, 81-2, 86, 94, 97, 106, 137-8, 142-6, 150, 153, 157, 171, 181-4, 189, 200-11, 215, 217, 223-6

Daewoo, 107
Daim Zainuddin, 188, 191, 195
Davis, Bob, 91
debt GNP ratio, 223
debt servicing, 7, 40, 200, 224
Deen, Thalida, 100
deflation, 12, 36, 37, 41, 42, 53, 58, 80, 88
depreciation, 4, 25, 53, 60, 75, 79, 96, 106, 153, 155, 184, 202, 212, 217, 219, 220, 227
depression, 200
deregulation, 3, 13, 38, 72, 93, 100, 123, 127, 141, 165, 219
Dertouzos, M., 230
devaluation, 3, 18, 39, 42, 53, 57, 58, 59, 81, 82, 85, 87, 99, 140, 142, 145, 147, 155, 158, 162, 193, 200, 204, 227, 212, 219
developmentalist, 3, 12, 24, 25
Diaz-Alejandro, Carlos, 36
direct foreign investment, 70, 171
discount rate, 51, 52
dollarisation, 36
domestic, 4, 9, 17, 35, 40, 45, 58, 60, 71, 72, 75, 78, 79, 106, 163, 165, 216
domestic savings, 3, 7, 8, 9, 23, 68, 70, 71, 76, 100, 142, 204, 210, 214
domino, 5, 10
Doner, Richard, 141, 142
Dresdner Bank, 67

Dutch disease, 163
East Asia, 1, 3, 11, 13, 14, 15, 19, 22, 23, 24, 25, 34, 36, 37, 38, 39, 40, 41, 67, 74, 154, 181, 199, 211, 216
East Germany, 60
Eastern Europe, 13, 19, 41
Eatwell, John, 11
Econit, 117
economic development, 2, 16, 22, 147, 158, 199, 220
Economic Planning Board, 227
economic policy, 12, 134
economic strategy, 194
EIU country report, 145, 147-51, 154, 156
Ekamol Khiriwat, 146
Ekran, 187
El Nino, 112, 116
Employees Provident Fund, 186, 187, 189
employment, 12, 18, 230
equity markets, 36, 44, 53, 54
ersatz capitalism, 194
ESCAP, 114
Euh, Y., 226
Eurobond market, 139
Europe, 19, 38, 39, 40, 41, 42, 44, 45, 101, 107
European banks, 41, 216
European currencies, 41
European Union (EU), 41, 81, 124, 133, 134, 155
exchange rate, 5, 8, 10, 75
export growth, 22, 63, 66, 67, 70, 71, 81, 101, 143, 152
export-oriented, 3, 4, 7, 18, 25, 34, 49, 67, 82, 132,
external account, 35, 37, 39, 40, 41, 42, 46, 47, 50, 57, 70, 75, 86, 105, 142, 178, 200, 211, 214, 215, 216, 217
external finance, 36, 40, 70, 75, 94, 138, 171, 179, 182, 193, 214, 233, 235

Far Eastern Economic Review (*FEER*), 124, 144, 145, 148, 149, 150, 151, 155, 156
Federal Reserve, 50
Feldstein, Martin, 40, 120, 121
Ffrench-Davis, Ricardo, 175
FIDF, *see* Financial Institutions Development Fund

finance capital, 9
Finance One, 50, 88, 147, 148
financial
  borrowings, 200
  collapse, 77
  capital, 7, 8, 9, 16, 190
  companies, 110, 141, 142, 144, 147-155, 157
  disintermediation, 16
  flows, 11, 24, 36, 66, 121, 226
  governance, 7, 9, 12, 16, 22, 87, 90, 102, 103, 133, 216, 226
  institutions, 6,11, 14, 20, 37, 38, 47, 51, 52, 69, 71, 72, 77, 86, 88, 90, 93, 97, 105, 106, 121, 126, 127, 131, 132, 140, 149, 150, 152, 157, 168, 189, 225, 226, 236
  instruments, 11, 165
  intermediaries, 14, 17, 69, 72
  intermediation, 15, 17, 157
  investments, 4, 52
  liberalisation, 3, 5, 6, 7, 10, 11, 12, 13, 47, 106, 108, 132, 138, 157, 168, 171, 175, 184 185, 191, 193, 203, 210, 211, 212, 216, 219, 235-6
  markets, 5, 10, 12, 16, 22, 36, 40, 42, 44, 45, 68, 70, 71, 72, 73, 76, 86, 87, 94, 120, 127, 225, 229, 232
  reform, 88, 125, 150, 166
  restructuring, 38, 90, 126, 151
  sector, 2, 3, 8, 10, 17, 19, 20, 35, 40, 49, 50, 71, 73, 76, 77, 78, 81, 88, 93, 94, 96, 98, 99, 105, 121, 126, 128, 130, 142, 144, 145, 148, 149, 150, 151, 154, 156, 165, 181, 185, 190, 202, 210, 211, 213, 217, 226
  speculators, 71, 75, 186
  system, 7, 10, 13, 16, 17,18, 19, 22, 38, 42, 48, 59, 71, 72, 73, 76, 86, 88, 137, 139, 140, 146, 155, 162, 163, 165, 168, 169, 175, 182, 184, 235-8
  turmoil, 216
Financial Institutions Development Fund (FIDF), 88, 147, 149, 150, 152, 154, 157
Financial Restructuring Agency (FRA), 90, 150, 152, 154
Financial Times, 106, 108, 120, 150, 151, 155, 156, 158, 193, 215
Finland, 162

First Bangkok City Bank, 92, 152
first-tier, 3, 13, 25, 33
fiscal, 1, 3, 9, 14, 16, 18, 19, 38, 39, 52, 57,
  73, 75, 76, 89, 106, 153, 202, 203, 204,
  210, 234
Fischer, Stanley, 10, 51, 123
Fisher, Irving, 58
fixed exchange rates, 6, 10, 153
floating currency system, 178
flying geese, 13, 39, 44, 45
Ford Motors, 154
foreign
  acquisitions, 36, 80
  banks, 4, 6 , 20, 21, 70, 73, 80, 87, 89,
    90, 92, 97, 98, 102, 105, 106, 131,
    132, 139, 151, 154, 169, 182, 210,
    214, 218, 224, 229
  borrowings, 4, 5, 40, 45, 52, 54, 58, 59,
    60, 68, 77, 89, 100, 108, 121, 132,
    142, 193, 202, 212, 213, 218, 219,
    223, 226
  capital, 6, 7, 35, 57, 71, 74, 78, 80, 86,
    88, 92, 100, 101, 102, 108, 125, 126,
    142, 157, 158, 211
  companies, 79, 191
  currency, 46, 50, 52, 87, 98, 98, 103,
    142, 150, 166, 210
  debt, 3, 50, 68, 78, 98, 99, 103, 104, 126,
    141, 168, 175, 181, 186, 199, 202,
    205, 210, 214, 219, 224
  direct investment (FDI), 3, 6, 12, 24, 34,
    41, 63, 66, 67, 75, 120, 149, 181, 182,
    218, 220
  exchange, 4, 10, 24, 40, 45, 46, 48, 50,
    51, 53, 54, 59, 70, 71, 73, 74, 78, 79,
    86, 87, 99, 122, 138, 139, 142, 145,
    149, 153, 155, 157, 163, 165, 166,
    168, 180, 185, 189, 205, 215, 217,
    220,
  funds, 17, 71, 73, 117, 182, 183, 193
  inflows, 214, 219, 220
  interest rates, 6, 8
  investment, 4, 21, 67, 79, 87, 93, 94, 97,
    122, 143, 205, 210, 211
  investor, 53, 67, 71, 77, 79, 83, 107, 121,
    126, 128, 138, 144, 151, 154
  ownership, 17, 21, 79, 97, 121, 130
  reserves, 51, 54, 68, 73, 83, 105, 138,
    148, 149

  savings, 3, 4, 7
  take-over, 105, 108, 131
  trade, 94
  workers, 194
Forum of the Poor, 114
Foundation for Children's Development,
  112
FRA, *see* Financial Restructuring Agency
France, 41
Friedman, Milton, 120
fund managers, 4, 5, 105, 182, 186
fundamentals, 3, 6, 8, 11, 12, 16, 18, 24, 37,
  162, 175, 179, 219

G7 governments, 133
GATT, 67, 82
GDP, 52, 66, 72, 73, 76, 77, 90, 91, 94,
  100, 105, 106, 115, 125, 138, 143, 144,
  145, 153, 154, 157, 171, 202, 203, 204,
  205, 210, 213, 214, 223, 226
Genting-Camerons, 190
Germany, 13, 104
Ghosh, Jayati, 22, 86
global, 10, 21, 33, 38, 39, 40, 41, 42, 43,
  44, 46, 47, 49, 54, 57, 60, 132, 134,
globalisation, 34, 44, 45, 49, 68, 102, 215,
  218
GM (General Motors), 154
GNP, 3, 4, 181, 182, 204, 210, 212, 213,
  214, 219, 223, 226
Goldman Sachs, 99
Golub, Stephen S., 48
governance, 22, 23, 25, 42, 43, 105, 134
government, 20, 114, 120
Great Depression, 53
Green, Duncan, 115, 116, 117, 129
Greenspan, Alan, 10, 36, 44, 51
gross domestic product, *see* GDP

Habibie, B.J., 99, 97, 129
Halim Saad, 187, 188
Hanbo, 50, 224, 225, 229
Hanlon, Joseph, 121, 123, 133
Harvard Institute for International
  Development (HIID), 120
Harvard University, 12
Hashimoto Ryutaro, 96
hedge, 5, 6, 145, 157, 213
Helleiner, Gerald, 35, 232

Helsinki, 121
herd, 4, 5, 7, 8, 10, 15, 24, 36, 67, 75, 182, 192, 215
high performing Asian economies (HPAEs), 2
Hong Kong, 1, 2, 3, 19, 24, 25, 33, 41, 47, 48, 53, 54, 78, 98, 185
House Ways and Means Subcommittee, 123, 130
Howard, John, 96
Human Rights Watch, 116
Hungary, 78
Hyundai, 107, 224

ICMI, 115
Iman Taufik, 128
immigrant labour, 194
impact, 18, 33, 35, 162, 191, 202
implications, 2, 15, 18, 20, 22, 23, 178
import, 22, 66, 194, 203
India, 86
Indonesia, 1, 2, 3, 5, 7, 16, 19, 20, 21, 22, 23, 24, 25, 33, 35, 37, 47, 48, 50, 52, 54, 63, 66, 67, 70, 71, 75-80, 82, 85, 89, 92-6, 98, 99, 101, 103, 104, 109, 112, 115-7, 120-4, 127-9, 132, 133, 162-80, 182, 184, 191-2, 194, 202, 204, 217, 224
Indonesian Banking Law, 168
Indonesian rupiah, 6, 37, 77, 78, 79, 80, 93, 94, 96, 98, 99, 162, 163, 165, 169, 171, 178, 202
industrial policy, 2, 227, 228
industrialisation, 3, 39
inflation, 3, 4, 16, 40, 42, 45, 46, 57, 76, 77, 81, 96, 97, 105, 106, 109, 115, 119, 131, 142, 150, 156, 193, 200, 202, 203, 204, 211, 213, 214
   control, 137, 227
   rate, 163, 179, 193, 195
Information Technology Agreement, 81
Institute of International Finance (IIF), 67, 69
institutional reform, 230
interest rates, 4, 6, 8, 11, 14, 35, 37-41, 43, 45, 46, 47, 49-53, 57-60, 69, 71, 76, 80, 82, 86, 88, 89, 91, 93, 94, 100, 105, 106, 108, 120, 125, 130, 131, 138, 140, 142, 143-5, 157, 158, 171, 178, 184, 189, 200, 203, 205, 212-4, 216, 217, 220
Internal Security Act (ISA), 189

international
   banks, 23, 34, 35, 67, 69, 126, 158
   capital markets, 162, 228
   community, 111
   confidence, 225
   corporations, 79
   credit markets, 70
   creditors, 126
   debtor-creditor, 22, 43
   economy, 72
   finance, 8, 9, 68, 69, 70, 73, 78, 85, 134, 162, 186, 226
   institutions, 123, 132
   investors, 74, 75, 78
   lenders, 18
   markets, 68, 73, 81, 100, 101
   monetary systems, 184
   offshore financial centre, 193
   private banks, 126
   reserves, 200, 204, 210
   speculators, 185
   system, 13, 73,
   trade, 10, 101
International Finance Corporation (IFC), 7, 182
International Herald Tribune, 146, 152
International Monetary Fund (IMF), 1, 2, 5, 9, 10, 15, 16, 18, 19-21, 23, 37, 47-9, 52, 54, 57-60, 69, 74-80, 82, 85-135, 137, 144, 147-50, 154, 155, 158, 178-80, 186, 191-5, 200, 202, 212, 222, 229-30, 237-8
   Articles of Agreement, 23, 121, 122, 133, 134
   Articles of Association, 19
   conditionality, 15, 21, 23, 37, 193, 196, 229, 234-5
   intervention, 19, 21, 191, 192, 194, 237-8
   Korea bailout, 21
   packages, 121, 123, 125, 234-5
   policy-making interim committee, 19
intervention, 20, 23, 24, 25, 33, 37, 141, 175, 192, 217, 219, 228
intra-regional
   investment, 39
   trade, 39, 81
investment, 3, 7, 8, 9, 12, 15, 17, 18, 21, 23-5, 34, 35, 37, 42, 71, 122, 134, 138, 139, 144, 151, 153, 156-8, 165, 181-4, 190, 193, 194, 200, 202, 204, 210, 211, 215, 216, 227, 228

investor confidence, 68, 76-8, 81, 120, 124,
130, 149, 158, 180
investors, 21, 142, 143, 145, 158, 182, 183,
185, 189, 213, 215
Iraq-Kuwait crisis, 204
Isthmus of Kra, 190

Jakarta, 77, 96, 115, 116, 163
Jakarta Post, 97, 117
Japan, 2, 3, 13, 24, 25, 38, 40, 42, 44-6, 51,
57, 80, 94, 101, 103, 123, 131, 140, 157,
180, 220
Japan Economic Institute, 104, 116, 149
Japanese banks, 225
Japanese yen, 40, 51, 54, 81, 184, 227
Jomo K.S., 3, 24, 25, 80, 183

Kaminsky, 16, 163
Kang Kyung Shik, 225
Kansai, 190
KCTU, 107, 118, 119, 120
Keynes, Maynard, 9, 10
Khazanah, 187, 189
Kia Motors, 225
Kim Dae Jung, 107, 108, 127, 131, 229
Kim Young Sam, 224-230
Klein, Lawrence, 11
Koener, P., 224
Kohl, Helmut, 96
Koperasi Usaha Bersatu (KUB), 188
Korea, 7, 48, 49, 50, 54, 59, 60, 178, 222
Korean won, 37, 54, 69, 79, 102, 107, 130,
222
Kregel, Jan, 22
Krissana Parnsoonthorn, 139
Krugman, Paul, 13, 14, 15, 21, 69, 143
Krung Thai Bank, 140, 152
Kuala Lumpur, 95
Kuala Lumpur Composite Index (KLCI),
181, 189, 193
Kuala Lumpur Stock Exchange (KLSE),
182, 185

labour market, 107, 108, 118, 129
Labuan, 183
Latin America, 19, 33, 40, 41, 47, 67, 74,
75
Lauridsen, Laurids, 68
Le Fort, G., 35

lender of last resort, 43, 57, 73, 148
letter of intent, 151, 153, 154
liberalisation, 8-11, 17, 19, 22-5, 34, 35, 60,
68-70, 72, 73, 76, 87, 97, 102, 121, 123,
124, 127, 132, 137, 163, 178-80, 193,
194, 205, 222
LIBOR, 69, 108, 131, 226
Liem Sioe Liong, 98
liquidity, 35, 43, 141, 145, 153, 154, 155,
165, 178, 185, 190, 212, 217, 232-4
Lissakers, Karin, 91
London, 5, 124
Lucky-Goldstar (LG), 101

Maastricht Treaty, 124
macroeconomic, 12, 14, 16, 18, 24, 40, 42,
157, 162, 175, 234
Mahathir Mohamad, 9, 13, 184-8, 190-2,
194, 195
Malacca Straits, 190
Malayan Banking, 188
Malaysia, 2, 3, 5, 7-10, 12, 16, 21, 22, 24,
25, 33-5, 37, 48, 49, 52, 54, 59, 63, 66,
70, 71, 82, 104, 112, 182, 184, 186, 187,
190, 192, 193-5, 204
Malaysia Inc, 195
Malaysian International Shipping
Corporation (MISC), 188
Malaysian Mining Corporation (MMC), 188
Malaysian ringgit, 10, 6, 184, 190, 193
Malhotra, Kamal, 23
Mar'ie Muhammad, 169
Marcos, Ferdinand, 200
Marks & Spencer, 156
maturity structures, 226
McKinnon, Ronald, 218
merchant banks, 20, 105, 131, 226
Mexican crisis, 5, 9, 10, 13, 22, 47, 57-8,
144, 145, 149, 157, 162, 214, 223, 224
Mexican peso, 44, 45
Mexico, 14, 35, 45, 46, 49, 52, 74, 103, 104
Ministry of Finance and Economy (MOFE)
(South Korea), 227
Ministry of Finance, 137, 142, 144, 157,
227
Ministry of Labour, 110
Ministry of Social Welfare, 110
Minsky, Hyman, 35, 58
Mirzan Mahathir, 182, 188

Mohamad 'Bob' Hassan, 129
monetary, 3, 10, 15, 38, 40, 45, 57, 94, 105,
    142, 143, 144, 150, 165, 183, 203, 204,
    205, 210, 234
money markets, 20, 54, 145
monopolies, 178
Montes, Manuel, 16, 18, 163, 175
Montgomery, John, 49, 50
Moody, 144
moral hazard, 15, 69, 108, 120, 126, 131,
    132, 179, 218
multinationals, 34
Muslim ulama, 195
Myanmar, 111, 156

Nan (Thai province), 110
NAP, 147
Naris Chaiyasoot, 138, 141
Narongchai Akrasanee, 147
Nasution, Anwar, 168, 171
Nation, 106, 108, 131, 156
National Assembly, 118, 119, 129
National Bureau of Economic Research
    (NBER), 121
National Economic Action Council
    (NEAC), 188, 191, 195
national income accounts, 14
National Law, 94, 97
National Steel Corporation (NSC), 188
NBFIs (non-bank financial institutions),
    166, 168
Neiss, Herbert, 91, 92, 153
neo-liberal, 2, 10, 13, 24, 120, 124, 218,
    228
nepotism, 189
net open positions (NOPs), 168
New Economic Policy (NEP), 192, 194,
    196
New Port Project, 119
New York, 53, 74, 108
New York Times, 94
newly industrialising countries (NICs), 1, 2,
    3, 13, 67, 217
newly industrialising economies (NIEs), 3,
    13, 25, 33, 40, 44, 45, 53
nexus, 3, 8, 181
Nikhom Chandravithun, 111
Nixon, Richard, 10
Nolan, P., 230

non-deliverable forward (NDF) cover, 217
non-exportables, 6
non-financial public enterprise (NFPE), 182
non-governmental organisation (NGO), 110,
    128
non-OPEC developing countries, 224
non-performing loans, 223
non-tradables, 3, 4, 181, 184, 211, 220
Northern Regional International Airport,
    190
Norway, 162
NU (Nadhatul Ulama'), 117

OECD, 34, 49, 66, 82, 100, 101, 223, 228
offshore 17, 24, 48, 138, 142, 144
Ostrey, Sylvia, 46

Pacific Chemicals, 187
PAKTO-27, 166
payment deficit, 45
Peerawat Jariyasombat, 155
pension funds, 6, 68
peso, 52, 74, 203, 205, 210-3, 215-7, 219,
    220
Petronas, 188
Philippines, 1, 16, 23, 24, 37, 48, 52, 63,
    67, 71, 93, 100, 104, 193, 199-221
Pichit (Thai province), 110
Pill, H., 218
Plaza accord, 42, 102, 157, 204
policy 5, 7, 9, 13, 37, 149, 180, 227, 228
political participation, 85, 133
portfolio, 6, 7, 8, 17, 75, 86, 143, 165, 205,
    212, 214, 215, 217, 218, 220
Prangtip Daorueng, 110
Prem (former Thai Prime Minister), 142,
    145
private debt, 4, 7, 12, 17, 34-6, 39, 93, 114,
    154, 229, 233
private sector, 12, 36, 132, 137-9, 149, 157,
    158, 165, 166, 179, 182, 214, 228
privatisation, 88, 94, 122, 127, 151, 154,
    182, 196, 202, 203
productivity, 2, 13, 18, 39, 139
profit repatriation, 12
property, 6, 8, 36, 154, 158, 211, 213, 216,
    217
Property Loan Management Organisation
    (PLMO), 147, 148

protectionism, 42, 67, 82
PT Bank Duta, 179

Quantum Fund, 186

Radhanasin Bank, 152
Raghavan, 5, 20
Ramos, Fidel, 188
Rangsit University, 110
Reagan, Ronald, 120, 121
real economy, 162, 222
real estate, 7, 14, 139, 141, 156, 183, 192, 211
recession, 19, 40, 92, 139, 142, 199, 204, 211, 214
recovery, 13, 18, 24, 37, 38, 145, 153, 192, 193, 199, 202, 214
Reinhart, Carmen M., 16, 163
Reisen, Helmut, 171
renminbi, 227
Renong, 185, 187, 188
rentier, 24, 25, 196
Rizal Ramli, 117
Robinson, David, 141
Rubin, Robert, 10, 124, 186
Russia, 13

Sachs, Jeffrey, 87, 89, 106, 107, 120, 122
Saito, Kunio
Samsung, 107, 225, 228, 229
San Francisco, 139
Sanger, 94, 127
Sanwa Bank, 92
Sap Poo Pan (Thai village), 110
Satya Sivaraman, 111, 112
savings investment gap, 3, 181
SBI (Sertifikat Bank Indonesia), 166
SBPU (Surat Berharga Pasar Uang), 166
second-tier, 1, 2, 3, 24, 33, 34, 44, 82
Securities and Exchange Commission (SEC), 146
Securities Commission, 182
securities market, 4, 36, 38
Sen, Abhijit, 86
Seoul, 101, 103, 130
Seoul–Pusan High Speed Railway, 119
short-run foreign borrowing, 220-1
short-term, 3-6, 8, 10, 11, 158, 181
   capital, 3, 8, 134, 157, 182, 192, 236

debt, 16, 18, 20, 21, 34, 38, 70, 108, 126, 138-40, 143, 175, 184, 211, 220, 224, 226
Siam Cement Company, 155,
Siam City Bank, 140
Siam Commercial Bank, 92, 140
Sime Bank, 188, 189, 192
Singapore, 2, 3, 5, 15, 24, 25, 33, 48, 94, 98, 129, 163, 193
Singapore Business Times, 187
Singh, A., 230
Siti Hardijanti ('Tutut') Rukmana, 128
Slade, Betty F., 168, 169
small and medium-sized enterprises (SMEs), 155
social costs, 20
social investment fund, 114
socialisation, 36,
Somprasong Land, 139, 147
Soros, George, 9, 185, 186, 216
South America, 44
South China Morning Post, 185
South Korea, 1, 2, 5, 15, 20, 21, 24, 25, 33-5, 38, 63, 66-9, 71-3, 75, 76, 79, 82, 85, 89, 100-9, 111, 118-20, 122, 123, 127, 130-3, 140, 157, 158, 171, 191, 199, 214, 217, 222-4
Southern Cone crisis, 36
sovereignty, 21
speculation, 15, 23, 132, 145, 149, 212, 213, 215-7
stability, 18, 42, 137, 142, 166, 179, 211, 212
state banks, 166, 169
state-business relationship, 228
state-directed economic system, 222
state intervention, 2
state-led economic system, 222
state-owned banks, 169
sterilisation, 17, 216
Stiglitz, Joseph, 2, 11, 121, 133
stock exchange, 168
Stock Exchange of Singapore (SES), 182
stock market collapse, 11, 36, 187, 193
stock markets, 1, 4, 7, 8, 14, 17, 21, 35, 37, 39, 53, 59, 66, 68, 74, 77-9, 93, 101, 103, 108, 130, 139, 141, 143, 145, 157, 166, 182-4, 188, 189, 192, 205, 211-3, 215

structural adjustment, 87, 199, 202, 203
structural change, 3, 16, 25
structural reform, 88, 105, 123, 143, 180, 222, 235
Suehiro Akira, 140
Suharto, 1, 77-9, 92, 94-9, 109, 124, 127-9, 132, 178, 190, 194
Sumarlin shocks, 169
Summers, Lawrence, 96, 123, 158
Supachai Panitchpakdi, 151, 153
sustainability, 18, 25
swap market, 6
Sweden, 59, 162
Swiss Bank Corporation, 69

TAFI, 168, 169
Taiwan, 2, 3, 24, 25, 33, 53, 54, 140, 157
Tarrin Nimmanahaeminda, 153
tax reforms, 203
Taylor, L., 230
Techapaibul family, 153
Telephone Organisation of Thailand, 91
tequila crisis, *see* Mexican crisis
Thai Airways, 91
Thai Bankers Association, 140
Thai Danu Bank, 154
Thai Farmers Bank, 140
Thai Military Bank, 140, 148
Thai petrochemical industry (TPI), 155
Thailand, 1-3, 5, 7, 14-6, 21, 22, 24, 25, 33-5, 37, 38, 44, 47, 48, 50-2, 54, 59, 63, 68, 70, 71, 76, 83, 85-7, 89, 90, 92, 93, 99, 103, 104, 109, 111-4, 119-27, 131-3, 137-61, 180-2, 186, 194, 204, 212, 214, 217, 223, 224
Thailand Development Research Institute (TDRI), 138
Thammavit Terdudomtham, 139
Thanong Bidaya, 89, 90, 110, 148
The Economist, 95, 120
Third World Resurgence, 21
Thurow, Lester, 139
Times of India, 20
Ting Pek Khiing, 187
Tobin, James, 10, 11
trade balance, 46, 47, 50, 59, 75, 141
trade deficit, 40, 42, 46, 210, 211
trade liberalisation, 105, 123, 124

trade policy, 155
trade surpluses, 40, 53
transparency, 4, 20, 57, 122, 132-4, 182, 189, 217, 237-8
Turner, Anthony G., 48

UEM-Renong, 187-9
UMNO, 187, 188, 191, 195
unemployment, 14, 16, 38, 41, 42, 156, 230
Unger, Roberto Mangabeira, 134, 141, 142
United Engineers Malaysia (UEM), 185, 187, 188
United Kingdom (UK), 13, 44
United Nations (UN), 11, 114
United Nations Conference on Trade and Development (UNCTAD), 34, 232
United States (US), 10, 11, 13, 19, 21, 23, 35-9, 41, 42, 44-7, 59, 74, 79, 80-2, 94, 96, 101-8, 120, 123, 124, 126, 127, 130, 131, 133, 149, 154, 156-8, 180, 194, 216, 228, 237
University of the Philippines, 216
Uruguay, 36

Vadarajan, S., 20
value-added tax (VAT), 88, 149
Vatchara Charoonsantikul, 89, 90
Voravidh Charoenlert, 112

Wade, R., 24
Wall Street, 5, 10, 11, 19, 186
Wardhanna, Ali, 168
Warr, Peter, 140
Washington, 74, 101, 133
Washington consensus, 123
welfare economics, 2, 33
White, G., 24
Wing Tiek Holdings, 188
Wolf, Martin, 108, 223
Wolfensohn, James, 117
World Bank, 2, 7, 11, 19, 24, 86, 92-4, 109, 110, 114, 115, 117, 121, 123, 128, 133, 134, 137, 150, 156, 158, 179, 182, 223, 224, 237-8
World Trade Organisation (WTO), 19, 43, 48, 67, 81, 82, 94, 236-7

Yamin, Kafil, 117, 128